★ NEW ENGLAND STUDIES ★
Edited by John Putnam Demos, David Hackett Fischer,
and Robert A. Gross

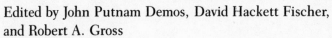

EDWARD BYERS
The Nation of Nantucket

RICHARD RABINOWITZ
The Spiritual Self in Everyday Life

The Spiritual Self in Everyday Life

THE TRANSFORMATION OF PERSONAL RELIGIOUS EXPERIENCE IN NINETEENTH-CENTURY NEW ENGLAND

Richard Rabinowitz

Northeastern University Press

BOSTON

Northeastern University Press

Copyright © 1989 by Richard Rabinowitz

Library of Congress Cataloging-in-Publication Data

Rabinowitz, Richard.
The spiritual self in everyday life : the transformation of personal religious experience in nineteenth-century New England / Richard Rabinowitz.
   p.   cm. — (New England studies)
   Bibliography: p.
   Includes index.
   ISBN 1-55553-022-2 (alk. paper)
   1. New England—Religious life and customs. 2. Experience (Religion)—History. I. Title. II. Series.
BR530.R32   1989   88-35706
248′.0974dc19   CIP

Designed by Richard C. Bartlett and Ann Twombly

MANUFACTURED IN THE UNITED STATES OF AMERICA
93 92 91 90 89   5 4 3 2 1

To my parents,
who meant it every time they greeted a sneeze
with a prayer for "life, health, and long years."

Contents

Preface

THIS BOOK has been very long in the making. It started a quarter-century ago in a college paper, an unsuccessful one written for a course on European romantic poetry. My theme was the evolution of the idea that the mind had an internal, expressive power to shape its own experience. Little did I know that a whole career of scholarship and teaching would be so powerfully shaped by this fragile effort, for almost all my professional work as a scholar and then as a dramatist of learning experiences in public spaces has stemmed from that central inquiry.

More immediately, this book started as a doctoral dissertation at Harvard. In looking it over, as if for the first time, I can see many things in it of which I was unaware when it was being written. Much of it flowed directly from my years as an undergraduate and graduate student at Harvard in American history and literature. That world was dominated for me by the massive presence of Perry Miller. By some strange convergence of Harvard's leniency on course requirements and my own audacity, I found myself an eighteen-year-old sophomore in Miller's last iteration of his graduate course on Romanticism in American Literature. Dutifully I attended every lecture, even as the old Titan was dying in front of us in Sever Hall. And dutifully I inscribed the master's orphic pronouncements: "Schiller's essay on the Sublime is the turning-point of Western civilization," a statement I could not verify, question, or comprehend. But more dutifully still, I mourned Miller's death in the middle of the semester—though I understood so little of what he had been talking about.

In those days, Miller's influence was felt in one absolutely basic assumption. If American culture had any significant humanistic interest, it came from the strain of religious rhetoric he had so magisterially limned. Andrew Jackson, Martin Luther King, Jr., indeed anyone worth caring about in our nation's history, was approachable chiefly through the thicket of Miller's definition of the Puritans' "Augustinian strain of piety." Gone for me, immediately, was the intellectual challenge of progressive thinkers, blacks, Jews—all would pale before what one of my professors announced were the "only three minds worth paying attention to in American history: Jonathan Edwards, Herman Melville, and William James." I can now only smile at my naiveté.

So, ever dutiful, my junior year was a whirlwind tour through James's psychological and philosophical writing, my senior thesis was on Melville, and I peregrinated from the Yard every day in graduate school up to the Harvard Divinity School to drown myself in Edwards.

I suppose that if I had stayed in Cambridge throughout my graduate years, I would have written a dissertation on Edwards's epistemology. As it was, I found myself captivated by teaching, and then beguiled on a winter's day in 1967 by the strange notion of teaching in a museum in Sturbridge, Massachusetts.

Old Sturbridge Village is an outdoor history museum of New England rural life during the early nineteenth century. Its collections have grown to include about forty buildings, carefully restored after relocation from all over the region. With equally careful research, many of these buildings and their surroundings are filled with re-creations of the work activities of Yankee farm families—crafts like blacksmithing and pottery but also more ordinary work such as laundry, dairying, and food preservation.

I had never been particularly drawn toward museums as a child, but Sturbridge came across as an almost overwhelming demonstration of the inadequacy of my academic training. Here I had been reading and writing about sermons that, I suddenly realized, were delivered in cavernous meetinghouses bereft of religious ornament and of almost every creature comfort. My beloved Edwardseans, I began to see, had wrought their revolutions in the minds of New Englanders above the chattering of unruly children, the shivering of fatigued men and women, the scampering of dogs, cats, and swine up and down the aisles—and yet the words had rung true. Those romances and novels we had carefully parsed in my American literature classes were written in those chambers, with those pens, on that paper, at so many days of an oxcart's journey from the metropolis. And yet written and read they were! And the work lives we had so blithely analyzed in our economic histories—what did we know of skills gained and forgotten, of tools improved and laid aside?

I proceeded to surrender my graduate fellowships, to the astonishment of my colleagues in graduate school. It must have seemed rash—there was a war on, and people didn't leave the banks of the Charles lest one misstep into the Mekong.

But if I forsook academe for that moment, I was still eager to learn. I loved the chance to share my enthusiasm for New England history with bashful ten-year-olds, brash teenagers, infatuated honeymooners, and beaming parents on family vacations. To my colleagues in the museum, the experts in historic architecture, technology, textiles, and ceramics, and the wonderful men and women I met on the frontlines of public interpretation, I owe an enormous debt. Every page of this book bears witness to an often witless query in their direction.

And once I had begun the research for the dissertation from which this book springs, I had posed a rather different question from that which might have come from my library carrel. Now I needed to know the mind of New England from the perspective of these farmers. I wanted to discover how the true history of the New Englander's controversy with his God had proceeded around the plain deal tables of kitchens and stores, as well as studies and pulpits.

Furthermore, Old Sturbridge Village was a bacchanalia of reconstruction. Everyone in the museum raced about putting together fragments of the past into clearly comprehensible experiences in the present. A general store from Dummerston, Vermont, was being reconstructed—not only its walls and roof and shelves but also the merchandise to be sold, its packaging, the business practices of its proprietors, and (to me) best of all, *its place in a rapidly expanding commercial-agrarian economy.* From this it was a small leap to try reconstructing the mental apparatus of New Englanders. True, I was reading Vico at the time and coming to share the perception of history as a process by which men and women make meaning out of the inchoate world. And my good friend Robert Post in Cambridge was periodically sending out the writings of French post-structuralist critics. But I was learning deconstruction and reconstruction firsthand in central Massachusetts.

Finally, a third and more subtle influence was being exercised on my scholarship. Though I hardly knew it at the time, I felt my scholarship freed from certain preconceptions that stemmed from the environment of study in graduate school itself. I came to conceive of a world full of miscommunications, misreadings—deliberate and otherwise, of unsteady foci, overstrenuous disagreements on trivial matters, and tacit consensus on issues of real consequence. This is not the intellectual history I was trained to study at Harvard. Most works in intellectual history or the history of ideas, especially those written by philosophers, construe the life of the mind as a perfect and endless graduate seminar—the coffee always fresh, the clock ticking away inconsequentially, with enough paper, ink, blackboard space, and chalk—and above all, an apparently eternal willingness of the parties to hear each other out. Such intellectual histories strive to transpose eccentric strokes of logic's hammer into rhythmic beats of a perfectly matched pair of wheelwrights. Every person reads another's work fluently and shoots his critical arrows exactly where the writer posed his key issues. In such portrayals of intellectual dialogue, the circle of logic is too round and continuous. Certainly that is not the way we *must* think of creative discourse. It isn't what we hear in the clatter of twentieth-century fiction, nor does it sound much like what happens in the course of a Socratic dialogue or a passage from the Talmud. We need to paint the interchange of ideas as fully human—with as much multidirectionality and chance, as much engorged with passion, ego, and willfulness as any other human acts, as recognizably experiential as coopering or cobbling. In the nineteenth century, no less than in our own time, logic was a luxury item, and logic-chopping to most people less necessary than putting the steel to onions, cordwood, or cotton.

Parents and children, we all know, speak to one another with admixtures of love, authority, deference, fear, and confusion—and so do intellectual elders and disciples. The longer I have stayed away from academic life, the more remote and incredible has its description of the world of ideas seemed.

Such detachment from my teachers' models, perhaps as much as the political furies of the late 1960s, led to the tripartite division of this work. My assumption was that historians could find material as fruitful in the uncomfortable inheritance of intellectual traditions as in the squabbles among heirs in the same generation. In the misconstruction of their teachers' words, the students created new meanings more appropriate for their own day. So, as this book says so often, the emphasis upon doctrine in the 1790s, for example, is itself a historical phenomenon—and the fate of such doctrinalism cannot be traced simply in conventional histories of religious ideas. Doctrine itself, in other words, does not always play the same part in religious life, even among theologians, any more than rhyme is an ineradicable element in poetry or economic interest in a government decision.

Needless to say, something may also be lost by this decision. This book does not stress intragenerational conflict, and hence it downplays the social dislocation that always impinges on intellectual life at any given moment. Historians have to make difficult choices between the figure in the carpet and its background, and I recognize that some will correctly chastise me for seeing the wrong element in the "optical illusion" that is the complicated historical record of New England consciousness.

Inevitably, then, as every work is autobiographical, these pages are deeply tinged with the experience of leaving academic life and of finding my domicile amid the woods and lakes of rural Massachusetts and my métier in the long, hard work of fashioning museums, exhibitions, multimedia presentations, and educational programs. I had been the youngest of Perry Miller's students, perhaps the last to absorb personally his enormous claim for the power of the human mind, but my personal experience had taught me to suspect, and sometimes to mourn the lost ideal of, a model of intellectual life based on the seminar room and Widener Library.

Though I can discover other traces of this odyssey in the body of this book, only two are worth mentioning. First, so remote was my career ambition from this project when the dissertation was completed in 1977 that I rather cavalierly put it aside. From time to time, I heard of readers who had taken the trouble to seek out a copy in the Harvard Archives, and there were references to the work in a number of books and articles—some whose genealogical relationship to my circle of friends mystified me. Robert Gross first concretely suggested that "we just publish the thing as is." Northeastern University

Press was kind enough to accept Gross's suggestion. And were it not for a certain ungraciousness on my part, this book would have been out two years ago. It is not exactly *as is*. Every page of the dissertation has been mined and refined, and the work in your hands bears the influence of several very helpful readers—among them Susan Geib, Bruce Kuklick, Daniel Calhoun, and Lawrence Buell. Ellen Fletcher has given a painstakingly careful reading of several key chapters, which only reinforced my envy of her special skills as a writer. Sanford Levinson and Robert Post have continued to be my most profound intellectual companions, on all matters American, historical and contemporary. Among an old teacher's blessings are the lessons learned from one's old students, and Philip Gura and William Breitenbach have been excellent critics. Sam Bass Warner, Jr., neighbor and friend, business partner and public citizen, taught me to honor the calling of historian more effectively than any of my own teachers. But what more than anything finally sprang the work from my word processor was a passing judgment from one reader who said it was valuable to publish even as a posthumous work. My heart leapt up at this challenge, assuring me that I (and my book) still lived.

In the place of the acknowledgments my university friends customarily offer to various funding agencies and faculty research and sabbatical-leave support, I have little to substitute. The American Society of Church History awarded this book its Brewer Prize ten years ago, but withdrew its financial award while I was about making a livelihood for myself in other ways. Mostly, those I have to thank are my colleagues at the American History Workshop, clients, and loved ones who put up with my distraction when I was thinking of New England history rather than dinner or our next multimedia presentation. Without Polly Price there never would have been a dissertation. Lynda B. Kaplan deserves enormous gratitude for her midwifery of the final draft. A special word of thanks to the librarians who've accommodated themselves to my hasty predations on their collections, particularly at Old Sturbridge Village, the American Antiquarian Society, the Congregational Library in Boston, and the Boston Athenæum. And great affection for the booksellers of New England and New York, whose courageous (if foolhardy) trade in old books has allowed me to do my research at the oddest of hours, in the comfort of my own library rather than that of institutions with fixed schedules.

My most profound debt is to my son Jonathan, born about the same time as this book and steadily its most engaging inspirer, competitor for my time, and now, astonishingly, its most strenuous (and helpful) critic. One of the amazing stories of my life has been the interconnection between fathering this work and fathering that child. Now, eighteen years later, when he is about to leave home to fashion his own habits of mind, this book has profited once more from its kinship with him—a parent of an adolescent child, like the writer of an adolescent book, cannot remake much of his offspring.

My final prefatory note has to do with religion itself, personal religion. I am not a nineteenth-century New England evangelical but a late twentieth-century American Jew. This work was and is a meditation on religiosity, on my grandfather's piety and my grandmother's social radicalism, on my father's mixture of moralism and economic ambition, on the inwardness and sense of personal destiny that legitimated my own generation's flight from the old neighborhood. I have been sympathetic to the Yankees as kinsmen in the struggle to find higher meanings in and for the ordinary clatter of life. For lapses of such sympathy, I can only claim the enormous difficulty of casting my empathetic net across these many generations.

Brooklyn, New York
June 1988

Introduction

THIS IS A STUDY of the personal experience of religion in New England during the years from 1790 to 1860.

For those who inscribe the title pages of textbooks like *The American Experience*, the word "experience" can simply be a vague synonym for "what happened." Taken any more precisely than that, the study of personal experience poses particular problems for historians, for the inner life of another person seems inaccessible even to his contemporaries. From the distance of a century, how can we hope to enter into a nineteenth-century New Englander's way of thinking and acting?

The problem is less severe if we understand that an experience always leaves traces, as soon as a person becomes conscious of his passing through it. These traces are the historian's sources. Among evangelical New Englanders, for example, a personal conversion experience, "being reborn in the Lord," was a necessary achievement before one was admitted to full communion with the local church. Records of church membership, then, can be used by social historians to determine how religious experience can be correlated with age or sex, family background, or economic and political interests. While this is valuable in helping us to see better the environment in which religious experiences occur, the complexity of individual experiences has to be ignored when conversion is equated to the simple act of joining the church.[1]

Psychohistorians, or more accurately, psychobiographers, overcome this deficiency by finding their "trace" evident in certain intricate forms of behavior or thought that strongly resemble symptoms accounted for in contemporary psychological and, especially, psychoanalytic theory. Psychohistory works best when its subject's life can be extraordinarily well documented, as in Erik H. Erikson's *Young Man Luther*, and where the intention is to explain the biographical consistency of particular historical actors whose lives were tumultuous. It is less effective in dealing with the historical changes that reshape ordinary action and thought.[2]

Psychohistory finds itself reducing (or equating) all experience to psychological experience. By contrast, phenomenological criticism, among which William James's *Varieties of Religious Experience* is a famous early example, is prepared to allow religious experience to stand by itself as a separate and internally consistent realm of meaning. Its evidence is generally derived from the verbal reports of those who have undergone religious experience, and its aim has often been to develop a typology of such experience. These typologies are by their nature ahistorical schemes.[3]

My approach shares the assumption of all these schools of thought that a person's religious experience, which may be ineffable within the mind, can be interpreted only when it enters some social sphere of meaning—either some aspect of the historical culture (like church membership) or some system of meaning in our own (like psychoanalysis). Like the psychohistorians, then, religion is here understood to be transacted within the individual consciousness. But my primary attention will be focused, like that of the "new" social historians, on the shared lives of ordinary people in the past and on the ways in which religious experience related to other aspects of everyday life. Perhaps most like the phenomenologists, I will try to distill from the historical articulations of personal religious events the common basic assumptions and leave aside those that are useful largely for explicating individual lives.

The World of John Phillips

Everything we know about an individual in the past is evidence of the social construction of reality in his world. Consider the case of Deacon John Phillips of Sturbridge, in southern Worcester County, Massachusetts.

From the town's vital records, we know that Phillips was born on June 29, 1760, and a visitor to the town graveyard learns that he died more than one hundred and four years later, on February 25, 1865. He married at twenty-five, fathered nine children, seven of whom lived to maturity, and lived with his wife for sixty-four years.

From the extant Sturbridge tax records, we can discover how much Phillips's property was worth, how much livestock and personal estate he owned, and whether he gained or lost wealth over time. Town meeting records indicate his election as a state legislator in 1814 and 1815 and as a justice of the peace from 1810 to 1824. The clerk of the Baptist Church entered his baptism on October 30, 1785, and that of his wife nine years later, and his election as deacon (to succeed his father) in 1799. We could probably learn more about Phillips by consulting the land and probate records in the Worcester County Courthouse, the federal and state census schedules, the extant account books of local merchants and craftsmen, and the collections of letters to and from town residents. By examining maps, Phillips's house and land might be found and explored, and with the help of local antiquarians and his descendants, it might be possible to locate artifacts that he once handled.[4]

This much we might discover of any man (though not of his wife) in nineteenth-century New England. But because of his celebrated longevity, we know more about John Phillips. In honor of his centenary, the town toasted him with encomiums and published a biography written by the local Baptist minister. Here we learn that Phillips had been born and had always lived and worked on the same two-hundred-acre farm he inherited from his father and passed down to his son. Even more interesting is the information that he was a lifelong "Democrat, or a Republican, of the Jeffersonian School. At the last presidential election [1856] he voted for Frémont and Dayton, and he hopes at the next to vote for Lincoln and Hamlin." In keeping with this, his biographer notes that his two years in the legislature were marked by strenuous opposition to the Hartford Convention, the attempt by New England Federalists to countenance secession from the Union because of their antagonism to the War of 1812.[5]

Living so long, Phillips personified the town's memory of the Revolution, and he recalled serving for seven weeks with the local militia company at Providence, Rhode Island, in the winter of 1776–1777. There is no mention of combat. Nostalgically he remembered being singled out as the biggest man in the regiment, at six feet and two hundred pounds, and being measured against the man who held the same honor in another company.

The Baptist minister also made important notes about Phillips's religion. Although he joined the church at twenty-five, he dated his conversion experience, in which he "met with a saving change, and his sins were pardoned," to a sermon he had heard and to his reading of the Gospels some fourteen years earlier. In thoroughly orthodox fashion, he listed "four of the leading articles" of his creed:

1. That God is good.
2. That Christ is divine.
3. That there is power and reality in revealed religion, and
4. That man, by nature, is totally morally depraved.

Finally, the biographical sketch provided accounts of both Phillips's physical condition and habits of life—he had foregone ardent spirits, but kept using snuff, always ate well, and so on—unusually detailed for ordinary folk. A daguerreotype of the old man was copied for this occasion. And, appended to all of this was a lengthy "Phrenological Character," apparently done by a professional bump-reader by examining Phillips's portrait. This indicated that "his Language appears to be full, his reasoning powers fair, his Benevolence rather large, his Veneration large, while Firmness is most enormously developed."

This much we know, specifically, of John Phillips. But because we are more interested in his world than in the man himself, it is clear that the details of his life matter less to us than that they met some standard of noteworthiness which caused them to be written down. If we try, as the anthropologist Mary Douglas suggests, "to think of cosmology as a set of categories that are in use," the kinds of things we know about Phillips light up his cosmos for us. All we know about him, in fact, arises from the social categories of his own age; his biography, or anyone's, tells us much about his society.[6]

For example, it was obviously a highly literate society in which written records served to fix the authority of such norms as private property, equitable taxation, political leadership, and one's role as a citizen of the town and a member of its various groups. His reference to the Scriptures and the polished form of Phillips's religious principles indicate further how significant the written word was in one's life. By contrast, quantitative skills in this society were rather crude, as one sees in the primitive form of tax calculations and in anecdotes like that about measuring one soldier against another.[7]

The basic social unit was the nuclear family, which held and transacted private property and around which all notations in the vital records were organized. In both legal and civil records, wives and children were always identified by reference to the head of household. The attainment of full adulthood in terms of both an economic competence (sufficient property to maintain a household) and church membership (among evangelical Christians, requiring a conversion experience) was entirely the responsibility of the individual, although, for both, a parent could bequeath considerable advantages in shouldering that burden. In fact, realizing both was sometimes problematical. Merely coming of age and performing certain customary rites was no guarantee of one's pecuniary or spiritual destiny, as it was for one's right to vote in a society with universal manhood suffrage. The original Puritan cosmos, which had linked these three forms of adult authority, had long been disassembled by the time of Phillips's maturity. But, once reached, the state of adulthood did not need continuing development. John Phillips, unlike his descendants today, was not charting a career, with various successes and failures along the way. If he had a "mid-life crisis," no one noticed it.[8]

The care with which Phillips's physical and temperamental characteristics were described is another index of this individualism, especially when we consider, as one nineteenth-century celebrant of the idea of individual personality did, that classical and Biblical literature are alike lacking in such exact depictions. After all, no source bothered to tell us either how tall or dark-complexioned Socrates or Jesus was or how gruff or smooth their voices were. All this zealous attention to Phillips is striking. At the same time, some things that the nineteenth century "knew" about individual personality, especially the phrenological reading, are no longer worth knowing in our own cosmology. Although we tend to view every episode of our lives as a further illustration of a developing, inner personality "structure," Phillips's peers thought of temperament as constitutional and permanent, essentially unaffected by biographical events. In most lives, the key markers were the traditional points of passage like birth, marriage, children's births, and death, as well as noteworthy public events like wars and elections, rather than the psychologically critical moments we emphasize. Perhaps Herman Melville was right in saying that "physiognomy, like every other human science, is but a passing fable," or, what is very much the same thing, a passing set of categories.[9]

By contrasting the categories of our day with those of Phillips's, we accomplish two things. First, each illuminates the other, allowing us to see such categories as human inventions, not eternal truths. For example, against the crude comparison of soldiers in distinct regiments, we might well imagine how easy it is today to compare statistically two groups of soldiers, hospital patients, or children. That says much about the expansion of not only our computational skill but also our techniques of record keeping, our tendency to visualize individuals as members of distinct groups, and our concepts of "average" and "normal." To take a more subtle example, we may wonder that the early religious experience of John Phillips, when he was only eleven years old, was nowhere mentioned as either childish or preparatory; in our cosmology, what happens to children has to be judged by a different standard from that applied to adults.[10]

Second, without such comparisons we can scarcely make use of the past in answering historical inquiries. Of what value, after all, are the scanty remains of John Phillips's life to any but the most ardent antiquarians? They lie in a useless waste, a tatterdown dwelling awaiting foreclosure and the wrecking ball, until we can move our own mental furniture into them by substituting our cosmologies, our categories, for his and his biographer's.

The most important of these substitutions is this: in Phillips's day, oddity was a stronger recommendation for an event's noteworthiness than typicality, but we think the other way around. Twentieth-century historians want to know that what happened to him was representative of some larger, well-defined social group of his contemporaries. Was it *common* to have nine children? (Yes, but much less so for his grandchildren's generation.) Did people *often* live so long? (About as frequently, probably, as they would today.) Were Baptists *usually* Jeffersonians? (Almost always.) Did Jeffersonians *generally* become Republicans in the middle of the nineteenth century? (A more difficult call, but about 20 percent of the Democrats in New England voted for the Republican Frémont; we would want to know how Phillips voted during the intervening Jacksonian era.) Was Phillips's experience *characteristic* of others in Sturbridge? of those who lived in nineteenth-century Boston or New York? of Southerners or Britons? And so on.[11]

Conversely, I can claim to know a great deal more about John Phillips by applying to him what was typical of New England rural communities. Without the hard evidence to say so, we may safely guess that he tilled no more than ten or fifteen acres of field crops on his farm, that he was most familiar with houses that had a central chimney when he was young and ones with a central hallway when he was aged, that he celebrated the Fourth of July and ignored Christmas, that he spent his winters performing handicraft work to earn some cash income, that until about 1820 he could repair almost everything manmade that he owned, and so forth. Here our notion of typicality works to imply much that is not part of their individual historical record about ordinary people.[12]

We may infer this much history because our cosmology emphasizes the connectedness of the entire culture. So did the nineteenth century's, but it still found the most likely connection in the universal subordination of all the world's pieces to the same ruling divinity. We tend instead to look for *lateral interweavings,* evidence that John Phillips "belonged" to the same political and intellectual world as men like the Adamses, or Webster, Jackson, and Calhoun. Or men like Joel Barlow, Sir Walter Scott, James Fenimore Cooper, or Ralph Waldo Emerson. What did he know, we ask, of Shays' Rebellion, of the Embargo, of the Nullification Crisis, or of the Fugitive Slave Act?

Finally, where Phillips might have felt an extraordinary stability in his rural life—a life in many ways closer, still, to that of Hesiod's *Works and Days* than to a modern John Deere instruction booklet—our interest, particularly as historians, is in *change.* We, of course, see changes that were imperceptible in Phillips's own day, though it is perhaps better to say that he saw the evidence of changes (and attributed meanings to them) which we interpret differently today. For if he was the town's memory, then his fellow citizens were his history, and he must have been able to notice and wonder at the changed lives of his townsmen: a son gone west to farm in Illinois, a neighbor's family gradually yielding farming to work in the local textile mills, the storekeeper's offering new goods and the new men setting up carriage and blacksmith shops when the Stafford Turnpike was opened into Sturbridge. For a child of the earliest group of the town's Baptists, persecuted in the 1750s for their deviance, he must have been pleased when the Congregationalists asked to worship with them forty years later when they were without a minister, or when the Baptists built a new Greek Revival meetinghouse near the town common in 1832, or when the odious Article III of the state constitution was finally repealed the next year, forever separating church and state in Massachusetts. But these passing events, which we seize upon as the pigments with which we can paint our picture of the past, were more likely only breaks in the stable patterns of Phillips's life, interruptions that made the rest of his life either easier or more difficult to sustain in its normal course. His great-great-grandchildren have no less trouble drawing coherent histories out of the details of their (our) lives, but they are more constantly inclined to do so because life is now understood to be a course of changes.

Although these twentieth-century assumptions about typicality, cultural interrelatedness, and historical change help expand what we "know" of John Phillips and his world, they also determine what we will find significant. We are looking for the evidence of typicality, of a connection to the most important events and changes in New England culture and society. Without such assumptions we might easily be awash in an immense tide of historical trivia. Our bias is inevitable. But our sensitivity to it can help us bridge the gulf between our cosmology and theirs, so long as we are ceaselessly aware that we are measuring (interpreting) according to our own standards of weights and measures.

Praxis and Theoria in the Evidence of Personal Religious Experience

The goals of this study are twofold. First, I want to reconstruct what New Englanders meant when they spoke of their personal religious experience during these three generations. Second, I want to connect their religious experience, as a variant of personal consciousness, to other ways they thought about themselves. Let me first explain my approach to this second goal.

The men and women who went to the meetinghouse on Sabbath-day for two sermons, read their Bibles aloud at home, retired to their "closets" for private meditation, underwent the stages of a conversion experience and made a public profession of their saving faith, gave hours and dollars to benevolent activities, and sought the salvation of the whole world—these were the same people who cooked and cleaned, harvested and traded, educated their children and tended their sick. A person is never only a religious person.

Religion is one way of exercising the mind, but only one. Like all forms of ordinary consciousness, all ordinary activity, it has its own realm of *praxis*. We may define praxis as the set of rules by which an activity is judged to have been done correctly. When the apprentice cooper was taught, for example, to use his jointer well, he was instructed also in how to distinguish a "square" or "true" cut from others done more poorly. This sort of "truth," which may be distinguished from the truth we seek in theoretical study (*theoria* was the term Aristotle gave to this realm), is inseparable from the art of coopering. Underlying all the practices of religion, all the personal experiences of faith and holiness, there is similarly a realm of praxis, by which whatever occurs is verified against the rest of our experience and that of our peers. When John Phillips read the last ten chapters of the Book of John, he said, he "came to and read that passage, 'It is finished,' [and] his burden left him.—He thinks he then met with a saving change, and his sins were pardoned." Reading the Scriptures was certainly a common practice in New England. But finding, amid a spiritual crisis, that one's condition was exactly represented by the language of the Bible was a part of the praxis of personal religion among late eighteenth-century New Englanders. If Bible reading was Phillips's "jointer," then recognizing himself in the verse was his notion of "true."[13]

Taken all together the praxes that order a person's experience form his cosmology. Every culture has a praxis that defines the boundaries of the self (the degree to which an individual person overlaps with others, or with the ground of Being); another that presumes the regularity of cause-and-effect relationships (hence the possibility of magical or supernatural intervention); and still others that postulate the overall benevolence, malevolence, or neutrality of man's environment, the stages of life history, and whether man is passive or responsible for determining his own fate. These assumptions are often so tacit that they escape articulation, but they crucially unite vastly disparate activities in the culture. For example, think of giving away your grown-up child's toys; reflect on what you are saying about yourself, your child, other people, the past, and the future in such an apparently simple gesture.[14]

The professional thinkers in every society seldom pay much heed to these implicit assumptions, but when they do the theoretical explication of them occurs separately from their life as the rules of social praxis. Intellectual debate, like every form of organized discourse, follows its own independent but usually parallel pathway. In the nineteenth century, for example, geologists and Biblical scholars puzzled over the age and provenance of the earth, but none of them denied that the planet and its creatures were well disposed toward man's energetic enterprises. Such assumptions were so widely shared that they could not be open to doubt, except, perhaps, by a fictional whaling captain setting off to test and avenge metaphysical affronts. And yet, according to twentieth-century environmentalism, the world is anything but limitlessly welcoming to human depredations. By this light, our intellectual ancestors had raised the wrong questions and were completely off the mark. Closer to our subject, the century-long theological debate over man's free agency in his own conversion and regeneration may have had something to do, tangentially, with the shift in praxis toward the voluntaristic backing of religion which followed the disestablishment (the end of tax support) of Congregationalism, but the theologians had to work through the issue within the terms of their own discipline.[15]

Changes in praxis, therefore, are more likely to reflect deep changes in social conditions than movements in the history of ideas. The cooper's sense of "true" could not, for instance, withstand the increasing precision of twentieth-century machine processes, and it has been replaced by a new praxis, called "tolerance" or "the margin of error," which must be designed into the production of industrial goods so that they will not be too good and too costly. That "quality control," as we euphemistically call this boundary on workmanship, should be a negative standard (how much error or deviance is permitted?) rather than a positive one (is this as good as possible?) is a sign of a deeper shift in the twentieth-century cosmology. Exactly the same shift may be seen in realms of life quite distant from manufacturing but sharing its attention to mass processing—witness public schooling or welfare. We "know" that we cannot provide enough money, technical support, and long-term professional guidance to educate every child to his full intellectual capability or to wrest every disadvantaged family from dependency on government, though we often profess to want to, so we employ a praxis that "accepts" a great deal of failure. We need more histories of what we do, rather than of what we want to do.[16]

This book proposes to locate the praxes for personal religious experience, the rules by which New Englanders during the years between the Revolution and the Civil War interpreted their encounters with the divine. *My aim and my method are to link the praxis of religious experience to that of other aspects of everyday life.* I hypothesize but cannot prove that the ways a person defined his individual responsibility in religious matters (for his salvation), in economic concerns (for his livelihood), in parenthood (for his children's well-being) were fundamentally interchangeable. Such fundaments shaped the cosmology or, if you will, the *economy* of experience. (I am thinking here of Thoreau's use of "Economy" as the title of the first chapter of *Walden,* wherein he established the interconnected material and spiritual bases for his experiment in living.)

I take it for granted that at every historical moment a specific economy of experience shapes the basic, everyday, wide-awake consciousness of the self as a working person. All the other ways one experiences oneself, as a religious or economic or legal agent, are equally variants from that one "attentive" self. But "the paramount reality of everyday life," as the phenomenologist Alfred Schutz calls this common province of alert consciousness, is not free of history. Because it depends upon the experience of the self in work—by which I mean all work, not only remunerated labor—changes in the way work is organized will change the basic "work consciousness" of a society.[17]

In 1790, New England was largely a society of rural freeholders. Perhaps 80 percent of the Massachusetts population lived and worked on family farms, and only 13.5 percent of the people lived in places that numbered more than 2,500 residents. Seventy years later almost 60 percent of the population lived in urban areas, most of whom were wage- and salary-earners.

Two economic revolutions had begun. New England, never a stranger to commercialism, witnessed an enormous upsurge in trade during the years after 1815. This reached into every household, while a regional and national market for agricultural and homecraft production was established. Rapid development of transportation systems—turnpike roads, canals, and railroads—forced the integration of economic activity. Grain imported from the Genesee Valley of New York and later from the western prairies pushed New England farmers into dairying, growing fruit, and raising cattle and sheep for meat and wool—agricultural sectors that still offered advantages to hill farmers close to urban centers, seaports, and textile factories. Basic agricultural equipment, cloth, and household furnishings equally became enmeshed in wider trade networks. The lure of cash income to be earned in production for market and to be spent in purchasing nonlocal products was virtually irresistible.

The second change was industrialization. Spreading outward from rural hamlets where waterpowered carding and spinning mills replaced the domestic preparation of fibers for weaving, New England textile manufacturing developed rapidly in these same decades. Great manufacturing centers for textiles, shoes, machinery, wood products, and other commodities emerged in the 1840s and 1850s. Although the proportion of mill workers in the population reached perhaps 20 percent by 1860, many of them recent immigrants from England and Ireland, the impact of industrialization was as powerful as that of commercial expansion.

In sum, work experience for many New Englanders was transformed from seasonal, task-oriented labor in the context of family livelihood and local exchange into clock-bound labor for cash income, in the company of relative strangers, with equipment owned by and for profits gained by capitalists. The change in the "ownership of the means of production," as Marx termed this transformation, made an overwhelming difference in the ordinary work consciousness of the society. By extension, every other kind of consciousness was also affected.

Interpreting the Language of Religious Experience: A Statement on Method

Let me turn now to my primary goal, reconstructing what New Englanders meant when they spoke of their personal religious experience. Although religion is arguably a self-contained realm of discourse, irreducible to other contexts, the expression of religious experience is still as much an entry into a social setting as walking through a church door. There is, in other words, no such thing as an account of personal experience unmediated by social and cultural forces, not the least of which is the lexicon available to its renderers.

I have sampled and referred to many different types of sources: diaries, letters, and conversion narratives; revival accounts and histories of particular churches; autobiographies and memoirs; hagiographies of pious "saints," missionaries, and martyrs; sermons, theological treatises, and philosophical disquisitions; manuscript collections of ministerial papers; advice manuals and devotional handbooks; church and moral society records; religious periodicals and ministerial association minutes; religious fiction and poetry; religious architecture, art, artifact, and music; and much commentary, contemporary and historical, on all of this. Every document frames its portrayal of religious life in the context of its time, place, manner, anticipated and remembered consequence. None is a "pure" account of "pure" experience, whatever that might be. A Gothic Revival church has meaning as a religious statement only in relationship to the Greek Revival churches it supplanted, and they in turn only when considered alongside earlier Federal-style meetinghouses, and so on. A revival account republished thirty years later is often interpretable as a polemic in a war declared by veterans against new recruits, especially when the sly devil of a compiler has taken liberties with the original text. A memoir adds the patina of later reflection onto the events recounted, almost always to vindicate youthful experience in the light of later wisdom.

Another way of saying this is to acknowledge the influence of Kenneth Burke's "dramatistic" method of literary criticism. According to Burke, every statement, in whatever genre, can be understood as a dramatic action. Even the most abstruse theological work—like Samuel Hopkins's *System of Doctrines*—is filled with images of the way man as an agent acts in regard to his God. Every statement has an *agent,* even if the subject is apparently unspecified. There is an *act,* a discernible movement in the world. The agent employs an *agency,* some instrumentality as concrete as a tool or as abstract as another person or a part of one's mind. The act occurs in a *scene,* which is both time and place. And, finally there is a *purpose,* a goal, some change in the world. All these terms are deeply interconnected in each statement.[18]

When a nineteenth-century theologian, as an example, wrote that a man is by nature either attracted to or repelled by God, his language presumed a form of dramatic action in which the sinner (his *agent*), seeking reconciliation with divinity (*purpose*), has to cross the divide between himself and God. The *act* of crossing such a *scene* employs the *agencies* of his good conscience and God's attracting power. Thus, the theological language can stand muster alongside (and be as useful to the historian as) more personal depictions of religious crisis; for example, a contemporary letter writer complains that he is "too far" from God. Both sources, and more than each alone, point to a praxis of religious experience in which the separation between sinner and God is metaphorically spatial as well as spiritual. To be sure, genre makes a difference. The theological analysis claims to be doctrinal truth; it refers, implicitly, to previous treatises and tracts; it can be tested against the "facts"—scriptural anecdotes, other doctrinal arguments, or observations about contemporary life—that it claims to explain. The personal letter exemplifies its loneliness and distance from God by being a private communication, written in the first person and sent to a person expected to understand and sympathize.

By encouraging us to view every document in this way, Burke's method allows us to translate the landscape of New England religion into a giant stage set. Hundreds of voices crowd our stage, each claiming that his or her experience comes directly from the hand of God but each related to every other.

A director's nightmare, the dread of every historian? At this point, a synthesis of these thousands of statements, in hundreds of voices, is needed. I will propose my synthesis in reference to the standard accounts put forward by historians of nineteenth-century New England religion.

The History of New England Religion, 1790–1860

There have been two conventional accounts of New England's religious history during this period. One has focused on the history of theology. The basic argument proceeds: The Calvinists were able to hold on to most Congregationalist churches in New England, despite the onslaughts of religious liberals like Universalists and Unitarians and of free-will advocates like Methodists and the Christian Connexion, only because they surrendered their Edwardsean Calvinist principles and became as Arminian as their foes. The historians of theology accept contemporary divisions among nineteenth-century heirs of the Puritans: Hopkinsians, Old Calvinists, New Divinity men, New Side and Old Side Presbyterians, Taylorites, Tylerites, Transcendentalists, Andover Liberals, and Perfectionists. As in more conventional political histories, there are kings (usually college presidents) and battles (pamphlet wars and contests over appointments to important posts).[19]

Such historians excel in the careful dissection of the premises of theological debate and sometimes in tracing the connections between religious thought and secular intellectual history. They fail, however, in assuming that doctrine meant the same thing in 1870 as it had in 1750. They ignore the way belief, or intelligence in general, changed. They assume that the audience for theological fireworks remained constant, instead of seeing that over time these flickers caught the eyes only of an increasingly isolated professional fraternity of professors and denominational leaders. The exposition of a theoretical argument, for characters like the politician Daniel Webster and the preacher Lyman Beecher, may have served to identify them with certain symbolic, patriotic causes, rather than expressing any coherent view of the way the world is ruled. For personalities like the writer Harriet Beecher Stowe and her celebrated brother Henry Ward Beecher, ideas often illustrated particular moods or were vehicles of individual expressiveness. Not every piece of intellectual work aims to refine dogmatic truth.

If the history of dogma has overemphasized conflicts among different schools of thought and undervalued the way each generation agreed upon the fundamental praxes of religion, the social, institutional, or ecclesiastical history of New England evangelicism has too often assumed the continuity of the social processes at work. In the standard account, the long religious revival called the Second Great Awakening, which began in New England during the late 1790s, sparked the next fifty years of religious innovations, including a vastly more instrumental form of revivalism, the extraordinary development of church bureaucracies to carry out moral reform and benevolent activities, the institutional arrangements by which modern American denominationalism and the "voluntary system" was established, and even the sentimentalism of midcentury women writers. For some historians who focus on the religious world itself, these seven decades have been interpreted as the steady if increasingly frantic effort of a ministerial elite to maintain its "social control" against the forces of American democracy, free thinking, and secularization. For others, newly emphasizing the role of religion in women's history or political culture, it is easier to see an unchanging religious backdrop for the changes they portray.[20]

But there was not just one economy of religious experience in this period, as social historians assume, nor is the history of experience encapsulated by the conflicts among doctrinal groups. In introducing my own synthetic structure, let me return to my example about the sinner's assumed need to close the distance between himself and God, for this is the central fact about the religious experience of evangelicals in the late eighteenth century. As Calvinists, they defined religion as the contrast between the absolute sovereignty of God and the infinite depravity of mankind. Implicit in this division, and in the lengthy Calvinist disputations upon it, were the notions not only that religious experience was a process of attaining a union with God but also that such faith was equivalent to a more profound knowledge of the workings of the universe. Belief in God was for them no pursuit down a blind alley; they would not accept dogmatic explanations that contravened the evidence of their senses and empirical reality. Instead, they believed that reality obeyed a perfect, if abstract, order—and that all the intricacies of that order were ultimately comprehensible by the human intelligence.[21]

Calvinists expected ordinary people to become modest metaphysicians, to be able to explain why God had been wise in permitting people to sin and then punishing them for it, and so on. This expectation was met with surprising success (by our lights); in the process, generations of followers of the Genevan Reformer perceived the world as constructed upon fundamentally consistent theoretical premises. The notion of totality was strikingly well understood and accepted.

New England evangelicals were also heirs of the Renaissance and Reformation developments of the idea of individuality; and certainly the praxis of early commercialism sharpened the perceived bounds of selfhood. The work of Hobbes and Locke, in sponsoring what has been called "the political theory of possessive individualism," strengthened these tendencies toward the idolatry of the isolated self. Henceforth the experience of one's personhood was most clearly revealed when it was demonstrated to one's internal self-consciousness, when one's economic or political interest most powerfully differed from others. The most important self became the "experiencing self" defining oneself largely in opposition to other people and progressively ignoring one's consanguinity with them.[22]

Not coincidentally, at this moment our modern notion of religious experience was first broached. The first recorded usage of "religious experience" in the *Oxford English Dictionary* dates from 1674, initially in a tract written by an English dissenter (as we call the defeated heirs of the Puritan revolution in England after the restoration of Charles II and the reestablishment of Anglican hegemony) and ten years later in the printed margin notes of John Bunyan's *Pilgrim's Progress*, a major classic of the dissenting tradition. At the same time, an enormously popular devotional literature sprang up among dissenters and evangelicals in the first half of the eighteenth century. Works like

Philip Doddridge's *The Rise and Progress of Religion in the Soul* were frequently reprinted both in Britain and America and served as inspirational models for evangelical Christians on two continents. The 1730s and 1740s saw an explosion of enthusiastic, pietistic religion throughout the Protestant world, even in central Europe, as well as among Hasidic Jews further east.[23]

The major American voice of that revival, the First Great Awakening, was Jonathan Edwards (1703–1758). It was still possible for Edwards, in the first half of the eighteenth century, to weave the Calvinist and Lockean threads together and to define religious experience as the affective apperception of the perfect aesthetic fitness between God's abstract Being and man's woeful finitude, but Edwards's rapturous vision was not easily replicated among his parishioners or his disciples. Edwards and Calvin came gradually to be seen as defenders of a barbarous notion of extreme divine authority, in which man counted for nothing. What had been for them a celebration of both human intelligence and the joyful possibilities of joining the human and the divine became simply a picture of metaphysical gloom to nineteenth-century optimists preferring the "liberal" view of man's individuality.[24]

The New England evangelicals, on the brink of the nineteenth century, faced this liberal dilemma in a peculiarly stark form. On the one hand, they insisted that each sinner work out his spiritual destiny through his own personal, interior, self-conscious experience; on the other hand, this destiny was supposed to relate to the total metaphysical meaning of the universe. Every single mind was expected to become the battleground on which the eternal war of grace and sin was fought. Liberalism had disassembled the mediating apparatus whereby the individual self could be integrated, piece by piece, in larger orders of meaning. Chief among such mechanisms for Americans had been the "covenant" theology of the Puritans, whereby a person was bound to share in the rewards and punishments of the community because *it* was collectively pledged to God's glory. Even before the end of the seventeenth century, New Englanders like Cotton Mather had turned from such systematic social intermediaries and drawn vastly larger meanings from the dramas of individual men like John Winthrop. By 1800, New Englanders could believe in either themselves or God; the challenge to evangelicals was to find a way to believe in both.[25]

Part One of this study concerns the efforts of New England evangelicals, around the turn of the nineteenth century, to reconcile themselves to this separation between the human and divine spheres. They accomplished this, and successfully initiated thousands of new members into their churches, by developing a praxis that urged Christians to become perfectly still and in their stillness to glimpse the totality of God's universe and their proper places within it. When parishioners and converts talked about their personal experiences, they preferred to use doctrinal or scriptural language;

their actions were most usually felt to be true when they accorded with the world view of orthodox Calvinism. For this reason, I have chosen to call this a *doctrinalist* or *orthodox* economy of experience, not because the evangelicals adhered more strongly to religious beliefs but because they felt that the end of experience was to exemplify the truth of the doctrines they espoused. Consequently, the faculty of the mind central to their religious enterprise was the understanding, rather than the will or the feelings; intellectual effort was necessary to determine the relationship between one's particular experience and the doctrinal explanations available from the pulpit, the Bible, or the minister's library.

The key word for the self in the doctrinalist economy was *soul,* which expressed well the sense that the person belonged to God and that the major events of one's life concerned that higher relationship, rather than the myriad ties of ordinary life. Still, the gulf between the metaphysical language of theology and one's personal way of viewing things could not be bridged forever by the doctrinalist method. And so, in the early nineteenth century, one finds the beginning of an effort to close the distance between the divine and the human. The first such strategy, which I call *moralism,* accomplished this by reducing the metaphysical range of the divine. Instead of appealing to doctrinal and scriptural statements to demonstrate one's essential correctness, evangelicals began to align themselves with the moral norms of their own communities. To be right and true, for moralists, meant behaving with propriety under all circumstances. Subjecting one's behavior to habits of rectitude counted for more than applying doctrinal notions to a midnight crisis of the soul. For moralists, the crucial human quality was the moral will, with which a man assented to the (divinely decreed) limits revealed to his conscience.[26]

Moralism, the subject of Part Two of this study, preferred to use the word *character* to represent the self. Character was implicitly both an empirical and a normative term. Moralism coincided as an explanatory scheme with the great nineteenth-century expansion of religious organizations, devoted to the reformation of morals and the expansion of evangelical Christianity. These organizational impulses provided the order into which one's personal experience could fit and safely allowed the magisterial aspects of the divine to go unheeded. I do not mean to suggest that the moralists were any less orthodox in their religious beliefs but only that belief as such meant less to them than to their doctrinalist colleagues and predecessors.

In Part Three I will address another way of foreshortening the distance between the divine and human spheres. The increasing tendency in evangelicalism, akin to romanticism everywhere, was to inflate the self so that it incarnated the divine within itself. Religious experience now became a self-contained world, exciting as an experience for its own sake. The dominant praxis of personal religion, especially in the decades after 1840, was a withdrawal from the social world and a dedication to devotionalist exercises within the privacy of one's own mind. Religious *devotionalism,* as I call this economy of experience, found its most consistent expression in the demand for one-to-one relationships between the self and its friends, the self and God as a companion, and the events of one's life history (in the increasing emphasis placed upon repetitive events). For devotionalists, each self was its own little universe, and the perfect individuality of that notion led to the use of the word *personality* as the most apt term for the self. In the devotionalist religious exercise, each experience was interpreted with chief reference only to other experiences, not to moral norms or theological dogmas. For this reason, devotionalism was a kind of "technical" religiosity, in which the ends of personal experience could be found in the process itself, in the techniques employed by devotees.

The doctrinalist, moralist, and devotionalist are, I should make clear from the outset, "ideal types," artificial constructions that serve as composites of the hundreds of voices and thousands of religious expressions I have culled. For convenience in argument, I imagine them frequently in heated dispute with one another. But it is just as true that each was an evasive language, a way of safely misconstruing one's antagonists by shifting the terms of the dispute onto experiential grounds. Orthodoxy, moral reform, and sentimentalism were not schools of thought but habits of action; each was recasting religious life on new terms.

In the Conclusion, I argue that the transformation of the economies of religious experience is a template for understanding parallel changes in other areas of everyday life—education, law, childrearing, literature, commerce, and industry. In the history of all these fields, recent scholarship has demonstrated the tremendous significance of this period of American life. I believe that the progression from doctrinalism, through moralism and devotionalism, broadly construed, is the process by which New Englanders experienced the changes wrought by the emergence of an urban, commercial, and industrial society, and, finally, that our history since 1860 has been powerfully shaped by the conflict among these three ways of organizing personal experience.

Those are my goals as a historian of the American self and society. The other part of me, an intellectual historian with a special fondness for Edwards and Melville, views this work as a prolegomenon for assessing the masterly artists of New England's interiority—Emerson, Thoreau, Hawthorne, Dickinson, and William James. More than the ink and paper they used, the publishers and audiences they needed, or even the sources of the stories they told, these dramatists of New England's faith and works need to be understood against the common language of religious life among their contemporaries. These great writers voiced the spiritual drama of New England in a way that would have perplexed old John Phillips, to be sure. But that he was their contemporary is a fact, though mysterious, that historians cannot ignore.

Nor can historians, pleased with their schematic reconstructions of past lives, neglect the way that religion—even in stable historical moments—is an unsettling and powerful challenge to the human intellect. It takes care to preserve and impart the past but even more admirable qualities to address the ultimate questions in our lives.

THE SPIRITUAL SELF IN EVERYDAY LIFE

PART ONE

SOUL
The Economy of Doctrinal Experience

Chapter One

Charles Backus and the Revival in Somers

ON AN EARLY spring day in 1791, the Reverend Charles
Backus stood in the pulpit of the little meetinghouse in the country town of
Bethlem, Connecticut, and addressed the assembly of ministers and towns-
people called to celebrate the ordination of twenty-five-year-old Azel Backus,
Charles's nephew, to the pastoral care of God's flock in that place. Seeking to
encourage the nervous young man, the elder Backus chose as the subject of
his sermon *The Faithful Ministers of Jesus Christ Rewarded.* "The prosperity of
the church in the present world," he advised, "is promoted by the services of
those who are pastors after God's own heart." What then, are the signs of this
prosperity?

> Visible success attends the ministry of some so soon as they enter on
> their work; a few, after spending many years in the vineyard, hear for
> the first time a general enquiry among the people of their charge,
> "What must I do to be saved?" And though many pass through life with-
> out seeing much fruit from their counsels and warnings, yet the seed
> sown by them may spring up in a glorious harvest after they are gath-
> ered to their fathers.[1]

In any case, the faithful minister will be blessed by God for his labors. But which fate, Azel Backus must have wondered, would be mine? Could I spend an entire lifetime in this frontier village and harvest not one more soul to add to the tiny band of Bethlem's saints? All the senior ministers present would have grimly nodded yes to such a question.

At least Azel Backus knew what job he had to do. A minister of the established Congregational Church in Connecticut or Massachusetts might be many things to his people. He could be a model of industry, tending carefully to his five or ten acres of field crops and his team of oxen. He could certainly be an example of patience and forbearance, especially if he did not press too hard for his claims for speedy payment of the five hundred dollars or so his parishioners had pledged to pay him every year. (By law, every town was obligated to support an "orthodox" minister and to provide land for a meetinghouse and burying ground.) He could be a counselor and consoler to the troubled families of his parish. He had to be a paragon of the strictest morality. His college training had prepared him to tutor the brightest lads, perhaps one every other year, on their way to his alma mater in Cambridge, New Haven, or Providence. More to the point, he was expected to expound the truth in three weekly sermons—the two on the Sabbath focusing on scriptural teachings and one, midweek, discoursing more freely on contemporary issues. In some places his political insight was valued, and his kind words about General Washington might sway some votes for ratification of the federal constitution.[2]

But all these plentiful duties were secondary. As Charles Backus said, Azel's primary task was the ingathering of souls, the reconciliation of individual sinners to God through the gospel scheme, the spiritual nurture of Christ's flock. That is what it meant to be an *evangelical* minister: to emphasize that sinners have "to make themselves a new heart." Encouraging conversions was primary. Nathanael Emmons, the dean of Calvinist ministers in New England, put the point bluntly: "The end which faithful ministers propose to themselves, in entering into the ministry is, to promote the salvation of souls." From the earliest days of New England, the Puritans had stressed the importance of a conversion experience, a personal pilgrimage through the Calvinist drama of sin, salvation, and sanctity.[3]

Even after the American Revolution, the ritual ordination of a new minister in Bethlem must have felt like a renewal of this, New England's errand. To work for the salvation of souls was to cultivate a well-traced furrow. The minister's tools, like his discernment of the difference between seed and fruit, were treasured legacies from the past.

Thus, we cannot fully explore the meaning of Azel Backus's career without looking back. For like everyone in the room that day, the young minister knew whose shoes he was filling in Bethlem. The town was tiny, and Backus was only its second minister, but how mighty had been the first! For fifty years, until the previous month, the pulpit office in Bethlem had been sublimely filled by the stout and imposing personage of Joseph Bellamy. All acknowledged Bellamy as one of the great minds of New England Calvinism, and all knew what the condition of religion had been in the year of *his* ordination, 1740, the *annus mirabilis* of New England evangelicism.[4]

Up and down the Atlantic Coast that year the magnificent preaching of George Whitefield attracted tens of thousands to outdoor worship services. Whitefield was nominally Anglican and a close associate of the founders of Methodism, John and Charles Wesley. But his doctrinal exposition did not impress Whitefield's hearers; instead, his preaching victoriously compressed the whole process of conversion into a single moment. Sinners, he urged, had the power to achieve a "new birth" instantaneously, sensuously, self-consciously. Thousands of them suddenly discovered themselves on the precipice of hell and witnessed personally the saving power of God's absolute sovereignty and Christ's ability to atone for all their sins.[5]

"In 1740," Bellamy once recalled, "every man, woman and child, above five or six years old, were under religious concern more or less." The effects were obvious: "quarrels were ended, frolics flung up, prayer meetings began, and matters of religion were all the talk." Consider what this yearlong universal concern about religion meant. Every neighbor's child, when inquired about, could be a source of surprising news about Christ's goodness. Old foes, long embittered about the location of a town road, could now exemplify similar illuminations of "gracious affections" on their hearts. From the stupors of taprooms and the slumbers of barn lofts there now could emerge the shadowy failures of Yankee towns, and they too could taste the universality of God's "covenant of grace."[6]

Nothing like this Great Awakening had been seen in Puritan New England. As the instances of Whitefield's triumphs, and then of other itinerants and settled ministers, began to grow, they were described, collected, and distributed in periodicals like *The Christian History*, published in Boston. Notices of revivals in other American colonies, in Scotland and Wales, encouraged some to think that the blessed day was near—the thousand-year reign of Christ on earth, the millennium promised in the Book of Revelation.

In most outward ways, the worlds of Joseph Bellamy and Azel Backus were consistent. Despite the furor of separatism, the Congregational clergy still retained the allegiance of 85 percent of New Englanders in 1760, according to Ezra Stiles, minister of Newport's Second Church. The ordinary rhythms of agricultural New England, in which the property sufficient to a competent livelihood was well distributed, seemed to go on as before. When external affairs intruded, as they did explosively in the campaign to capture the French fort at Louisbourg in Nova Scotia in 1745, the French and Indian War in 1756–1763, or the resistance, rebellion, and revolutionary war dating from the Stamp Act Crisis of 1765, New England's "black regiment" of Congregational ministers still spoke with one voice to shape local opinion in support of the autonomy and traditions of the region.[7]

But beneath the surface of such consistencies, the religious world of New England had changed considerably during this half-century. From the Awakening four distinct clerical parties had emerged, though they had not yet taken a distinctive institutional form. First, the rationalist ministers, focused at Harvard, were strongest in eastern Massachusetts and in coastal towns. Like Charles Chauncy of Boston, they were open to liberalizing currents in theology, leading them to self-proclaimed Unitarianism in the 1820s. But their preaching was more often directed at encouraging habits of moral rectitude than at high-flown theologizing. Second, in western Massachusetts and Connecticut, the dominant party was Edwardsean, variously called New Lights, New Divinity men, or Consistent Calvinists. Hating the self-serving strivings of "unregenerate" people for their own reformation, they called upon their parishioners to enact the Calvinist drama of reconciling God's absolute sovereignty with man's infinite sinfulness through an experience of "new birth." Influential at Yale, Princeton, and newly established Dartmouth, they retained an institutional conservatism about local church government. Their new doctrinal emphasis brought them into a conflict with a third group, the Old Calvinists or Old Lights, still powerful at Yale. Closest to the pre-Awakening Puritans in theology and ecclesiology, the Old Lights feared that innovative doctrinal speculation would disrupt the harmony of local churches. Finally, there were the Separates, some still Congregationalist but increasingly Baptist as the years went on. Instrumental in the founding of Brown, their theology resembled Edwardseanism, but as closely knit communities of sectaries they fought hard for the disestablishment of religion and freedom of conscience. Strongest in eastern Connecticut, they were becoming a dominant voice on the northern frontier of New England. In Vermont and Maine, where the population was increasing rapidly, Baptists and other radical "new lights" took advantage of the Congregationalists' failure to recruit enough ministers for every new settled town.[8]

Each party supported the movement to independence. Each articulated a rhetoric of liberty that identified American republicanism as a crusade against the Antichrist. Together they sponsored the *rage militaire* in 1775–1776 that animated the struggle to wrest control of America's destiny from British hands, to defend the holy integrity of New England's divine mission as a Bible commonwealth.[9]

But New England evangelical religion had fragmented sufficiently so that there was no mistaking the leanings of the group that convened for Azel Backus's ordination on that April morning in Bethlem. They were Edwardsean to a man. For them the experience of the first-generation Puritans was a hallowed memory, but the memory of the Great Awakening was a vivid model of experience. They saw religion through the lens, particularly, of the post-

Awakening writings of Jonathan Edwards and Joseph Bellamy. They considered themselves the children of the Awakening, and they prayed for its return.

When Edwards died in 1758, shortly after becoming president of the college at Princeton, he left Bellamy and the other defenders of the Great Awakening to reshape a social world around the intense personal exercises of religion he had outlined. A new kind of community was needed to comprise and encourage this kind of benevolence and inner conviction. These men, the New Divinity ministers, knew that individual conversions and modest behavior were not enough. In a powerful 1758 sermon, Bellamy called for something even greater than a great awakening. "Nor can the salvation of their own souls, although ever so safely secured," he noted, "satisfy their minds, without a clear view of Christ's final victory over all his enemies."[10]

Bellamy used this sermon, entitled "The Millennium," to demonstrate that the collected saints would do much more than glory in their common godliness. They would enjoy a world of wonder and loveliness, in which poverty, sickness, ignorance, and despair would be conquered. This world would be brought about by God's blessing the exertions of Christians united in the holy cause. As Bellamy promised the saints,

> in a firm belief that the cause they were engaged in, and for which they spilt their blood, would finally prevail, and prevail in this world, where they then beheld satan reigning and triumphing, I say, in a firm belief of this, the whole army of martyrs could march on to battle courageously, willing to sacrifice their lives in the cause, not doubting of final victory, although they themselves must fall in the field.

This language rings with such urgency that it's hard to imagine that Bellamy had no specific battles in mind. The battle, of course, was to find "the cause," for it was in the heat of contention for the church militant, finally, that the excruciating pains of personal conversion would be redeemed.[11]

Gradually, perhaps inevitably, certainly with tragic results, the evangelicals began to believe in the 1760s and 1770s that the struggle for American independence was the cause they were seeking, the social "glue" to make permanent the collective enthusiasms of the Whitefield year. In 1762, Bellamy gave an election sermon before the governor and general assembly in Connecticut, urging Connecticut's people to "stone [sin] until it is dead," and three years later the colony's evangelicals were at the forefront of the Stamp Act protesters who surrounded the tax agents, despoiled the churches and rectories of the Anglican officials in the colony, and forged the chain of radicalizing choices that led to a revolution a decade later.[12]

This ideological association of evangelical pietism with the radical politics of the Revolution can best be seen in the 1774 sermon "Liberty Described and Recommended," delivered by Levi Hart to the freemen of Farmington, Connecticut. Bellamy's student as well as his son-in-law, Hart anointed the resistance to British oppression as "the sacred cause of liberty." But the liberty Hart recommended was not the sort to set Farmington men free from all obligation so that they could do whatever they wanted. Instead, Hart found his definition of liberty in Edwards's twenty-year-old treatise, *Freedom of the Will*. A moral man is not free to make up his own mind, out of thin air as it were, but only to enact the moral inclinations within him. A good man is part of the moral order, moved by its urgencies and guided by its dictates. He feeds upon the leadings of his moral perceptions and in turn makes the world moral by his actions. Thus Hart could say, in a way unfamiliar to most modern Americans, "civil liberty doth not consist in a freedom from all law and government, but in a freedom from unjust law and tyrannical government." [13]

The individual citizen is never alone. Insofar as he is "considered a member of society, he hath no interest but that of the whole body, of which he is a member." Society is not a composite of atomized men, each pursuing his private interest. It is an organism of vastly greater significance as a whole than in its individual parts. "The crime of every private member in opposing the interest of society," Hart warned, "is greater than that of the opposition to the interest of an individual, as much (other things being equal) as the interest of society is greater and of more than that of an individual.' "[14]

For Hart, slavery is a bondage to sin. He starts with physical servitude (in almost every New England rural community, ten to twenty African-Americans belonged to the richest families) and reasons from there to civil liberty and ultimately to spiritual freedom. Emancipation is progressive. "With what a very ill grace," he asks, "can we plead for slavery when *we* are the tyrants, when we are engaged in one united struggle for the enjoyment of liberty." But it would be an even greater madness to "prefer the guilty slavery of sin and satan, to the glorious perfect liberty of the children of God!" [15]

Thus the battle against Lord North and General Gage is only a first step, though it may lead to something greater. "What is English liberty?" Hart asks, "What is American freedom? When compared with the glorious liberty of the sons of God." [16]

The question for evangelicals in 1774, as resistance was leading to rebellion and rebellion to full-scale revolutionary war, was this: Would the sons of liberty be the children of God? Would the American Revolution be a victory of communal over private interest? Would the Americans, in the exertions of military strife and political contention, devise a civil society dedicated to the common welfare?

By the end of the war the answer to all these questions was clearly no. Far from launching the work of redemption, the war for independence nearly destroyed the religious life of New England. A crusade for righteousness devolved over eight years into an astonishingly bitter internecine struggle. Corruption, chicanery, profiteering, treason, and cowardice evidenced the failure of war to sustain, much less to purify, the moral bearings of the patriots. So inflated an expectation led less often to self-sacrifice than to accusations of betrayal. The Hessian mercenaries were scarcely less hated by civilians than were the continental troops, or the officers by their men, or the soldiers by their leaders. Everyone, including its members, scorned the Continental Congress.

Nathanael Emmons of Franklin, Massachusetts, recalled that the war

> diverted the attention, and even the affections of the people from me. They were so much embarrassed themselves with the experiences, labors, and fatigues of the war, that they neglected to attend public worship, and became very indifferent to every thing of a religious nature. Those who had been apparently warm friends, became cold and distant in their behavior towards me, and sometimes, indeed, treated me with real disrespect and contempt.[17]

Emmons tried to resign his charge in 1781 and 1784, but his people refused his requests for a formal dismission. (He served until the year of his death, 1840!)

Another leader, Samuel Hopkins of Newport, Rhode Island, whose name was placed at the head of the Edwardsean party around this time, saw his parsonage and meetinghouse utterly ruined, his congregation dispersed, and the efforts of his preaching swept away by the British assault and the French occupation of the seaport town. A devout layman, Captain James Morris of Litchfield, Connecticut, wrote of the town next to Bethlem: "Profane swearing and open Sabbath-breaking and drunkenness were not uncommon among professors in religion. About the year 1780 South Farms [Parish] was a stench in the nostrils of all good men." Eminent ministers suffered, churches were abandoned, and meetinghouses fell into disrepair, burying grounds into unweeded disarray, and local manners into decay. Ministerial salaries went unpaid year after year, and new college men chose the secular pulpits of political and military office rather than the sacred calling.[18]

The economic dislocations that came with the return of peace were, if anything, worse than the deprivations of war. Many in the countryside could not meet their obligations for debts and taxes. The privileged and well-spoken seemed free of communal restraint as they speculated in depreciated notes or finagled land grants for their associates. Ministers, of course, could only appeal for voluntary contributions and community obligation to stay their families' destitution, but merchants and town officials took the quicker, harsher path of legal action to seize their neighbor's goods and land in lieu of repayment. The new American states, far from being commonwealths of civil self-sacrifice, seemed to set the pursuit of private interest as their highest value. Around this time Noah Webster coined the word "demoralizing."[19]

By the summer of 1786, the debtors' resentment exploded in mob disruptions, led by Daniel Shays and Luke Day, of county court sessions held at Northampton, Worcester, and Springfield, Massachusetts. For six months, until the insurrection was crushed by a private army of gentlemen (recruited and reimbursed with state funds by Governor Bowdoin), the Shaysites threatened Massachusetts with civil war.[20]

Few evangelical ministers, especially those of the established Congregational church, sided with the Shaysites. For almost all of them the events of 1786–1787 sealed further talk of the "sacredness" of liberty's cause. There was more talk now of the sacredness of obligation and obedience, of peace and quiet. New England seemed further than ever from a sure and progressive evolution into the Bellamyite millennium. Some began to abandon Bellamy's hopeful assumption that the millennium would be *followed* by the Day of Judgment and began to look for omens of the coming cataclysm, the Apocalypse, which would *precede* the thousand-year reign of Christ on earth.[21]

The followers of Samuel Hopkins still avowed the ideal of disinterestedness, asking his famous question of all prospective converts, "Are you willing to be damned for the greater glory of God?" But now the weight of the question seemed to tip toward its harsh opening words rather than the promise of its conclusion. The church, after all, also had its interests, apart from those of secular men and women. It needed to look out for its own. And that led Charles Backus, standing in the Bethlem pulpit in April 1791, to urge the assembled clergy forward: "The prosperity of the church in the present world is promoted by the services of those who are pastors after God's own heart."

After they had each extended the right hand of fellowship to Azel Backus, the ministers who had come to Bethlem prepared to depart for home. Some, including Charles Backus, had a considerable distance to ride, and the time from Wednesday's ordination ceremony to the following Sunday's sermon in their own pulpits was not very long in those days of poor roads. Still, as he rode eastward with one of his students through the spring mud to the Connecticut River Valley, where they could pick up the smoother road north to Somers, near the Massachusetts border, Backus was crossing a comfortable landscape. The crazy quilt of Connecticut town roads led him past meetinghouses and parsonages occupied by men whose temperamental and doctrinal peculiarities were as familiar to him as the members of his family, as the characters in his well-thumbed Old Testament.

To an orderly and sober fellow like Charles Backus, there was a seemliness to things that April. He took a special pleasure in seeing Azel settled at Joseph Bellamy's Bethlem, for that post fittingly closed a circle. Charles had been a student of Levi Hart at Preston, and so in sponsoring Azel he had trained a successor for the teacher of his teacher. But his own calling was not satisfied by closing such tidy historical circles. Had he been the "faithful minister" his ordination sermon had celebrated? Surely his own ordination sixteen years earlier must have come to mind as he rode home. "I hope," he later wrote of the event, "that amidst all my wickedness, I have not forgotten the weight of my charge." He could tick off his accomplishments. There had been a long succession of young men, straight from the mild tutelage of Ezra Stiles at Yale College, whom he had tutored in the Edwardsean way of interpreting texts and recommended for licensing by the Tolland (North) Association of ministers. There had been his successful contention in Somers against Separatism, early in his tenure. [22]

But a revival, a general awakening like that of the 1740s, had always escaped him. Backus had been a lonely convert himself, whose tortuous path through the agonies of self-renunciation had been accompanied only by the guidance of a handy copy of Edwards's *Religious Affections*. One or two similarly isolated cases of spiritual turmoil might find their way each year to the door of the Somers minister's study. But a general revival never came, and by the time Charles Backus helped ordain his nephew, as we have seen, he could ponder the possibility that it might never happen.

Almost six years would pass, and then suddenly, in February 1797, "a serious attention to religion began in this town," Backus wrote. Coming on the heels of "a season of awful security," in which not one convert had come forward in three years, it was a great surprise. The Somers revival was neither the first nor the most powerful of the 1790s in New England, but it will serve us well as an example of the local awakenings that exploded all over the region during the decade that crossed into the nineteenth century. Together we call these the beginnings of the Second Great Awakening in New England, which ushered in a new kind of spiritual economy. The personal experience of religion, the social and institutional forms that accommodated that personal experience, the relationship of religion to the world of ordinary affairs—all were transformed in the Second Awakening. And in that transformation, as we shall begin to see in this and the next chapter, the nineteenth-century New England "self" began to take a new form. [23]

Something new was occurring in Somers. "There was not at that time," Backus reported, "any uncommon serious thoughtfulness within fifty miles of us." Yet, just two years later, Edward Griffin announced that he could stand in his doorway at New Hartford, Connecticut—close to Somers—"and number fifty or sixty contiguous congregations laid down in one field of divine wonders, and as many more in different parts of New England." [24]

Backus and Griffin wrote these reports for the *Connecticut Evangelical Magazine*, founded in 1800 because "such displays of divine power and grace ought to be faithfully narrated to the world, for the purpose of awakening the secure." Backus's account, the first published, set the pattern for many to follow. "The revival," he began, "was not rapid in its progress, and never became general in the town. Here and there one, in different parts of the place, were seriously impressed, within two or three months from the beginning of the work. It continued to increase for almost a year. It then began to decline." We can hear the minister marvel: this revival has a life of its own; it is not my doing; it belongs to God. Like a gardener gleeful at news of the first spring wildflowers, Backus was heartened by news of "seriousness" in a household near the Enfield line, then another over on the Stafford road, then one in the center village. Who was being converted?[25]

"This awakening," Backus wrote, "began with the youth, and afterwards extended to the middle aged, and to a few who had passed the meridian of life. The greater part of the subjects of this work were heads of families. More than half of the whole were under 35 years of age." The church and town records confirm this account. As the revival continued, more and more men in their late twenties, thirties, or even forties professed, whereas five of the first six were between nineteen and twenty-two. Conversion was an interruption in their lives, arriving as a momentary reprieve from the course of ordinary mortality, an unanticipated chance to set all things straight.[26]

But if the appearance of the revival surprised Backus, it hardly caught him or his congregation unprepared, intellectually or organizationally. Backus's role, particularly, was markedly restrained. Far from taking credit for the awakening, he represented himself only as the "discoverer" of the seriousness in his midst. Clearly he was not out prowling for distressed local sinners; discoveries were better made by watching those people already in the pews who had never been converted. If they could be awakened through the regular "means" of two services on the Sabbath day, then Backus saw little need for unusual methods to press their cases along. Thus, he instituted only two extra weekly meetings, one for the young on Wednesdays and the other for "the church" (those already communicants) on Sabbath evenings. Both were conducted at the minister's house. He made little effort to push the inquiring further along, to inflame their passion in the cauldron of community fervor. The Somers revival was no camp meeting extravaganza, like those of the Second Great Awakening in Kentucky or western New York. A biographer notes that Backus "wished those who were impressed with the importance of religion to have time for retirement, for reading the Scriptures and other books, and for reflection and prayer." As a follower of Samuel Hopkins, Backus believed that the unregenerate (the unconverted) could do little to advance their own causes. Rather than spur them to fruitless action, it seemed more profitable to encourage their gradually deepening understanding of the course of faith.[27]

The minister's reticence was mirrored in the stillness of his parishioners. "This awakening," the magazine account reassured readers, "was not, in a single instance, attended with outcry or noise. The subjects of it appeared very solemn while attending public worship, and conferences." No itinerants were invited in to rant, no one accused the minister of lacking gospel faith. Backus would not even permit people to speak of themselves in the first person singular, feeling that this was a sign of "egotism and self-display."[28]

But a coolheaded conversion was in no way an easy personal experience. While converts were restrained, they were emotionally rapt. The first stage was a sense of alarm: "they wondered that they had not before seen themselves on the brink of everlasting ruin." As the awakened came to accept the language of the church for their plight, they had two choices: they could either slip back into a "state of carnal peace" or press onward to a "more full discovery of their moral pollution." This latter experience, getting an eyeful of one's own tainted nature, involved a violent self-rejection called "conviction." In this largely intellectual process, one became committed to change or "repent" by repeatedly dredging up and "discovering" one's own vileness.

No accusation was too damning. "They confessed," recalled their pastor, "that they felt themselves to be enemies to God, and wholly opposed to the plan of salvation revealed in the gospel." But phrased in this way, no accusation was actually very personal. To be an enemy to God was to oppose his gospel plan, not his person. Their disloyalty was to the doctrinal "plan of salvation," to the road map of regeneration, not to its publisher. The sum of their self-vilification was to say no to divinity.

Thus, whatever pain the awakened felt was constrained by this dispassionate way of depicting their sinfulness. "They were distressed," for example, "because they had no proper conviction of their sins." And, when they began to attain this depth of conviction or self-knowledge, and "their consciences told them they should receive no wrong if they were sent to hell," then the affections reached their crest: "their hearts rose against the justice and sovereignty of God."

So even as they became emotionally provoked, their hearts found objectionable the abstract qualities of the deity or rather of the doctrine. In that sense, the heart, although the apparent center of the self and the single faculty that required change in the process of salvation, was still an intellectual organ. For Backus and other disciples of Edwards, Bellamy, and Hopkins, it represented a kind of final judgment of the soul about its maker. It was pointless to be "true to one's heart" if the heart were not true to God.

And then? About the moment of crossing from conviction to conversion, Backus was silent. His next sentence confirmed the importance of ideas, but it did not attempt to venture into the mystery of the divine change that was rebirth. "The hopeful converts," we read, "in general observed that when divine truth first appeared in a new and pleasing light, they scarcely thought of their personal safety; or whether they were, or were not, converted." Now, *the divine doctrines were perceived to be pleasing*. Past reason hated, and, no sooner had, past reason loved. Was one's change of heart only a change of opinion? Well, not if an emotional change followed the intellectual one. "They discovered a relish for the doctrines of the Bible." As before they had been frightened by what they knew, so after the crucial moment they could relish those same truths.

As the only emotion allowed to converts was their disapproval and subsequent approval of the terms of the gospel plan, the experience could not be personally painful. One's case always and only illustrated the rules set forth in Scripture, Backus believed. And so he was not surprised that converts were not assured of their salvation. Having no language to describe their feelings but the one legitimated by doctrine, they apparently had no selfish stake in the outcome. They were not so much tasting the joys of salvation for themselves as personally agreeing that the recipe was right for everyone. While God's power was evidenced in his work on individual souls, they were none the worthier for their personal triumphs.

This was important, for the last thing Backus wanted from the refreshing shower of divine grace was social atomism, with puffed-up converts pronouncing themselves intimates of the Lord and freed from the laws binding all finite souls. Like other Consistent Calvinists, Backus was glad that none of his flock "manifested high confidence of their conversion." Such self-assurance might make converts believe that they "should not live agreeable to covenant bonds" and then fail to appear at Sabbath worship, take communion, baptize and instruct their children, and so on.

Conversion was more than winning a place in eternity: it also fastened the loyalty of Christians to the institutions of the local church. Beyond that, the impact of conversion on personal behavior was left rather vague. "The hopeful converts were reformed in their lives," the pastor claimed, "and appeared desirous to know and practice all the duties both of the first and second table of the law." The primary social experience of conversion lay elsewhere, in taking sides with God's party at the local level. From the meetinghouse porch, Backus's converts were said to "tremble at the thought of reflecting dishonor on his name, in the eyes of a scoffing world." Charges of disloyalty and treason had been flung back and forth for a generation of revolution, war, and political turmoil; it was easy to divide the town between those who honored God and those who scoffed. For the orthodox Congregationalist ministers of Federalist New England, acts that affirmed one's loyalty to the godly were more significant than proper behavior or constrained manners. Within the church community, the Lord's Supper and other ordinances like family prayer and scriptural readings outweighed commitments to temperance or industriousness.

The ends of religion were in a worshipful and holy, not a morally instrumental, life. Instituting household prayer, for example, was better directed at obtaining the children's conversions rather than at improving parental discipline or family intimacy. These last were decidedly secondary ends. To join the church, therefore, was less to embark upon improvements in all of one's

life, although this was occasionally said to happen, than to see one's personal
glory in everything touched by the favor of God's love.

"The first warmth of young converts," Backus warned, "is but of short con-
tinuance. It is soon exchanged for the conflicts of Christian warfare." The
path of the Christian was not easy, and salvation was never entirely secured
in life (or at least, never theoretically assured to one's own knowledge, according to Calvinist orthodoxy). "The followers of Christ are conducted towards heaven, in a way which teaches them their perfect dependence on the
riches of divine grace." All along the road were further rebukes to one's own
pride. What made this tortuous progress conceivable at all was that such
rebukes were themselves evidence of God's involvement with oneself and one's
people, that he governed the world a man inhabited. In sum, the evangelicals
in Somers, even in travail, retained their proprietary feelings about the spirit
of God.

Thus, the surprising explosion of the experience of holiness in Somers
revealed a minister and his community prepared to order that experience
through church procedures, theological and psychological explanations, and
a sympathetic social and political framework. All these ways of ordering were
stamped by their consistency with Calvinist theological doctrine. Religious
experience—as an internal, personal, or social affair—was a chance to demonstrate that correct doctrine could embody itself in the lives of real men and
women.

Such enormous assurance in the truth of Calvinism, such deep faith in the
capacity of language to shape experience, such intense interest in the power
of the human mind to comprehend divinity in this way, such dedication to the
idea of fidelity as the proper bond of society—these were the elements of the
economy of religious life we call *orthodoxy* or *doctrinalism*. They were the rules
by which orthodox evangelicals like Charles Backus reorganized religion in
the Second Great Awakening. To see the boldness of their claim, we must
now move beyond Bethlem, Somers, and the winter of 1797.

Chapter Two

The Power of the Understanding

THE NARRATIVES OF THE REVIVAL of 1800 bespeak a world very different from ours. We come to them curious about life history. We want to know how individual people were changed by the shower of divine grace, how this Zephaniah finally stopped tippling, or that Deborah grew more sweet-tempered to her neighbors' children, how the widow Marcy became reconciled to her husband's early death, or how an impious storekeeper rolled on the floor until he found peace in the arms of Jesus. Instead, the heroes and villains of the vignettes recorded by Charles Backus and his clerical colleagues are the "internal operations" of the converts' minds. The pilgrim in this progress is not the man Christian but the heart and the understanding. In these adventures, they encounter not Lilliputians but the conscience and the imagination. Open any page, and the human faculties dance before us. "Their hearts would recoil at the thought of being in God's hands. . . . The subjects of this happy change exhibited sentiments and feelings widely different from those above described. . . . Their hearts are peculiarly united to the people of God. . . . Another, accustomed to contemplate moral truth in the light of a clear and penetrating intellect, had mistaken the assent of the understanding for the affections of the heart."[1]

The Primacy of the Understanding

Although the Puritans had talked at length about the workings of the mind, it was Jonathan Edwards who had so powerfully imbued New England evangelicism with this fascination for the epistemology of grace. The soul might be said to gain its salvation during the conversion experience, a person's character might be improved, the most egregious defects of temperament and constitution cleansed by this operation, and the possibilities of human brotherhood and charitableness made most wonderfully apparent in the moment of communal awakening; but the experience of regeneration itself was for Edwards a simple mental process. Grace was neither a thunderbolt nor a rattling of one's nerves but rather a "new, simple idea" grasped firmly and clearly by the ordinary powers of the mind operating at their best.[2]

Edwards spoke in many different ways about the religious mind, using one set of terms in his treatises, another in his notes and miscellanies, a third in his sermons, and probably a fourth in his pastoral counseling. Sometimes, as in *Freedom of the Will*, he depicts the mind as having two faculties, the (cognitive) understanding and the (volitional) will. But even here, by assuming that "the will is as the last dictate of the understanding," he fiercely binds the two together. He always seemed reluctant to allow the understanding to stand totally apart from the world; it always inclines toward or away from its objects—it is always already determined to act. Thus a cold-hearted indifference, neutrality, impartiality, or disinterestedness is impossible. In *Religious Affections*, Edwards insisted that "true religion, in great part, consists in holy affections," and these he discovered in "the more vigorous and sensible exercises of the inclination and will of the soul." This definition of religion is tied to his distinction, in a note on "The Sense of the Heart," between a "speculative" and a "sensible" knowledge. The former is only an intellectual manipulation; the latter is a full-minded appreciation, engaging the whole self in a single instant. If grace is a "sensible knowledge of divine things," as he says, then the heart, the moral dimension of the will, is also a cognitive faculty. The saintly heart's knowledge and love of divine reality, and their expression in holy practice, are the goals of true religion.[3]

Edwards's philosophy served his theological ends. Calvinism insisted that the heart or the will had to be changed in the new birth. To make this point, Edwards's successors argued more and more strenuously that the understanding was merely a natural, amoral faculty, not the seat of sin in the soul. Salvation did not come by convincing the understanding of divine truth, insisted Samuel Hopkins in his *System of Doctrines*, the chief reference book of the Second Great Awakening. Indeed, intellectual conviction was useless. In the natural (unregenerate) man, Hopkins argued, the mind was subject to "moral blindness," even though it was physically clear-sighted. Moral blindness was "wholly owing," he wrote, "to the opposition of the heart [the will's moral quality] to the light of moral truth." A man's understanding could not, then, see "disinterestedly" (which was Hopkins's ideal) until his corrupt will ceased to interpose its selfish or emotional bias between it and the truth.[4]

Hopkins was thoroughly orthodox, according to Edwardsean standards, but a subtle change had taken place. Years of theological disputation had led Hopkins and his followers into an implicit elevation of the respect accorded the natural understanding. First, emphasis upon the will's sinfulness had left Hopkinsians more tolerant, even admiring, of the cognitive powers of the mind. Edwards's blistering dismissal of speculative knowledge was relegated to a footnote.

Second, it seemed harder in revolutionary America to discount natural phenomena. Although the Hopkinsians were always skeptical of appeals by deists like Jefferson to "Nature's God" and talk of "natural rights," they seem to have softened the Puritan's traditional disdain for the natural world, that is, the physical universe without God's redeeming power. Calvinism had a ready schema for explaining this: The world, it taught, was rigidly divided into two spheres, that of nature and that of grace, and the Holy Spirit contrived to rule by two distinct methods. By its "common operations," it sustained the uniform connection of cause and effect, of means and ends, in the natural universe. In this providential manner, God gave men the understanding to note the signs of spring, to plant, to cultivate, and then to harvest their crops seasonably. This, too, Edwards had taught. But, again, Hopkins's doctrinal exegesis was forged in combat with men who greatly respected this aspect of natural philosophy, and he had relented a little.[5]

The Hopkinsians could accede because they so firmly insisted that the act of regeneration, the salvation of a soul, was an event in another realm. It was not necessarily based upon any causes in the natural world. Grace was entirely unmerited. Nothing the sinner did could influence God's sovereign power to save or damn that sinner. "Nothing which goes before the new birth," Charles Backus said flatly, "can be considered as a *part* of that change." Salvation was the task of the Holy Spirit's "special operations," its redemptive powers, which were reserved for these moments. The act of regeneration, occurring in an instant not measurable in human time, was itself imperceptible. How God wrought such changes in a soul's destiny was inexplicable, but that he did so was clear from Scripture.[6]

Still, in the full glare of the American Enlightenment, Hopkins could not so easily overcome his desire to explain spiritual events in terms of their effects in the natural sphere. Although regeneration is imperceptible, its effects are not. "Nothing is perceived but the effect, which in the adult consists in perception of truth, and answerable exercises. The cause is to be learned and known only by the effect." In other words, though we have not the power to know the mechanics of God's redeeming power, we may yet witness its work on the human understanding.[7]

The Hopkinsians therefore adopted a double method of analysis with two different vocabularies. When they were relying upon revelation to describe what God accomplishes in the moral sphere through the Spirit's special operations, they spoke metaphysically, calling the events *regeneration* or *salvation*. But when they wanted to describe the effects of this moral change in terms of human experience, their language was empirical; the key events of that human change are *conviction, contrition,* and *sanctification,* summed up in the term *conversion*. How regeneration occurs is a divine mystery, revealed only in Scripture. By contrast, how conversion happens is philosophically verifiable through self-consciousness.

Speaking two languages at once, the evangelicals could meet every objection to their system. Are sinners merely passive in their salvation? Why should they then even bother to attend the meetinghouse and listen to sermons? Yes, of course, in metaphysical terms they can do nothing to help their own progress; everything that a sinner does is sinful. But, practically, empirically, however, it is possible to trace their activity in conversion. They listen to the soul-humbling doctrines of divinity, repent, give up their own claims to sovereignty over the soul, and begin to apply themselves to holy acts.

Inevitably, in the revival season, when sinners were asked to explain themselves and ministers to explain their congregations, this proud effort to trace the natural history of conversion often pushed aside the exposition of the theological doctrine of regeneration. No matter how much they could theoretically distinguish between acts and mental exercises of the unregenerate and the saved, the orthodox preached and wrote relatively little about the latter. They promised that converts would conduct themselves in holiness, and they had the theological terms to describe the continuing development of saintliness, or sanctification, but their emphasis upon the importance of conversion seemed to leave these issues for another day.

Third, and finally, the very stress upon doctrinal knowledge propelled evangelicals toward a greater regard for the cognitive faculties of the mind. So important was the verbal expression of belief in Fitzwilliam, New Hampshire, that a convert was required "to present a written statement of his doctrinal belief, and of his religious experience, to be read to the Church as his profession." Ebenezer Porter found no better way to stimulate piety in his congregation than to assign its young people the responsibility of preparing "written compositions" on religious themes, and these were read aloud at church conferences. "The time was," Elihu Baldwin, born in 1789, recalled fifty years later, "when every child among us was thus instructed in the doctrines of our faith. That education was incomplete," he continued, "which did not lodge the Assembly's Catechism in the memory of the child. It was taught in the day-school and at home; it formed a part of the duties of the parent, to inculcate its truths upon the minds of his children every Lord's day, at least."[8]

Thus, even if their ideology led them to discount the understanding in favor of seeking a regeneration of the heart, their practical philosophy of mind stressed the primacy of the understanding. Doctrinalism as a form of living piety tended, paradoxically, to contradict the doctrines it enshrined. That conundrum is the focus of this chapter.

Although they never believed that religion was a matter of the natural understanding, the orthodox evangelicals continued to stress examining one's mental life as a key to the process of regeneration—but more often now as an end in itself.

Nothing was worse, Edward Griffin complained in 1797, than "to have forgot the way around the different apartments of my mind." So evangelicals went about scrutinizing their thoughts and those of other people, always asking whether they were proper for regenerated Christians. Even a courtship was not exempt from these probings. In a 1798 letter to Roxana Foote, his intended wife, the young Lyman Beecher could "not dispense" with one question: "'When you feel calm, and a degree of joy, what does it arise from? Something you see in the character of God that charms you, or something you see in yourself that you think charms God?'" Roxana, less evangelical than he, refused to be caught in this Hopkinsian snare, with its too rigid dichotomy between self-love and the love of God. "Our love of happiness and our love of God," she responded, "are . . . inseparably connected," and she insisted that "in contemplating the character of God, his mercy and goodness are most present to my mind, and, as it were, swallow up his other attributes."[9]

She was closer in spirit to Edwards than was Lyman Beecher in his junior year at Yale. He would probably have wanted her to say, as did another convert, "I cannot see half enough of myself. I want to see the very worst of my heart." These introspective exercises and presumptuous inquiries shared several basic assumptions about the human mind. First, if one were to be able either to see one's very worst or to have internal evidence of one's best, that assumed the mental apparatus could stand apart as a kind of detached observer of itself; in other words, an idea could be investigated apart from the mind that conceived it. And second, as Beecher later realized with regret, such introspection effectively denied the relevance of mental exercises to one's conduct; ideas were to be studied as they sat passively enthroned in the consciousness, not as they could be expressed in practice. As Beecher later would say, "Some people . . . keep their magnifying-glass ready, and the minute a religious emotion puts out its head, they catch it and kill it, to look at it through their microscope, and see if it is of the right kind. Do you not know, my friends," he said, "that you can not love, and be examining your love at the same time?"[10]

This detachment of doctrine from practice gradually led to a new picture of the mind. Instead of locating religion first and foremost in the heart's immediate apperception of divinity, as Edwards did, evangelicals now created a *sequence* of mental operations, in which the heart came second. "In every case," Edward Griffin noted of his New Hartford parishioners, "after their understanding assented, the heart rose against God's sovereignty with indignation." For Griffin the heart still acted directly in response, though only negatively, to divine reality. Other writers, probably less imbued with Hopkinsian rigor than he, encased the heart spatially within the understanding. "The truth," William B. Sprague believed, "can never find its way to the heart, except through the understanding." Gradually, as more evangelicals adopted a faculty psychology of mind—compartmentalizing the intellect, the emotions, and the will into three distinct phases of mentality—they pushed the heart into a secondary role and made it only an emotional afterburner for a primary intellectual engine. Thus, Timothy Dwight calmly and logically explained that "saving faith is always a speculative belief, joined with a cordial consent to the truth, and a cordial approbation of the object, which that truth respects." Here "cordial" evidently referred to the heart's secondary and subsequent approval of the "speculative belief" regnant in the understanding. Dwight's diction itself reflected this interpretation of the mind. The two phrases about what is "cordial" (a Latinist's euphemism, of course, for the heart) modify only the main independent clause, which is about the activity of the understanding.[11]

Such Augustan cadences demonstrated a resolution to slow down and cool religious energy. Each of the three mental activities in Dwight's significant definition is said to coexist; they neither stimulate nor affect one another. Saving faith was simply the addition of three mental gestures: a scrupulous adherence to doctrinal truth, plus two rather genteel approving "thumbs up," one for the scriptural doctrine and one for God himself. Compare the language of Dwight's grandfather, Jonathan Edwards, who caught the affections as kinesthetic products (or "sensible exercises") of the will's ceaseless inclining toward or away from an object in the world.[12]

The Transforming Power of the Understanding

The evangelicals' picture of the mind, like their image of other natural phenomena, expressed a profound gratitude to God's providence. It was a blessing on the New England orthodox that sinners were susceptible to the operations of the spirit by their nature. Given the social situation of the New England clergy, it did not have to look far to find souls willing to undergo the torment of contrition. Every meetinghouse had many in its pews who, though devoid of a saving experience of grace, still dutifully attended the teaching of the law each week.

In the minds of these men and women, the evangelicals knew, the groundwork for divine truth had been naturally laid. Each had an unimpaired understanding, as we have seen, and a conscience that could reliably spur the self-examination necessary for conversion. The relationship of the two was considered in Charles Backus's treatise on regeneration:

> All men, whether good or bad, are capable of distinguishing between holiness and sin, and of knowing their duty. This faculty is called *The Understanding*. The pleasure or pain which the mind feels in a review of its actions, is stiled [*sic*] *The Conscience*. This, in some instances, operates to a high degree, in the worst of men while in the present life, and will be like a worm that never dies, to the impenitent in the world to come.

The conscience registered the mind's feelings about its own actions. To do so it had to be independent of one's will, and in fact it brought great pain to those unrepentant. The conscience had to obey, if not oneself, something external.[13]

What outside the self commanded obedience? Apparently the conscience sought to obey divine revelation, especially scriptural law, not the attractive promises of the gospel. Hemen Humphrey, the chronicler of the Second Awakening, called it a "law revival." And "the law," as another commentator wrote, "is the great instrument which the Spirit of God wields in producing conviction of sin. Let that never be brought in contact with the *conscience*," he warned, "and the sinner would go slumbering to his grave." The conscience did not belong to oneself; it was, instead, the part of the mind where the ideas of divine decrees would find residence.[14]

In fact, the conscience seemed to be God's possession. This generation of evangelicals may have been among the last Americans to believe that the mind, as well as the body, was so utterly a part of the divine estate. Their view of the conscience was a throwback to concepts that reigned in the seventeenth century, before Locke had so stringently set apart the mind from its world and made the former uniquely human. By contrast, as the historian of political theory Sheldon Wolin notes, "The 'Puritan conscience' has been conceived by its defenders as a disciplined mode of judgment, one controlled by the 'objective' standard of Scripture and steeped in religious instruction." Even Edwards could not accept such a positive view of the natural conscience, but once again his disciples did. Their conscience did not partake of Locke's new definition of it as (again in Wolin's words) "the subjective beliefs held by the individual." From this definition, Locke had argued that in matters of conscience each man has "'the supreme and absolute authority of judging for himself.'"[15]

At the turn of the nineteenth century, the Lockean view was still not widely accepted in the Congregationalist community, which evidenced its discomfort with such ideas by continuing to restrain complete freedom of conscience in the constitutions of the New England states. By midcentury, as later parts of my study will show, the prevailing view of conscience had changed: not only could one avoid penalties for dissidence or unbelief, but the conscience was now said to be an inborn moral sense that did not need the authority of revelation to legitimate obedience. In fact, once we reach Thoreau's generation, the conscience becomes synonymous with the obedience of the self to almost any moral ideal higher than pure selfishness; then conscience might serve as a personal line of defense against even God's revealed dictates or the demands of society.[16]

But in 1800, the only "conscientious objection" possible was still an objection to one's own impious willfulness. The moral faculty was designed to remind one always of the deviations the will had taken from the perfect pathways disclosed in orthodox doctrine. Although since then we have come to imagine the conscientious person as entirely alone and poised against the world, in 1800 the true role of the conscience was to help a person acknowledge his firmly rooted place in the world, in the plan of creation and salvation.

Small wonder, then, that ministers used doctrinal teaching to disturb the consciences of their parishioners during the revival season. In the case of Somers, for instance, Backus perceived the onrush of "an excess of animal emotion and a flood of tears. . . . He conscientiously restrained his own feelings, and instead of labouring to heighten the excitement, he aimed to enlighten the understanding and conscience, to make deep and permanent impressions of Divine truth." Refusing to admit his own sympathy with his parishioners' feelings, Backus took the opportunity to instruct the rational faculties and, by this, actually to impress divine truth in their souls. In this way, he would be "conscientious," the biographer notes, at the same time he was making his flock so.[17]

It is well to compare Backus's view with the emotionally charged accounts of religious experience that effused from the First Great Awakening. Samuel Buell, for example, was then led in conviction "to the most affecting discoveries," his memorialist wrote, endowing these intellectual glimpses with an inherent affectional or emotional quality. "His spiritual discoveries," it was said, "of the glory of the divine character, perfections, and law of Christ, and the way of salvation through him, and his consequent joy and peace in believing, were proportionate to the pungency and terror of his antecedent convictions." In fact, this account confirmed, Buell's entire conversion experience can be understood as a single piece only if we see that its continuity rested in the strength of the affections throughout. Initially, in conversion, these were terrifying; later they became joyful, but they were always strong.[18]

In 1764, when Buell led his own Long Island congregants through one of the most exuberant religious revivals of the eighteenth century, he focused on the affectional core of religious change. "The Lord's people," he wrote, "did not know how much joy was theirs to enjoy, on this earth. . . ." So affected were the hopeful in East Hampton, Buell recalled, that "words seem to fail as to expressing their ideas and views of the infinite glory of divine objects, and the everlasting importance of things eternal; and while they beheld them in such a clear and strong light, it often appears to them, as though others must, as it were, be powerfully impressed and affected with them."[19]

"Words seem to fail. . . ." In that phrase lies the heart of the experiential difference between the two awakenings. The First Awakening, and its offshoots like this one in Long Island, felt the power of divine intervention as a gust that spun weather vanes too quickly for any to discern its direction. Thus, so much writing about the First Awakening is by way of report or commentary on how the signs of grace may be discerned by man's limited intellect. What we cannot examine, the Edwardseans seem to have said, we will trust as the work of God, even if (or because) its mystery escapes us.

In 1800 words never failed. Because the doctrines of orthodoxy perfectly expressed a view of the world as a consistent whole, anything that contradicted orthodoxy was senseless and unacceptable. God simply did not appear outside his laws, and the laws were available for human inspection in his inspired Scriptures. The Bible caught the entirety of God's breath for man. Incomplete testimonies were valuable only as parts of a more thorough account, like Hopkins's *The System of Doctrines, Contained in Divine Revelation, Explained and Defended. Showing their Connection with Each Other.*

More important than a change of doctrine between the First and the Second Great Awakenings was the increased significance of doctrine to the conversion experience. In the 1740s, evangelicals could love the world because they could use their heart's knowledge to feel God's immediate presence in it. In the 1790s, using one's own understanding and its divinely connected partner, the conscience, an evangelical could discern the total meaning of the world. God was no longer immediately apparent in everyday life; he had become, as I will show, a distant ordering principle in the universe.

The evangelical's understanding/conscience was more than a perceiving machine, a sense receptor, or the stimulus part of a stimulus-response reflex arc in the mind. This understanding/conscience was more like an instant translator, converting miscellaneous sensations into a set of logically coherent statements about the nature of things. Working properly, in the moral person, it could make instantaneous connections between worldly moments and heavenly eternity.

It is hardly surprising that people who discourse with ease about mental philosophy should advance strong claims about the powers of the mind; that is, after all, their bread and butter. Few philosophers make their way in the world by either defending or explaining ignorance. The history of mental philosophy is a fascinating dramatization of the social and political claims of intellectuals. Every account of how the mind works is a kind of mini-drama about the possibility of intellectual life in the social world.

In developing their philosophy of mind, the orthodox evangelicals worked within a tradition of Anglo-American thought that stemmed from the work of John Locke, though they had considerable sympathy, as we have seen, with pre-Lockean notions of the conscience. Locke had cleared away the detritus of scholastic philosophy and claimed that the mind was originally free of all innate ideas. Every phenomenon in mental life was the product of experience, the inscription of simple ideas on the mind's blank slate; the combination of these simple ideas resulted in complex notions, like the doctrines of theology or politics. Jonathan Edwards, who first read Locke as a young student at Yale, reshaped the morphology of Calvinist religious experience on Lockean lines. Grace, he asserted, was a new simple idea. In practice, this allowed Edwards to insist that divine illumination could occur in a sinner's mind instantaneously, without the long period of "preparation" that his Puritan predecessors had prescribed. Revivalism, in which religion was evidently a powerful mental experience, was an ideal proof of Edwards's philosophy of mind.[20]

In England, Locke's work stimulated a greater interest in the subjective experience of thought. The writings of George Berkeley and David Hume, contemporaries of Edwards, cast doubt on the mind's ability to capture the actual reality of the external world. Hume's ensuing skepticism about the truthfulness of religion was particularly frightening to late eighteenth-century thinkers on both sides of the Atlantic. In Scotland, Thomas Reid and Dugald Stewart responded by claiming that the unaided human reason had the ability to discern certain "common sense" realities. Looking at the ordinary experience of people, they insisted that the mind was constituted to know what was true and what was false. Thus the claims of religion, insofar as they were based on fairly simple precepts, could be sustained without recourse to metaphysics.[21]

The Scottish Common-Sense School would dominate American philosophy well into the mid-nineteenth century. Taught to virtually every college student in the nation, Scottish philosophy legitimated personal experience while limiting the destructive individualism that free thinking might produce. Men were free to see the world on their own, as Locke had insisted, but, in fact, they would tend to see it much the same way.[22]

In the 1830s, Ralph Waldo Emerson would push Scottish realism even further. Emerson posited that the ordinary human understanding gave only a fragmentary view of the world, "all buzz and din." His transcendentalism required a higher reason, almost German or Coleridgean in its vaulting romantic ambition, to discover the ideas that underlay ultimate reality.[23]

Without saying so, the Hopkinsians were making the same epistemological concessions to the power of understanding as the Scottish philosophers. Needing to emphasize the significant effect of the religious "new birth" on the mind, they inflated the complex cognitive powers of the saint's mind. In this way, they could reward Christians with an enhanced view of their own abilities and thereby justify their own roles as teachers. Without challenging the simplicity of grace, the evangelical orthodox believed the natural mind capable, if the saint's conscience was working properly, of discerning the complex reality of Calvinist doctrines. So conversion, in a sense, became the installation of an interpreter. In grace evangelicals learned how to substitute a scriptural, authoritative, universal, and conclusive vocabulary for a personal, private, sensual, and confused one.[24]

Their diaries and other records of religious experience trace this substitution of one language for another. One of the best comes from the pen of

Edward Griffin, the young minister of New Hartford, Connecticut. For a week in August 1797, Griffin's diary recorded the way he wrestled with the problem of Christ's atonement. "The need and fitness of Christ's dying to atone for sin," wrote the preacher, "has appeared the gordian knot in divinity." He wanted to feel, as any evangelical would, that personal experience gave meaning to all religious truth and complained that "it was hard to see, how *my* sins were properly punished, or any frown properly manifested against them, by the sufferings of Christ." On this simplest level, he was bothered that he was not being sufficiently chastened for his own sins when Christ assumed the burden of atonement for him. He wished to deny neither his sinfulness nor God's readiness to pardon him, but he still felt personally and troublingly unresolved if his absolution were to be won with so little punishment. Pain, some private pain, was necessary.[25]

Why, we might ask, did he not just forget the whole question and enjoy his reprieve from damnation? That, of course, would have admitted doctrinal confusion in order to live an uncomplicated Christian life. But the whole point of his Christian existence, we have to understand, was to clear away these confusions and to see his eternal destiny clearly. So Griffin had to press on.

His first step was to cast Christ in the the role of Griffin the sinner in suffering God's wrath for his sins: "If I am to be pardoned by Christ," he wrote, "the Lord expressly and avowedly laid his wrath on him as a substitute for me, as though I was the only sinner to be redeemed, and as much as though I was present on the spot attending on the sacrifice." But this was only a partial solution. Christ, like a second killed in a duel in place of one of the principals, permitted Griffin to suffer his punishment vicariously. He could be absolved, the young man thought, by observing this act of surrogate punishment. But the punishment itself still seemed inadequate. Could the whole metaphysical transaction of redemption come down to this—Jesus serving as a scapegoat for every sinner's transgressions? As a stand-in, Jesus was only a single human figure crucified for a particular person's violation, and worse, God's wrath seemed to be reduced to the level of a provincial governor's sentence of death. Why should Jesus Christ have undertaken such a burden?

Finally, one night, in the most offhanded way, Griffin closed his prayers with the phrase "for Christ's sake." Suddenly "the propriety of Christ's advocacy rushed on my mind with new light."

> It appeared undesirable that any blessing should be bestowed on me for my own sake; for this would be patronizing my iniquity, which is the whole of my natural character. It appeared desirable that they should be bestowed avowedly for Christ's sake, that it might be publicly understood that they were bestowed in consequence of what took place on the

cross, and out of respect to a perfect righteousness, that they might be removed the farthest from the appearance of being a favor to sin.

This was better. The atonement was not a reward for Griffin's "natural character," after all. His nature was entirely sinful and undeserving of divine attention. But if Griffin's case, and that of every other sinner, could be bound up within the metaphysical relationship between God the Father and Christ, then the atonement could make sense. Redemption had nothing to do with the sinner's motives, acts, thoughts, need for punishment, or anything. God had his own reasons for acting this way. Christ neither as man nor as surrogate principal, but rather as perfect righteousness, earned the favor of forgiveness for his people. The human case history was thus linked to the divine plan of redemption. By scriptural revelation and doctrinal reasoning the links could be understood within the human mind.

This is not a fair representation of Griffin's theologizing skills. Many years later, in fact, he wrote a subtle treatise on the subject of the atonement. But it is interesting to see how theological doctrine emerges in the course of personal experience. For Griffin, reconciliation with divinity followed his disavowing personal ways of interpreting his own experience and emerged by substituting doctrinal for personal explanations.[26]

As he began this introspection Griffin was thinking of atonement as a question about the fate of a single human being; at the end, man's puny state was absorbed totally into the larger and more logical drama of the universal operations of the Lord. Distinct ideas about one's own exercises of mind were transmuted, through the alchemic influences of Calvinist dogmatics, into distinct ideas about God's holiness. Grace had nothing to do with perceiving the self. "When comfort was obtained," observed Alexander Gillett of his converts in Torrington, Connecticut, "it did not seem to arise from mere impressions on the imagination, but from such a view of God and divine things as they never before experienced."[27]

We tend to associate introspection with self-absorption, but these evangelicals thought otherwise. Salvation, their Calvinism taught them, meant destroying their self-interest, even their interest in being saved. "Their minds were so engrossed by the great truths of the Gospel," one minister wrote proudly of his parishioners, "that they thought little or nothing about their own salvation." Despite the clergy's encouragement to sinners to examine their inner "views and exercises" carefully, evangelicals did not view introspection as a personal exploration. An article on "Self-Examination" in 1804 offered this advice on being too personal: "That a man may examine himself to any good effect, it is necessary, that he should fix upon some standard, by which to try himself, and compare his heart, life and conversation. Indeed," the writer concluded, "there can be no judging ourselves, but by some standard in view, which is accounted perfect, and to which we may bring ourselves for trial." Self-examination was not designed to reveal things about ourselves we did not know before. It was a judicial, not an analytical, proceeding. Up or down, yes or no, that is all that one could discover in this way.[28]

The "perfect standard" to which the author referred, of course, was the Bible or at least what the evangelicals did with the Bible. In practice, for all their references to the gospel truths, the language to which saints compared their own assessments was less often verbatim scriptural text and more often evangelical exegeses of the Bible. The verdict could only be guilty. Compared to such a divinely decreed standard, all men and women would invariably be found wanting. But the judgment, though harsh, was scarcely personal. Converts did not dwell on their own sins after their scrupulous self-examination. Instead, their self-condemnation drew upon the impersonal diction of the sermons; for example, "Her righteousness was but filthy rags," "I found I was building on the sand," or "They felt themselves to be enemies to God."[29]

The purpose of introspection was to have sinners exchange the monogrammed robes of personal description for the universal cloak of doctrinal language. Edward Griffin used a different metaphor: "I had been searching for the door of deliverance, on the wrong side of the room, in seeking a sense of the evil of sin from examining what I had done rather than what God is. I was convinced," he concluded, "that a view of the purity of God would best discover [i.e., uncover] the awful nature of sin." He did not need to consider his sins biographically as incidents of personal weakness. By better fixing his attention on the "purity of God," he would learn more about the "evil of sin" than confessions of lust or worldly ambition.[30]

I will summarize the evangelical position in these years: Experience is not real until it is verbalized, and words are not true until they are refashioned into their scriptural or doctrinal equivalents. Such precepts were neither proclaimed baldly nor disputed in pamphlet literature, but they prejudiced every account of religious experience. They were the implicit rules for proper religious life—the dining table etiquette, so to speak, for the feast of salvation. Furthermore, they fit into a much larger set of equally unexamined rules for conducting the religious self in the Federalist era. Let us explore some of these.

Disciplining the Mind

Orthodoxy thought of religious life not as a fulfillment of one's personal destiny so much as a limitation on individuality, a harnessing of the private self. In the religious revivals of the Second Awakening, evidently few solitary pilgrims retreated to their "secret groves" for prayer, as was much more common sixty years earlier. In his chronicle of this awakening, Ebenezer Porter claimed that "not a single instance appears, in all these narratives, of any person who was apparently converted to God, without a previous solemn excitement to attend on the means of salvation," that is, to go to church and listen to sermons.[31]

Of course, converts suffered privately during the process of their conversion. But privacy was associated only with the painful phases of conviction and contrition, never with relief and assurance. "To hide her convictions from the eyes of the world," a young woman in Wintonbury, Connecticut, "spent all her spare time, in a chamber by herself, in reading the bible and in prayer to God." Once she could emerge, she was ready for the instruction and counsel of others, relieved by the minister's sermons, and reconciled to God. Her private language of self-condemnation was left behind at the threshold to her private chamber, and in church she was at one with others in the use of scriptural language.[32]

Church membership required that one accommodate oneself to the official vocabulary. This requirement was enforced through the examination of candidates by a committee of the minister, deacons, and other learned laymen. Such examinations were as crucial to the elite of the evangelical Calvinist churches as baptism or communion and probably as well attended. All church members were invited to participate. The minister began by asking, " 'What are the reasons, which have led you to suppose or hope, that you are reconciled to God?'" Then each would tell his experience. As one cynic later recalled,

> This consisted almost universally in telling how they had been "under distress of mind"; how deeply and how long they suffered before conversion came; what first threw them into this distress, which was often some dream, or vision, or death, or sermon, or prayer, or remark, or text, flashing suddenly upon them. Then came a sudden rebound of the spirit, the shoutings and hallelujahs. I have heard many of these new converts relate their experience in my childhood, and it usually consisted in passing through the above process.[33]

The testimonies of candidates for church membership were verbal transformations affirming their links to the community. The church did not sanction many different kinds of spirituality. All the distinct paths of conviction led to one place, a town common of religious uniformity. This, indeed, proved the divine origin of the revival. As Nathan Perkins of West Hartford surmised, "the very great uniformity in the views, feelings, and impressions of those, who have been the subjects of it . . . is no slight evidence of its being a real and genuine work of the grace of God." Doctrinalism protected evangelicals against the possibility that their religion was a self-delusion, "If it," Perkins said of the revival, "had been the effect merely of enthusiasm, or a heated imagination, it is not at all probable there would have been such an uniformity."[34]

Again and again, in the accounts of Perkins, Gillett, and others, we see the proper security of verbal formulae contrasted to the self-indulgence of a "heated imagination." Edwards had also warned Christians of his generation that the imagination, by presenting images to the mind that did not correspond exactly to their external reality, was a deceptive guide, unworthy of being compared to the richer sensible knowledge of the divine meanings surrounding real things in the world. By 1800, the imagination had reasserted its older, seventeenth-century meaning as a faculty engorged with dangerous phantasms. The mind, viewed as a finite storage room, would then be filled with false representations. There would be no room for reality, correct perceptions, or the truths of doctrinal knowledge. " 'Can *I* be a *new creature*,' " a man in the throes of conviction asked in Torrington, Connecticut, " 'and have my heart filled with so many vain tho'ts and strange imaginations.' " The imagination was an interior labyrinth of sin, evangelicals like Lemuel Haynes knew, and when he debated the Universalist leader Hosea Ballou he could accuse him of nothing worse than "walking in the imagination of your own heart."[35]

The strange imaginings of the sinful heart were not of man's devising. They were, in fact, the products of invisible spirits seeking to overturn the clear thinking of proper men and women. "To the rational mind neither angels, nor devils, have immediate access; nor can they excite volition, nor move the affections, but by the medium of the imagination, that faculty in which ideas are formed, by the exhibition or impression of external sensible objects."[36]

Nathanael Emmons, the magisterial pastor of Franklin, Massachusetts, was well versed in the epistemology of John Locke, but this did not explain why "Satan should have access to our minds, yet it seems confirmed by daily experience." Arguing that "The Scriptural Account of the Devil Ought to Be Believed," Emmons asked rhetorically, "Why is the chain of our thoughts so often and so suddenly broken? Why do new, unconnected, and unexpected thoughts so frequently rush into our minds? Why do thoughts, which the mind abhors and endeavours to banish forever, so repeatedly and repeatedly recur?" To Emmons, there was but one conclusion to draw: "These things favour the account, which the scripture gives of Satan's tempting power over us."[37]

This same loss of directedness in thinking, this irrationality and bewildering start-and-stop of coherence, had been the subject of Locke's famous chapter "The Association of Ideas" in the *Essay Concerning Human Understanding*. Locke had seen the chance connection of ideas as a form of madness, universally inwrought in the human constitution, which was responsible for most of the unreasonableness abroad in the world. For David Hartley, James Mill,

John Stuart Mill, and other British followers of Locke, the association of ideas was at the heart of correct reasoning. Later chroniclers of the "stream of consciousness," like William James, "expect," as Michel Foucault writes, "our intelligibility to come from what was for many centuries thought of as madness."[38]

Emmons returned to Locke's distrust of the breaks in our logical processes, but he added the evangelical dictum that such errors must be rooted in man's original tendency to corruption. And he assumed, as did most of his contemporaries in the New England churches, that Satan used this corruption to his advantage. Imaginings emerged from the "constant intercourse between the inhabitants of this invisible world, and those of this inferior globe."[39]

So, too, did dreams and visions. They were completely illegitimate. Although the folk literature of New England has plenteous tales of ghostly visions and customs of divination, the evangelicals forthrightly condemned the authority of such oracles. "No person is warranted from the word of God," wrote one, "to publish to the world the discoveries of heaven and hell which he supposes he has had in a dream, or trance, or vision. Were any thing of this kind to be made known to men, we may be assured it would have been done by the apostles, when they were penning the gospel history." Note how much priority is given here to the word, especially the written word (*"penning* the gospel history").[40]

This antagonism to the imaginary sets the evangelical orthodox apart from the radical dissenting sects of revolutionary America. For the Baptists and Separate Congregationalists, groups that emerged from the schisms of the First Great Awakening, as well as Arminian (anti-Calvinist) enthusiasts like the Methodists, Free-Will Baptists, and Christians (later the Disciples of Christ), visual imagery was crucial to religious experience.

A young woman participating in a Baptist revival in Litchfield, Maine, for example, used language never allowed among the stolid Calvinists of Massachusetts and Connecticut:

> The 6th day of last February, I was taken as it were out of the belly of hell, and my feet set upon a rock, and a new song put into my mouth, even praise to the Most High. The heavens, which I before thought wore a gloomy aspect, now seemed to glitter with the glory of God. And the animal creation seemed jointly to whisper praises to their Creator. This new scene reminded me of man in his first happy state. In this frame I had a view of the justice of God, and of Christ's sufferings, which I can describe to none but those who have drank of the same fountain. February 9th, I was enabled to follow my blessed Saviour into the water; but I have since been brought to feel that I am nothing, and to abhor myself.

The sacrament of baptism itself, as this account shows, was a scene constantly available to Baptists for graphic representation, and Baptist sermons, like those of Episcopalians at the other end of the spectrum of American Protestantism, were rich in metaphor and image.[41]

Visual thinking was an integral and legitimate part of many other conversion experiences among these groups. Heman Bangs, the Methodist hero, recalled that "one man drew an exact *picture* of my own feelings, and I thought if I could only say 'that is my case exactly,' I should find relief." John Colby, later to attain significance as a great preacher for the Free-Will Baptists, "had every feature of [the whole work of regeneration] painted out in my mind; but when I came to compare my then present feelings with the picture I had drawn in my ignorance, they did not agree." The young Elijah Shaw, who later was the organizational genius of the Christian Connexion in New England, recalled that at age fifteen he "dreamed one night that he saw a star arise as large as the sun" and thought this was a sign of the judgment day. An unconverted hired man working alongside the young Shaw told him, "'If you had then begun to pray, you would have been converted.'" Evidently it was commonly believed among the folk of the New Hampshire hills that such dreams and visions were indeed God's chosen paths to grace, although they varied with scriptural orthodoxy.[42]

Most examples of the visualized divine promise took place in northern New England, and one can also find regional Congregationalist accounts that ignore the verbal biases of the learned clergy in the more established towns of Massachusetts and Connecticut. The power to receive such special revelations from God, which called upon the faculties of mind most suspected by the theologians, survived as a significant religious tradition in the most northern states. This tradition was important in shaping the experience, we might speculate, of young Vermont boys like Joseph Smith, the prophet of Mormonism, in the following generation.[43]

By contrast, evangelical Calvinists insisted that visual illuminations were a deceptive snare. In a 1793 entry in the diary of Nancy Pomeroy of Middletown, Connecticut, she confided that during Sabbath worship one week, "My eyes were wandering, I did not studiously avoid the most conspicuous place.—Satan took advantage of my too easy unwatchful frame. That time which I intended to devote wholly to God (O dreadful to repeat) was too much taken up upon sublunary objects. . . . Have not my eyes been amused by vanity, and my heart drawn off from thee by idle and distracted ideas," she asked God. "How often have I resolved to keep a strict watch over my eyes and heart in the house of God, and to let no thought be found in my heart which was inconsistent with thy dying admonition: Watch and pray—that ye enter not into temptation." Nancy Pomeroy was deeply anguished by her transgression and spent the following Wednesday in fasting and prayer to repent. On that day, she hoped to "let no mortal eye intrude upon my retirement"; while she prayed, she asked God to "keep me also from those secret sins of the heart, which, though hid from the eye of short-sighted mortals, are yet open to thee."[44]

What does it mean for her to say that she should have been more "watchful" and that her sins were so deeply involved with allowing her eyes to wander? The danger of the visual, evidently, was its distraction by the myriad details of ordinary life. Not only did this inattentiveness yield a meaningless jumble of perceptions, rather than the concentrated delight she should have sought in God's singular and "holy word," but, in addition, her distraction masked a deeper sin. Vanity amused her eyes and brought her short-sighted pleasure when she focused on "the most conspicuous place." (Was that focus the minister, a suitor, or, most likely, herself in the eyes of others?) Like a good Hopkinsian, her grossest sin was to be self-regarding.

Against this, she should have been "studious," she said, and every thought in her mind should have been worthy of Christ's scriptural admonition to "watch and pray." In her plea to God for forgiveness, she asked, "Where shall I find language to express thy unbounded love to such a polluted dying worm as I am." Not her love for God, notice, but his love for her. The problem of the saint, then, was to substitute sanctified language, the gospel expression of God's willingness to love and save sinners, for her own selfish and unholy glances.

Nancy Pomeroy's sin must have been common in the New England meetinghouses of her generation. Almost nothing in these cavernous, unheated buildings was conducive to an orderly perception of the scene. Not even a cross characterized the use of the meetinghouse for religious purposes. Inside the high-walled box pews were seated parishioners laden with caps, cloaks, blankets, foot warmers, and even the family dog, to avert the autumn chill; the pews themselves were often irregularly arranged, some finely and others poorly crafted, some endowed with beautifully stitched cushions and others bare of all ornament. What a lot there was to look at, but how little sense to make of this jumble of sights![45]

The sense came, of course, from the pulpit, which, in those eighteenth-century meetinghouses, was perched far above the congregation and canopied over by a giant sounding board. These New England evangelicals, after all, were children of the Puritans and heirs of that seventeenth-century attack on the visual luxury of the Anglican liturgy and the metaphorical splendor of the Anglican sermon. "Faith cometh by *hearing*, and hearing by the word of God," New Englanders still loved to read in Romans 10:17. The auditory experience, listening carefully to the minister's exposition of the text, doctrine, and reasons, was still the key element in Congregationalist worship at the end of the eighteenth century. One could have sat blindfolded through the four or five hours of such worship each Sabbath day, kept awake in some communities by the prods of the tythingman's stick, and have missed nothing. Nothing, that is, except the sinful delight of looking around aimlessly, like the daughter in Adino Pomeroy's pew. Letting her eyes wander provided an avenue, Nancy Pomeroy understood, for Satan to take command over her.

During the Revolution, according to the historian Harry S. Stout, the evangelical clergy had faced a new and powerful challenge to their primacy as the chief media of communication in their own communities. Mass gatherings for political and religious purposes called forth innovative forms of public address and oratory, in a voice that broke with the "polite style" of colonial New England literature. Many sermons delivered by the evangelical supporters of American independence shared this more direct appeal to the senses. In the Second Awakening, however, the clergy of the Standing Order was reasserting the dominance of a print culture that depended upon significant "book learning." Hegemony over public language would evermore escape the evangelical Congregationalists, while dissenting Jeffersonian and even Federalist politicians continued to expound their polemics in a new orally focused rhetoric. But by repudiating the need for huge revival assemblies and by constraining their converts' accounts of personal experience within the strictures of Calvinist theology, the orthodox party preserved a form of expression they believed inextricable from gospel truth.[46]

The Experience of Orthodoxy

How did it feel to experience orthodoxy as a religion? Can it make sense to participate in a community not only by sharing but also by worshiping one's beliefs? It is vital for us to see that orthodoxy, as a form of religious life, was quite different from the Calvinism it espoused. Orthodoxy was not a system of beliefs but a socially situated response of a group of evangelical Christians to the problem of living piously at a given historical moment. Preaching, thought Charles Backus, was more than a communication of doctrinal truth to minds that might or might not accept it. Doctrine shaped every moment of one's life.

"The knowledge and conviction," Backus explained,

> which are obtained and impressed during what has been called the *preparatory work*, are of no small use; in disclosing to sinners their real character, in teaching them that they must be wholly indebted to sovereign grace for salvation, and in assisting them in their walk when brought into cordial submission to the divine will. It has often been remarked that those whose minds had been most stored with doctrinal knowledge, are, other things being equal, the freest from imaginary flights during the ardor which young converts feel, and shine brightest in the school of Christ.[47]

Preaching was only one of the "means" that the church pressed upon sinners as mandatory for their conversion. All the others—Sabbath worship, regular communion, fasts and thanksgivings, conferences, prayer meetings, and the baptism of children—were similarly valued for their instructional merits. Although later voluntary societies considered moral reform and charity as their highest ends, the very first of them in the nineteenth century seemed to concentrate on assisting members to a more profound understanding of their spiritual conditions. Just before she left Sturbridge in 1812, Nancy Coburn wrote to the Female Society of the Congregational Church to thank the women for admitting "of my meeting with you the short space of time that I tarried here which has been very pleasing and I hope instructing to me[;] perhaps you may think that I had better not exposed my ignorance before so many that are of so much greter knowledge and understanding than myself. . . . I consider it A great privilige that you do enjoy in meeting togeather to convers upon a religion a privilige which but very few in this world do have & why it is we are set apart from the world to enjoy it."[48]

The proper behavior of church members, then, was a continuing catechism lesson. These evangelicals were conformists not only in belief but also in believing in belief. By contrast, they tolerated all sorts of deviance in personal habits. Local eccentricities of dress, diction, and manners occasioned little comment and were certainly not threatening. Perhaps they were seldom noticed, so minute was their significance in determining one's eternal destiny. At the very least, such oddities did not warrant exclusion from the society of the churched; however, those whose religious sentiments were heretical seemed to warrant less brotherly or sisterly compassion.[49]

Eventually doctrinal proficiency, initially only an advantage in gaining grace as when Backus promised that the studious were "freest from imaginary flights," became a hard and fast test for admission to the church. By the time Ebenezer Porter came to reflect upon the triumphs of 1800 in his 1832 Letters on Revivals, he would "not scruple to say to any one who remains altogether uninstructed and uninterested on the subject of religion, that there is no present prospect of his salvation." But, of course, this was obvious; an "uninstructed" person simply could not give evidence of the requisite experiences, which included aligning one's self-scrutiny with the standards of revelation.[50]

Although it is hard for us to acknowledge that farmers in the remote communities of rural New England could have such an abiding faith in abstruse doctrines, it is nonetheless true. Many nineteenth-century men and women remembered the religion of orthodoxy, fondly or angrily, as a remarkable human phenomenon. Henry Clarke Wright, later an anticlerical abolitionist, poured out great venom on the imageless conception of God he was taught to worship in such an evangelical congregation:

We are told to fix our thoughts on God when we pray. It is impossible to form any distinct idea of a spirit aside from matter. God, when we think of Him as something distinct from duty, justice, love, and human sympathy and kindness, always assumes the form of a human being. So that, in formal prayer, we are addressing a self-existent, omnipotent, omnipresent, omniscient MAN—for such is the form given to the Deity, when children or adults try to fix their minds on an abstract divinity in their prayers. . . . But I never could hear persons pray without asking myself, "Are they speaking to the true God, or some image, or unnatural, unreal conception of their own brains?"[51]

As a child of the evangelicals, Wright knew exactly how to hurt his teachers. These self-proclaimed advocates of disinterestedness were wholly wrapped in a mental selfishness. But his memory failed to recapture the grandeur of the evangelicals' effort to translate the quotidian into the Word. Horace Bushnell, the greatest theologian of nineteenth-century America, recalled his young days in a similar meetinghouse much more favorably. "Under their hard, and, as some would say, stolid faces," he mused, "great thoughts are brewing, and these keep them warm. Free-will, fixed fate, foreknowledge absolute, trinity, redemption, special grace, eternity—give them anything high enough, and the tough muscle of their inward man will be climbing sturdily into it; and if they go away having something to think of, they have had a good day." For the parents of Wright and Bushnell, evangelical Calvinism created a spatial scaffolding out of the verbal doctrines of orthodoxy. As Christians heard the familiar language leap off pages of treatises and sermons, they were carried higher by each stage in the argument, until they felt themselves at the steeple top of truth. In a revival, with a single deep breath of the Holy Spirit, evangelicals raised themselves into personal realizations of the architecture of God's eternal grace, each scheming at Babel in the hinterland of New England. Edified by doctrine, they boldly transformed themselves into edifices of divinity.[52]

Chapter Three

A Revival of Stillness

FOR NEW ENGLANDERS the 1790s were, finally, prosperous. Exports and the carrying trade had revived. The population grew, and emigrants replicated New England villages in the valleys of Maine and Vermont, western New York, and the Ohio country. Although much had changed, the stability of prewar life had returned to much of southern New England. Among the well-to-do, impressive Federal-style farmhouses were the first new residences built in almost a generation. With light-filled rooms set symmetrically on either side of central hallways and twin chimneys thrust through their gently pitched roofs, the houses symbolized a new prosperity and a rational ordering of private life. Their doorways were decorously trimmed with side lights and topped with fan ornaments. The front rooms were more formal—a parlor on one side, a dining room on the other, both designed for the company of respectable neighbors and guests. The family now gathered in other spaces behind the first, to read aloud, to share its meals at a more leisurely pace, to spin globes, and to look over engraved plates of the wonders of the natural world.[1]

The restoration of private pleasure, after so much public turmoil, felt like a blessing. The renewed traffic of wagons on weekdays and of families walking or riding to the meetinghouse on Sabbath days evidenced a restoration of private concerns. Town meetings returned to the subject of roads, schools, and the care of the poor. Little was heard of national events. Local contests for power had more to do with what part of town each side lived in than with what someone had done in the war. The best news for such Yankees was no news.

For the orthodox evangelicals, the challenge of the time was to submerge this private world in the comprehensive gospel plan of salvation. Don't read newspapers, they advised, especially on Sundays: "Will earth's low scenes thy soul prepare / For Heaven's eternal joys?" an evangelical poet addressed "a Person who employed himself every Sunday in reading News-Papers." Attribute nothing to chance or luck. Don't say, "I wish it had not rained," advised Alvan Hyde; God had his reasons for everything.[2]

Everything in daily practice could be acceptable, so long as it taught the truth of divine doctrine. Natural history taught God's providence. Education could open the young soul to God's wisdom. An oil lamp, lighted at sunset, was worthy, as it "resembles the introduction of the morning sun, which draws aside the curtain of the night, and makes the day." Art and artifice, said the *Massachusetts Missionary Magazine*, are only "works of admiration, accordingly as they answer to the archetype, or the wise and benevolent design of nature."[3]

The quotidian world was thus a series of entries that fit perfectly into the all-encompassing crossword puzzles of orthodox theory. A doctrinal reading could be applied to anything, in the natural as well as the religious sphere. The key was, do not let yourself be overtaken by events. Look at the landscape as if it were covered with a winter's snow, leaving evident only God's landmarks. Then the riot of summer weeds would be blanketed into oblivion.

Orthodoxy had prepared itself well, through decades of disputation and debate, for such a systematic accounting of reality. It plotted every path of the soul's pilgrimage on the Calvinist map, tracing every twist and turn of religious agony and triumph on the palimpsest of consistent doctrine. Knowing reality with their eyes closed, limbs locked, mouths stopped, with only their ears open to the most familiar words, the orthodox evangelicals boldly walked a narrow line.

In religious life, they prayed for revival, heightened attention, a lively regard to divine concerns. But equally they prayed to be spared a repetition of the excesses of the First Great Awakening and "the great disorders," as one man wrote, "which became mingled in various forms of fanatical excitement with the genuine and glorious work of the Holy Spirit, and which produced a deadly reaction upon the churches."[4]

Nothing heartened them so much as the quietitude of the revivals of the Second Awakening. In Charles Backus's Somers, stillness and solemnity reigned. The jubilation that had affected revival congregations in the 1740s and the personal sense of "enlargement" that had then come to converts were nowhere to be found in the well-established New England churches of 1800. Like many others, Alvan Hyde thought of the revival in Lee, Massachusetts, as "a still small voice." Simon Waterman, the minister in Plymouth, Connecticut, bore witness "to the order and decency, the silence and solemnity, with which, and the numbers by which these meetings have been attended." A revival meeting was a converging of two opposites. The greater the number of people attending the minister's sermons, the more stunning was the noiselessness of their gathering. To see the meetinghouse filled with people and empty of tumult made ministers exultant.[5]

The revival in Goshen, Connecticut, for example, "was not the work of enthusiasm," according to Asahel Hooker, the local minister, "nor but slightly, if at all tinctured with it." Hooker continued:

> Hence, the subjects of it pretended neither to *see*, nor *hear*, nor *feel*, any of those things, which denote a disordered state of the understanding. None were carried away by impulses, or the flights of an ardent imagination. None were disorderly, or indecent in their behaviour, either in public, or private. Their passions were not generally wrought upon, to any considerable degree. Hence, instead of being noisy, or much inclined to communicate their feelings to others, they were commonly silent and reserved, except where they had opportunity of conversing with those, whom they thought able to instruct them.

All the enemies of true religion—visions, voices, jerky movements, disorder, impulse, imagination, passion, noise, even sociality—all were driven away, and stillness reigned in their place.[6]

The awakened were encouraged to confess their helplessness, their passivity. At a "season of life which is attended with uncommon temptations," one young woman cried out painfully, "How much do I need the protection of Almighty God!" For another woman in Coventry, Connecticut, paralysis seemed to follow upon her withdrawal from the world's social pleasures. "I have been crucifying the Savior afresh," she wrote, "and I still go on adding sin to sin. What an awful condition I am in. If I stay here, I shall perish. If I go back to the vanities of the world, I shall certainly perish. Now what shall I do?" Or, as a man in Goshen, Connecticut, scrawled on a note and handed to Asahel Nettleton, some had to cease from the merely formal observance of religion. "I have been laboring to convince myself," the man said, "that I was not a very great sinner, but the more I read my bible and attended meeting, the greater my sins appeared to me, till they seemed to rise like so many mountains before me. I know not what to do." In one personal narrative after another, conversion was a process of locating one's strongest impulse, one's most characteristic quality, and learning how to hate and resist it, to divorce oneself from it, to become, instead, totally passive.[7]

In this way, each individual case embodied the Calvinist precept that all activity was in the hands of the Lord. Merely one's fleshy sins or even one's vanity, pride, formality, did not need expunging; *sinners had to rid themselves of human activity, all of it.* Even when a minister, already converted himself, was leading others to Christ, as Edward Griffin revealed to his diary, he "was very fearful of pride and every movement of animal affection because they should lessen a sense of my ruined condition and total dependence on sovereign mercy." Griffin confessed that he could be "so fearful of selfishness and pride that I have scarcely dared to move."[8]

Silence was as necessary as prostration. While in his meetinghouse, Simon Waterman noted, "nothing was said but by the minister; for so little disposed were people to take an active part in any religious exercise, except singing, that it was difficult to get one publicly to propose or ask a question. Many were swift to hear, but all slow to speak." Were the ministers suppressing speech merely to advance their own standing? True, pastors always spoke of their role in strong terms. "The power of divine truth," Edward Griffin claimed in one sermon, "made deep impression on the assemblies." But if the congregation was only to feel impressed upon, passive under the instructions of the minister, the intent was not primarily to celebrate the latter's skill. Asahel Nettleton, who became the most famous evangelist of this revival, preferred not even to ask parishioners questions, "lest by this means he should turn the attention of sinners from their own wretched state to think 'how they should reply to the minister.'" Instead, Nettleton directed his conversations, his biographer said, "to produce silence and self-condemnation." Not to the minister's skill but to "divine truth" was the honor of silent parishioners paid. Sinners were instructed in being still so that they could properly allow their understandings and consciences to receive and be transformed by doctrinal truth.[9]

The worst ploy of the sinner was actively to seek for peace, in every corner and in the middle of the darkest nights. A man in Killingworth, Connecticut, wrote, "A pained conscience would not suffer me to rest, and the fear of Atheism aggravatedly oppressed me, till it pleased the most High, in sovereign manner, graciously to enable me, as I hope, to stay my soul on Jesus Christ." The long nervous battle within his own mind—his conscience constantly taking the side of doctrinal truth against the temptations of unbelief—ended when God exercised his sovereign power and brought him to "stay his soul," or, as it was sometimes said, to "arrest one's attention," to "fix one's heart," in other words, to stillness.[10]

The apotheosis of stillness, of course, was death, and in metaphors of morbidity evangelicals found their most powerful representations of religious awakening. Edward Griffin was delighted that his New Hartford congregation was "as still almost as a burying ground." Simon Waterman of Plymouth, Connecticut, was even more graphic: "The silence observable among those who were going to or returning from those meetings, was very impressive, and frequently noticed with surprise and pleasure. Little or no tumult, or noise, and the appearance of most, much as if they had been going to, or were returning from the funeral of some near relative or friend."[11]

The death bed became the ultimate sanctum for evangelical experience. The Hopkinsians of 1800 differed from their Victorian grandchildren in this regard; they were not at all interested in the sentimental, tear-inducing possibilities of the last moments of life. The final words of dying Christians were savored but not for their emotional effect on the survivors; instead the pure rationality of the expiring saint was treasured. "Admonitions from the Death-Bed," an article in the *Connecticut Evangelical Magazine* in 1801, advised "that the state of men's minds at that hour is often such as affords a solemn and weighty argument for the reality and importance of religion and divine truth. Then the appetites are cooled;—then the world and all its pleasures and interests appear in their true light; then the mind solemnly pauses and considers, and consideration is most favorable to rational and sincere conviction." The moribund soul, purged of all self-interestedness and tendencies toward corruption, was especially capable of the rational conviction of divine truth. But more important than such rationality was that a dying person understood the cardinal fact, "the reality and importance of religion." [12]

Stillness, then, was an experimental dying in the midst of life, a temporary abstractedness from biological momentum that could, like the approach of death itself, be used to glimpse eternal destiny. Only if one's appetites were cooled, and one's interests suspended, was rationality possible. "Death," Jacob Catlin of New Marlborough, Massachusetts, said, "is a detecter of the heart." [13]

Stillness proved Calvinism true. It proved that you could not get to heaven by any of your natural abilities. Like the thrashings of a drowning man, a sinner's energetic pursuit of his own salvation only drew him further under. It was necessary to stop, to arrest one's life, to call a halt to time.

The evangelicals were not otherworldly men and women. They had great respect for the consistency with which God, like the Great Artificer of Newtonian physics, kept the cause-and-effect relationships of natural life going. Their sermons depended as much upon the proverbial expressions of this faith in natural order as they did upon biblical catchphrases—"what you sow, so shall you reap," "the fruit falls not far from the tree," and so on. The evangelical ministers promised their flocks that faithfulness, which they epitomized in going about one's seasonal labors industriously, would inevitably be rewarded. [14]

But all these things were mundane. They were the province of the "common operations" of the Holy Spirit and had as much effect, obviously, on the fate of heathens as on God's own people in New England. Far more important, the evangelicals insisted, were the "special operations" of the Spirit, the saving energies that redeemed sinners in conversion and brought them to the promise of paradise.

The high drama of evangelical experience relied on a. single, immutable circumstance: one's eternal destiny, with all its attendant glories and endless splendor, rested upon getting saved during this earthly existence. The more sensible you were of the passage of ordinary life, the more concerned you were about economic and material problems, the greater was the danger of neglecting the task of salvation. "'You have no time to spend in conversation,'" Nettleton told an awakened sinner, "'before the salvation of the soul is secured.'"

Calvinism denied that the awakened were suspended in some special limbo between sin and grace. They were entirely sinful until the moment of regeneration. If they died before that moment, their Bible reading and fervent praying would go for nought—they would be lost forever. Whatever town road had brought the Somers people to their meetinghouse on Sabbath day, Charles Backus told them, "every person in this assembly, or anywhere on the earth, is either in the road to heaven, or in the road to hell." [15]

Ministers need not preach the terrors of hell; it was far better to appeal to a person's prudence. Now, this brief now, was the only moment for salvation, and it was passing. "This, probably, is not the first time you have felt concerned about your soul," a frightened sinner was admonished, "but, perhaps, it may be the last, if you quench, or disregard it. If you do not receive Christ now, and turn to God by unfeigned repentance, you have reason to believe, that you will never be awakened again; but that you will be left to perish in your sins." Why depict graphically the horrors of the nether region? It was simpler and more rational to contrast the quickness of earthly time's passing with the greatness of the opportunity about to be lost. Religious magazines told how rarely conversions came after age thirty-five. "It is but a short winter's day," wrote dour Fanny Woodbury to a friend in Beverly, Massachusetts, "that we have to spend on earth." And, continuing the metaphor, the harvest of souls had to occur, against the course of nature, during the brief daylight of this cold season. [16]

Stillness was the wintering of the body so that the soul could blossom forth. Evangelicals liked this metaphor. It helped to explain both why the present was not so brilliantly sunny as it once had been and why the future, equally, would shine even more. In his treatise on the millennium, published in 1793, Samuel Hopkins found New England's ecclesiastical fortunes on the same astronomical orbit. "As the winter in the natural world is preparatory to the spring and summer, and the rain and snow, the shining of the sun," he predicted, also

> the wind and frost, issue in the order, beauty, and fruitfulness of the vegetable world, and have their proper effect in these, and the end of winter is answered chiefly in what takes place in the spring and summer, and the former is necessary to introduce the latter, and in the best manner to prepare for it; so in the moral world, or the church of Christ, what precedes the millennium is as the winter, while the way is preparing for the summer, and all that takes place has reference to that happy season, and is suited to introduce it in the best manner and most proper time, when the gospel, so far as it respects the church in this world, and all the institutions and ordinances of it, will have their genuine and chief effect in the order, beauty, felicity, and fruitfulness of the church. [17]

Hopkins sounded confident, but compared to the millennial fervor of Bellamy and Hart in the 1760s and 1770s this is a dreary report on New England's spiritual weather. Hopkins was accepting the frozen state of New England religion. The millennium, he knew, was far off. And yet, God's faithfulness made it sure. Just as any rational New Englander could look out on fields covered with snow drifts and know that God would reward his patience with renewed verdancy, so even in the present condition of quietude there was a way to build up true faith. The still revivals of the Second Awakening confirmed the wisdom of this scientific sounding prediction.

Stillness was more, therefore, than an observation about religious practice. It embodied a whole way of looking at the world. It was a strategy for personal salvation and a theory of history at the same time. The quiet Christian was no mystic. He did not cultivate stillness in order to transcend ordinary reality. His orthodoxy was designed to get things right rather than to make them better and better. He did not abandon formal observances of piety and gave no heed to meditation.

On the simplest, behavioral level of analysis, stillness may have been part of a longer trend in American Protestantism toward order in the religious service. With the advent of singing schools and church choirs and the later introduction of the bass viol and pipe organ into New England meetinghouses, the quality of the hymn singing improved immeasurably in the first half of the nineteenth century. As middle-class politeness softened the manners of Yankee churchgoers, congregational silence became commonplace. The unheated eighteenth-century meetinghouse, with dogs scurrying about, the windows rattling, "thumping of feet on the floor, and the bustle in wrapping the capes of great coats around the ears," was increasingly scorned as inappropriate for divine worship. But something deeper than gentility was at stake. Stillness allowed evangelicals to accept the factual givenness of their universe and to subordinate every fact to the totality of divine providence.[18]

Almost to a man, the orthodox evangelicals were Federalists, and like other Federalist intellectuals in New England they spent the last two decades of the century assiduously cultivating a detailed reading of their region and nation. But while they spent most of the 1780s arguing for an innovative American-ness in politics, culture, and education, they were far more conservative a decade later. Civic virtue, either of the Boston liberal variety or the evangelical kind, was not in the wind of Shaysite or Whiskey Rebellion, or in the upheavals plotted by French Jacobins or Bavarian freethinkers, or in the fire of Jeffersonian "mobocracy"—but only in the "still small voice" of New England's orderly life. Speculative and utopian philosophy was to be abandoned in favor of a historical approach that sanctified the New England way. Timothy Dwight, minister in Greenfield, Connecticut, and future president of Yale College, attributed near perfection to his adopted state. "The happiness of the inhabitants of Connecticut," he wrote in 1794,

appears, like their manners, morals, and government, to exceed any
thing, of which the Eastern continent could ever boast. A thorough and
impartial developement [sic] of the state of society, in Connecticut, and
a complete investigation of the sources of its happiness, would probably
throw more light on the true methods of promoting the interests of
mankind, than all the volumes of philosophy, which have been written.

"To facts alone," Dwight concluded, "ought we to resort, if we would obtain
this important knowledge." Dwight's social science was, in essence, a con-
noisseur's appreciation of a fine still life painting. Because Connecticut was
presumably the happiest abode of mankind on earth, all future studies of
human happiness need only be explorations, gazetteers, and histories of Connecticut.[19]

Finally, consider Noah Webster. In 1789, the great lexicographer had proclaimed that "a *national language* is a bond of *national union.*" But when Webster sat down in 1800 to begin his quarter-century's work on the great American dictionary, his goal, as Richard M. Rollins notes, "was anything but a
new 'American tongue.' "

He did not advocate the development of a new language, or even a new
dialect, separate and distinct from that spoken in England. Instead, he
perceived himself to be writing merely an *American* dictionary of the
English language, which is of course a very different thing from creating a whole new language. And he further explained his position, noting that the body of the language was basically the same as that of England. He added a revealing statement: "It is desirable to perpetuate
that sameness."[20]

In 1808, Webster was converted to evangelical Calvinism, and many definitions in his dictionary reflect his encouragement of quietude and deference
to established authority. The phrases he used to illustrate his definitions are
telling. Quoting Alexander Pope, he urged, "look through *nature* up to *nature's*
God.' " In Psalms, he found that "Great *peace* have they that love that law."
"*Reconciliation* and friendship with God, really form the basis of all rational
and true enjoyment," according to Samuel Miller, the evangelical divine. Edwards helped define the soul, for example, "Such is the nature of the human
soul that it must have a God, an object of supreme affection." But "the eyes of
our *souls* then only begin to see, when our bodily eyes are closing." To what
should we pay heed? "God is the *sovereign* ruler of the universe. . . . God is
the *sovereign* good of all who love and obey him." How shall we relate to him?
"Entire and cheerful *submission* to the will of God is a christian duty of prime
excellence." Webster's work could truly be called an orthodox evangelical dictionary of the English language.[21]

Between 1780 and 1800, the Federalist intellectuals loved the same things about New England: its hardy independent farmers, its deeply rooted respect for language and learning, its concern for order and method. Although they loved these things in the 1780s because they were American traits and Yankee facts, by the turn of the new century they were more appreciated for simply being facts—final, certain, unquestioned, revered. To gain the respect and to demand the obedience of its citizens, New England needed to be converted into a single, immutable fact; the researches of this generation of New England scholars became a way of freezing everything they discovered—theology, law, public institutions, social customs, language. Nothing was true, as we have seen, until it was written down.

Reality was inevitable. It was consistent. It was rooted in God's law. A key evangelical term for such a view of things was "constitution." "The 'divine constitution,'" the historian Bruce Kuklick summarizes,

> was a key phrase in Bellamy's *True Religion Delineated*, as well as in Hopkins's *System of Doctrines*. Bellamy interpreted God's covenant with Adam as a constitution and declared that Adam "broke the original constitution." For Hopkins, people were "constituted" sinners, but Christ's work was "constituted" to save them, and baptism was "constituted" as a seal of this work. . . . The constitution was a rule of God's conduct that could be read from the nature of the moral universe; the constitution was his law-governed mode of operating. . . . for the New Divinity men, God operated on law-governed principles—a constitution—in both the natural *and* moral world.

In the decade after the adoption of the United States Constitution in 1787–1789, the word became even more heavily freighted. Whereas the framers in Philadelphia thought of the structure of government as mechanical, complete with "checks and balances," their evangelical supporters in New England loved the Constitution for its stabilizing, static quality. Now that the nation had a near perfect structure of government, only obedience to law was necessary. Virulent opposition to President Washington's administration, of which there was a great deal, was perforce an irrational denial of reality.[22]

Even before he reached the political meanings of the word, Noah Webster defined "constitution" as "the state of being; that form of being or peculiar structure and connection of parts which makes or characterizes a system or body." The evangelicals went far beyond their Federalist allies in counseling stillness and submission to this lawful ordering of the universe. God's law is now understood to be a constitution, but this constitution, unlike the one drafted in Philadelphia, is not a human construction of reality. It is in fact the given constitutiveness of the world. How can mankind be located within the constitution of a universe it has neither made nor even ratified? Through the strategem of stillness, man ceases to see himself at all. His view is transformed during the act of conversion to include everything in his ken, comprehensively, the all rather than the one. His conscience construes the constitution of the universe to be God's creation, and he names it as such.

This interpretive act, this literary transmutation of personal experience into divinely given meaning, was sustained by the faith that revelation and reason are entirely compatible. If there is sin in the evangelical scheme, it must belong to the order of nature; if there is salvation, it must belong to the order of grace. The association of sin with nature was a radical assumption that tied Calvinist doctrine to the ultimately constituted reality of the world. The saint learned to use his morally clear understanding to see himself only through the lens of orthodox dogma.

The analogy would be to construe the United States Constitution as a totalitarian and systematic description of ordinary reality. Citizens could then understand themselves only as members of the polity. The evangelicals had hoped the Revolution would in fact bring on a millennium to establish America as a purified community of virtuous saints, linking religious virtue and citizenship forever. But the federal constitution from the outset was viewed by its framers as quite limited in its applicability, and both Hamilton and Madison stressed the extra- and non-political life beyond the scope of citizenship. By contrast, Samuel Hopkins actually defined his millennium as a complete transformation of the conditions of ordinary life.

A basic fact distinguished the United States Constitution and the "distant logic of the gospel plan": the latter was supposed to be constitutive of reality, not merely a human mechanical arrangement. Small wonder that the evangelicals should denounce Jefferson for his speculative energy, for orthodoxy felt enormously threatened by the relativism implicit in such manmade meaning.

Thus did the evangelical orthodoxy try to see the world rationally as expressive of divine reality. Its soteriology, or theory of salvation, worked, as long as men saw truth in just this way. Disloyalty or infidelity, to them, was a distrust of the way things actually were, a setting-up of the world on entirely opposite principles. The saint, instead, was confirmed in his faith that he understood the world perfectly from his own stance; free will was for him as legitimate a description of human reality as brawny or industrious, and a recriminating conscience as hard to cross as a swift-running brook.

The quiet Christian lived in a world of absolute providentiality. Everything was a given, explicable, rationally comprehensible. The textually determined, imageless divinity of New England's orthodox evangelicals fulfilled William James's "first practical requisite which a philosophic conception must satisfy: *It must, in a general way at least, banish uncertainty from the future.*" [23]

But what would happen when certainty was no longer the central problem? In the next generation, the children of the orthodox, as well as many converted in their revivals, wanted greater risk, wanted to feel themselves alive to unassured possibilities. "The young men were born," Emerson recalled, "with knives in their brain." Then the 1790s constitution of divine reality would feel like an empty void, a vacuum to be filled by the prodigious energies of young nineteenth-century Americans. Activity, not stillness, would become the religiosity of men and women.[24]

Chapter Four

The Distant Logic of the Gospel Plan

A TASTE FOR CONTRADICTION must be acquired, and New England Calvinists spent many hours training themselves to puzzle through the paradoxes of their faith. Once acquired, though, this penchant could be indulged endlessly, and its flavor pervades their accounts of religious experience. In Somers, Charles Backus loved to say that the shower of divine grace was an unexpected confirmation of his twenty years of doctrinal preaching. In Granville, Massachusetts, the revival began when "a number of young people met for a civil visit, and the violin was introduced, which instead of producing the usual hilarity, occasioned a flood of tears." Such ironic rebuffs to sin always made the orthodox feel that they had chosen the right side in an endless struggle.[1]

Choosing right from wrong was, as we have seen, the function of the understanding, which proved its power by picking its way through these "seeming contradictions" in the way of faith. This was no easy task, for to the evangelical in the Second Awakening the world was a place of deceptions and snares, and no inborn moral endowment in one's mind could succeed, without the aid of divine revelation, in finding its proper course. Contradiction was everywhere. The language of conversion narratives was twisted with phrases like "what you are you will not be, and what you now love you will soon hate." A widow in Litchfield, Connecticut, for one, unfortunately "believed that to live uprightly, and deal fairly and honestly with mankind, was sufficient to entitle her to salvation. But at this time, she found that her former hopes were nothing, and that her righteousness was but filthy rags."[2]

Ministers took a somewhat supercilious attitude toward such sufferings and seemed glad that their familiarity with doctrinal explanations of personal experience was verified by these pains. For them, contradiction was more than a tone; it was the center of their experience of faith. For example, Edward Griffin generalized about the convictions of his parishioners during the revival at New Hartford:

> The order and progress of these convictions were pretty much as fol-
> lows. The subjects of them were brought to feel that they were trans-
> gressors, yet not that they were totally sinful. As their convictions in-
> creased, they were constrained to acknowledge their destitution of love
> to God; but yet thought they had no enmity against him. At length they
> would come to see that such enmity filled their hearts.

And so on. The yielding confessions in each sentence, we see, are broken by
the repetitive "yet" clauses. One did not instantly fall headlong into the arms
of Divine Providence, according to this description; at each stage, the convict
stopped and refused to go beyond the minimal concession required. But such
a concession was itself only a point of logical perplexity, a contradiction of
what had preceded and the material for a future rebuff, and soon it too would
have to be abandoned. [3]

The question arises, how could Griffin get into the minds of his parishioners so that he could detail their personal thoughts with such precision? And
then the oddity of his way of speaking becomes clearer. Although individual
parishioners are said to have thought this and that, the words their ministers
cited do not seem very personal to us at all. Instead, the converts' accounts
sound more like recitations from an ancient catechism than like revelations
of personal distress. To Griffin, the key events in his people's conversions,
apparently, were these verbal formulations. Each was a step in the logic of a
Calvinist argument and could be used to predict the next. The minister was
therefore hardly troubled by this series of contradictions. He knew there was
a plan to them, and he was master of the plan. When a parishioner acknowledged that he had sinned on occasion, Griffin's Calvinism pressed for a further
admission that this transgression was rooted in the man's sinful nature, not
in some momentary passing temptation. Orthodoxy "knew," again, that after
the understanding was convinced, the heart would object and have to be subdued in turn. And on and on, until the stillness of a comprehensive understanding was achieved.

Aside from making one's personal case exactly like that of other converts,
the import of this doctrinal language was felt in many ways. From Griffin's
words, we can discern that the movement of their thoughts was from the
particular to the general, from the partial to the total, from their lack of good
to their fullness of evil. A sin here and there had to be transmuted into a
general condition of sinfulness; it was not enough that they did not love
God—they needed to acknowledge that they were nothing but enemies of
divinity. In this way, a man's private case could be fitted up to scriptural spec-
ifications. When that was done, one was pressed to reverse the process and
see the scriptural label firmly attached to everything one was. In another place
Griffin said men might plead that they could not repent precisely "because

their nature and heart were so bad; as though [the minister glowered] their nature and heart were not they themselves." Not only, in other words, were they sinful, but also Sin was They. And if God was to extirpate sin in the world, they too would be doomed to perdition.[4]

That is, unless they repented and were changed by divine grace. In the end, the clear progression of Calvinist lessons in Griffin's description was not altogether disheartening. It did move to the fruition of conversion and holiness. And all along the path to that end, the sinner had a certain security in knowing where he was in the logic of Calvinist theology. With Griffin as counsel, one might be pained but never entirely lost or left to one's own devices.

There were, indeed, contradictions between one stage of the Calvinist argument and another. But Griffin's account can be read on a second level, as a description of ordinary human acts. What did the converts do? They "were brought to feel," "were constrained to acknowledge," "would come to see"; although these surely were not strong verbs, nonetheless they were acts of real people. The positions of the Calvinist argument, phrased in the sequence Griffin found in the mouths of his parishioners, might better be read down a page of catechistic questions and answers, but the actual experience of the converts who held and gave up these positions occurred over the course of time. In fact, these verbs and some of the other terms used—"increased," "at length"—stress the duration of these mental exercises.

When we look at the events in New Hartford from this light, the conversion experience becomes a series of long, drawn-out, uncomfortable rebuffs. We might surmise that sinners felt the same way about each of these stages—a modest assent to the next logical doctrinal tenet, combined with some gratification at the progress made and some frustration at the apparent endlessness of the process. Immediately, it must have seemed, the minister or some doctrinally proficient church member was back, again suggesting one's incomplete orthodoxy and urging further improvement. In this sense, the conversion experience was almost repetitive despite the progress made toward doctrinal truth. Furthermore, it seemed to contain no excitement, no peaks of particularly intense love or pain, but only a succession of still points from which one could reflect on the irony and futility of one's previous exercises. If we were to give Griffin's "gospel plan" a visual form, to map his geography of grace, we would have to imagine the scheme as a well-marked, if long, horizontal route—always on the same flat experiential and chronological plane.

The doctrinal interpretation of the evangelicals' experience was derived from Calvin and Edwards and other theological eminences. The sources of these more ordinary interpretations, which spaced and paced the stages of the Calvinist argument within the frame of human experience, are much harder to pin down. But clearly the ways of construing time and space relationships in one's religious experience were homologous to the ways these categories operated in other aspects of everyday life, particularly in agricultural work. In this chapter, I will focus on the convergence of theological and ordinary language in the praxis of the doctrinalist evangelicals, that is, how their faith was shaped both by doctrine and the assumptions of ordinary life. I will look at the problem of faith as three questions: of space, of time, and of authority. In each case, I intend to point to the consequences of this praxis of faith in both religious and mundane life.

Distance

Triumph in conversion meant mastering the labyrinthine details of the whole gospel plan. Failure could come in two ways. In the beginning of one's awakening to sin, before one became familiar with the scheme, it was possible to feel totally lost. Young John Todd, for example, found himself "involuntarily weeping very freely, for I did not know what nor where I was." Once the awakened souls entered the logical conversion path, their greatest worry was the loss, not of their places, but of their distinct ideas about God and sometimes even of sensibility altogether. Lyman Beecher confided to his diary in 1799 that "I can not feel. God is distant. I can not realize, can not get into his presence." But such troubled cloudings of Beecher's distinct ideas of divinity did not lead to doubt. Instead, he concluded this entry by affirming, "But God is: he is just; he will do right. I am a worm, and deserve to be unhappy." Even in such pain, then, Beecher was able to locate himself in relationship to God.[5]

Still, a convert's progress along the route did not mean closing the distance between convert and God. Familiarity with God's plan did not imply intimacy with the Lord. Grace was the precise clarification of both one's distance from the deity and one's place in the divine order. This distance from God did not imply his entire absence from the world; rather, it suggested that, as one traveled horizontally toward grace, God remained the same distance from that path. He appeared as a plan, a principle, a law—not a being intimately involved with his people.[6]

Therefore, what Beecher and other evangelicals sought was a more precise perception of God. When Timothy Cooley wanted to describe the signs of grace, for example, he went for evidence to "the views and exercises of those who obtained hope" during the Granville revival. "Some obtained relief," Cooley reported, "by a view of the glory and excellency of Christ; others were led to see the excellency of the gospel plan and its fitness for sinners; others felt a happy and joyful submission to God as a sovereign, and were willing to be entirely in his hands." Cooley intended this report to exemplify the "great diversity as to the manner in which divine light was let into the mind," but all three alternatives have the same grammatical structure and seem to represent the same kind of action. What is that pattern?[7]

Grace in each instance is a *perception* ("view," "to see," "felt") of the *moral quality* ("glory," "excellency," "sovereign") of the *divine* ("Christ," "gospel plan," "God as a sovereign"), and this in turn produces a *sensation of appropriateness* ("relief," "fitness," "submission").

Taken together, Cooley's words represent a static mode of religious apprehension, extremely quiescent in its epistemological assumptions. Like Griffin's wording in the passage we explored earlier, Cooley's verbs were all weak, revealing his sense of the human mind's relative passivity in conversion; all people had to do in grace, apparently, was to be led to (or to let in) correct impressions. These impressions of the divinity were not to burn with passion. A new Christian did not perceive God or his activity directly—the Christian could not see Christ, only his "glory and excellency." In two of these cases— "the gospel plan" and "God as a sovereign"—the terms for God were theological terms. Thus, all that converts could see was mediated by this screen of moral and theological labels.

Still, the evangelicals did not ignore the ordinary aspects even of this holy experience. First, they were implying that grace, a spiritual condition, was evident in the use of one's natural faculties; somehow simply having the proper "views and exercises" in one's mind was tantamount to having secured the great gift itself. Second, the result of such views was, as I have called it, a sensation of appropriateness—one's fitness or relief or submission. These terms were particularly suspect to double meanings. Relief, for example, might just as well have related to the psychological relaxation that followed the tense, long night of conviction as it did to shirking one's eternal metaphysical condition as a sinner.

Fitness was an even more powerful, and perhaps even more ambiguous, term. The evangelicals meant neither that the gospel plan fit sinners as individuals nor that it responded to their private conditions and their individual needs. All this they would not have understood in the least. By fitness they meant the appropriateness of the plan for all men and women, not that it could be adapted for each, but that each person would find the same salvation available therein. The gospel plan was not flexible; it was immutable, comprehensive, and thus allowed men to fit *its* terms.

The person who achieved a proper fitness with the gospel plan was not absolved of all sin and given a new, more godly, self. Instead, the extreme distance from the divine character was preserved in a kind of theological amber. And, yet, God would still save the sinner. The most common expression for this was the sinner's acceptance of criminality. The *Connecticut Evangelical Magazine* observed,

> When any one submits to the grace of God, he freely consents to be
> considered and treated and pardoned, as a criminal, deserving endless
> wrath, and to be so considered forever; and to be fixed as a pillar in the

house of God—a living monument, to perpetuate the memory of such grace, to the glory of Christ: he cordially submits to this way of salvation, and prefers it before all others which his imagination can invent.[8]

Through this notion, the evangelicals warned people that their self-interest would be ignored forever; they were not to look forward to their time after conversion and imagine themselves living wonderful and carefree lives as active Christians. Instead, always known as criminals, they would realize that God had saved them despite their criminality, redounding only to his credit, not to theirs.

The most common term for regeneration during this period was *reconciliation*. To be reconciled to God implied both a prior period of estrangement and a legal settlement. But reconciliation was in addition a process involving independent entities; as compared to *union* or *infusion* or *image*, or even *participation* or *commitment*, it left untouched the individual's personal identity. There was no question of interpenetrating divine and human substance, no transcendence and no immanence. Man's splendid understanding could welcome the rationality of God's ordering of the world, patching up their quarrel and providing an eternal connection.

Although the gospel plan encompassed men and women, was appropriate for, and enfolded them, they were not changed by it. To understand the plan—and a convert wanted to understand it more than anything else in the world—the convert had to step back from it, keeping distance from its ruling principles and fields of force. The Christian had to see the divine order as entire and be content to locate the self, with all its isolated human frailty intact, within that order. "The only way of securing real happiness to ourselves," Charles Backus emphasized, "is to feel satisfied with our proper place in the system."[9]

Nothing so well expresses the profoundly conservative quality of doctrinalism as this emphasis upon the "givenness" and unchangeableness of the gospel scheme. Religion was not a way to change the world, or even to change oneself, but only to find and accept one's place—as a pardoned criminal—within it.

There is some evidence that men and women took different approaches to this process of location and acceptance. Of the eight women, for example, whose conversion narratives were recorded during the 1814 revival in the village of South Farms (Litchfield), Connecticut, only one—a twelve-year-old girl—was said to have been deeply distressed. For the others, conviction of sin meant accepting its doctrinal meaning rather than finding one's personal faults. For example, one was said to "hate sin because it is exceedingly sinful," another said that "she then hated sin, because in its own nature, it is odious," and a third had "a high sense of the malignant nature of sin." Calling sin sinful, of course, meant locating oneself in the orthodox party, and this could produce a sense of one's fitness in the divine order. Typically, a woman became "submissive to the divine will—[with] a disposition to resign herself into the hands of God, feeling that the judge of all the earth would do right." Another, in even more orthodox fashion, "was made . . . to submit to the terms of the gospel." [10]

These acts of submission allowed women to rationalize and organize their religious lives, without forcing them to abandon the other forms of submission which they had already assumed in their ordinary work. There was little violence or self-hatred in their accounts. They acknowledged a surprising serenity as well as their benevolent feelings to God and to others in the community. Women rather often stressed the "divine consolations" that accompanied and highlighted conversion. Piety for them, therefore, was a mode of explanation, powerful enough to bring them restful "confidence in God through Christ."

By contrast, for the four men whose accounts are included with these, conversion demanded the subjugation of an explicitly rebellious heart. Their crises came more sharply and quickly, whereas the women had gradually awakened to the new truths the gospel offered to their lives. One hardened sinner of thirty-seven reacted to the chidings of his conscience with ever more violent and profane behavior and even planned suicide. Finally, "it seemed to him that the torments of a future world for sin, could not exceed the pain of mind which he felt." This was said to have broken his pride, "and he was made to bow at the footstool of sovereign grace on the 10th day of March." "He admires, and adores," it is recorded, "that such an awful, heaven-daring, and heaven-despising wretch, should be plucked as a brand out of the fire." Three of the four men also reported remarkable changes in their temperaments as a result of such experiences, corresponding to the consolation that attended their female coreligionists.

For men, there were no ordinary impulses of submission to strengthen. Instead, males actually needed to be stopped, threatened with the direst consequences, until their lives were changed. They needed to purge themselves of activity itself. As Charles Backus wrote, "You know—you feel, that if God had not stopped you in your dreadful career, and silenced your objections by his spirit, you would have remained his enemies, and have gone on to fit yourselves for everlasting destruction." In 1800, when this was published, "career" did not yet carry the significance of one's work history; its older sense, derived from its racetrack ancestry, was that of an "uninterrupted course of action." The reordering of grace, therefore, was a redirection of one's activity. One traveled in a horizontal world of sin, on the road to hell, until God changed the landscape of one's life; one continued to proceed horizontally, but now one knew the precise distance from the ordering sun of God's light. [11]

Women, whose work lives were more ordinarily circumscribed to the farm-house and the barnyard, could be confirmed in the stillness of the central places of their lives. Religious experience for them was both a relief from having to "tend" so many things at the same time (house, children, animals, fire, garden) and a newfound power to concentrate their loyalties precisely on God. Women often "dwelled" on the Word, rather than rebelling against it. Through religion women discovered a safer, quieter quarter, where passing time counted for less than it did in a farmwife's kitchen.

Doctrinalist religion was, on the basis of this evidence, remarkably atten-tive to the ordinary spatial lives of the two sexes. Its gospel plan took account of the fact that men's work was centrifugal, needing redirection, and that women's work was centripetal, needing focus. The irony of this should not go unnoticed. For if religion was so scrupulous in observing the traditional pat-terns by which men and women moved through space, then it offered no fundamental change to those patterns. Once a person was converted, he or she still had to pursue the traditional pathways of life, and the evangelicals did not promise that God would be an intimate companion on those paths.

In a way, doctrinalists were advising converts on how to rationalize and to comprehend their ordinary lives without the immediate presence of the divin-ity. Henceforth they would have to see, in their spiritual lives as well as in their mundane economic labors, that God's will was expressed in their newly won stability in the conventional way. God was willing to save a person and leave that person far off, just as God would reward planting and harvesting, simply by maintaining the regularity of natural principles in the universe. God would neither "disrupt" the spiritual lives of his people by sudden inter-ventions, nor would he arbitrarily destroy the fruits of a family's spring labor. Although the evangelicals were more insistent upon the primacy of the reli-gious sphere of life than upon anything else, their advocacy of a praxis of distance ironically allowed people to live more coherently without God in their daily lives.

New England society changed over the next half-century; people moved into the cities, industrial jobs, new and more confined work spaces, and more highly regulated work rhythms. Their basic passages through time and space were also altered. To many, God seemed entirely absent from ordinary life, as much from the fruition of man's work as from its initiation. "Life in the city," writes J. Hillis Miller, "is the way in which many men have experienced most directly what it means to live without God in the world." For the evangelical moralists and devotionalists, as I will show in Parts Two and Three of this study, preserving the role of divinity in these new circumstances implied bringing God into a closer relationship with humanity, into a more personal and intimate kind of companionship amid the hostile godlessness of surround-ing events.[12]

The Authority of Logic

Evangelicals thought that nothing was more important in obtaining salvation than neglecting one's self-interest, even an interest in being saved. "Their minds were so engrossed by the great truths of the Gospel," one minister wrote proudly of his parishioners, "that they thought little or nothing about their own salvation." We have already seen how ministers encouraged introspection and how that self-examination was designed only to yield self-condemnation. But this condemnation was not a confession of specific personal errors; it rigidly adhered to the formulae of Calvinist doctrine.

The same aversion to thinking and speaking personally shaped the way evangelicals prayed. They were not supposed to ask for personal favors from God or to explain anything extenuating or mitigating about their individual trials. "It is not the design of prayer," noted one writer, "either to inform the Divine Being of what he knew not, or induce him to change his mind, and bestow favors contrary to his previous intention." The proper thing to do was rather "to express a becoming sense of the divine perfections": speak to God only of God, not of oneself.[13]

What could this mean in practice? How could Christians speak of divine perfections they had not personally felt? By removing the natural self so far from the subject of introspection and prayer, how did the evangelicals expect that people could represent their own relationships with the divine? The clue lies in the link made in this last passage between God's "previous intention" and his "divine perfections." Only in the logic of Scripture and Calvinist doctrine could the perfections of God be equated with his previous intention. People were not to speak of what had happened to them personally but only of the plan God had once promulgated in Divine Scripture, presumably to accommodate every sinner henceforth.

The notion of obeying the logic of Christian doctrine was a splendid compromise for the orthodox evangelicals. Their theological instincts led them to stress man's submission to the deity, but their ordinary sense of God's distance made it necessary for some substitute to appear in place of the divinity itself. That substitute was his gospel plan as an articulated explanatory scheme for the way the divine witness was felt in human history.

The same procedure worked in the puzzling case of man's responsibility for his own salvation. Recall, if you will, that Calvinists distinguished between regeneration and conversion, "meaning by the first," as Charles Backus explained, "the energy of the holy spirit in changing the heart; and by the last, the holy exercises of the heart which follow; such as love, repentance, faith, and other graces." According to this theological reading, then, the soul was passive in regeneration, which was wholly the work of God. Only when the heart was changed would human activity have any virtue. "In conversion,"

Backus said, "men are active, and are as free in turning to God as in any exercises whatever." [14]

Amazingly lengthy theological controversies swarmed around this point, but it is more profitable to contrast the theological notion with what actually occurred. In practice, sinners were led to perform all sorts of activities on their own behalf before they were regenerate. Most of these entailed employing the "means," like attending church, reading Scriptures, and conducting family prayers. Ministers encouraged this "because," as one wrote, "the intellect of the sinner, not being the seat of depravity, his reason, memory, conscience, &c. are directly accessible by means." In other words, it worked. "While his heart is still unsanctified," wrote Ebenezer Porter, "he may make great attainments in doctrinal knowledge, and have deep and solemn conviction of the truth." As we saw in our discussion of the understanding, the industrious application of the sinner's mind to doctrinal matters was crucial in winning a place in eternity, although for doctrinal reasons all this endeavor had to be regarded as without merit. And when a person could at last act freely and virtuously, according to the theological dicta, after regeneration, that person did not seem to do so. In practice, the need for a convert to be perfectly still paralyzed the convert at the moment he was free to act. [15]

We can see here how the theological and the ordinary senses of activity and passivity in conversion were exactly reversed. In the theology, one was passive before conversion and active thereafter; in common parlance, one was active before and paralyzed afterward. The importance of doctrinal knowledge throughout gives coherence to this process. As the sinner began to understand the doctrinal logic, he had to pursue these truths actively; most activity before conversion was in disavowing self-interest and accepting the scriptural descriptions of sinners as appropriate. In conversion, one's way of thinking gradually became entirely enmeshed in the logic of one's religion. And because a Christian saw his deviance less frequently after conversion, he was in fact less sensitive to his own activity. He seemed now more genuinely if passively to espouse the accepted doctrines. In this way, the evangelical practice of religion as obedience to the gospel plan, rather than directly to God, worked to reverse the implications of the evangelical theology.

In the secular lives of New Englanders during this period, there was, of course, nothing like the Scriptures or the volumes of Calvinist apology to supply the directions for ordinary life. But insofar as we can discover their views on ordinary matters, evangelicals appreciated the person who went industriously about business, keeping careful track of personal gains and losses. But they were even more pleased if such industry were in tried-and-true paths of economic activity like farming ten acres of field crops each year, rather than striking out in speculative ventures. In this way, the praxis of the gospel plan, in which religious activity was sanctioned so long as one remained within its logic and valued one's place in the divine system above all things, overlapped with an equally conservative stance toward ordinary life. If one's livelihood, like spiritual salvation, could be achieved by a scrupulous attention to the traditional verities of the New England agriculture and commerce, then such a person would be double rewarded.

Books like Timothy Dwight's *Greenfield Hill* spelled out these connections very well and encouraged New Englanders to see that doing things in the traditional way was a reverence for established truth. Respecting tradition was not prescribed because the past was better than the present but rather because the endeavors of the past had resulted in a present probably superior to any other possibility. Like Burkean conservatives without Edmund Burke's admiration for emotional ties, the orthodox evangelicals presumed that if the past persisted it did so because of its correctness and rationality. Error, they believed, could never have survived generations of hard testing on the soil of New England.[16]

The work diaries of New Englanders were filled, then, not with notations of what God had done for them, but of what they could do for themselves. And yet all that activity, they felt, had in some measure approximated God's expectations of them. Small wonder, then, that many diary entries concluded with the phrase, "I leave the event with God," as though only the divinity could judge the rectitude of one's having sowed properly. The moment of success, when the reaping was to be done, was God's justification for one's labors. The enactment of God's providential plan—in both ordinary and spiritual pursuits—had the same pattern. In both cases, the success was God's and exemplified his wisdom in providing a way for men and women to follow.

The Gospel Plan (Time)

Evangelicals frequently commented on the heightened diligence in worldly matters of those who had passed through a conversion experience, but they never doubted that the spiritual sphere was the higher realm of man's life. "The people," complained Giles Cowles of Bristol, Connecticut, when the revival in his church was waning, "appeared to be uncommonly inattentive to their eternal concerns. . . . The concerns of the present life appeared to engross the attention of most." A saint like Jeremiah Hallock of Canton, Connecticut, who turned to farming to eke out his scant ministerial earnings, wept that he had "spent the day in worldly business, and found it morally impossible to keep the world, as I ought, out of my heart. Had but little time or life in prayer," he told his diary. "O how doth the world impoverish my soul."[17]

Settle your eternal affairs first, congregants were advised, and then attend once again to mundane matters. In the "short winter's day" that is mortal life, nothing else counted. Underpinning this pressure for an immediate attention to salvation was the evangelical doctrine of "instantaneous regeneration." Asked, for example, in 1828 to account for the success of American revivals, Edward Griffin credited the "distinct apprehensions which prevail in New England about the instantaneousness of regeneration, the sinfulness of every moral exercise up to that moment, and the duty of immediate submission. Such a view leads the preacher to divide his audience into two classes, and to run a strong and affecting line of demarcation between them." The practical effects of this preaching were significant. One could see one's neighbors and one's family members on the other side of the dividing line, and those on the side of perdition must have resented the line that could keep them from joining their loved ones in holiness. Furthermore, the idea of instantaneousness seemed to convince sinners that their grace was only a moment away, that what could happen in a flash would have eternal consequences for them.[18]

In evangelical literature, children wept over their parents' lost condition—as they would over drunkenness a generation later. But conversions did not come quickly. They were lengthened, delayed, deferred excruciatingly. The extraordinary significance attached to professing faith made it harder, not easier, for awakened sinners to carry themselves through the final stages of the process. As the self tried to discover stillness and adapt its understanding of all things to the measure of orthodox doctrine it often became stuck.

Although there was no distinct theological condition between sin and grace, large numbers of parishioners stayed there nonetheless. Attending to the "preparatory work" was so important for their doctrinal instruction that they could win the sympathy of their fellow congregants, if not their scriptural approval. Each week's discovery of the applicability of the gospel plan to one's own case was welcomed but also subjected to the narrow scrutiny of ministers like Edward Griffin. Even when they seemed ready to profess their faith, the repentant were warned about being too hasty, and many churches forced such recently relieved souls to put off their first communions for two months or more to allay fears of hypocrisy.

Conversion, in sum, could become a seemingly endless confrontation with the intricacies of doctrine, and revival narratives spoke feelingly of those who incurred danger by cyclically awakening, coming near to fruition, and then falling back into slumber. Lyman Beecher complained that some parishioners seemed to "stay so near the boundary-line [between sin and grace] all their lives that they hear the lions roar all the while."[19]

A good example of a long deferred conversion is that of James Morris. His father had been converted under the ministry of Joseph Bellamy in Bethlem, Connecticut, in 1740. Born in 1752, Morris was attentive enough to religion in his youth to consider studying with the aged doctor of divinity himself. The revolutionary war intervened, however, and by the time Morris returned home in the early 1780s, he was too old to resume his study of theology and

turned instead to tending his family's property and adjudicating local disputes
(as a justice of the peace) between creditors and Shays-like debtors in the
town.[20]

Morris was an upright man, and, though inclined to religion, he was disgusted by the vulgarity of the church members in South Farms parish. "The
church in this place," he wrote, "was made up of numbers of ignorant, un-
principled and unexemplary men. They voted in Church Meeting that conversion should be no requirement of Communion at the Lord's table, and the
Society ratified the vote." But he himself was not yet a church member, as his
standards were higher.

> As to my head knowledge, I was a Christian [he recalled], while my
> heart was estranged from holiness. . . . My father dated his conversion
> at the time of the general outpouring of the Spirit on the churches in
> the years 1740 and 41, before he was twenty years old. My mind was
> anxiously impressed with the idea that presently I should be forty years
> old, and if I sinned away the day of Grace till after that period, my
> crimes would be sealed in the book of God against me.

He was the perfect subject for the religious revivals that came in the 1790s.
Seeking both social and gospel order, a well-read and doctrinally expert parishioner, already delayed too long in his conversion by the vicissitudes of the
world, Morris finally made his profession and joined the church in 1790,
when he was thirty-eight.[21]

It would not be too much to say that such evangelicals thought so highly of
conversion and so narrowly of the frame of life around it that they might admit
that conversion could fill an entire adult lifetime. For one thing, the exercises
of converts after their supposedly instantaneous changes differed little from
the discipline, self-doubting, and mental gymnastics of the months before.
And the orthodox thought little and spoke less about all the other moments of
Christian experience—the sacraments, sanctification after grace, charity.
They were entirely absorbed by the question of conversion, and as it swelled
in importance it became the apotheosis of the human condition itself.

In the contrast between the theological doctrine of "instantaneous regeneration" and the praxis of a lengthy conversion experience, one can discern
the orthodox evangelicals of the Second Great Awakening apart from their
Calvinist heritage. It might have been possible for Calvinists, at other times
and with other social intentions in mind, to offer the possibilities of conversions that occurred as quickly and mysteriously as did regeneration. But the
revivalists of 1800 feared the anarchic enthusiasm of such sudden changes,
and thus they constructed a way of bringing sinners through a long conversion
in which their minds would be insistently fixed upon the demands of doctrinal rigor. It is likely that this arduous religious praxis emerged from an

inclination among the evangelicals toward the stability and severity of traditional agricultural life. Harvesting, for example, was as powerful a metaphor for the spiritual cultivation of souls as it was in economic life, and the continual succession of planting and harvesting seasons, or of the diurnal rhythms of household maintenance, provided evangelicals with strong illustrations of how men and women could be faithful through uncertainty.

Despite their attentiveness to Calvinist dogmatics, the orthodox in 1800 were not prepared to take the theology literally. Their notion of faith as the Christian's appreciation of the distant logic of the gospel plan distilled their assumptions of ordinary life as much as it derived from their doctrinal teachings. The gospel plan, to put it bluntly, was not itself gospel truth. It was, like every attempt to order religious experience in the course of human life, a cultural conceit that took account of the "facts" of ordinary life as this particular culture understood them.

It is worth stressing this point, lest one lose sight of the real contribution of these evangelicals. They could not find the imperishably true path of Calvinism. But they could adapt their Calvinism to an ideal of rural economy in which people would ceaselessly pursue hard truths despite the absence of a wrathful God in their midst. They wanted people to act like players in an immense metaphysical drama at the same time they toiled in their earthly vineyards, both without direct apperceptions of the divine.

The contrast with their mentor Jonathan Edwards is instructive. Like Edwards, the orthodox evangelicals believed that God could be known in one's consciousness. But Edwards had gone much farther than this; he insisted that the spiritual exercises of the mind were in fact interrelationships with the Holy Spirit. The aesthetic aspects of the divine, he believed, had an ontological status. God *was*, in other words, his beauty and excellency and harmony. Furthermore, people were endowed with a sensibility capable of apprehending that beauty directly and hence experiencing the actual *being* of God. Within their own minds, in fact, they could discover aesthetic correspondences that linked them to that Being. Grace for Edwards, then, was the "consent," the harmonious connection, of one's finite "being" to "Being-in-General," or God. There was no question, therefore, of one's distance from God; one existed only in being constituted of the stuff of God's beauty, never merely in rational contemplation of it from afar.[22]

Even among the most loyal Edwardseans, God as being-in-general gradually paled in the late eighteenth century before God as moral governor. Joseph Bellamy, whose words breathe a purer Edwardsean spirit than any other disciple's, assisted this progression by arguing for a general view of the atonement, that is, that Christ died for all sinners rather than only for the elect. This made the gospel plan effectual for all mankind, not merely for those decreed for heaven, if only sinners would accept it. Sinners were suddenly citizens of the spiritual world by this revolution, rather than nonentities outside it. But the talk of God henceforth was more of his legal proceedings and decisions than of his infilling presence. With so much work to *do,* the divinity came less to be what everything *was.* His gospel plan, the outline of this work, became more important than the love that had promulgated it in the first place.[23]

At least for Bellamy, though, God as judge remained a being. With Samuel Hopkins, as one historian has written, God became a "cosmic destiny before which he [man] could do little but gladly resign himself." In Hopkins, the impulse to separate the human and divine realms became central to the religious life. Hopkins's God *is* the logical order attained when people overcome their natural tendencies. For example, a natural sentiment like gratitude would, of course, lead people to love God if they knew that he designed to save them. Such love, said Hopkins, "is nothing but self love." However, "He who has a new heart and universal disinterested benevolence," Hopkins asserted, "will be a friend to God, and must be pleased with his infinitely benevolent character, though he see not the least evidence, and has not a thought that God loves him, and designs to save him." Such selflessness seemed, in fact, to preclude having any evidence of God's love for oneself. Edwards also had downgraded gratitude or reciprocal love, but only as inadequate to regeneration, not as primary signs of sin.[24]

How far could this selflessness go? Hopkins continued on, approaching the maxim his partisans made famous, "And if he could know that God designed, for his own glory and the general good, to cast him into endless destruction; this would not make him cease to approve of this character; he would continue to be a friend of God, and to be pleased with his moral perfection." People should be willing to be damned, the Hopkinsians thought, for the "greater glory of God." All that mattered was their willingness to overcome all their natural impulses to care about themselves, even to care what God did to them. Religious life, becoming a friend to God, then, was entirely a matter of expunging self-regard from human consciousness.[25]

Despite his talk of God, Hopkins provided little positive sense of the divine in human life. His sense of either deity or godliness was simply abstracted from his negative interpretation of the human heart; it was the product of doctrinal exegesis rather than personal experience. God was pure and holy and perfect and excellent and glorious, to be sure, but orthodox evangelicals could understand all that only as logical inference or by seeing God's character as humanness turned upside down. Griffin's "view of the purity of God," remember, was as much logically dependent upon his perception of the "awful nature" of one's sin as it was the other way around.

The orthodox still talked of a universe ruled by an absolute sovereign, but he was now a formless and impersonal deity, whose chief characteristic was the absence of any natural human feature. More to the point, by this way of thinking, the Hopkinsians had ceased to think about either God or God's personal relationship with man. "To these Calvinists," Daniel Day Williams has written, "the essential fact underlying all doctrine and all religious practice was man's status as a moral being who either has a primary affection for God or who does not have it, and whose eternal blessedness or damnation is to be determined by his primary choice." The contrast in the evangelical mind, then, was no longer between one's participation in the divinity or one's dissent from it, as Edwards had suggested, but rather between two types of beings—one freed of self-regard and another mired in it.[26]

In order to see God more clearly, the orthodox evangelicals had to step back from him, to see him as an explanation rather than a living force. Man's chief end, one evangelical remembered bitterly from his childhood lessons, "was to 'worship and glorify God,' as a Being entirely separate from all human relations and duties." Having views of such a God in one's mind was no longer a way of sharing the divine being.[27]

Thus, although the doctrine of instantaneous regeneration was continually preached during the seventy-five years after Edwards began to articulate his sense of religious experience, the practical immediacy of the divine in Christian lives diminished constantly. Instead, the clarity and comprehensiveness of the logical plan of salvation came to be the object of worship. In one sense, the orthodox evangelicals were providing a more consistent view of life as a natural process, with God's activity chastened by his previously expressed intentions. On the other side, they were delineating a way of thinking about human life in which people were forever straining to overcome their mere humanness. The orthodox, designating the spiritual landscape in which one traveled as a divinely decreed version of the New England countryside, hoped that by constantly striving against selfish instincts one might think it possible to live on this higher plane, even when encumbered with earthly cares. Twentieth-century Americans tend, I think, to shrink from such presumption, to doubt that people could so overcome their human natures and see their lives compressed (or expanded) into the outlines of a Calvinist drama. But one must admire the courage with which the evangelicals, understanding and admiring so much of their human environment, vowed to live beyond the limits of human nature, to introduce into that nature a higher possibility for perfect obedience to scriptural truth.

Chapter Five

Espousal with the Local Community

BENEATH THE SURFACE of appearances, the orthodox evangelicals faced a problem new in American religious history. Particulars were everywhere; choice weighed down every moment. There was no longer a single way to worship piously, to act politically, to establish oneself economically, to define oneself socially. Conventional patterns were not less attractive, only less coercive. In the 1790s orthodoxy answered a question that still plagues us: How can the fragments of experience be fit together?

The orthodox can be defined less by their doctrinal tenets, their ecclesiology, or their theory of the mind than by their characteristic answer to this question. The rhetoric of all religious relatedness shared the same aesthetic. The single unified particle of experience was always understood to fit perfectly into a larger, equally unified, plan: each conversion fit into the gospel plan; each idea fit into the doctrinal truth. But this "fitness" was usually a distant relationship. Orthodox Calvinism bridged ordinary human experience and divine reality, without erasing the deep divide between them. The one could not be understood without the all, and vice versa.

Unity bridged to totality: that was how the orthodox thought about everything. Rid religion, they would say, of all the extraneous fragments of experience and find instead a precise, singular, right way. There were several minidramas in which the unified self related to a coherent universe: when the understanding integrated diverse messages into a unified assent to correct doctrine; when the conversion experience swelled to occupy one's full attention, and maybe one's whole life; and most of all, when the "perfect standard" of biblical rectitude purged the self of more personal insights.

By contrast, the religion of Jonathan Edwards was more comfortable with the abstract. Edwards thrilled at the aesthetic contrast of absolute divine sovereignty and human finitude. But he seemed able, always, to see the divine clearly. He could catch totality with his rope without ever burning his hands. His disciples at the turn of the nineteenth century, after years of misbegotten millennial fervor, were much more scarred by grand truths. Stamp Acts and

64

Bunker Hill, Yorktown and Barbary pirates, funding schemes and impost duties, iron plows and the China trade: events of such distracting particularity
made the evangelicals hard-pressed to force reality into their systems of belief.
The aspiration remained, but the strain showed.

The social dimensions of doctrinalist religion were similar. This concluding
chapter on the orthodox evangelicals focuses on the institutional arrangements by which they fixed parishioners in a correct relationship to the
church. I want to elucidate how the evangelicals conceived, particularly, of
privacy, sociality, and authority. And because these concepts carried over into
the evangelicals' sense of secular society and politics, it will also be possible
to see orthodoxy in the context of the political culture of the Federalist era.

Congregants became members of the church, of course, when converted,
on the "day," Charles Backus wrote, "in which they were espoused to Christ."
Espousal is a helpful metaphor for understanding their social religion. Converts associated themselves publicly with the church for eternity, arranging
to live under the constraints and with the privileges of its household. As with
marriage, church membership began with great celebration. Terminating it
before one's death was a tiresome procedural affair. Finally, like marriage,
church membership was a publicly recorded change of status, a permanent
link with the people of the Lord.

The church was central. No solitary figures are recorded in meditation
amid the rocky pastures of New England's farms; spiritual pilgrims did not
retreat, as we have seen, to private chambers or "secret groves" for prayer.
"The revival," Samuel Shephard of Lenox, Massachusetts, proudly exclaimed, "began in the church, as I believe is almost always the case when
God pours out his Spirit." Religious experience was personal but invariably
public.[1]

Our tremendous respect for the inner, private sphere emerged from the
mid-nineteenth-century collapse of faith in the ability of "external" institutions to express unique points of view. In the 1790s, ideas meant public ideas.
Because individual expressiveness was as illogical and unwarranted as un-
grammatical diction, religious experience became real only when it verbally
conformed to the public standards of the church. About articles of belief,
there could be no diversity or dissent. Calvin Colton caustically explained the
system of examination of these points.

> Having been satisfied on the great point of the new birth, the candidate
> is then examined particularly as to his knowledge and belief in all ar-
> ticles of the creed. Under this head I have always noticed, that the lay
> officers [deacons in the Congregational and Baptist churches], and some
> other members, are disposed to be very particular; especially on those
> points which they deem most essential to orthodoxy, and which with
> them are favourite points; and it is remarkable how they select those,

which are most difficult of apprehension, and which have most embar-
rassed the minds of leading theologians—as if children, youth, and
other ignorant persons—ignorant in theology—could be expected to
make an innocent profession on the highest and most abstruse points of
Christian doctrine! Or as if these examiners themselves were perfectly
at home in such a field![2]

Because the uniformity of belief proved its validity, joining an orthodox
church was more a question of attaching oneself to the doctrine than to a
community of fellow believers. Religion was simply not a matter of dealing
with other people. As Henry Clarke Wright recalled, "When asked, 'What is
Effectual Calling?'—'What is Justification?'—'What is Adoption?'—'What
is Sanctification?' the thought of my duty to my fellow-beings never entered
my mind."[3]

One's personal relationships could even get in the way of a proper connectedness to the church. A magazine article on revivals reported,

> One [woman], on pretence of a visit, had left her father's house for sev-
> eral days, because she supposed that God had bestowed saving mercy on
> one of her sisters, and had left her in a state of condemnation, which so
> exasperated her heart against both God, and the subject of his grace,
> that she could not endure the sight of her. Another, when he had heard
> that a neighbour had obtained a hope that he was renewed, secretly
> wished that it might prove false; for then, he tho't, his condition would
> be no better, but worse than his own.

Autobiographies and memoirs tend to overlook these episodes of conflict, but
diaries show that during the period of conviction sinners frequently expressed
their alienation from their parents, siblings, or peers. Sarah Connell of Newburyport reviled herself for being surrounded by men like her father who
spurned religiosity; the worst moments came when she yielded to these
worldly temptations and forwent the observance of her proper duties. "I was
dissatisfied with myself," she told her diary, "how I have misspent this Sabbath! Instead of devoting it to religious duties, I have been engaged with
company, joining the trifling conversation of the gay and thoughtless." Among
girls, especially, the conversion of a friend or a sibling usually generated considerable anxiety about one's own destiny. It was, for example, after her friend
Harriet Osgood had obtained a hope of grace that Sarah Connell pledged "to
devote more time to the reading of religious books than I have done." But this
anxiety could be transmuted into simple rivalry, as each friend counted every
sacrifice of worldliness as evidence of a deeper piety.[4]

Children sometimes felt that their parents' lassitude had been squandering
both their own and their offsprings' destinies. Brothers reacted jealously to

one another's religious attainments, as though the birthright promised each was now in danger of being stolen by one. Finally, converts always impatiently deplored any signs of unconcern in their own families or social circles as representative of the worst, almost unforgivable, sins.

Some converts seemed to discard all their familial and fraternal relationships in turn, until they achieved a sufficiently isolated sense of themselves. Harriet Lathrop, a young woman in Norwich, Connecticut, for example, went in her religious anxiety first to her mother, then to a set of peers, and finally to a group of local women exemplary for their piety. Each time she took flight. "I seemed to expect," she remembered later, "some special revelation from Him of my adoption, and often prayed that some angel might come and give me the so-much-desired assurance." Eventually, such an adoption did occur, although it was not quite as personally dramatic as she had fantasized. Harriet Lathrop could end her reclusiveness when she was reconciled—not to her parents or friends, but to God.[5]

It was not a good time for friendship, familial affection, or good feeling in the local community. Close and emotional relationships menaced the primacy of ecclesiastical loyalty. Because they exposed one's strong natural affections, they threatened to loosen the ties to doctrinal orthodoxy and right practice.[6]

In cases of church discipline, offenses against other members of the congregation counted for less than breaches of the church's own ordinances. Dyer Hughes refused to take communion with the Congregational Church in Hampton, Connecticut, because he had been grossly insulted by William Brewster, a leading member. The church agreed that Hughes had been wronged but excommunicated him anyway because he had no right to absent himself from these ceremonies. In Bristol, Connecticut, Doctor Josiah Holt angered the community by attempting to seduce seven of his neighbors' wives and by cavorting in bed with the widow Ruth Ives; but he got away with an admonition and a forced confession. Soon after in the same town, Joseph Stone and his wife were excommunicated for avoiding public worship and communion and for believing in universal salvation.[7]

When the General Association of Connecticut, the assembly of the state's ministers, met in 1808 to spur "united endeavors to revive gospel discipline," they complained that "so many sit at our communion tables, who are so ignorant of each others real characters." To remedy this, they suggested more frequent meetings for Christian conference and social prayer and a closer supervision of "each others spiritual state." But all this was, in a way, an afterthought for the association. When they sat down to deal with the problem of church discipline, they showed that institutional regularity, not interpersonal intimacy, was their highest goal. First, they recommended caution in administering communion to members who were not truly sanctified because they would not submit as well to church discipline as others. Second, they called for the extirpation of heresies from the church. And third, they complained of "covenant-breaking," by which they meant the failure of parents to baptize their children or to submit their families and themselves to the proper instruction preparatory to a conversion experience.[8]

The ministers did not complain about fleshly sins. They worried only about the spiritual instruction of their children. They were silent on the responsibilities of church members for one another or for the unfortunate in the community. A minister who walked more than five miles a day to visit the sick in his Beverly, Massachusetts, parish was regarded as quite eccentric; "ministerial visiting was not so much required in those days." But if one questioned doctrinal orthodoxy and the outward duties of church attendance and Bible reading, the clergy were quick to act. In church after church, the two most common sins submitted to church discipline around the year 1800 were "embracing universalist sentiments" and "failing to observe covenant obligations." During the previous half century the record books had been rife with cases of fornication, as obviously pregnant brides could not avoid the detection of deacons and parsons. Now prenuptial conceptions were fast disappearing. And the great worry over public intemperance would await the 1820s. In 1800, "infidelity" was the greatest threat to church order.[9]

The evangelical orthodox, although they represented themselves as defenders of the "faith once delivered to the saints," set new and higher doctrinal standards in order to stamp out dissent in their congregations. When Samuel Worcester succeeded to the pulpit in Fitchburg, Massachusetts, in 1797, he discovered a church without formal articles of faith. The "half-way covenant" still prevailed, allowing unconverted members of the congregation the privilege of having their children baptized. Membership was available to all who sought it. The free and easy custom of "exchanging pulpits" found Worcester sitting one Sabbath morning in his own church listening to a preacher espouse deistic and universalistic sentiments. Worcester's ire rose, and in his study that evening he exploded, "Yet this is the man, to whom I was called upon to give the right hand of fellowship, as with me a fellow-laborer in the vineyard of Christ! Be offended who may—I affirm, that, as are his sentiments, so is his character, notoriously vile, licentious, and infamous."[10]

Worcester, only in his late twenties, proceeded to propound a new confession of faith for the church, in the strongest Hopkinsian language. Although those already members were not forced to renew their vows, new candidates would be required to assent to these articles of doctrine. "The impression generally obtained," said a pamphlet about the ensuing controversy, "that a voluntary consent to the new forms was the only satisfactory evidence of a person's really possessing the Christian's temper." The parish erupted. A group of dissenters seceded to form a Universal Christian Society in Fitchburg. The Congregationalists then voted to excommunicate seven men, all of good character—three for universalist opinions, three for irregular attendance on church ordinances, and one for attending the neighboring (and more liberal) church in Westminster, Massachusetts. This led to a church council, composed of ministers and deacons from other towns, which overturned these exclusions, arguing that "we are of [the] opinion that every man may exercise the right of private judgment, without offence to a brother, provided he appear to be conscientious and conduct in a Christian manner." The doctrine of universal salvation was judged insufficient ground for either church censure or denying admission to a Christian church. The council then voted to recommend that Worcester's relation with the church be dissolved, and the Fitchburg town meeting, still a party to tax-supported established churches, concurred.[11]

The strict evangelicals could not "conceive a greater absurdity, than to suppose that a man's religious opinions do not affect his religious character." For the orthodox, opinions were crucial. "'No Union with Error' was the watchword [Worcester reported]; it was caught up and echoed from pulpit to pulpit through New England, till the separation was made, and the Gospel again had free course and was glorified."[12]

Such splits within Congregationalism were painful because most New Englanders still wanted to identify their towns with their churches. Voluntarism and denominationalist pluralism were, despite their obvious reality in fact, still objectionable in theory. Liberal Congregationalists were as elitist as their evangelical opponents. But after the Revolution, such liberal congregations seemed to countenance more individualism among their parishioners. Their churches, like their new social and reading circles, became refuges of respectability. Membership conferred the benefits of social prominence, while constraining few from a more assertive expression of their private economic interests.

For the evangelical orthodox, religious society implied the denial of private interest. They thrilled instead to the liveliness of the church as an organism with its own vitality. The proper role of members was to watch quietly as the institution enacted its rituals. For example, Charles Backus describes a triumphant communion day at the culmination of the Somers revival:

> It was animating to meet at the Lord's table, in this season of refreshing. Old Christians were enlivened, from the beginning of this work. It rejoiced their hearts to behold souls flocking unto Christ, and coming to his table. The old and the young appeared to feel the worth, and to taste the sweetness of the Saviour's dying love. The spectators were more numerous than they had ever been; and not a few of them were in tears. In several instances, persons had their doubts removed, and were emboldened to join the church, by what they saw and heard at the administration of the Lord's supper.

Indeed, there were many spectators. It is hard to conceive who was doing anything in the Somers meetinghouse that Sabbath day; instead, everyone was a witness, being "animated" and "enlivened" and "emboldened" by what they "beheld" and "appeared to feel" and "saw" and "heard." Always slow to acknowledge his own importance, Backus drew this picture of an impersonal body acting on its own account. His people were detached from the activity of the church, and that activity became subjectless, an abstract articulation of divine truth.[13]

The active church, though, was not an instrument devoted to human ends. It was the embodiment of communal order, most often called, simply and exclusively, "The Church of Christ in ———." Christians did not alter their place in the social world because of church membership; rather, it confirmed their place in the given social order of the town. True, in the conversion experience, children threw off the authority of their parents and the companionship of their friends, in order to accept the dominion of divinity. But once converted, a child returned home to face a father as unrelenting in his authority as ever. The new convert doffed his cap as well as his opinions when scrutinized by those theologizing deacons in the meetinghouse. Grace was not an equalizing ointment. It restored the full authority and hierarchy of the rural community, but with the added blessing of the gospel truth.

It was a special moment in the history of a religious revival, then, when God changed the hearts of the "natural" leaders of the community—heads of households, wealthy merchants, and well-educated lawyers and doctors. One minister recalled how "the conversion of a sedate, influential lawyer was announced. I was at the meeting when he first made known the fact, and gave a most stirring exhortation. This 'brought out' others under distress of mind." The revival seemed at such moments to rivet the social order of the agricultural community to its gospel order. In parishes that still "dignified" their meetinghouses, social superiors sat front and center. Religious attainments did not win you more highly prized pews.[14]

All Congregationalists prized such social stability, but only the orthodox insisted strenuously that the gospel order was primary. Although rich men be respected, their riches were as nothing compared to the bounty of God's grace. "Vanity," Alvan Hyde warned, "is stamped upon every thing terrestrial. Riches are as fluctuating as the waves of the sea. Honors are as fading and temporary as the flowers in the spring. The pleasures of the world are as short-lived, as the beautiful prospect afforded by the morning-sun." Piety, the same piety, was for all the most important blessing. Lawyers and laymen, parents and children, deacons and dullards—all were asked to manifest the same submission to the Lord. The experience of children was always understood as precociously adult, not as a distinctly juvenile form of evangelical faith. In the next generation, as we shall see, religious life was adapted to different ages, classes, genders, and economic communities. In 1800 such distinctions would have been incomprehensible.[15]

Anonymously, quietly, the church defined and sanctified the town. At a time when New England town leaders—selectmen, clerks, school commit-teemen, tax assessors and collectors, and inspectors of all sorts—were occupied with their duties for only a few hours a month at most, ministers of the established church were the only essentially full-time, paid public officials. Their meetinghouses in the eighteenth century were often on windblown deserted hilltops, rarely visited except on the Sabbath. But by making a round of all the schoolhouses in a dispersed settlement like Lee, Massachusetts, convening religious conferences at each, young Alvan Hyde could remind people of their allegiance to the town in 1792 and spark a religious awakening.

Ministers were the chief spokesmen for local pride. "Localism," says the leading historian of the clergy during this period, "was the essential characteristic of the clerical office in eighteenth-century New England." As opposed to lawyers, whose political and legal interests drew their attention to shire towns and state capitals, or merchants, whose goods and credit came from seaport cities and river entrepôts, ministers had most to gain from the insularity of the New England town. They took every occasion, therefore, to praise their communities as internally unified and coherent models of Christian polity, as "peaceable kingdoms." Elijah Parish of Byfield, Massachusetts, renowned locally for his excellent business advice in addition to his spiritual standing, even refused to deliver homegrown sermons to other congregations. And whenever they were asked to comment on the town's history or economy, as in the questionnaires sent out to leading citizens (and often to local clergymen) by the Connecticut Academy of Arts and Sciences or the Massachusetts Society for Promoting Agriculture, they responded with strong localist prejudices. Each town had, it would appear, a particular method of harvesting corn or maple sugar as much as a characteristic topography of "gentle declivities and fast-running streams." In each, the salubrity of the air, the longevity of the denizens, the breed of cattle, the yield of oats, or the prevalence of the wheat rust were all as peculiar to the spot as the legendary first white settler, the date that the present meetinghouse was erected, or the total assessed valuation. These returns were like treasured bits of exotica. Was Connecticut or Massachusetts, then, a country of myriad wonders? Or was this extravagant localism itself a strategy for defining the defensible limits of the minister's, the church's, and the saints' domain?[16]

If you follow Yale President Timothy Dwight on his travels through New England, you can glimpse his sense of the wide geographic separation between towns, and his willingness to make wholesale judgments of them as integral communities. Passing from one to another by horseback or in a chaise, Dwight evidently witnessed widely dispersed communities, but he was thankful that the country had been settled in "a village manner" so that he could perceive its moral quality immediately upon arriving at the home of a fellow clergyman or Yale graduate. The four volumes of the *Travels* carefully present the divergent characters of each town and then pass on to the most sweeping summary statements.

> The parish of West Hartford, for the fertility of its soil, the pleasantness of its situation, the sobriety, industry, good order, and religious deportment of its inhabitants is not, so far as I know, excelled in the state.

> The morals of the inhabitants [of Exeter, New Hampshire] have been much improved during the last half century. . . . [They] have been distinguished by a meritorious attention to their schools. . . . A number of intelligent, genteel, and very respectable families reside in this town.

How could Dwight have been so sure of himself to make such assessments? He used no notion of comparative statistical significance; the remarkable phenomena for each place contribute to an overall impression that is tested against the ideal "compact settlement," not against one another. Sturdy fences, well-painted houses, respected clergy, farmers in intelligent intercourse with one another, children taught piety at home and at school as well as in the meetinghouse—all these interchangeable and mutually dependent indexes of social stability shaped the aesthetic of the *Travels,* as they had of Dwight's *Greenfield Hill,* his long poetic tribute to his own parish, in 1794.[17]

The evangelical clergy said that the entire town would be taken as a religious unit and that the praxes we have discerned in personal religious experience—the importance of stillness, the primacy of intellectual and rational faculties, an obedience to the distant order of the gospel scheme—could be applied as well to the spiritual condition of communities. The implicit sociology of New England villages, as of their religious revivals, then, prized their quietude, their deference to citizens of accurate understanding, clear conscience, and logical facility, and, most significant, their total, shared subordination to the demands of the revealed plan of redemption.

The theological basis for this localism can be found in Dwight's lectures to his Yale students, published as *Theology Explained and Defended.* The moral benefit of Christianity, he showed, would not be found in palaces and courts, where kings and courtiers put on beliefs like garments but rather "in still life, quiet society, peaceful neighbourhoods, and well-ordered families." But, in fact, Dwight noted, people cannot share their benevolence universally. "The mass of concerns would be immense, could never be comprehended by the mind of man, and could, therefore, never be arranged into any order or method." The need for an orderly arrangement of our concerns, Dwight was saying, forced people to restrict their energies to those within view. The New

England town, fortuitously, was about as large a unit as one could scrupulously discern.[18]

Dwight, it should be noted, respected the ability of natural (unregenerate) people to advance their own spiritual condition. But even the Hopkinsians, who would have questioned this theological point, agreed that the limits on human perceptivity were the chief determinants of the proper scale of communities. Sounding exactly like the Yale president, Samuel Hopkins wrote, "The mind of man is not omniscient, and cannot have a full, comprehensive view of all men, and their circumstances, at the same time; therefore those who are nearest to him, and most in his sight, must be more the objects of his benevolence, than others." So, despite the fact that he defined virtue as universal disinterested benevolence, Hopkins was emphatic that a man should be primarily concerned "with whom he is most acquainted, whose wants, dangers and miseries, and whole capacity of happiness, are most in his sight."[19]

Hopkins and his followers always defined self-love and self-interest as the essence of sinfulness; all their religion was a reaction to that condition, saving people from their natural proclivities. But they were willing to think people virtuous if they could overcome their selfishness and act with benevolence to anyone, even a neighbor. It was not necessary, they thought, that holy people express their love universally, only that they no longer always heed the corrupt heart.

Here the Hopkinsians parted ways with Edwards. In *The Nature of True Virtue*, the latter had argued that people are endowed with sufficient "natural instinct" to "have a determination of mind to union and benevolence to a *particular person*, or *private system*, which is but a small part of the universal system of Being." But unless this disposition to love a particular person was "subordinate to benevolence to *Being in general*, such a determination, disposition, or affection of mind is not of the nature of true virtue." Edwards did not despise the love of one's country, of one's town, and certainly of one's own spouse or children—perhaps the loveliest passages in his writing are tributes to the divine benevolence that provided these natural aids to happiness in a world of pain. But unless such private and limited affections were based in, and subordinate to, a comprehensive benevolence to all of being, they were not virtuous. Ultimately, the love of a few others would resolve itself into mere self-love. Holiness was not reached, Edwards always knew, by adding one particular to another; only a commitment of love to the whole could justify one's tenderness to the partial.[20]

Like other Federalists, Dwight and Hopkins feared the consequences of an unleashed affectionate energy that might overspill the boundaries of a decorously governed community. Like Madison, in the tenth number of *The Federalist*, their greatest enemy was faction, "a number of citizens, whether amounting to a majority or minority of the whole, who are united and actuated by some common impulse of passion, or of interest, adverse to the rights of other citizens, or to the permanent and aggregate interests of the community." But unlike Madison, the evangelicals wanted to advocate the possibility of small communities in which the permanent interests would be defended by clearsighted and responsible citizens who could overcome their self-interestedness and passionate inclinations by subscribing to the gospel plan. Even the differences among them that stemmed from distinct economic interests, which to Madison were ineradicable sources of conflict, did not alarm the orthodox evangelicals. In a small New England town, so long as citizens did not pursue profit too avidly, economic antagonisms would not be severe. For example, the local merchant would perform valuable services for the farmer-craftsman in supplying imported commodities and purchasing surpluses for distribution elsewhere. The mutual benefits derived from exchanging goods and services would outweigh, they assumed, the potentially divisive debtor-creditor relationships that developed along with such commercial transactions. In any case, preferring religious to mundane affairs would prevent excessive strain among social groups in the populace.[21]

The evangelical orthodox considered their religion the best guarantor of social order and public morality. The most ardent Calvinists among them, the Hopkinsians, felt that religion offered people a chance to overcome their narrow self-interestedness and attain a wider social and metaphysical coherence. Less orthodox in this regard, Dwight and his followers seemed confident that a prudent and rational self-interest would not differ markedly in its social effects from an attention to scriptural truth. But both groups hoped to give New England farmers a sense of community without demanding (as enthusiasm had) a surrender of the self's independence. The local authorities, while expecting deference from believers and citizens, would not impose onerous demands upon them. It was loyalty, not painful sacrifice or even time-consuming participation, which such a church and municipal polity asked from its members. Moreover, this was loyalty to a set of complex abstractions, not particular social leaders. Because of their intense suspicions of the dangerously explosive affections during the First Great Awakening and the Revolution, the evangelical Federalists wanted an impersonal authority to rule in even the most local polities.

They sought not a vigorous but a safe and permanent leadership. On July 4, 1796, when Samuel Worcester mounted the Fitchburg pulpit to reflect on the twentieth anniversary of the Declaration of Independence, he fiercely delimited his definition of democracy:

> The right of election is the most important of any, which a people can enjoy. It in fact involves everything, which appertains to the free citizen. It is in the exercise of this right only, that the people can feel and act as sovereigns; for so soon as they have elected their officers into

place, they step, as it were, into the subject, and have nothing further
to do with the government, so long as constitutionally administered, but
to strengthen its influence and submit to its operation.

The analogy of politics and religion was perfect. Men were free, naturally,
to choose God in conversion or their representatives in congressional elections. But once they did, their citizenship instantly became subjecthood. Because God would treat them with constitutional exactness, as would the government, subjects had henceforth only to submit, lacking any further part in
determining divine or political policy. The gospel plan was like the hallowed
federal constitution, a verbal charter of limited powers and a government of
laws, not of arbitrary men or gods. Thus did the Enlightenment meet the
Puritan ecclesiology.[22]

The evangelical orthodox probably represented one fifth of the population
in most rural towns, but that minority status did not prevent their speaking
for the whole community. So long as religion conformed to the scriptural truth
and politics subordinated itself to the same authority, all those who opposed
could only be irrational infidels. Political life was just like the struggle inside
the Christian's mind: root out the pockets of disbelief, and a single-minded
attachment to correct judgment remains. "Though every man has a right to
judge according to evidence," one writer warned, "yet no man has a right to
judge contrary to it. . . . The Bible is superior to any man's private judgment."
Hence Noah Webster's virulent distinction between a republic, in which sovereignty is vested in representatives of the people, and a democracy, "in which
the people exercise the powers of sovereignty in person." The political theory
of the evangelicals, like their religious doctrine, was designed to promote obedience to a sacred and permanent constitutional order.[23]

That is why the orthodox Standing Order stigmatized its opponents as infidels. Opinions were crucial, the ministers warned. In Farmington, Connecticut, Julia Cowles shrank before her minister's "exhorting all to avoid evil
company as much as possible, as those of different opinions have a great tendency to lessen our firmness in a good cause if we are engaged in one." Profli-
gates and intemperates did not worry him, but one must watch for those of
"different opinions."[24]

Excluding infidels from power, and even from social company, was thus a
way to defend righteousness. In the early years of the Second Great Awakening this worked well. The evangelicals succeeded in winning back the commitment of lapsed believers in New England's social stability. Churches that
had been reduced to destitution were flooded with new members. Many of
these, in all likelihood, were simply men and women like James Morris of
South Farms parish in Litchfield, Connecticut, whose long delay in being
converted was described in Chapter 4. Their memories of preaching heard in
childhood had already implanted the "five points" of Calvinism in their minds.

Now, through hard-won conversions, they could succeed to their own proper inheritance as God's people and the leadership of their towns. In many places, two thirds or more of the new church members were the children of religious parents. For them, joining the orthodox church restored their claims to a legitimate place in their family's communities, after the long disruptions of the revolutionary era.[25]

What became of the more numerous who had no such claims? Here the politicians parted company from their religious allies. Young Federalists, knowing that political power required more than a once-in-a-lifetime pledge of allegiance, quickly established a new apparatus of popular electioneering. Districts and towns were divided into nominating caucuses, which were then knit into state party organizations. A more or less constant political process ensued—a permanent campaign. In many towns, Federalist clubs were rivaled by organizations of enthusiastic Republicans or Jeffersonians. These groups began to have a social function, with taverns, debating societies, and balls serving as occasions to associate with the like-minded. The clergy, horrified by this espousal of factionalism by their allies, drew back. Would they become only a bloc vote, subject only to manipulation by the young Federalist politicians?[26]

In the more instrumental age that followed the turn of the nineteenth century, the orthodox began to respond to this challenge by machine crafting their own organizational engines. But first they had to try the strategy of stillness and religious rectitude. In the process, they lost the allegiance of those who wanted to experience the contagious affections of popular enthusiasm. Such people drifted into either the Baptist and Universalist camps, or Jeffersonian politics. Those who abhorred stillness but preferred an equally disciplined personal regimen could now join together in small Methodist or Free-Will Baptist groups meeting in schoolhouses and barns. There were still others, equally prominent socially, who forged a tradition by dissenting. In Somers, for example, the Kibbe family, as a recent town history says, "almost certainly supported the Jeffersonian Republican minority" against Charles Backus's Federalist orthodoxy. The Kibbes were Universalists, apparently, in the 1790s, and Episcopalian Jacksonians in the 1830s. All these anti-Calvinists, the targets of the campaign against infidelity, were tarred with the deistic brush of Tom Paine, Ethan Allen, Robespierre, and Thomas Jefferson and baited as visible examples of the international conspiracy to overthrow true religion.[27]

The orthodox needed such local targets. For if politics outwardly expressed the Christian's inner turmoil during this first era of true religious choice, the reverse was also true. Only by seeing their own minds as battlefields with social and political adversaries could the orthodox reaffirm the "reality and importance of revealed religion." One's own conversion made a difference in showing the proper way to loyalty. If a loved one could be lost, it might mean the loss of everything. Chaos and chance would rule in the place of God. One's town could be drowned by divine retribution. The orthodox evangelicals were not smugly confident but eternally combative, indeed self-combative. The enemy was within and without. Infidels worshipped what the saints knew from their own inner reflections and what they had forsaken in regeneration. Bar the door to selfishness, stop the pendulum of earthly time, and close one's eyes to ambition and temptation. The meaning of the whole world was there in one's hands, in black and white, as crisp as Caslon type on vellum paper, and forever.

PART TWO

CHARACTER
The Economy of Moral Experience

Chapter Six

Lyman Beecher and the Remedy for Sins

AFTER A YEAR studying with President Dwight, Lyman Beecher's ministerial career began quietly, in the remote Presbyterian church at East Hampton, Long Island. His predecessor in the East Hampton pulpit was Samuel Buell, whose enthusiastic account of mid-eighteenth-century revivals has already served as an instructive contrast to the more solemn renovations of the Second Great Awakening.

Beecher came to East Hampton with a revival in mind and soon won over a divided congregation by his energetic preaching of the hard Calvinist, Hopkinsian doctrines. Temperamentally, he was ill-suited to expound the Hopkinsian theology of stillness. "I was made for action," he later wrote. "The Lord drove me, but I was ready. I have always been going at full speed." For most orthodox evangelicals, the world seemed to lie still in a flat plan, to be traversed by sinners on their way to grace. In Beecher's mind, by contrast, everything was in motion, spinning toward glory or toward doom. Even the virtuous, he once complained, "are insensible of the constant motion of the whole body towards the vortex of ruin."[1]

But in the heyday of Hopkinsianism, young Beecher was a Hopkinsian and earned the sobriquet of "snow-bird" among his East Hampton neighbors for flitting about with the gospel of man's passivity even on the most wintry days. Beecher refused, as his more lax predecessor had not, to baptize the children of those who were "half-way" (still unconverted) church attenders. And when his deacon's two sons began to sense the "great change" of conversion for themselves, during Beecher's second winter in East Hampton, the ensuing revival was conducted on strictly orthodox terms: no clamor, no special protracted meetings, but much self-condemnation. One young woman, in good Hopkinsian fashion, declared that she was glad to be a sinner so that God could evidence his mercy in saving her. In being redeemed, she came to love God selflessly and to see him glorified by her submission. Eighty were converted in the East Hampton church that winter and spring, and fifty of them joined the church.

And then what happened? As the revival faded, the community drifted back into its customary apathy and isolation. And what a depth of stillness that was! When Timothy Dwight came to Long Island in 1805 to visit his old pupil, he considered the town a museum of eighteenth-century manners. Beecher never appreciated the compliment. In that flat, virtually treeless landscape, farm families lived languidly, apart from one another. They seldom traveled, except to church, and there were more geese than gossips along the roads. Along those weedy lanes, the young minister rushed around the township. Emboldened by his conviction that "the conversion of the world to Christ was near" and enlivened by his sense that the East Hampton pastorate was the theater in which he would make his mark, Beecher sought converts everywhere. He visited and lectured, lectured and visited, at each of the six or seven villages within an hour's ride from the town center. He preached to the blacks at Freetown and to the Indians at Montauk. He indulged himself in the company of the lordly Gardiners, who lived on Gardiners Island in Gardiners Bay. But nothing much happened. In East Hampton, as Lyman's sister-in-law, Mary Hubbard, would write, "the man that took ten steps yesterday taketh the same today. . . . A kind of torpor and apathy seems to prevail over the face of things."[2]

What could exuberant Lyman Beecher do in sleepy East Hampton? His first three years had been occupied with his ordination and his leadership of the revival. He had married Roxana Foote and fathered Catharine Esther. He tried to teach in the local academy and hated it. Occasionally, Beecher's pulse raced as he responded to the signal of a whale offshore and joined the rowers in the local boats to chase the giant creature. But Beecher's Leviathan, the conversion of the whole world (much less all of East Hampton), was no closer, and Lyman must have felt himself a little cramped. Perhaps this contributed to the severe illness that kept him abed and out of the pulpit for almost a whole year in 1801–1802. "Every body seemed to think, and I thought myself, that it was a gone case with me."[3]

Beecher recovered, and in his recovery he apparently began to puzzle out the answers to four questions that struck at the heart of being a passionate evangelical in a country town: How could the church be the center of community life? How could everyone in the town become involved in church life? How could what happened in East Hampton be connected with what occurred in the rest of the country, in the rest of God's Kingdom? And, how could a name be made for Lyman Beecher?

Proving himself a disciple of Timothy Dwight, Beecher's strategy was to call the community together and urge common action upon them. In 1803, he established a moral society in East Hampton. Beecher suggested that at regular meetings the society would conduct several inquiries: What evils of moral nature, are now existing in this community? What is the most probable cause of those evils? And in what manner can they, with the most probable cause, be remedied?[4]

In the following year, Beecher published his very first sermon, celebrating the Moral Society in East Hampton. *The Practicability of Suppressing Vice, By Means of Societies Instituted for that Purpose* is an instructive document. It is much less concerned with the dangers of vice than with the virtues of organization. Discarding his Hopkinsian tone, Beecher was seeking the largest, most inclusive body of the town's citizens to join his group. "In our communities," he boasts, "the body of the people are sober, honest and moral. Even among the immoral," he asks confidently, "where is the hardened, open champion of vice?" One need not, evidently, be a church member, touched by divine grace, to enlist in the work of the moral society. In fact, it only institutionalized respectability in the country town, a "moral majority."[5]

Beecher succeeded. The citizens gathered—almost all, one account said, of "the respectable inhabitants of the town." And, further, "They have not merely formed a constitution, assembled, deliberated, and resolved, according to the spiritless and useless examples of too many such societies, but have executed their resolutions in a manner highly honorable to their character."[6]

There had, indeed, been many precedents for Beecher's engine of vigilance. Nathanael Emmons, the stalwart of Hopkinsian theology, had sponsored a moral society in his Franklin, Massachusetts, parish in the early 1790s. Acknowledging that "a few men of influence in every town govern the town, and a few men of influence in every society govern the society," Emmons asked such notables to exercise their leadership on behalf of strict morality. They could, for instance, stop the use of imported cloth by the force of their own restraint. The moral society, then, was to serve as a rostrum for the pronouncements of moral obligation—by the minister and the social leaders of his community. Membership, and the activity of members, were less important than leadership and natural superiority.[7]

Beecher was a more democratic spirit than Emmons. In his meetings, all were invited to speak, even to criticize others, even to comment on the misbehavior of those with higher social standing. The terribly impersonal theological language of the revival meetings of the 1790s had masked the personal and social antagonisms within the community. A new sort of formality had emerged, keeping citizens from both honesty with one another and, more important, vigorous defense of the cause of virtue.

In East Hampton's society, Beecher noted, "the reluctance of the individual to reprove is diminished; he speaks more readily, and with greater efficacy because he speaks the sentiments of many and is conscious that numbers are prepared to uphold him, and back his reproof." On the surface, Beecher seems to be prefiguring Alexis de Tocqueville's famous notion of the "tyranny of the majority."[8]

"In societies of the description we are considering," Beecher said, "every member is a soldier, every soldier a centinel [*sic*]." There were no places reserved for the inactive, the passive, the still. By posting themselves as sentinels, ready to call out warnings of danger, the members themselves shaped the boundaries of permissible behavior. This insured that no one left the circle, for all their eyes were cast inward, toward their neighbors and on themselves. When one spoke, one looked about for confirming nods, for mirroring sentiments. Before long one's behavior, too, conformed to local norms.[9]

It was important, while sitting in these meetings, to catch the drift of social sentiment, variously called "common sense," "public opinion," "respectable notions," "moral influence." But you knew it when you had it. Common sense was an ethereal substance produced by two physical motions—one person's speaking and another person's nodding assent. You speak, and I nod knowingly. I reply, and you nod knowingly. Soon the space between us is suffused with common sense. It gently cloaks both of us in the same ghostly mantle of propriety.

Common sense may include pieces of knowledge, but it is different from knowledge. A person may entertain bits of knowledge when either alone or in hypothetical conversation with an author; furthermore, any piece of knowledge always has logical and symbolic connections to other pieces of knowledge. Common sense is an ephemeral experience of consent; its sense is always secondary to its commonness. Unlike doctrine, common sense cannot be authenticated by reference to special texts and symbols. It is self-justifying.

Common sense or public opinion could be profoundly democratic. A wealthy landowner and militia captain, a Harvard-educated lawyer, even a clergyman could not command respect until his words could win approval from his neighbors, and that was often only by falling in with local prejudice. Beecher was insisting that the force of tradition give way to the force of public opinion. Of course, in the early nineteenth century, and probably for a generation after, the same social leaders continued to lead public opinion. But to be an opinion leader was more hazardous and transitory than to be a "leading citizen" in the eighteenth-century sense.

Beecher's moral society reflected the altered political conditions of the first decade of the nineteenth century. It was increasingly impossible for the Federalists or the evangelicals to dream of restoring the perfect unity of their towns under their political and religious leadership. The "infidel" party did not disappear in the Great Deistical Scare of the 1790s, and the "chief infidel," Thomas Jefferson, had actually been elected president of the United States in 1800. Universalist churches were being established in dozens of towns, and they were audaciously building meetinghouses in several. These in turn were made available to newly formed groups of Methodists and Free-Will Baptists. In seacoast communities from Fairfield County in Connecticut to York County in Maine, the evangelical drama of sin and redemption was rarely a subject for pulpit instruction, as anti-Calvinists dominated religious life.

With so much diversity, it was not hard for a citizen's absence from church on Sunday to go unnoticed—who knew where he was? With so much political discord, it was not unusual to hear some profanities associated with the names of various public officials—who could blame a man for that? With so much news to share, of Napoleonic upheavals and Barbary pirates, of ships arriving from China and new turnpikes, would not the flow of conversation be eased with some liquid refreshment?

Beecher hoped to stem not only such misbehavior but even more the laxity and tolerance that permitted it to continue without criticism. Stillness was no answer. In the manner of a latter-day slogan, it might be said, if activity is outlawed, only outlaws will be active. A more vigorous enforcement of the laws was needed. The moral society would be the grand jury's grand jury, presenting evidence that could not fail to indict and convict for immorality. All the people would then proceed more prudently, testing themselves in the eyes of their neighbors and drenching their views of things in the local ether of common sense.

The center of religious life shifted, under this innovation, from the immortal souls of the parishioners to their moral characters. When, for example, Beecher suggested his "remedy for duelling" in the 1806 sermon that made him a clerical celebrity, it was by fixing on moral character as the basic criterion for judging a man's worth. "Let it once be known that a fair private character is indispensable to the attainment of public suffrage," he flatly predicted, "and reformations will take place." Publicizing private character became the key technique of evangelical moralism. [10]

This development of a behavioral, interpersonal, inclusivist, and active religious life, comprised in the shift from soul to character, is the movement I label *moralism*. For moralists, the chief referents for human action were moral norms, not orthodox doctrines. Evangelical moralism in the United States found its most powerful expression in the explosion of moral and social reform groups across the nation in the generations before the Civil War. At the same time, moralism was altering the orthodox religious experience of one's mind, one's fellows, and one's God. The next five chapters explore these changes.

Moralism, I will repeat emphatically, was not a theological dissent from orthodoxy. It was, instead, a this-worldly movement within American religion, and so its arguments with the orthodox were not about theological questions at all. The moralists continued to worship the same God, but now they discovered his will in proper behavior rather than in doctrinally consistent credos.[11]

Evangelical moralism must be contrasted also with its contemporary competitors—liberal moralism or Unitarianism. Within both evangelical and liberal theological camps there was a transition from an orthodox or doctrinal mode of religious experience (e.g., Hopkinsianism and Universalism) to a moralist mode (e.g., "Beecherism" and Unitarianism); subsequently there would be a shift from moralism to sentimentalism. Evangelicals and liberals did, of course, battle over theological questions like the Trinity. But more often than not, the deeply wrought expectation that religion involved a personal experience of change drove evangelicals away from the loftier and cooler respectability of Unitarian moralism.[12]

Was moralism a single phenomenon, clearly articulated, defended and unchanging over its three or four decades of hegemony? Of course not. But for reasons of clarity, I will stress the continuities of this form of religious rhetoric. There is precedent. In 1838, Lyman Beecher's 1806 sermon against Aaron Burr, "The Remedy for Dueling," was reprinted in its entirety. But in every place that Beecher had written "duelling" and "duellist," the latter version supplied "slaveholding" and "slaveholder." "It appears to us," the 1838 reviser noted, "that the Doctor's [Beecher's] arguments, if they were *conclusive* to dueling, must be admitted to be absolutely INVINCIBLE in their application to slaveholding. . . ." In 1838, this may have been embarrassing to the ancient champion, but it is conclusive proof that the structure of Beecher's thinking remained applicable for many years.[13]

I turn, then, to the era of American moralism. Once again much evidence is drawn from diaries and memoirs, but the tone even of personal documents in this period is admonitory. Rather than offering many revelations of self, of the sort encountered in studying orthodoxy (and to be found again in sentimentalism), moralists were always giving advice, especially to themselves. The reader of these pages should be ready with some defense against all these judgmental turns of phrase.

Chapter Seven

Faith as Confidence in Character

FOR YOUNG EVANGELICALS like Lyman and Roxana Beecher, on the verge of the new era of moralism, orthodoxy had driven will out of the world. All that eighteenth-century talk about the freedom of the will had left evangelicals treasuring talk rather than will. From one's own still center, one could look far off and locate the world's meaning. But a world so fitting for one's metaphysical condition of sinfulness and redemption was not a place for human action. To experience God was to purge humanness.

Most religious liberals objected to worshipping the Calvinist's God. They pointed, as William Ellery Channing said, to the "inconsistency of the system with the divine perfections." They chided evangelicals for having "ascribed to the Supreme Being the most detestable practices." For another apostate from orthodoxy, Henry Clarke Wright, theology brought the opposite of relief. Instead, he recalled, that "my anguish was the result of my theological belief, rather than of conscious wrong-feeling or doing. I was in a distracted state," he continued. "My heart was at war with my *head*. My theology said I was 'under the wrath and curse of God.' My heart said No to that. My head said, I had 'lost all my communion with God.' My heart said that I loved to be close to him, and to feel that I lived and moved in Him. Thus I was sorely distressed; my heart an utter infidel to my head, and my affections pouring contempt upon my theology." And still another, Orville Dewey, shared the sense that "religion had a sort of horrible attraction for me, but nothing could exceed its gloominess." Consequently, when Dewey was converted at Williams College, he did not receive grace in the orthodox form, as a "consoler of grief" or "as the deliverer from terror and wrath"; instead, to him God's love "came as filling an infinite void, as the supply of a boundless want, and ultimately as the enhancement of all joy."[1]

In all three of these cases, the Calvinist void between humanity and God had seemed itself the barrier to salvation. They each escaped the rigors of the creed entirely and became religious liberals. But there were also many evangelicals, still loyal to "the faith once delivered to the saints," who were both-

85

ered by the too wide and seemingly impassable gulf between sin and grace in the orthodox scheme. In the first quarter of the nineteenth century, many evangelicals turned away from the privation, passivity, and void of orthodoxy toward a more active religious life. These moralists could not tolerate the unrelieved absence of human emotionality and, even more, the obscure place of personal responsibility in the orderly orthodox universe.

Moralists saw will everywhere. God's gospel plan now became his moral will. A once passive acquiescence in criminality now became active and willful obedience to specific commands. Now the relationship between God and man achieved a new symmetry, as each party applauded the tenor of each other's acts. Theological debates reflected this shift, but theology was increasingly a peripheral concern. Moralism, like orthodoxy, could embrace every jot and tittle of Calvinism while revolutionizing its notion of the Calvinist saint.

Why does a young man see a gloomy void where his father saw a bounty of stillness? The orthodox fathers lived in a world in which creatures died; their moralist sons threw themselves into a world in which men lived. These differences were not the sort of fiery theological disputes that led family members to throw the table china at one another. But when both men heard the tall clock strike the half hour, one said it was half past the hour, and the other that it was half till the next. The elder leaned back, pondering how to make his peace with God in the time remaining; the younger leaned forward, pulling up his boots, straining toward the door to get a start before a moment more was wasted.

The moralist generation understood evangelical faith in a new way. It redrew the orthodox images (or imagelessness, rather) of divinity and humanity. It caught men and women in midstride and reassured them that they were already on their way. The moralist path was well-marked, but it had none of the dead ends and hidden alleys of orthodoxy. The test of religion, for evangelicals like Beecher as much as for liberals like Channing and Dewey, became the sense of human voluntarism and divine reasonableness.

Once again Timothy Dwight, with his translation of Edwardsean doctrine into the concrete realities of postrevolutionary America, provided a bridge. "The Faith of the Gospel," Dwight said in his Yale lectures, "is that emotion of the mind, which is called trust, or Confidence, exercised toward the moral character of God, and particularly of the Saviour." As always, Dwight simplified and humanized divinity. He had no trouble locating the idea of confidence in the most familiar experience of his listeners. "Look into your bosoms," he advised, "and examine what is that exercise of the mind, in which you trust a man for the sake of what he is: a parent, for example, or a friend. In this exercise you will find a strong illustration of the faith of the Gospel." Where his Hopkinsian clerical brethren loved to contrast divine affection with family bonds, Dwight worked outward from the universality of natural emotion. As logicians, the orthodox viewed similes of ordinary life only as useful figures of speech. Dwight, although not contesting the theological difference between nature and grace, believed that his analogies and metaphors actually worked. Fearful that the orthodox had defined faith too mysteriously, Dwight insisted that it could be felt in one's heart. Every member of Dwight's congregation could use the confidence he or she already felt to temper the frequently intolerable idea of redemption.[2]

Dwight's rhetoric helped fill the orthodox Calvinist distance by making reciprocal the relationship between man and God. In exchange for grace, man conferred confidence upon his Creator. But Dwight was careful not to make the relationship contractual. As a Calvinist, Timothy Dwight could not accept the notion that God might be bound by a person's works; mortals were justified by faith and faith alone. Confidence or faith was both the requirement and the evidence of divine grace. But in his zest to make the virtuous relish for spiritual things seem as familiar as the love of families or friends, Dwight skirted the Hopkinsians' constant, complicated reaffirmation of the primacy of grace.

God's sovereignty was as absolute as ever, but humanity could now worship him full-heartedly, as emotionally as did the Christians of the First Great Awakening. To place confidence in God was neither to diminish him in any way nor to make God and humanity equal. A conservative eighteenth-century mind, living in a world that accepted superiority and subordination as natural facts, Dwight did not confuse affection or reciprocity with equality. Honoring one's parents, one's king (at least until 1775), one's ministers, teachers, and political leaders did not imply regarding oneself as their equals. Significantly, the Yale president concluded his sermon by suggesting that "Confidence is also the highest honour, which an Intelligent creature can render to his Creator." What is honor but to admit superiority, or as Noah Webster put it, "to treat with deference and submission"?[3]

Timothy Dwight remains a transitional figure. Confidence is an "emotion" or "exercise" of mind, not yet an act in itself. But confidence, even for Dwight, legitimated activity, human activity, which could be one's responsibility and serve one's eternal interest. His sermon contrasted confidence with "a mere speculative assent to probable evidence" and found the latter wanting in virtue because it left the mind entirely passive toward God.[4]

Confidence or trust in the Lord was an old Calvinist theme. In his biography of Sarah Osborn, an exemplary women in his congregation, Samuel Hopkins had found a "remarkable instance of humble trust in God, and resignation and acquiescence in his will." It seemed that almost every three months the elderly Mrs. Osborn was short of the five dollars rent she owed for her Newport rooms. But in responding to her neighbors, she was confident.

> I do not doubt of my having the whole of the money at the time in which it will be due, or near it. God has given me a constant and ear-

nest desire to do justice, and pay when any thing is due. This is a just debt, and God has been pleased hitherto to gratify me by enabling me to pay, when it is due; and I believe he will still continue to do it. Perhaps I shall not live to the end of the quarter. I shall then leave enough to pay this debt. I desire to leave it with God.

For Hopkins, Mrs. Osborn's rent was a perfect illustration of the debt we all owe to God. It is just. As we approach our deathbeds, we can see more rationally that the debt can be paid only through divine intercession. And, indeed, somehow the money always found its way to Mrs. Osborn, as would divine grace. Contributors in "Quebec, from the West Indies, and from various parts of the United States," even without knowing of her recurrent straits, would rescue her every time from homelessness.[5]

Timothy Dwight would not have looked askance at such pious confidence, but he certainly did not think this a good tactic for paying the rent. Whereas Hopkins's saint is awed by the just debts owed her unnamed and aloof landlord, preferring the mysterious interventions of God's spirit to help her pay, Dwight warns his parishioners to stay out of debt altogether. His kind of confidence is best exemplified in the man who enters God's country store with hard coin, earned in the sweat of his brow, and proceeds to look for good value among the merchandise. Go ahead, Dwight tells him, make your deals; have confidence in the Storekeeper.

But how would an enterprising Yankee farmer know that he could trust the Storekeeper? Here Dwight helps by defining faith, you will remember, as "Confidence, exercised toward the moral character of God." Thus, one must trust neither God, who was a mystery, nor God's plan, which was too highly intellectualized, but God's moral character. What did this mean? He spoke at length to this problem.

> Moral character seems not, in its nature, to be an object of science, properly so called. Spirits by every eye, except the Omniscient, are discerned only through the medium of their actions; which are proof of their natural attributes, and expressions of their moral character. Moral character is the amount of all the volitions of a moral agent. As these are free and independent, they are incapable of being known, but by the voluntary manifestations of the agent himself. United, they form, and exhibit, the whole moral character.

It is impossible to examine moral character directly, Dwight says. Although spiritual, moral character has natural and visible effects, seen in the actions that stem from it. Moral character is, then, both the source and the sum of volitions. The moral dealer does not hide his rotten apples at the bottom of the barrel.[6]

The ability to infer the root of action from the evidence of diverse actions was basic to the idea of character. God's actions, and thus his intentions, were visible in every aspect of Connecticut life. Dwight thereby assumed that all these volitions emanate from a single source, as consistent and reliable as the elaborate gospel plan of the orthodox. This source could not be God himself but his knowable moral character—that is, all the actions of the divinity comprehended and judged as a whole. Because God's will was always subservient to God's moral character, a person could be fully confident that his God would not be arbitrary and erratic.

The steady intentions of the Lord were expressed most perfectly, of course, in Scripture. "The *word* of Christ," Dwight wrote, "is the only ultimate evidence, by which he [the human being] must be governed; and this word depends, for all its veracity and convincing influence, on the moral character of Christ; on his goodness, faithfulness, and truth." Man and woman are governable, then, not by the intricate plan of redemption exemplified in Scripture, as the orthodox had argued. Instead, the Bible reveals the quality of God, especially the character of Christ, and the terms used for that character—"goodness, faithfulness, and truth"—are words that might just as easily be applied to people.[7]

Dwight's reasoning altered the purpose of Scripture. For the orthodox, biblical texts were used largely to verify the theological or theoretical structure of the revealed plan of redemption. The passages were instructive but only if interpreted as proof-texts for Calvinism. For Dwight and the moralists who learned at his knee, Scripture was instead an endlessly entertaining collection of instructive tales, literally a compendium recounting the actions of God, Jesus, kings, prophets, saints and sinners, each tale richly and individually informative. The Bible was more like a father's storytelling than an alchemist's mysterious formula. It was not useful merely in exemplifying principles that could be stated most clearly in the dogmatic theology of Calvin or Edwards. Literal believers in Scripture could discover positive and exact directions for everyday life.[8]

Such a God was inherently more anthropomorphic than the orthodox deity. The latter had been a moral governor, but his decrees evinced a philosophical grandeur that swept far beyond the ken of ordinary men; the moralist's moral governor seemed more like a legislator interested in providing solutions for the pressing problems of daily life. For Bellamy and Hopkins, God was a moral *governor;* that is, he governed the moral or spiritual sphere in which men and women gained salvation. For Dwight's favorite students, the evangelist Lyman Beecher and the theologian Nathaniel William Taylor, God was a *moral* governor, a Creator who acted justly toward his creatures. Whether the moralists' God was also in command of the entire universe, and whether people could become part of the total meaning of the world by joining the party of Christ—those were questions seldom asked any longer.[9]

Even in Taylor's most profound explorations of how God could have permitted sin to exist in the world, a new reluctance to engage mystery is apparent. To make the point, the Hopkinsians would have thrown open their windows in the severest thunderstorms, as if to say that the best interior light was that explainable only as the direct expression of God. At the moral reform meetings that justified their activity on Taylorite grounds, the windows were best left closed; the best light was sparked by human understanding and learning. Taylor retreated from the traditional passion of Calvinist writers to explain how God behaved. One of his *Practical Sermons* counseled, "Well, then, let God, I say, be responsible for his own work. If he has made men sinners, it belongs to him to unmake them." And then, impatiently, "To talk of a work which God only performs, as my duty, is out of the question." Trust God; even if you do not know him, trust him. [10]

Although Taylor spent many years in doctrinal exegesis and doctrinal controversy, he exemplifies a shift of theology away from metaphysics toward religious psychology. A new picture of people as moral beings was emerging. Lyman Beecher's famous sermon, *A Reformation of Morals Practicable and Indispensable,* defined God and humanity through corresponding commitments to each other: "The commands of God are the measure and evidence of human ability. He is not a hard master, reaping where he has not sowed, and gathering where he has not strawed. The way of the Lord is not unequal. He never demands of men the performance of impossibilities." [11]

The stability of God's intention, as expressed in the commands of his law, was thus linked to the parallel stability and rectitude of the human constitution. Men and women were made both for the purpose of obeying and with the capacity to obey God's demands, which made sense to Beecher only if men and women could meet them. I might also say that human ability is both the measure and the evidence of God's commands. One's constitution, obviously more knowable than God's gospel plan, is now the given; God's dictates could be inferred from one's ability. Active obedience is therefore the touchstone of one's power, just as God is known by his reasonable commands: the two poles were perfectly reciprocal.

This implied even more about the moral condition of mankind. Beecher's conjunction of the normative (measure) and the descriptive (evidence) ways of assessing one's ability was important in the moralist credo. He inferred that man *is* what he *should be,* and deduced that henceforth man's success or failure lies in what he does rather than what he is. The activist encouragements of moralism were hinged upon this strong defense of human ability. [12]

Just as God's will had to be stabilized in his moral character, and that located in specific scriptural illustrations, so human ability needed a more certain base. This was typically achieved by pointing to the constitution of the human mind as confirmation of this fitness for obedience to God. Beecher's 1817 sermon, "The Bible a Code of Laws," is an excellent example of this argument.

Beecher began by assuming that "a moral government is the influence of law upon accountable creatures." God may be a moral governor, but he needs moral citizens to show that his is truly a government. He could expound laws from dawn to dusk, but that would be fruitless without a submissive polity. Reciprocity was confirmed when Beecher set out the requirements for effective governance: "a law-giver, accountable subjects, and laws intelligibly revealed, and maintained by rewards and punishments, according to the character and deeds of the subjects." Not only must God have subjects in order to rule, but he must also have laws *and* a system of rewards and punishment appropriate for those subjects. While this satisfied the evangelicals' need for a scriptural, not a natural, law, it also assumed that scriptural law works because it suited nineteenth-century American Christians as much as the people of ancient Israel.[13]

Accountability is therefore derived from neither the law itself nor an orthodox reckoning of one's dependence upon God but from human psychology. To prove his point, Beecher speaks as if he is making a wiring diagram of the mental faculties.

> To accountability in the subjects are requisite,—understanding, to perceive the rule of action; conscience, to feel moral obligation; and the power of choice, in the view of motives. Understanding, to perceive the rule of action, does not constitute accountable agency; choice, without the capacity of feeling obligation, does not constitute accountable agency;—but the capacity of understanding, and conscience, and choice, united, do constitute an accountable agent. The laws of God and man recognize these properties of mind as the foundation of accountability.

In order then to illustrate his diagram by concrete examples, Beecher takes us on a brief tour of a nineteenth-century cabinet of (mental) curiosities.

> A statue is not accountable, for it has no perception or choice; an idiot is not, for, though he may have choice, he has no competent understanding to perceive a moral rule, nor conscience to feel moral obligation; and a lunatic is not, because, though he may have choice and conscience, he has not the unperverted exercise of his understanding.[14]

Beecher's tripartite division of the mind into the faculties of understanding, conscience, and will (which he significantly called "choice") was much like those contemporaries similarly influenced by the Scottish common sense philosophy. Like them, he emphasized that the understanding was unimpaired and would deliver proper messages to the conscience; if approved there, the will would then choose positively or negatively but always freely. The Hopkinsians, following Edwards, had limited this free agency by claiming that the will of sinners had a moral, if not a natural, inability to choose the good. Sinners were blocked by the innate sinfulness of moral blindness. Beecher and Taylor wanted to escape this two-sphere business altogether. Men and women could act both morally and freely by their very nature; if they could not, then they should not be called human.

Sinners would choose evil, probably every time, the moralists conceded, but they could choose good. Freedom was an essential characteristic of the human frame. The world was waiting for free people to act well; henceforth nothing could keep them from acting freely. Nor did they have to wait upon God's grace to do so. The orthodox had reveled in discovering that one was divinely ordained to act for the good; the moralists, however, wanted to build their religion on the constant internal sense of a free choice. The consciousness of being able to act freely and morally was, for American moralists as for the Scottish philosophers, the key to imposing a sense of moral responsibility upon all mankind. Almost all Americans came to think that one would refuse personal blame for one's errors without the feeling of commanding a choice. Free choice was only common sense.

But how did they know that men and women were free? Beecher and Taylor found freedom within the mechanics of the faculty psychology. Hopkins and even Dwight understood virtue as one's outlook toward divine things; if one felt right, that was a sign—however imperfect—of moral health. Dwight's students worked from a different way of reading the self. Each of us has different motives and alternatives (or as we might say today, options). Now, a motive is an unexercised direction of the will. It just sits there, a live potentiality. Jonathan Edwards would have regarded this as nonsense. If the motive did not move one anywhere, then it was not, inherently, a motive. Beecher and Taylor thus built their sense of internal freedom upon the contradictory sense that alternative possibilities might exist in the mind, side by side, going nowhere. Only the coexistence of these distinct motives at the same moment permitted one to feel, in the next moment of choice, that one could be free. In Beecher's wiring diagram, one could prove ability—the free passage of current in and out of the mind—only by assuming the "resistance" of the diverse mental faculties.[15]

The Beecherite conception of personal freedom in action thus paradoxically and necessarily depended upon the existence of a stable, resistant, or unmoving core within the mind. Freedom was the choice of A or not-A, or, as Taylor argued, the "power to [act] the contrary" of the way one had acted. But we can imagine many more extravagant possibilities for human freedom than the choice between purchasing or not purchasing an item on the Storekeeper's shelves. Emerson's call, just a few years later, to "build therefore your own world," was an expression of a much bolder faith in human possibility than that of the evangelical moralists. Will for Beecher and Taylor was simple choice, not an explosive inner creativity.[16]

This simple view of the will as an on-off switch effectively legitimated and limited human freedom at the same time. Now people could "feel" free without threatening to unleash dangerous desires. In fact, the key mechanism of choice could now be interpreted simply as the indulgence or repression of various impulses. The conscience became the mechanism for selecting what should be obeyed and what should be suppressed. In the moralist scheme, then, the conscience or moral sense stood guard over an internal conflict between moral intentions and immoral desires. Such freedom was ripe for moralist second-guessing, or for juridical review. It was only common sense, moralists would say, that one's better half was in perpetual warfare with one's worst qualities. The orthodox insistence that the whole self could have a single metaphysical label like sinful or holy was lost in the shuffle.[17]

The evangelical moralists, of course, did not mean that people could not be saved or damned. In some sense, they had traded the carefully constructed knowledge of the stages of orthodox argument for the ceaseless feeling of internal freedom. The test of virtue was defined not so much by doctrinal consistency, then, as by inner confidence. Unitarians like Aaron Bancroft of Worcester, Massachusetts, encouraged parishioners to look for the general pattern of morality or vice within themselves. "Every man," he noted, "may for himself determine whether it be his sincere desire and habitual endeavor to do the will of God, and to walk in the commandments of Jesus Christ blameless. If, on the examination of himself by this rule, the heart of an individual condemns him not, then may he have confidence towards God. . . . If he is conscious that religion has an abiding and universal influence on his heart and life, then he had evidence within his own mind, that he is qualified to join the heavenly society."[18]

As we shall see in the next chapter, Beecher and other evangelicals would have supplemented Bancroft's inner test with a requirement of a public profession of "saving grace," at least in theory. But, like the Unitarians, evangelical moralists wanted to glimpse the positive inklings of godliness in a person. Working upwards from the slightest evidence of an inclination to follow scriptural rules, moralists could test themselves only against their own possibilities of being more sincerely and habitually observant, and they could work to improve themselves. Unlike the orthodox evangelical, whose inner exercises were holy insofar as they mirrored the conventional form of doctrinal language, the moralist was the best judge of the battles within his or her own heart. Eventually, a positive sense of self would lead to confidence in God, and that in turn to an even greater self-confidence. Where the doctrinalist aimed for a perfect fit in a distant order, always confessing to criminality, the moralist pugnaciously sought out God's laws as a personal challenge. In becoming the field of contest between habitual constraint and impulsive waywardness, the moralist's self-mastery proved the self worthy. By increasing this self-confidence, the moralist had turned God's confidence to a healthy profit.

Self-confidence was not valuable as an object of smug satisfaction to the moralist. Forged in a relationship between the created and their heavenly Creator, self-confidence had to be expressed outwardly in the world. Christians would feel even more energetically committed to social causes. As Lyman Beecher said in an 1819 sermon, "He [the Christian] needs the confidence for action which a profession of religion only can inspire, and the faculties and excitement to action which social enterprise alone can afford." In Beecher's language we can see a whole new way of connecting religious and earthly affairs. Religion was now preparatory: it readied the self for the ordinary combat of life, rather than establishing one above it. Having dealt confidently with the divine Storekeeper, one could now traffic equally well with secular merchants in the same street. With a proper moral character formed first in conversion and then in sanctification, Christians would be propelled into the world. Far from immobilizing them in contemplativeness, their confidence in the divine would bring them "confidence for action" in the social world.[19]

A Whig like Beecher would have extolled the link between religious and economic confidence. As Daniel Webster told the United States Senate in 1838, "Credit and confidence have been the life of our system, and powerfully productive causes of all our prosperity. They have covered the seas with our commerce, replenished the treasury, paid off the national debt, excited and stimulated the manufacturing industry, felled the forests, and multiplied our numbers and augmented the national wealth so far beyond all example, as to leave us a phenomenon for older nations to look at with wonder."[20]

Prosperity in both economic and religious spheres rested, in other words, on confident risk taking. The risks of moralist religion involved taking upon oneself the responsibility for faith. It was, as we have seen, a free act of the human mind. The risks of the market were similar. They too involved taking responsibility for initiating and fulfilling contracts. Furthermore, confidence acknowledged that man could never have sufficient *knowledge* upon which to act. As the sociologist Georg Simmel once wrote, "As a hypothesis regarding future behavior, a hypothesis certain enough to serve as a basis of practical conduct, confidence is intermediate between knowledge and ignorance about a man. The person who knows completely need not trust; while the person who knows nothing can, on no rational grounds, afford even confidence."[21]

In the place of sure doctrinal knowledge, the moralists had substituted confidence in God. Orthodoxy had prided itself upon men's and women's superb cognitive faculties, and its boldest claim was to their ability to perceive the order of the universe and the limits of the human mind. In goading men and women into action, moralism unavoidably diluted the intellectual coherence of evangelical religion. In the place of magisterial treatises or tightly reasoned sermons, the moralists in the 1820s and thereafter distributed little tracts filled with moral homilies; these encouragements to tidiness and good character were appropriate for every distinct age and condition of life. No longer were Christians at large expected to master doctrinal arguments for themselves. This became the exclusive function of the seminarian and biblical scholar. The mental skills needed to compute risk were different from those required to discern certainty.

Most historians have emphasized the fearful, backward-looking, conservative stance of this generation of evangelicals, even when treating their commitment to social and moral reform causes. But the rhetorical analogies between religious and commercial confidence should allow us to see, at least for the first quarter of the nineteenth century, a steadily growing emphasis upon the power of positive human willfullness. Moralists, even while adhering to Calvinist doctrine, radically uprooted the postrevolutionary aesthetic of stillness.

Yet, around 1830, a change was felt. The terms of moralist discourse were now less often designed to encourage adult Christians in the midst of their active lives. Instead, as the historian Karen Haltunnen brilliantly shows, a whole industry of avuncular sages emerged, all of them dramatizing one single moment as the culture's moral crisis: the entrance of a young man, fresh from the countryside and eager for a career as a merchant clerk, onto the streets of America's rapidly growing cities. In his path, the advice writers noted tremblingly, lay a whole succession of man traps—the smooth-talking stranger offering instant companionship; the political demagogue quick to enlist the young man in his partisan machinations; and the gambler or speculator, offering the sure ruin of profit without labor. And beyond were the hideous allurements of prostitution, intemperance, street crime, and other unmentionable dangers.[22]

The young man's problem, of course, was that he came to the city already imbued with a propensity for action. Beecher encouraged his rural parishioners to combat local vice through moral societies, employing peer pressure. But the negative peer pressure of the urban boardinghouse, where young men lived apart from the supervision of their parents, neighbors, employers, or ministers, was rather different from the positive peer pressure of the rural parlor meeting.

If anything, so far as the moralists were concerned, the young man already had too much confidence. Lacking even a modicum of knowledge about the people he met, lacking any practical way to test moral character by slowly and carefully reading the sum of a stranger's volitions, lacking the time and space to frame issues in a simple, Taylorist, yes-or-no contest between indulgence and restraint, the young man was easy prey for "'the goodnatured civilities of persons you have never seen before.'" These last had the appearance of probity, but appearances were deceiving. To their horror, the moralists discovered that one's character, rather than being the self's subordination to the principles of rectitude, might be only an external imposition on the self, an insincere role put on and taken off for the effect.[23]

By 1849, these deceivers were called "confidence men," and only eight years later Herman Melville etched their methods in his poisonous satire, *The Confidence-Man: His Masquerade*. Here the multifaced hero, spouting moralist slogans as he offers his splendid nostrums for sale, deceives his fellow passengers on the steamboat *Fidèle* into thinking that their self-confidence is contingent upon their confidence in him. In the course of Melville's book the social faith of those who figuratively shared the ship called the *United States* was also called into doubt. As long as men sought personal advantage by investing in one another without knowledge or a sense of common risk, Melville seemed to say, a complete personal withdrawal was preferable to the hypocrisy that ruled in society.

At least that was the path Melville took, for *The Confidence-Man* was his last effort to write for a general public. There were other Americans, as Part Three of this study will show, who wanted an even more intimate relationship with God and with one's friends as compensation for the lost security of locating oneself in the same gospel order as everyone else. Faith as confidence in God had been Timothy Dwight's way of making religion concrete; his students Beecher and Taylor had found human accountability and freedom compatible with such confidence. Encouraged in their activism, moralists went out into the business world mentally equipped for combat. Now, ironically, their unleashed energy needed a sounder source of constraint than the individual's free choice, lest moral young men be overwhelmed.

Moralists developed other strategies to overcome the dangers of the insincerities they encountered in their ventures into the marketplace. Although the fixed standard of orthodoxy was better in grasping the meaning of a star-filled night on a New England farm in 1800, some much more active way of securing an allegiance to God and his support in everyday life was needed for those who traveled on the railroads and canal boats of the next generation. That was the purpose of moralism.

Chapter Eight

Sudden Conversions and Steady Characters

ALTHOUGH THEY RESEMBLED the Unitarians in defining faith as confidence, the evangelical moralists in New England still firmly believed that a personal experience of rebirth was necessary to achieve such faith. And their practical bent made it obvious that the way to bring the largest number of parishioners through that experience was by a religious revival. The moralists were splendid revivalists. Their preference for a world of activity made them more amenable to the emotional excitement of the revival season, and accounts of their work in the 1820s and 1830s never mention the "stillness" of the participants. On the contrary, the moralists were loath to permit a sinner, during his conviction of sin, to dwell passively, contemplating his infinite weakness before the Lord. Instead, they insisted increasingly upon segregating sinners in different stages of conversion away from the whole of the congregation and impelling them rapidly on the road to salvation.[1]

This mission was accomplished by introducing techniques to divide the congregation by its diverse psychological conditions. An intensely emotional sermon, for example, might cause some listeners to break out in tears or cries of distress; these were removed to an adjoining "anxious bench" or "anxious room," where they were skillfully and personally addressed. The accumulated tension might explode into a condensed version of the orthodox conversion sequence—fury at God's decreeing power, frustration at their own weakness, self-hatred, conviction of the rightness of their personal damnation, repentance for their myriad and magnified sinfulness, an exhausted surrender of all other sources of self-esteem, the relief that came with recognizing that God would accept them, and the tears of joy from the first inklings of personal assurance and confidence.[2]

Again converts, separated from those still agonizing, began a process of mutual support and celebration through individual testimonies of experience and hymn singing. The converted were tended by assistants to the evangelist or exhorter who had presided over the earlier stages of the conversion ordeal, which, incidentally, might be continuing as before in the church itself. Once

97

the converts had been adequately encouraged by their progress, they were discharged to carry the message of the revival house to house in the community, especially to their neighbors and relations. "For the period," wrote two British visitors, "but one object is before them, and it *possesses* them. They have found mercy, and they thirst to bestow it; they have dishonored God and they thirst to glorify him. They become missionaries for the time; and they move about in their families and their connexions, warning, teaching, and entreating, with tears, that they would be reconciled and saved." "Such visitations," concludes Charles I. Foster, "provided energy to keep a revival going for some time." To accomplish this, "protracted meetings," lasting from four days to four weeks or more, were instituted to carry forward the work in particular communities.[3]

All these techniques were described as "new measures," innovations of the 1820s and 1830s that were often pioneered by Charles G. Finney and his associates in upstate New York's "burned-over district" (so named because of the frequency with which the revival fires burned across the landscape). The new measures were initially resisted by New England divines like Beecher and Asahel Nettleton. But in practice, the new measures depended upon an increased sense of man's personal responsibility for his conversion, making these tactics less objectionable to those who, like the Taylorite professors at New Haven, shared the moralist faith in the human will. Eventually, Beecher parted way with conservatives of Nettleton's stripe, much to the bitterness of the latter, and adopted new strategems in his own preaching at Boston and Cincinnati.[4]

Although the new measures respected the sequence of psychological states as enunciated by the orthodox evangelicals, the techniques depended upon an immense expenditure of human instrumentality: the clever specialization of prayers, exhortations, and activities for converts according to their distinct stages; the provision of specially designated times and spaces for these specific stages; and the delegation of responsibility to men trained and certifiably skillful in particular aspects of the work. This program gave opponents (and many historians) the idea that the revivals were wholly engineered phenomena. More probably, the distinctive cognitive style of the new measures revivals gave such offense. By passionately setting religion so sharply off from the day-to-day "dull round of chores," the protracted revival meetings of moralist evangelicism and its sudden conversions threatened to disrupt the way orthodox religion had accommodated itself to the pace of ordinary life. So much specialization also violated the emphasis upon consistency, coherence, and unity in the orthodox understanding of religious experience. And furthermore, the self-evident willfulness of such revivals was a major factor in their acceptability to the moralist party. The exercise of will, after all, presumed a person's responsibility, giving that person the feeling of freedom in activity. These were significant recommendations to moralists. In sum, the logic of religious conversion, as it had occupied the minds of the orthodox evangelicals, had been overwhelmed and diminished by the mechanics of the process.[5]

For the participants, the methodology of the 1820s revivalism was less important than the intensity of the experience. Most converts still came from religious households, and many had been imbued with the lessons of Sabbath schools and charitable works in childhood. Conversion, however, now became more strictly a rite of passage associated with late adolescence. For this generation, the triple pulls of westward expansion, urban development, and rural industrialization meant that few young men and women would follow their parents in the conventional paths of single-family farms and independent household economy. One's early twenties were made savagely uncertain by leave-takings.[6]

The road out of town ran through a landscape crowded with crossroads. Where to go, what to do, where to live, whom to trust, whom to love—life was chock-full of choices. News of a neighbor's arrival and success in a distant place inflamed possibilities. The mails were jammed with letters of inquiry and introduction, promises of backing, and disavowals of responsibility for debts incurred. Second-guessing became second nature. A sense of sin flowed from failure to realize parental hopes. A letter from home was a guilt-provoking double bind, urging one onward and pulling one back. Combined with the injunction not to waste one's time in indulgent introspection, such anxiety set the stage for these youthful conversions.

The protracted revival meeting, whether it occurred in one's home village or in a new setting, addressed these anxieties directly. Filled with stories of sin and redemption, revivalists tried to impart a stable and collective narrative structure on the quaking shoulders of lonely young men and women. They aimed not at reconciling universal truths but at providing usable equipment for active lives. The revival worked by recruiting the unconverted as hoped-for heroes of these new sagas of salvation. Hatred of one's mistakes—and everybody made mistakes—could justify seizing the opportunity to make a clean break with the past. Rebirth assumed the whole drama within oneself. One's new calling as a soldier for Jesus could justify the pain of dislocation and disloyalty. Thus the moralist machinery aimed to turn out Christians fit for a long life of service and commitment.

Ebenezer Porter, writing in 1832 against the new measures, warned that men converted so rapidly would neither support the institutions of the church nor submit to church discipline; their church membership would wither as soon as the heat of their excitement had dissipated. To this the moralists replied that in sanctification, the progressive development of one's holiness after receiving the first infusions of grace, not in conversion, patterns of stability would be attached to the convert. In fact, the moralists soon expected converts to modulate their crisis energy into scrupulous and consistent observance of religious obligations. To do this, the new members would need the confidence of having undergone the trauma of spiritual rebirth. The stability of their confidence, thus, was the equivalent of the placid and well-ordered comprehension of the whole meaning of the universe through the "gospel plan."[7]

In the next three chapters, we will analyze the way in which the life of the stable Christian character was organized and understood, especially in the period of sanctification. But before that discussion, it would be useful to explore the dynamics of particular moralist conversion experiences in greater detail.

In his account of his work during the revival at Westfield, Massachusetts, in 1839, Charles Henry Porter began by acknowledging that "God's Spirit was the prime mover of the whole." But Porter, who had been Taylor's student at Yale, also "did not fail," he said, "to press home upon the sinner's conscience the absolute necessity of his giving his heart to Christ; his guilt in putting it off; his desert of damnation if he neglected this great, this simple, this excellent, this *only* salvation."[8]

What held the notion of God's power together with that of man's responsibility was the trustworthy nature of the divine "character." God's character was such that a man could approach it in confidence; if he did not come forward, it was his own fault.

Porter's efforts to dislodge paralyzed parishioners by his strenuous invitation to them to "give their heart to Christ" was met, on one occasion, by a young woman who claimed "that she had done all she could." "I asked her," Porter responded, "if she was in the habit of retiring alone, and upon her knees begging God's mercy, and then tried to show her the guilt of living without prayer, and the folly of expecting forgiveness without asking it. As I left her, she seemed to feel that she was a rebel against God. I met her about dusk. She choked for utterance, and asked my forgiveness. She came out a sweet, decided, humble Christian." This rather sudden reversal of her spiritual fortunes occurred, at least in Porter's account, through her submission to the young minister's demand. It is his forgiveness, for example, which she asked, not God's. And, further, this touch of romantic atmosphere in Porter's account—"I met her about dusk"—made his mediating role even clearer. Her reconciliation, then, was rather different from those orthodox women whose conversions, as we saw earlier, were often embodied in their passive submission to the language of the Bible and the gospel plan. Porter's young convert was a more personal triumph.[9]

But he did not treat male parishioners in the same way. "I found one young man fighting with God's purposes," he recorded. Porter told him bluntly that "God had a right to reign and rule, and would do it, whether he opposed or not." Setting up the struggle as between two wills, Porter advised the young man purely and simply to yield, even if he could not understand why. "If he could not understand God's purposes," Porter told him, he must be willing to wait and learn; that he could understand far more now than when he was a child, and if he continued from the present time diligently and prayerfully to read the Scriptures for ten or twenty years, he would then probably see many things clearly which he could not now understand. That it was unreasonable for a child to look into the back part of an arithmetic and at once reject it because he could not understand it, when, by beginning right and patiently pursuing it, he might in time understand the whole. So with the Bible. If people were willing to begin with its most simple parts, and gradually learn by patient study and prayer, they would in a few years arrive at great knowledge, compared with their former ignorance. I saw him the night I left, and found him in a very different state of mind, apparently submissive to the divine will. He said hereafter he was determined to devote his days to God. He is about seventeen. I directed his attention to the ministry.

The advice to undertake patient study was a characteristic of moralists. Although the minister was thinking of biblical knowledge here, proper behavior was also frequently thought a matter for textbook learning. Porter's message, although initially quite harsh, was ultimately encouraging, for he could lead the man to make his way one step at a time into a thoroughgoing religious life. There was less personal self-loathing in this process and much more self-confidence. And finally, the young man's submissiveness, we note, was linked to his determination to seal his conversion by dedicating himself to divine service. Rather than press the young parishioner to ever more painful forms of self-renunciation, Porter's aid was to give him real tasks on which to start immediately. They would, as surely as any of God's natural laws, lead directly toward the consistent practice of virtue.[10]

Although they did not demand that males stop dead in their tracks, as did the orthodox ministers, the revivalists who subscribed to moralism did demand that men redirect their lives. Men were still to be more *active* than women in the pursuit of greater holiness, but men's pace would be more effectively regulated by the instruction manual regimen of moral discipline. When asked how to proceed in the way of grace, moralist ministers were fond of suggesting that "you must put one foot before the other, and the Lord will take care of you." So activity was sanctioned but, as always with moralism, carefully circumscribed and directed along proper paths. The moralists' conversion, then, was aimed at producing both human activity and the limits upon it. The imposition of those limits on experience was called the fixing of one's character; to that process we now turn.[11]

Chapter Nine

The Ways of Fixing Character

MORALISM, as we have seen, was a way of looking at God and the world as if everything were in motion, as if both God and people were active and actively related to the other. Its premise, though, was that such activity could be confined within proper channels because God and man or woman each had a "moral character" as an integral part of their beings.

Their doctrinalist predecessors had taught the moralists that God was absolute; to which they replied, as Timothy Dwight demonstrated, yes, and he is also trustworthy. This was surely not the most direct answer and hardly the most controversial, but such shifts in language—in the way such questions are phrased—indicate basic alterations in the structure of religious experience. The opponents of the doctrinalist Calvinists, like the Universalist apologists, would have argued the main point and suggested that God was less than absolute. The Universalists, mirror images of the orthodox Calvinists, posed an alternative but equally abstract system for consideration by New Englanders. For moralists, the absolute sovereignty of God—or virtually any other doctrinal point—begged *their* main question; accordingly, they ignored dogma whenever possible. They wanted to find ways for men and women to feel personal responsibility for their lives on this earth. And when they in turn were faced with strenuous opposition from Unitarians, it was not, characteristically, over the truth of the divinity of Jesus—or any other truth— which they fought but rather about which belief had the best "moral tendency."[1]

The doctrinalists would have scoffed at the idea that they were lax in matters of morality; conversely, the moralists could generally defend themselves against charges of heresy. But there were sharp differences in emphasis between them. The orthodox commonly distinguished between the pious and the merely respectable and found the moral behavior of the two either indistinguishable or even to the latter's advantage. The moralists could later denounce mere "opinion" (by which they usually meant belief) as an impediment to the ends of religion in promoting virtue.[2]

Such shifts in religious sensibility are seen both when controversies dissipate and when new ones emerge. For a generation, for example, Hopkinsians had fenced with their opponents (the Old Calvinists) about the spiritual quality of acts of obedience performed by the unregenerate. With the success of the revivals around the turn of the nineteenth century, and particularly with the ingathering of those upright local citizens whose conversion was so long in coming, the problem became in large measure moot. Moralism felt that it was more important to identify how the spiritual could be moral than it was to know how the moral could be spiritual.[3]

Instead, they asked what could be done with the mass of recent converts once they were safely ensconced within the church. Orthodox Calvinists maintained the grip of doubt over converts by forcing them to compare their personal exercises always with the "perfect standard" of the Bible, against which Christians would again be humbled. But facing increased competition in the nineteenth century from the Methodists, who were quick to harp on the backsliding of less-than-persevering Calvinists and equally quick to teach their own converts to practice a strict behavioral rigor, the evangelical moralists within Calvinist churches also looked for a more positive way of securing the moral confidence of their parishioners. They, too, then began to understand church life as an ongoing course of instruction, not in the intricacies of the creed but in the proprieties of the sanctified life.[4]

Furthermore, many potential converts in their communities, who could never reach the requisite peacefulness of reconciliation with God through the orthodox plan, were clearly willing and capable of leading lives of peerless Christian character. Among the most tortured keepers of nineteenth-century New England diaries were many who could articulate orthodox belief superbly but never validate a claim to church membership through personal experience. For the children of ministers like Lyman Beecher, Joel Hawes, or Alvan Hyde or children like Edward Payson, Susan Huntington, and William Hallock, it appears that growing up in a ministerial household must itself have been a block to fulfilling doctrinally defined conversions.[5]

Thus, in both moral discipline for sudden converts and inclusion of those loyal nonconverts, moralism accommodated itself to a different sort of religious experience. Neither of moralism's constituencies thought much about their "souls," but both constituencies were well aware of the need for a good "character." In this chapter we will explore the notion of character as it became the keystone of the moralist's redefinition of religious life.

We may begin by looking at a case of a failed conversion. William Hallock was born in 1794 to the Rev. Moses Hallock and his wife of Plainfield, Massachusetts. Hallock's biographer, writing from the vantage point of the 1880s, says, "With such a nurture, we might naturally expect to find this eldest son of the pastor early entering the church fold."

> Not so, however; partly, perhaps, because children were not then
> thought capable of apprehending the nature of either the sacraments or

the vows of the church; partly because "conversion" was beset with a greater degree of ideal distress and deliverance than the common experience of most children in Christian families was able to reach. Short of this many a thoughtful and earnest young person has suffered years of delay to go by, shorn of the help and strength which the communion and fellowship of the church would have afforded them.

William looked for a marked and sudden change in his inner life, which never came, and he reached manhood "secluded from the hopes and privileges of the child of God." Indeed, he gave up his early classical studies, feeling that they would be not only no benefit in this world, but would rather "enhance his misery in the world to come"; relinquishing study, he devoted himself to the labors of his little farm.[6]

If Hallock's story had ended here, it would have illustrated the cruel rigidity of evangelical orthodoxy in denying a religious life to a young man who could neither comprehend the theological subtlety nor feel the personal anguish demanded of converts to his father's church. But Hallock was only temporarily deterred. Vowing to press on further in hope of that elusive encounter with grace, he entered Williams College and then Andover Seminary and even embarked upon a career as an ordained minister. Committing himself to labor in the cause of Christian evangelicism, Hallock served the American Tract Society for forty-five years before his death in 1880.[7]

To live the Christian life without undergoing a Christian conversion was to mock the pretensions of orthodoxy. But William Hallock would have been the last to mock orthodox Calvinism. Instead, his life demonstrated a new mode of religious affiliation and experience. The new method, his biographer notes, was "that *practical* consecration that kept him day and night at work for Christ." Unconsecrated by divinity, his own exertion sanctified his service.[8]

The power of personal effort to shape one's own character is one way moralism restructured religious experience. Hallock's case also demonstrates two other ways in which moralism revised the personal experience of religion— that is, rejecting both introspection and theological sophistication and turning toward usefulness in Christian service as a personal goal.

Three other patterns concerning personal experience and characterizing moralism will be discussed here. First, there is the tendency to value habits and routines rather than events. Second, future-oriented concerns, especially those of one's "purpose" or plan in life, are interposed in present considerations. Third, pressure is exerted to model one's behavior on leaders in one's own community rather than upon such abstract or perfect exemplars as biblical or classical figures. Together, these six ways of thinking about oneself created a new "character" to occupy American pews.

The Revolt Against Introspection and Theology

The orthodox had treasured their researches into the workings of the mind but not because they accorded the capacities of human intelligence a holy standing in their theology. On the contrary, the mind unaided by divinity could only flounder in error and sin. Orthodoxy's reverence for the understanding was more subtle; the human mind was wonderful because God was understood in the compass of its thought. A thought of God had intrinsic interest, and discovering God amid one's mental life was invariably riveting.[9]

Moralism, by contrast, wanted results, and it tended to view the mind merely as a mechanism to process the sensations of the world into actions. Moreover, moralists had confidence in the natural mind to judge some actions as moral, thus giving more credit to mental life than did the orthodox. But intellection, inherently different from and even opposite to action, was unworthy of high regard.[10]

The moralists understood the mind as a structure in which first the understanding perceived and then the moral sense (or conscience) acted as a screen or judge upon such perceptions. Together the understanding and the conscience provided motives, chosen or rejected in the volitional faculty or will. If this mechanism operated perfectly, there would be no immorality at all. From where then did error come?

Joel Hawes, the minister of Hartford's First Church, expressed some common opinions on this score in describing the season of youth.

> Then [during youth] the passions, budding and hastening to ripeness, acquire new vigor, become impatient of restraint and eager for gratification. Then the imagination, unchecked by experience and unrestrained by judgment, paints the world in false and fascinating colors, and teaches the young bosom to sigh after its vain and forbidden pleasures. Then springs up in the mind, the restless desire of independence and self-control;—a disposition to throw off the restraints of parental counsel and authority, and to think and act for itself. "Then the social impulse is felt, and the young man looks around for companions and friends;" then the calling for life is chosen, the principles of action adopted, habits acquired, and those connections in business and society formed, which usually decide the character and fix the condition, both for this and the future world.

For Hawes, like other moralists, the young men coming to the city were menaced not so much by their new environments as by their own minds. Propriety was threatened by the eruption of passions, the imagination, and a premature desire for independence. Hawes described each of these as interruptions within the mind itself, as in the phrase "springs up in the mind." Such intrusions obscured the proper functioning of the understanding and caused the will to choose incorrectly; the failure may be represented as indulging a passion already within the mind and always threatening to lead one's character astray. With an eye to duty, the will would, as we have seen, "switch off" such passions.[11]

Compare these erratic ways to the positive actions taken in Hawes's last sentence, beginning with "the calling for life is chosen." Here the mind acts as a complete and integral organ; it chooses, adopts, acquires, forms, as if without possible internal divisiveness or conflict. Hawes's language implied that proper behavior emerged from the mind considered as a whole and that impropriety came from internal fragmentation.

Moralists always advised their auditors, then, to remove obstacles to clear thinking and smooth action. Intoxicating drink, Justin Edwards wrote in 1832, would be sinful in itself, but it also served to "darken the understanding, scar the conscience, pollute the affections, and debase all the powers of the soul." Gradually, through such language the organs of the mind became associated with the difficulties and dangers of incorrect behavior. When upright behavior was praised, no mention was made of the understanding, the affections, the conscience, or the will. A *man* was good; if not, his *conscience* was scarred.[12]

The young were advised to leave well enough alone, pay no attention to the internal operations of the mind. But there were difficulties with this approach. Timothy Dwight, for example, had urged a model of regeneration in which the sinner was active, and such activity was placed in the unsanctified will. But all the moralists really needed was the *feeling* that one had free choice. Furthermore, one did not have to feel this way until after one had acted; the sense of one's freedom did not play any particular role in one's choice. After one had acted, it seemed sensible to presume that one could have acted differently; this was all that the sense of freedom was expected to connote. Consequently, one need neither explore the mind in the process of decision nor allow any feelings to surface before the correct decision was made. In this way, both unnecessary emotionality and introspective delay could be averted.

This inattention to the interiority of experience depended, as we have seen, on the notion of the mind as a smoothly working mechanism. To propel the mind's proper choice, all that was needed was the presentation of truth. Sidney Mead has written about Nathaniel William Taylor, Dwight's successor as professor of theology at Yale:

> Basic to the thinking of Taylor and his fellows was the conception of fixed and eternal "truth," to which all reasonable minds must give assent as soon as it is made clear to them. Hence as revivalists they sought, first, to make their doctrines conform to this "truth" and sec-

ond, to present them so clearly that the common mind could understand them. Once the "truth" was seen and understood, acceptance was automatic for a rational mind, and only perversity and unwillingness could account for its rejection.

In Lyman Beecher's crisp terms, "I can know, if my opinion *be* correct, that it *is* so, because evidence seen and felt creates a moral certainty."[13]

The evangelical moralists thus transferred to the idea of truth the sense of absoluteness that had previously belonged only to God. The mind's "automatic" acceptance of truth eliminated the need for God to have an immedite effect on the convert's mind. God could work more simply and effectively through the means of the mind because it was so fortuitously constituted to respond to truth. Taylor, Beecher, and their allies in the moral reform movement could thus be as thoroughgoing in their naturalism as the Unitarians; for both groups, God acted in the same manner in grace as he did in the ordinary affairs of life. The distinction between the common and special influences of the Holy Spirit was gone; and gone with it, in all likelihood, were both the notions of instantaneous regeneration and of the dual structure of a theological and an ordinary experience to which it gave rise.[14]

The orthodox doctrinalists, quick to leap upon Taylor's "heresy" in this regard, used it as the basis for the Taylorite-Tylerite split that tore apart Connecticut Congregationalism in the 1820s and 1830s. (Almost exactly the same issues led to the Old School–New School division in Pennsylvania and Ohio Presbyterianism in the same decades and after.) The conservative group, forming itself around Bennet Tyler and Asahel Nettleton, established its own theological seminary in East Windsor (later the Hartford Theological Seminary) to counter the influence of Taylor's teaching at Yale Divinity School. In fact, the threat of Taylorism led to the reprinting of the theology and the revival narratives upon which I have based my study of the doctrinalists.[15]

But my purpose here is not to trace the history of theological disputes or ecclesiastical politics. Ultimately the results of Beecher's and Taylor's ways of thinking were registered most forcefully in the religious experience of almost all members of the mainline Protestant denominations. What effect did Taylor's picture of the mind have on religious experience?

Clearly the rejection of introspection was synonymous with the rejection of doctrinalism. Concern with the intricacies of one's innermost thoughts and feelings was generally accompanied by a concern with the most fundamental orderings of the universe. If you give up wondering about the logic of God's gospel plan, you then cease to worry about which part of the mind responds to it.

In addition, the moralist's position, emphasizing as it did the unique power of the truth to compel personal acceptance, actually added to the stature of the Bible. It was now less clear why the Scriptures contained the fundamental truths, but because they did they carried more weight. The evangelicals, to distinguish themselves from the rationalistic religious liberals who shared their moralism, emphasized the role of revelation in religion. Without the saving hand of divinity actively and immediately felt in every single case of conversion, no other path was open except to proclaim one's adherence to "the faith once delivered to the saints."[16]

Defending the old faith (but with new methods) was Lyman Beecher's task, in sermon after sermon, and in Beecher's words, too, we find the clearest reflection of the moralist revolt against introspection and theologizing in everyday religion. In recalling his own all-too-painful introspection during his conversion and courtship of Roxana Foote, Beecher disdained his early discouragements. " 'Some people,' he would say [to his children], 'keep their magnifying-glass ready, and the minute a religious emotion puts out its head, they catch it and kill it, to look at it through their microscope, and see if it is of the right kind. Do you not know, my friends, that you can not love, and be examining your love at the same time?' "[17]

Given the choice, Beecher would rather have loved than examined his love. Moralism always pointed one way, and the movement provided anyone with the self-confidence to love without careful examination. Accepting and disregarding one's mind in this way meant that religion ceased to be a sphere to which one escaped from the deficiencies of one's natural (sinful) condition. Instead, as Lyman's most famous son, Henry Ward Beecher, said, "religion is the right using of the whole mind and life." To the moralist, faith had become a way of acting, not a mode of thinking.[18]

This emphasis on action signaled the demise of the "epistemological" self, the way of looking at man as if he were chiefly known by his constant reception of sensations from the world and his constant response to them with self-determined or divinely determined volitions. From the time that young Jonathan Edwards read Locke or, even before, until the second quarter of the nineteenth century, questions of theology and morality had invariably focused on a person categorized by his way of knowing. Moralism dethroned the "epistemological self" and replaced it with a "behavioral self," to whom not ideas but events occurred. It mattered less what was happening within his head than how he demonstrated his thoughts in the world. In the end, the "epistemological self" attracted the concern only of experimental psychologists and analytical philosophers.[19]

The Primacy of Fixed Principles over Experience

The behavioral self lived in a world dominated by the concept(s) of character. An excellent example appears in Catharine Beecher's account of the loss of her mother.

> It was at an age when I knew my character was forming in the eyes of the world—when I was expected to throw off the character of a girl

and assume that of a woman—when every action of my life would be regarded, not as the impulse of an uninformed child, but as springing from the fixed principles of an established character.

The word *character* is used three times in this sentence, and each time a bit differently. In the first instance, Beecher seemed to mean that her social reputation was being made; in the second, her persona or role was being exchanged for another. In her last phrase, she implied a permanent moral quality to her fully formed self.[20]

All these varieties of character refer to a quality that not only stands for the self but also stands in judgment over the self. From its original literal meaning of a mark or stamp, *character* had had a rich development as a figurative expression. In the sixteenth and seventeenth century it meant the distinctive mark of a person—a trait, the essential nature, the sum of such qualities, a description of those qualities. In the eighteenth century, the word came to refer more often to whole persons—as reputation, as good moral quality, as a part in a novel or play. Finally, in 1773, Goldsmith completed this shift by using "character" as "an eccentric person" in *She Stoops to Conquer*. But in all these meanings the word had never lost its stable or static sense. One's experience shaped or emerged from or could be described as one's character, but character as such was always to be differentiated from experience.[21]

By stressing these stabilized aspects of her development, Catharine Beecher could thereby gain command over her experience. She could see herself more clearly apart from the events like the death of a parent that tossed one about dangerously. We want here to focus particularly on how the third of her uses of character—as in the phrase, "the fixed principles of an established character"—was capable of confining her experience.

The basic strategy was to refer present choices to the test of "fixed principles." Catharine Beecher contrasted such principles to "the impulse of an uninformed child," presuming that *information* led to establishing a principled character. But, as we have already seen, one's acts could not be referred to such data as introspective or cosmological statements about one's spiritual condition, as these were unsuited for the analysis of human behavior.

Needed, instead, were principles to serve as behavioral norms. *Principle* in the days of Edwards had meant the same thing as moral character—the essential quality of one's interior spring of action. Since then it had become detached from the self and now stood for an external ideal to which one could subscribe. The question for moralists could therefore be seen as establishing certain principles upon which to make proper choices.[22]

In addressing the young men of Hartford and New Haven, Joel Hawes considered in turn the possible merit of a number of such principles. *Honor* he found offensive because "it has no reference to the law of God, nor to the established laws of morality." *Pleasure,* or *the love of money or human applause,* were similarly contemptible. He came then to a principle of "very extensive influence, . . . adopted and acted upon, by multitudes who claim to be respectable and intelligent men. . . . They call it prudence, discretion, wisdom. But in plain English," Hawes exclaimed, "it is cunning, duplicity, deception. Now this principle of double dealing, of artful accommodation and management, is, if I mistake not, eminently characteristic of the age in which we live. . . . Instead of acting in open day light, pursuing the direct and straightforward path of rectitude and duty, you see men, extensively, putting on false appearances; working in the dark, and carrying their plans by strategem and deceit." The main danger from playing the role of an "intriguer" or "manager" in those dark Jacksonian days was its inconsistency. Such principles were destestable because they were not principles at all; they could be judged by no other standard than immediate utility.[23]

In the place of such inadequate, even immoral, principles, Hawes wanted one principle that would be firm, easily comprehensible, and capable of illustration by scriptural models. He advised his auditors to subscribe therefore to "the principle of unyielding rectitude" and recommended it particularly because "it is always easy to know what is right; but often very difficult to know what is for our present interest, or popularity."[24]

Hawes noted further that three aspects of rectitude were requisite for attaining moral principles. First, one needed "a clear and well defined knowledge of the proper rule of life."

> The distinctions between right and wrong, in your mind, must not be
> vague and fluctuating; but clearly ascertained and thoroughly settled.
> Your views of duty must be derived, not from the maxims of a loose and
> pliant morality, but from the word of God and the dictates of an enlight-
> ened conscience. There must be a quick perception and a lively feeling
> of obligation,—a moral sense that would "feel a stain, like a wound,"
> and cause you to shrink at the very appearance of evil.

To adopt such fine principles meant, we may infer, that one would not waver before changing circumstances but instead would quickly apply the proper dictates of the moral code derived from both revelation and one's own conscience.[25]

Second, Hawes expected that a commitment to rectitude relied upon a sense of one's accountability to divine government, particularly to God's retributive justice. Obeying a fixed principle, then, meant seeing each situation as subject to judicial review. Because error was now more a case of misbehavior than of wrong opinion, the principles had to be moral norms rather than doctrinal standards.[26]

Finally, Hawes demanded "a deliberate and settled resolution" always to act as if one's destiny was at stake. This reaffirmed the previous two points, but it also implied that destiny stood or fell on the basis of success in following such behavioral norms. Later, Hawes stated the point more baldly. "On the character you are now forming," he warned, "hangs your eternal destiny."[27]

By interpreting one's present experience according to these three tests of rectitude—locating it in the code of life provided by Scripture, feeling each act as a test of one's standing before divine justice, measuring each as contributing to one's salvation or damnation—the experience was inevitably controlled. The present was bent to the future, the facts of the situation to the standards of eternal judgment. The behavioral self, then, though built upon a concept of free will, acted less and behaved more. That is, it followed obediently the expectations of the moral norms sustained by the churches.

To the moralists, the opposite of the life of character was a life "without plan and without object." Their doctrinalist forebears had also praised the merits of a plan, but in those days they meant the "gospel plan," distant and even tangential to man's immediate circumstances. The moralists substituted a plan wholly fitted to the natural lifetime. And its object was not the greater glory of God so much as the ability to walk one's own straight path.[28]

The economic metaphor most applicable to the doctrinalist mind was that grace was an inheritance; once received, it would continue to enrich one's life until a full estate in heaven was achieved. For the moralists, rectitude was a continuing investment, slowly building one's fortune by continuing exertions. In that way, the middle-class emphasis upon savings could be applied equally to one's religious experience and to one's property and emotional reserves.[29]

The reward of the strategy of deferred gain could, like the investment itself, be comprised in the good word *character.* In the following passage, Joel Hawes translated character from a qualification for success into its own crowning achievement.

> No young man can hope to rise in society, or act worthily his part in life, without a fair moral character. The basis of such a character is virtuous principle; or a deep, fixed sense of moral obligation, sustained and invigorated by the fear and the love of God. The man who possesses such a character can be trusted. . . . Such a man has decision of character;—he knows what is right and is firm in doing it. Such a man has independence of character;—he thinks and acts for himself, and is not to be made a tool to serve the purposes of party. Such a man has consistency of character;—he pursues a straight forward course, and what he is to day you are sure of finding him tomorrow. Such a man has true worth of character;—and his life is a blessing to himself, to his family, to society, and to the world.
>
> Aim then, my friends, to attain this character.[30]

The Preference for Habitual Conduct

The moralist's antagonism to experience was expressed, as we have seen, by denying its interiority and then by subordinating events to the "fixed prin-

ciples of an established character." Another, perhaps even more popular avenue of assault upon personal experience was the preference for habits over
momentary events in the life of the behavioral self. Again a perfect illustration
comes from the Beecher family, this time from Lyman. One child recalled,
"He was in the habit of saying to me that the kind of religious experience
which supposed God sometimes to shine, and sometimes to darken himself
without any accountable reason except a mysterious sovereignty, was an entire
mistake;—that the evidence of religion should not lie in these changes, but
in the mind's consciousness of its own steady, governing purpose, as witnessed
by the *habitual* course of life." Do not be alarmed, Beecher assured his family
and parishioners, by those shifting perceptions of God's moods, no matter how
powerful these momentary experiences are. Instead, concentrate on the way
you habitually act as the proper "evidence of religion." These words inevitably
dimmed conversion as the highlight of the religious biography. In fact, now
no individual experience could count for much.[31]

There were two main reasons to challenge the emphasis upon conversion.
First, an almost endemic infirmity of evangelicalism at any time or place was
simply the problem of how one could derive a Christian life from even the
most overwhelming event. How was a whole way of life triggered by a single
day or week? Second, pertaining more particularly to the moralist revision of
evangelicalism in early nineteenth-century New England, many failed painfully to have the expected encounter with grace at all.[32]

Each reason tended to press the claims of habit against experience. Even
from the most orthodox of pulpits there had been many warnings about relying too heavily upon conversion. As Charles Backus, in closing his narrative
of the revival in Somers, somberly confessed, "It is to be expected in the most
promising religious appearances, that there will be tares with the wheat.
False brethren have mingled with the true, ever since there was a church on
the earth. If any professing Christians rest in past attainments, and become
habitually indifferent to holy diligence and watchfulness, they make it manifest that their hope is the hope of the hypocrite." For Backus, hypocrisy could
be identified by too heavy a dependence upon one's "past attainments." No
matter how exciting the initial encounter with grace, it was important to be
habitually diligent and watchful ever after.[33]

To the orthodox, conversion did not release personal constraints. Orthodox
converts were reminded that "this is not an hour of boasting, but of putting
on the harness; and that it still remains to be proved from their fruits whether
they have true religion or not." Improving the fruits of one's religion was called
sanctification. The nineteenth century, perhaps because of its success in attracting converts, strained ever harder to center religious life on the sanctifying process, the means by which the new saint deepened his experience of
divinity.[34]

Sanctification for Calvinists was inextricably connected, also, to the theological doctrine of the perseverance of the saints. If the experience of regeneration was to have any real meaning as a sign of God's decree of one's salvation, then it mandated (for Calvinists) the accompanying proviso that one could never lose one's grace once conferred. But no one in the evangelical community seriously contended (in an antinomian vein) that the Christian life was entirely without sin. Methodists, among the chief competitors for converts in the revivals around 1800, continually chided Congregationalists and Baptists for including among their numbers blatantly back-slidden (and even obviously besodden) heroes of earlier revival seasons.[35]

The dilemma of transforming a single event into a life was addressed by applying the model of associationist psychology: namely, each event contributed, piece-by-piece and cumulatively, to constructing a total pattern. The process of sanctification was therefore a course of life in which proper associations (or what is the same thing, good habits) were established.

Sanctification was therefore a gradual, not a sudden, change in one's life. This pattern of behavior was learned, neither immediately attained by divine illumination nor inborn. As Aaron Bancroft described the Christian's life,

> By the diligent study of the truths, and by the serious observance of the directions of the gospel, he acquires the qualifications of the Christian character. By adding to his faith the graces and virtues of his religion, he makes his calling and election sure. Having learned how he ought to walk and please God, he abounds more and more in every good word and work. From the commencement of the Christian life, he makes constant progress in the path of goodness; and with quickened steps he presses toward the goal of perfection. . . . This purpose cannot instantaneously be accomplished. Christian qualifications are slowly acquired.

Of course, Bancroft was a Unitarian; he viewed this gradual growth in grace as *both* conversion and sanctification. Nothing about religion was instantaneous to Bancroft; all good things were learned through disciplined study and expressed in habitual exercises of virtue, not in grand gestures of affirmation to God's way.[36]

This liberal model of progressive regeneration was naturally abhorrent to Calvinists. But the orthodox picture of the *sanctifying* phase did not differ markedly from that of their Unitarian or Universalist antagonists. Charles Backus conceded that "the work of *sanctification* is carried on progressively in the hearts of the renewed, and will be continued until it is completed in the concluding moments of life; but *regeneration* is the beginning of holiness in the soul, and admits of no progression."[37]

The contention between Calvinists and liberals focused entirely, then, on whether the conversion experience was instantaneous and hence characterized by a special act of the Holy Spirit or progressive and therefore simply another (and indistinguishable) religious experience. But even within the Calvinist camp, those who had dethroned the epistemological self and who thought instead of selves as whole participants in events, slowly abandoned the distinction between conversion and sanctification.

For one, Nathanael Emmons, who led Massachusetts Calvinism from his parish in Franklin, assumed that all experiences depended equally upon divine power, that one "exercise" was therefore much like any other. Timothy Dwight, who disliked the flamboyant arbitrariness of Emmons's divinity, came to believe that sanctification was but a second dose of the same medicine that brought conversion. "Our Sanctification," he wrote, "consists supremely, in *enhancing* this relish [for divine things], in rendering it more *intense,* more *uniform,* more *vigorous,* and universally, more *operative.*" These adjectives are significant because they suggest that Dwight understood holiness as the muscular development of a power first given in the moment of grace. The habitual Christian was simply more practiced than the novice; the difference was in degree rather than in kind.[38]

Gradually the message was clearly conveyed. Even if one were converted, one still needed further development. Stronger habits could be imprinted on the self by continuing to learn the right way and sticking to it. But, of course, even if one had not been converted, it was still possible to establish habits of rectitude in the same manner. This sort of life history was the second fundamental challenge to the primacy of the conversion experience among evangelicals.

For those whose early encounters with religion had been unsatisfactory, or had not heralded the intended life of Christian endeavor, dismissing individual events was a fine self-justifying strategy. John Todd, by then an aged minister, recalled that even after his conversion and communion with the church, "my interest abated, and I fell into old ways. And then," he recounted, "when I was in college, there was a revival, and I was stirred up again. And then I grew indifferent again. And so it has been all along. I don't know—perhaps it is better to rest my hope upon the general aim and endeavor of my life, and upon the mercy of God, than upon those early experiences." The blunter Elijah Shaw of the Christian Connexion advised reluctant members of his religious group that "It is not what a man was, but what he is, that renders him acceptable to God."[39]

By loosening the weight of past experience in the life history of a Christian, moralism was also expanding the realm of present-mindedness for the virtuous. Because the gradual development of proper behavior could happen even to those who had not undergone a powerful moment of enthusiastic paroxysm, no one could escape the attentions of the church due to a seemingly endless failure to convert. Thus, moralism shifted to the discipline of habit and threw a net around the religious community, even those not members in full communion. One might be willing to count oneself as permanently outside God's net, but that of the moral society was wider still and harder to avoid. As in the economic life of the commercializing nation, simply remaining in the "market" was an important moral norm. Success or failure, in this sense, was less vital than participation.

Furthermore, downgrading past experiences meant that the virtuous had to bear all their moral responsibilities in every present moment. In fact, a proper life history put every experience in a proper context. One's present impulses would continually be chastened by rules derived from prior experiences, but the present was all that counted.

Moments of intensity, if inconsistent, were thus foolish and regrettable episodes. Baron Stow, growing up in New Hampshire, remembered that,

> while our dear father was ill—I think in 1815—he read the Life and Diary of David Brainerd. One morning very early, as Royal and I lay in the trundle-bed, I was awake, and overheard father say to mother that he thought Brainerd "made too much account of frames and feelings, for his hope rose and fell with his happiness or unhappiness." That remark I have pondered much in my heart. Hope is the effect of faith. Joys are incidental things, of very little worth as evidence of Christian character.

The attack on moods as evanescent and insignificant deserves to be placed next to the passage from Lyman Beecher with which I began this little section on habits. There Beecher advised the saint to avoid God's inconsistent shining and dimming; man's and woman's fickle mirroring of those changes is rejected. As always, moralism built its religious language upon this correspondence between the divine and the human, ever seeking to see action, but only in its most stabilized and consistent form.[40]

The stability and consistency of action derived from its submission to the "fixed principles of an established character." *Habit,* then, was the repeated bending of one's actions before the principles of rectitude. Or, rather, it was not the repetition itself, for the moralists did not insist that the actions themselves were each exactly alike. To have done the same thing twice or a thousand times was not the same as to constrain oneself within steady habits. For moralism, events were linked instead by their common subordination to the same principles.

For example, look once again at Beecher's words. The evidence of religion, he noted, lay "in the mind's consciousness of its own steady, governing purpose." Such a purpose was the immutable but learned set of moral norms by which the Christian's life was governed. And if each of his days evinced an obedience to these principles, his acts qualified as habits and certified him as a reliable member of the community.

Note, finally, that the mind possessed its own consciousness of moral principles; though such ideas might be taken from Scripture, they resided and were controlled from within the human mind. Habitual virtue was thus a way of equipping oneself for a self-regulated journey through the moral landscape, a fitting preparation for a society of men increasingly "on the loose."

Social Models and Personal Experience

For moralists, piety could be displayed by the exercise of habitually good behavior, showing off one's good character, and so reputation became an important concern. Members of competing religious groups began in the 1810s to turn away from using contests over scriptural interpretation to enforce their parochial claims. Instead they tossed accusations back and forth, arguing that the reputation of a church's members was the best sign of its truthfulness.

Thus, Susan Huntington, the wife of an evangelical minister in predominantly liberal Boston, constantly complained of the reigning formal morality of her city. Her diary rankles with suspicion about men well known in public for one or two charitable acts. Deeply concerned with the applicability of evangelical religion to family life, she secretly puzzled over whether the hearthside scenes of such men were equally moral. "Character," she vowed to teach her children, "is not what a person does, or is, once a year, or once in half a dozen years, but what he is and does habitually."[41]

Wrong as public opinion might be, however, it played a crucial role henceforth in judging moral character. Remember that Catharine Beecher spoke of her character "forming in the eyes of the world." Such a conception had great importance as the moralists reshaped personal experience. Moralism, in externalizing religious obedience through its emphasis upon behavior, also liberated parishioners' eyes to watch other people carefully. The orthodox, we recall, had pressed all to inquire into anyone's spiritual condition, even a stranger's, in the hope of clamping the gospel scheme upon him. But as the case of Nancy Pomeroy showed, it was sinful either to watch oneself or to watch oneself being watched.

In the new Federal and Greek Revival meetinghouses of the early nineteenth century, it was more legitimate to look at others and only proper to be seen. Just as the buildings were themselves built from design books, copying details, so the moralist parishioners worshiping within could begin to copy the details of their lives from one another. Reputation, then, was a reciprocal activity. In being aware of one's local character and that of another's, one could unhesitatingly watch the watchers and, most important, model oneself on the best of them.[42]

As we have seen in our discussions of the moralist's aesthetic of the divine-human relationship, this picture of a bipolar correspondence between two bodies, each trusting the other and reciprocating with acts of mutual confidence, was fundamental to a moralist's mental habits. The claims of reputation allowed this modal relationship, this way of construing the self in relation to the world, to be applied to the social setting of behavior.

The effect was powerful. Behavior could be constrained at the same time it was being pushed toward greater holiness. The social world of religion became an arena for enforcing conformity. As the *Panoplist*, a Massachusetts evangelical journal, put it, "Conferences are eminently and peculiarly social. Different persons express their minds; different persons engage in prayer; the observations of one are often the means of leading others into a new train of thought; attention is kept awake; the fire of the more ardent is communicated to the more lukewarm; the caution of the more prudent is insensibly imparted to the more adventurous." Insensibly, moderation and uniformity emerged from such sharings. Even without saying so out loud, the moralist was able to enforce the claims of normative religion on everyone.[43]

This required substituting the method of imitation for the orthodox "fixed standard of the Bible" as the best judicial rule. "We are, by the very constitution of our nature," the moralists said repeatedly, "creatures of imitation." Therefore, the trick to obtaining virtuous habits was placing oneself in the company of the virtuous, watching them carefully, and modeling oneself upon them. Because their actions could be more clearly seen in such behavior as abstaining from ardent spirits, collecting dimes and shirts to support young men studying for the ministry, or sewing garments for sale to assist missionaries in converting heathen Hindus and Burmese, it was much easier to emulate the pious of the 1820s than those of 1800.[44]

Conversely, it was easy to fall prey to vice and corruption simply by frequenting their local abodes. As hoards of young country boys flocked into the cities, their abandoned rural parsons painted gloomy pictures of the deprivation awaiting the young in cities like Hartford and Boston and New Haven, and especially New York. The lonelier haunts of rustic depravity were more easily ignored.[45]

This worship at the shrine of imitation implied an environmental determinism, to be seen also in the way reformers designed asylums, prisons, schools, and even parlors to enforce moral norms. But equally important was the implicit change in how personal experience and mind were understood. If a hearty confidence rather than passive appreciation of the total gospel scheme had become the essential form of religious faith, so too had emotional leanings toward other people become the basic mode of social bonding. If two events were linked into a habit by their common subordination to the same ruling principle, then two people might become inextricably tied by following the same habits.[46]

As terrifying as the Calvinist test of orthodoxy had been, at least it had the virtue of being offered independently to each sinner. One came to grace all by oneself, each person face-to-face with the God of all. Moralism inevitably diminished standards of piety by substituting the imitation of human models for trying oneself against the purity of gospel doctrine.

Of course, the method of imitation had the advantage of social conservatism. The most withdrawn and ascetic members of congregations were seldom the recommended models. Power passed inevitably either to those who were assertively active in their moral habits or to those most willing to watch the habits of others. As the historian Charles I. Foster summarizes, "This alliance of wealth, energy, and intelligence devoted itself to the inculcation of certain attitudes and values in American society. Genuine religious conviction was, of course, one of them, but it had to find its expression in conformity to a pattern of behavior. And even without the conviction, conformity would serve. The enforcement of conformity," Foster concludes, "brought into play pressures probably stronger than any that the United States has seen before or since." In some measure, this judgment must be tempered by recognizing that moralism helped shape standards of propriety for many generations of Americans who could never have mastered the puzzles of doctrinalist faith.[47]

A Commitment to Usefulness

William Hallock, disarmed from religious life by his failure to undergo a conversion experience, enlisted in Christian service anyway by "personally consecrating" himself to such work. Validated only by their own commitment, Hallock and many other charitable characters were soon acting in ways indistinguishable from those who had suffered the pangs of conviction and repentance before being saved. Evangelicals of a more orthodox stripe had always worried that "some worldly men preserve a character with fewer blots, are more generous, more socially sweet, &c. than many christians." One accounted for this as the greater power that (sinful) *pride* had in controlling the self than did *grace*. But for moralists, when such attributes of charity became the stuff of many Christians' lives, proudly being committed to service could itself be the practical equivalent of grace.[48]

The testimony of many who entered the Lord's service as ministers or missionaries, or as their wives, demonstrated that such commitments sealed off further doubts about their calling. In 1815, Nathaniel Bouton, a young man in Bridgeport, Connecticut, was in the deepest throes of a conviction of his sin when he said, "I further resolved to engage at once in every Christian work, and especially to try to bring others, my relations, and young companions, to a knowledge and experience of religion." His resolution to service, in other words, *preceded* his reconciliation with God. And only after continued work in this way, he united, in great ceremony, "with the First Congregational Church of Bridgeport, Rev. Elijah Waterman, pastor."[49]

Usefulness, then, was a strategy for ending one's interior confusions about religion. Serving others could relieve one of the pain of too much introspectiveness. In another Connecticut town, young Harriet Lathrop came home from a meeting of the local Society for the Relief of Poor Women and Children and announced to her diary: "I found pleasure as usual in attempting to do good. Oh that I had a heart to improve every opportunity of usefulness to my fellow-creatures; but *self* too much engrosses my thoughts, my time and my labor. For self I sigh and toil, regardless of the suffering multitude, and more frequently neglectful of the few who are in my own family, and who might be benefited by my exertions." Harriet's devotion to duty deepened as she grew up, purged her of self-regard, and led her to marry the Rev. Miron Winslow; they spent her last thirteen years as missionaries in Ceylon.[50]

Harriet Winslow's life was not focused around any single event; it was organized as a commitment to an ongoing work. Such a moralist pattern transformed the evangelical notion of life history. In 1800, when conversion was the major experience in a life construed as a "short winter's day," Christians had to see everything else as secondary. The turn toward Christian enterprise altered this perspective on time. By 1842, Elijah Shaw stressed instead that "there is a day allotted us to do all our work in."

> That day is our natural life. It is a short day at the longest, but its duration is to us a matter of the greatest uncertainty. But sure we are that it will end at death, and then our work must cease. . . . Had we a long day, and but a half day's work to perform, there would be some apparent excuse for neglect and delay; but it is not so. Our life is short, and we have a full day's labor to perform.

Life was now more clearly bounded by birth and death and less by the eternal destiny that Shaw neglected to mention. A moralist's attention was not fixed on the bounds on life but instead on the tasks to be accomplished. One had to do as much work as possible within the (mysteriously) allotted time. For the orthodox, we recall, all one did was subordinated to the one great task—and a passive one at that. The fear of dying before salvation made the event of death more crucial than it would be for moralists whose daily "errands of mercy" seemed to accumulate heavenly credit for them regularly.[51]

There is one more point of contrast. In the mind of the evangelical orthodox, the image of Christ had been fixed on his atonement for sinners. Again, Christ's atonement was a single act with overwhelming metaphysical significance. But, as the rest of this passage from Elijah Shaw tells us, Jesus was now to be cherished for other reasons: "Our Lord improved every day, and the whole of every day, and sometimes he rose up to his work 'a great while before day,' and at other times continued all night in prayer, and even performed a sea voyage by night to get from one congregation to another. What an example of industry and perseverance is this! How should it stimulate us to improve every moment to advantage!" In 1842, Christ was a model worker in the vineyard of the Lord himself. And given the imitative impulse of moralism, emulating Christ's work became a common personal goal.[52]

In summary, practical commitment was a powerful guide to the moralist redirection of personal experience. The idea of usefulness took people as actors rather than as thinkers; giving them a task that brought them into conformity with others and relieving their anxieties about the condition of their souls, it helped them fashion a life of service with immediate and ongoing gratifications. "Usefulness" released much energy from the frozen earth of the orthodox winter.

The Omnipotence of One's Will

"Indeed, my friends," said Joel Hawes to the young men of Hartford and New Haven, "in the formation of character, personal exertion is the first, the second and the third virtue." All the structures by which moralism ordered personal experience depended upon human will.[53]

Of course, the willfulness that moralism encouraged was not a personal reconstruction of the world; it needed to be subordinated to a scripturally instructed principle of rectitude. Or it could be channeled by copying the character of a well-reputed Christian in the neighborhood. Or it could be disciplined by being placed in the service of an acknowledged Christian cause like temperance or Sabbath keeping. Thus, the will for which moralism spoke was inherently bound by the moral norms of American evangelicism. Still, such an eminent place for the volitional faculty did redraw the picture of the self offered by orthodoxy. Now, for example, religion was implicitly within the self, not external to it. The moralists could easily toss off the criticisms of religious liberals like Orville Dewey, who was outraged by what he condemned as the revivalists' view that "religion is some divine *afflatus*—breathed into the mind—having nothing in common with it—existing independently and alone—not incorporated with the mind and dwelling in the most intimate friendship with it, but maintained within it, as an abstract principle or ethereal essence, by a foreign and preternatural influence." Instead of this view, moralism stressed the capability of the human will to act in accordance with correct principles *from its own power.*[54]

In fact, the gradual and painstaking development of that internal power for good within the self was needed. Rectitude, it was commonly agreed, needed exercise to become easy and proficient. And each exertion built upon the last to solidify character; as we have said, each act was an investment toward the accumulation of a proper accounting of one's virtue. It was not so significant that one improve one's actions all the time; a longer series of visits to the local poorhouse was not so important as the consistency with which one undertook them at all. The activity, thus, mattered less than the will to do it. As Aaron Bancroft said, a person needed to "be conscious of a sincere endeavour to live in the habitual exercise of all Christian graces and virtues."[55]

Conversely, a man's failure might now be reckoned as simple weakness rather than wickedness. Of course, wickedness was still the proper doctrinal position, but sometimes a little ministerial coaxing helped parishioners to see their sinful lives in the proper way. Here is an an example from the memoir of Charles Henry Porter, a young minister, in the midst of a revival in Terrysville, Connecticut: "I have made so many good resolutions that I am almost afraid to make any more. I feel weak and utterly incapable of keeping them, or rather, I should say, that my wickedness prevents me from keeping them."[56]

Porter's point suggests, too, some important problems for moralism. It was all very well to say that "you may be whatever you resolve to be. Resolution is omnipotent." But was this in fact a positive strategy for personal life? From where was the energy to come to enact these consistent resolutions to habitual virtue? By placing religion so much within the self, did not moralism close off the power beyond the self that is always crucial to spiritual life?[57]

In the moralist plan of life, one thing became certain. The choice of unyielding rectitude as one's fixed principle meant that succumbing to vice was much harder. Taking the first step of becoming a moral character did not insure that one would lead a positively normal life; it did, however, seem to foreclose the alternative option.

Moralists lived in a world where religion and sin were alternative paths. By switching off one's indulgence of sinful tendencies, one could choose the road of religion. But where that road went, or how one could define virtue except by one's companions along the way—and by the ever-present specter of the alternative route just over the tracks—was a more difficult question. Staying on the road, though, seemed to become an end in itself.

These six ways of redefining personal experience find unity when they are seen as an approximation, in religious life, of the new, secular sense of life history gaining favor in early nineteenth-century America. The dilemma of orthodox doctrinalism might have led to certain alterations in the fabric of a religious life built around personal stillness and the immutability of the gospel plan. But that such changes took the form provided by moralism was an accommodation to the larger culture in which religion now played a significantly reduced, if intensively enriched, part.

First among these accommodations was the translation of experiences into behavioral acts that could be observed and tested by others. This implied a redirection away from too much concern with the interior quality of one's experience, or with the systematic and theoretical structures by which it could be understood. Instead of relating to theology, then, each of a person's acts produced a "manner," a consistent pattern, that could itself be a clue to one's social status or personal power. Conformity in behavior, but also in dress and speech, became critical indexes of personal worth.

Once behavior was the focus, then a person's life was constituted by the events of his life history. These events had now to be understood as belonging to the same order: they had antecedents and consequences; they had a specific duration; they were all equally sacred and profane. In sum, they were the pieces by which one's entire life, including one's eternal destiny, was constructed.

But the events were not merely a series of discrete building blocks lined up in a chronological ordering. They were linked developmentally. Early experiences anticipated and determined later ones; later happenings revived memories of the past. Life was the natural course of events that ensued upon birth. The immediacy of God and his power to alter that course anywhere along the way were more and more difficult to integrate into the moralist explanation of human development.

In one's memory, it was not so much that the events themselves were recalled, at least not in their particularity. Events were tied together into a consistent life history by their common organization around certain principles or moral norms. Such norms fundamentally operated to assert the sovereignty of mind over events; no experience was worth having if one could not discern what ideal it served. Consequently, moral norms did not need to be overtly specific; they did not need to outline in precise detail the thousand obligations to which the self was bound daily. Instead, the essential moral norm was that one's life have a plan and an object and that one be willing to take blame or accept credit for each act. Although the norms suggested by moralism in this period of American reform were certainly sexually and emotionally repressive, that was not their basic character; an act's "principle" was more important.

It is easy for us to see how such devotedness to moral ideals could mask a hypocritical and haughty meanness. But moral truth was thought to have a privileged access to the human mind, according to moralism, and standards of behavior could be clearly understood and accepted by all. All men and women were equipped to act properly; their "instinct" was for the good. They needed only the will to follow these instincts.

To be sure, moralism—like most systems of ordinary language—took the customary morality of stable society, organized around nuclear families as the units of work and economic transaction, and incarnated that as immutable dicta revealed in Scripture. But in doing this moralism advanced a form of religion that crossed the lines between denominations and even between believers and nonbelievers. The primacy of moral rectitude was a cardinal tenet of all of American society, and there were few disagreements over the details of propriety. The contests over which path led to the strongest character did not obscure the essential agreement that virtue was the chief end of religion.

All parties argued that their form of belief encouraged the most active and assertive devotion to moral principles. The evangelicals accused the liberals of harboring beliefs about the power of the human mind to achieve good without striving; the liberals firmly contended that evangelicism discouraged men from trying to be good because of its gloomy statements about sin and the need for personal redemption.

Both were agreed, however, that a man's character and his life were his choice. He could not make of them what he willed, entirely, for that opened too many possibilities for aberrants in the American moral landscape. But a man would be judged on the basis of what he had willed and on the quality to which his actions had habitually been directed. Life was a chance to make something of oneself. Religion had become, through the offices of moralism, an alternative struggle for success.

Chapter Ten

Consecrating Character in Everyday Life

Alvan Bond and "Night Meetings"

Reverend Alvan Bond, twenty-six years old, assumed the Congregational pulpit in Sturbridge, Massachusetts, in 1819. Almost immediately, he discovered how quiet a local church could be. "Any special awakening of religious sensibility in the case of individuals or in the church," he later remembered, "was characterized as an effervescence of animal feeling." Few in the church were young, and those of middle age were mostly "unaccustomed to personal activities in the work of religion."[1]

Alvan Bond had recently graduated from Andover Theological Seminary, and before his ordination he had organized charitable work among the poor of Boston. Others in his class at Andover had journeyed to the West, bringing the gospel to bands of settlers on the American frontier. A few had even sailed to Ceylon or Palestine as missionaries. One had dedicated himself to the education of the deaf. These were not men likely to appreciate the sluggishness, the passivity, the deathlike stillness of a congregation.[2]

Alvan Bond came to Sturbridge looking for activity. What had been a cherished quietude to his predecessors in the 1790s was to him only a void which needed to be filled quickly. And fill it he did. Soon the Sturbridge town common was being crossed morning and evening, weekday and Sabbath day, by church members and their families on their way to education, missionary, and temperance society meetings, or to Sabbath schools, or to gatherings for intimate prayer.

Rev. Alvan Bond and his young wife are greeting the women at the doorway of their parsonage in Sturbridge as they arrive one by one on a damp March evening in the early 1820s. Several have their daughters along, and the girls steal a few moments to share a secret before the meeting is called to order. A dozen "stick" chairs are arranged in the parlor facing the fire. The intricate black lines in framed engravings of the Prodigal Son story are scarcely distinguishable in the light of the three or four candles set around

124

the room. Brightest are the faces of those assembled, and these draw the attention of everyone.[3]

As night falls, the curtainless windows become black, and slowly the corners of the room, the floors and wall coverings, the ceiling and the wainscoting, are all lost to view. Each person is fixed in place, for the light is immobile. Sally Bond recalls that she intended to pass along a tract she had recently received to one of the members, but there is no point in getting up and looking for it in another, pitch-black room. Instead of fidgeting, one's hands are put to better use in some inconspicuous handwork—darning or knitting—and the silent rhythms of hand movements help warm the whole body.

The setting, remember, is ordinary; the time is stolen out of the regular work of New England kitchens and sheds. Only by an act of will, beginning with Rev. Bond's opening prayer, is the meeting sealed off from the secular life of the community, raised above it. The voices of the meeting and the words are familiar, belonging to neighbors and friends, but they are delivered in a more reverent, uplifting intonation.

One person shares a piece of recent news, another recalls a related incident, and a third wonders aloud about her confusions or doubts. Present success is contrasted with past inaction, local triumphs with the waywardness of heathen lands. In the dark, the village outside the window is reimagined, made to seem tidier, more enterprising; its shameful detours and embarrassing pitfalls are erased from the maps engraved in orderly minds. Even in that cold, dark room, its floors wet with boot mire, mention of "the vermin in the streets of Smyrna" brings instant revulsion. Even when the cries of drunken pleasure ring from the tavern nearby, it is not hard to feel superior to "the filthy stealing habits of the Nestorians in Persia." The candles shine brighter in earnest faces.

More encouragement brings pledges of redoubled efforts. The enlistment of each person to the goals of all is recognized with a nod. And then the group is consecrated with a final closing prayer. All depart, to light up the night with their fervor, to stride in the paths they have imagined, and to promise, if it is Monday, to make Tuesday another moment of holiness.

Such evening meetings often stunned the rural community. Even decades later, the furious growl of local antagonists resounds through the memoirs of ministers ordained during the 1810s and 1820s. "Night meetings" would be the ruin of religion, they were told. They would be wasteful, for who could afford the extravagant use of tallow candles for these purposes? They would be insulting to the memories of the town's fathers, for they had not had to show their piety under the cover of midweek darkness. They would be heretical, for where did the Bible offer authority for such repeated exercises of Christian public worship? They would be dangerous to the morality of youth, for dusk would be a convenient excuse for yielding to promiscuous temptations. They would even be cruel, for the overworked sexton would never have a day's rest if such meetings continued.[4]

For these young ministers, these meetings were both the first great battle of their clerical careers and their first proud triumph. But what did this victory mean? What did the onset of evening meetings of charitable societies mean to evangelical religion and to the rural communities of New England?

To answer that, we must compare these meetings with the other prevailing forms of sociality in these villages. The most frequent occasions for festivity in rural New England were outcroppings of the work experience, and hence of the calendar of the agricultural year. Most of the time, farm families trod parallel but separate paths through the calendar with their neighbors. All in the appointed times they planted seeds, cultivated, harvested, preserved, and prepared food; they cleaned the fibers, and carded, spun, wove, and sewed the cloth; they cut the timber, hauled, split, stored, and burned up the cordwood. There were few opportunities to make light of this work, and even less often did work bring one's peers together. But some tasks were too large to be performed within single families, and these became the "times" for the greatest merriment and sociality as well as the most awesome labor. At midday, the hardy men or the dextrous women would gather for some undertaking requiring concentrated and cooperative labor—raising a barn, quilting a coverlet, clearing or rolling the roads after a snowfall.

As night approached and the work was completed, members of the opposite sex were admitted to the company, rum and cider were handed around, and a fiddle and some new dance steps were taken up. The inhibitions of work dissolved. The roughest lads drank to excess and boasted of their physical strength to the point of combat. The giddiest girls played at divining the names of their future husbands. And while the company's eyes were elsewhere, some swains and some maidens stole away into the night, having eyes only for each other. "Quilting was a real festival," Samuel Goodrich recalled, "not infrequently getting young people into entanglements which matrimony alone could unravel." The word "bee," an American coinage for these work parties (as in corn husking bee, spinning bee), is a sign of the link of New England sociability and leisure to busyness and work.[5]

Compare the night meetings of religious societies. They come as complete breaks from the work of farming and housekeeping. They are regular, prearranged, held throughout the year without regard for the seasons. Chastity is one of their most hallowed goals, intemperance one of their great foes. Eloquence is the only prowess allowed, but a proper mien and a gentle, impassioned tone of voice are great blessings. Like a barn raising, a night meeting is a work experience, but raising money for missionaries is abstract work. Although never completed, it is always cherished more for its process than for its product; it is part of a new order of life.

The evangelicals did not attack the forms of rural society directly. Their strategy was to kill the "bee" with scrupulosity. First, ardent spirits had to be renounced, isolated from "good company," then removed from the workplace, and finally banished altogether. In the 1810s, the first generation of temperance reformers piously removed decanters of sherry and Madeira from the sideboards of the genial clergyman who hosted the ministerial association meeting. Next, cider was absent from the communal "wood-spell" which furnished the pastor's fuel each autumn, and rum no longer lubricated the steeple raisings of the new-style Greek Revival meetinghouses. In the 1820s, the ministers and their allies campaigned against the age-old association of alcohol with such cooperative adventures as the summer haying and the winter "breaking out." Then the parlor and dining room were scourged in proper homes, segregating spiritous drinks from proper ladies (except for their patent medicines, which were often more than half alcohol). By the 1840s, the evangelicals had located the melodrama of drunkenness in the barroom, and their last campaign led eventually to the Eighteenth Amendment to the Constitution.[6]

Dancing was a more elusive target for the evangelical reformers. The evil of intemperance showed its effects everywhere in New England—in tumble-down houses, battered wives, filthy and brutish children. Cotillions and contradances, on the other hand, were increasingly ensconced in the most respectable, most highly ornamented places in the center village. Among socially prominent citizens, including some church members, it was not rare to convert upstairs chambers in their Federal homes into ballrooms. The birthday of George Washington had quickly become a traditional (and implicitly Federalist-boosting) occasion for balls in country towns.

Though they could not find scriptural examples of "social dancing for amusement," evangelical ministers did not think balls were sinful. Still, gently at first, vigorously later, self-righteously in some places and half-heartedly in others, they began to attack balls and other so-called innocent amusements. Their attack was couched in the tone of a sour taxpayer rather than an enraged pulpit dragon. Balls were a waste of time, a waste of money. "Trifling as is the expense of a single Ball," grumbled one minister, "it is often sufficient . . . to defray the whole expense of a common District-School a month." (This comment may say more about education in New England villages than about recreation.)[7]

Perhaps the best key to the evangelicals' true interest is the text Jacob Ide used for his two sermons against balls. "Prove all things" (I Thess. 5:21), he told his young parishioners in Medway, Massachusetts, in 1818; subject everything you do to the test of religion. Any amusement that distracts you, as dancing does, from a "serious reflection" on eternal concerns is not innocent. Find your enjoyments in the course of your work, your family life, your reading in God's book, and God's creation. Life, as the old New Englander would always say, was its own greatest entertainment, were we but conscientious enough to know it.[8]

The attack upon drinking (and card playing, horse racing, and other diversions) showed that the evangelicals were less interested in reforming behavior per se than in altering the community's sense of social time, social occasion, and social place. More important than what transpired at night meetings, then, was the way they organized New Englanders into regular meetings for mutual conscientiousness.

Before meetings could be called to order, they had to be called to mind, contemplated, anticipated. Balls and bees were few and far between; as special events, they were longed for and remembered. Night meetings were like stagecoach runs; when scarcely passed they were anticipated again. As much as they occurred in the parsonage parlor, then, night meetings also occurred in a specific time, a Monday or a Thursday. The time itself had become a space. It accommodated a woman's reforming energies fully as much as her sitting room. The perfect modern illustration of this idea of time as space is our "week-at-a-glance" calendar.

Deep in the Puritan consciousness it had been registered that time was an instrument, to be used for good purposes, to be "improved" by man's proper uses of it. Almanacs constantly urged rural New Englanders to bend their time, not merely their backs, to the plow. Valuable moments could not be allowed to evaporate into the void that was idleness, for there Satan resided, tempting men and women to their annihilation. The moment itself was ripe for Puritans. In the best of souls, every minute was quickly indentured to some important work. Most fittingly, that was the work of the seasons. A moment, then, was like a sinner in eighteenth-century America—to be seized, convicted, then reconciled to the immutable order of God's universe.

Work was to stop on the Puritan Sabbath, as would travel, sociality, childish mirth, and all the other necessary but trivial aspects of secular life. One went to meeting with one's family, prayed in orotund tones, and conversed in prayerful ones. Reading was either from the Scripture or from commentaries and tracts adhering to gospel truth. The pace of life slowed, refreshing one with concentration rather than diversion. But the Sabbath did not order the week; it only slowed down the press of a season's constant labor.[9]

The moral laxity of the revolutionary war years, the economic dislocations of the postwar scarcities, the confusions of political strife, and the muddled anonymity of denominational identification all contributed to the slow degradation of the Sabbath stillness. By the 1820s, the evangelicals had decided to crusade for restoring the Sabbath in New England to every bit of its former rigor. They were appalled that certain merchants opened their shops for Sunday business, or that canal boats still operated, and vowed boycott. As United

States citizens, they were abashed that the mails were carried and even distributed on Sundays, and they pledged political reprisal.

But the Sabbatarian campaign was only in part a movement to restore what had been gradually lost. Now Sabbath keeping was prized for new purposes. It adorned the whole week with moral purposiveness. "Nothing furnishes so sure a protection against the allurements of the world," Joel Hawes told a group of youths on the verge of being allured in 1826; "nothing tends so much to invigorate private virtue, and diffuse around, a healthful, public sentiment, as a serious observance of the Lord's day."[10]

To Catharine Beecher, Lyman's eldest child, the establishment of the Sabbath was proof that God was a "Being of perfect system and order." Adopting his method, we too could subdivide the remainder of the week and consecrate which parts we would to divine service. From the peak of Sunday evening, we could look out over the landscape of the week and espy the time given to procure livelihood and to prepare food, raiment, and dwelling. But the leisure of two afternoons and evenings, Miss Beecher said, might be ours for "religious and benevolent objects, such as religious meetings, charitable associations, school visiting, and attention to the sick and poor." Other leisure moments might be devoted to intellectual improvement and social enjoyments.[11]

The new evangelical week, then, was itself a void, time to be filled with a person's activities. Morally neutral, time itself had no obligations. But as much of it as we wanted could be consecrated to God's work; our will decided.

Evangelicals like Hawes and Beecher were addressing a population that was moving from the seasonal rhythms of country life to the schedules of urban society. The work of a merchant house or a city household had a different sense of time from the farm. By and large, the work was less strenuous, and the daily tedium was offered bold contrast only by the chance triumphs of financial speculation, or by more corporeal extravagance. Moralists wanted young men and their wives to satisfy themselves with the steady growth in fortune that came from regular labors and the steady growth in virtue that came from both regular attendance at religious meetings and a scrupulous observance of the Sabbath day.

The triumph of the hebdomadal, or weekly, regimen synchronized religious time with the schedule of the emerging commercial system. In a sense, all Americans were now to live by the rule that had once characterized only their Protestant ministers: every day should have its special moments and every week its momentous Sabbath. But in the process religious life, too, became a bound set of weekly appointment books, as blank before man's will as nature around him.

The opponents of the evangelicals, the religious liberals, upheld an older sense of time. Aaron Bancroft, the Unitarian minister of Worcester, Massachusetts, deduced in 1817 that "as we may not carry the labours of the week into the Sabbath, so we may not carry the rest of the Sabbath into the week." Instead, our weekdays are to be spent, he suggested, in faithfully performing the business work we had contracted to do, "as a duty enjoined by God." Restating the old Puritan ideal of the calling, Bancroft noted that "the careful and conscientious discharge of domestick duties is religion in practice."[12]

As a Unitarian, Bancroft feared enthusiasm, religious fervor, and zeal more than he did heresy. It could only be pretentious for a Christian to devote himself to religion so willfully. "Those who attend these meetings," he complained, "are apt to consider themselves more religious than such as discountenance them; and they often abound in severe censures and uncharitable judgements."[13]

But as a conservative, in social if not in theological terms, Bancroft's fears went deeper. What chance did the obligations of ordinary life have if the evangelicals thoughtlessly made every moment so fungible? Did they not realize that by loosening the ties a person had to diligent labor the worst kind of materialistic self-seeking might also be encouraged? Like a good seventeenth-century Puritan, Bancroft reminded congregants that their chief good was in the hereafter. "Habitual employment on the six days of the week is inculcated as an important duty; but the work is not represented as the abiding place of man, nor its goods recommended as the ultimate objects of human pursuit."[14]

The evangelicals were quick to respond. If liberals like Bancroft were afraid that precious time would be diverted from labor, one asked, why did they judge harmless such raucous recreations and entertainments as a "gang of equestrian performers"? If they feared religious conferences so much, why did they not speak out against balls and other festivities? Such sport, we conclude, was excusable to the Unitarians because it expressed man's continuity with ordinary nature. It was just part of the innocent metabolism of work, play, and food that composed earthly life after the Fall. But if evangelicalism meant anything, it meant that there was nothing innocent; everything was either sinful or holy.[15]

To the evangelicals, one's behavior on the Sabbath became a perfect test of one's character and a sure index of one's likely success both in this world and the next. "No habitual Sabbath breaker," Joel Hawes warned flatly, "can be permanently prospered." And with the air of a dour political economist, he passed along the report of a distinguished gentleman "that those merchants in New York, who have kept their counting rooms open on the Sabbath, during my residence there, (twenty-five years), have failed without an exception." And this was also true for other worldly concerns. "Shall we not press upon him [the sinner]," the Spirit of the Pilgrims asked in 1833, "the claims of the Sabbath as a test of his character in the sight of God, and a means of bringing him to a just sense of his sin?" The key term is "test of his character." If the Sabbath did become such a perfect and convenient test, what effect did this have on the practice of religion? Could the converse also be true? that is, could one's righteousness be declared or one's fortune made simply by passing the test of such observances?[16]

Furthermore, because secular and spiritual success both seemed to depend upon consecrating particular hours to God's service, did one become the reward of the other? Obedience to a moral duty surely became requisite to social and economic achievement. But was the true end of religion to assist young men in attaining wealth as well as virtue? And was the highest place in the temple of the righteous to belong to the richest money changers?

These were some vexations of American moralism as it brought the moth of spiritual experience closer to the flame of economic ambition in the decades after 1815. Treasuring regularity in all spheres of life, it encouraged a remarkable outpouring of diary resolutions to organize one's time more effectively in the future and to devote oneself to regular exercises of devotion. "There is no point in Christian experience more settled than this," wrote one man, "that there is an intimate connection between enjoyment in closet devotions, and *their return at regular seasons.*" In a way, the power of religious life became the product of one's dedication to its regular exercise.[17]

So, too, with spaces. The more intently one underlined the expected moral purpose of new churches, meeting rooms for religious societies, even parlors and libraries, the more likely they were to inspire moral lessons. The result of this approach was a remarkable development of specialized spaces in every part of the community. The old New England meetinghouse had commonly been the province both of religious services on Sundays (and perhaps on Thursday evenings for the minister's "lectures") and also of town meetings to discuss such secular concerns as schools, roads, poor relief, and, of course, taxes. This overlapping was a survival of the Puritans' disdain for religious artifice and willingness to lump the support of religious teaching among the municipal responsibilities of the town government. Such responsibilities, as we have explained, had generally disappeared or become less stringent as disestablishment came to Connecticut in 1818 or to Massachusetts in 1833; by that time, few ministers drew their salaries from town coffers. But even before, some new meetinghouses being built by Congregational societies were specifically excluded from use by the town "rabble" at town meeting time. Gradually, the Episcopal custom of "consecrating" their churches was emulated by lower-church groups, especially in cities. Similarly, the use of graveyards as playgrounds for the young and courting lanes for the romantic slowly faded with the recognition of their singular and specialized roles as repositories of the dead and reminders of mortality. And, within houses, the common parlor or sitting room was divorced from the formal parlor in these years, and the latter was often specially devoted to religious events and moral instruction, especially on the Sabbath.[18]

The strategy of consecration could be applied as much to one's own self as to the time and space around one. In so doing, moralism had to detach the will from the self. Then virtue could be defined as the self's compliance with the will's decision to serve God. Edward Griffin, for example, was aroused by reading a piece urging the distribution of religious tracts, and he decided to add this effort "to my other attempts to promote (what I now hope I can say is my favorite object) the salvation of men. . . . O to employ every faculty during life, and to seize every new measure to promote this object."[19]

But this implied, did it not, that religion was only an object, an end, not a kind of act or person? Would it not be possible to devote the same faculties to other ends? To keeping a clean house or making money? Here was a dilemma; it resulted from the moralist impulse to enlist in the service of religion all sorts of new instruments—organizational skills and technical proficiencies— that were emerging in nineteenth-century America. So what if religious life became progressively involved with such nonreligious acts as fund-raising and publicity campaigns, rather than prayer, contemplation, reading Scripture, hymn singing, or even visiting the unfortunate? As long as the funds raised were dedicated to furthering Christ's kingdom, what did it matter that the acts one performed or the faculties one employed were not traditionally thought of as spiritual in character? Did the coming of the kingdom not deserve the best talents of Americans, at least as much as secular ends?

Inevitably, moralists found themselves condoning the most private and self-aggrandizing kinds of business practices, then, *so long as they served religious ends.* As Justin Edwards wrote to his wealthy brother-in-law, a New York merchant, in 1828, "But if he [the businessman] is active and acquires property for the sake of honoring God, and doing good, his very activity will tend to promote his salvation, and while diligent in business he will be fervent in spirit, serving the Lord." The more successful his business exertions were, in fact, the more fervent would be his religious life. Although the equivalence of cash and grace was only hinted at here, that between economic energy and spiritual engagedness was clear enough.[20]

My intention here is not to impugn the charitable motives of businessmen like Edwards's brother-in-law but only to show that such consecration of his business activities to religious purposes effectively absolved those activities from moral tests. Therefore, a little chicanery in the import trade or in the treatment of one's workers, so long as one contributed one's time and money sufficiently to the church, did not disqualify one from godliness. This chain of reasoning had an important effect in accommodating evangelical religion to expanding capitalist commerce in the nineteenth century.[21]

In addition, the idea that one willfully committed oneself to God or to religious ends confirmed the moralist picture of the self as morally neutral. Only one's purposes in acting had a morality. Lost was the sense, so strong in Jonathan Edwards's writing, that human being was only part of the same stuff as God or being-in-general. For Edwards, the infusion or illumination of holiness in the soul was only a "remanation" of God's emanating holiness, and virtue was the conjunction of the lesser being with the larger one, their "consent." Now, in the tide of the moralist revision of the evangelical experience, a Christian could connect himself or herself by the wonderful act of will to a wholly distinct religious purpose—higher and better but quite different. Men and women took on the moral character of the ends they willed—if the ends were those revealed in Scripture their wills were accounted good—but they themselves could be neither good nor bad.

A revealing episode in the moralists' struggle to adapt religion to the power of the self-consecrating will occurred in Justin Edwards's parish in Andover, Massachusetts. In 1816, the Society for Doing Good, composed of adults, sponsored a Bible society for several hundred parish children. The *Panoplist* reported:

> At the opening of the schools in 1816, each teacher was furnished with a blank-book ruled with eight columns. On the first column was to be written the name of each scholar; on the second, his age; on the third, the number of times he had been at the head of his class at the last spelling for the day; on the fourth, the number of books which he had taken from the library; on the fifth, the number of verses of hymns and divine songs which he had learned; on the sixth, the number of answers which he had learned of the shorter catechism; on the seventh, the number of verses which he had learned of the Bible; and on the eighth, the number of cents which in the course of one year he had given to the Bible Society. When any scholar had in the course of the week saved any thing for the heathen, he was allowed on Saturday, when he took a book from the library, to hand it to the teacher, and the sum was recorded against his name in the eighth column, as a donation of his to the Bible Society.[22]

Such charts, here described in such detail that the author must have presumed little acquaintance with their form, were becoming extremely popular in these years. Minutes of ministerial associations, which had reported the verbal accounts of local pastors about their parishes' growth and decline, were in the 1810s substituting enumerations on charts. Phrases like "we are thankful for divine blessings" were replaced by columns listing the number of new members received by baptism or by letter (recommended from another church), or exclusion, and even the money raised for charitable endeavors. At a single glance, one could now see that some churches were thriving and others declining; one could even discern patterns, like the obvious relationship of Sabbath schools to increased church membership.[23]

In the Andover case, this statistical reckoning went further. Given the limited resources of the children, "the great question was," according to the

Society, "*How shall we get money to give?*" The committee then outlined an elaborate plan by which children could transfer money in their name from the treasury of the Society for Doing Good to their Bible Society by attaining a certain score in the columns of their teachers' books; for example, "each scholar who should be at the head of his class more than six times, should be considered as earning six cents," and so on. "In these ways," the reporter noted, "they might by their diligence and good conduct greatly benefit themselves, and at the same time be constantly earning something for the heathen. Both teachers and scholars when the system was unfolded entered into it with very great ardor, and the result has surpassed the most sanguine expectations." The magazine account concluded, naturally, with a numerical accounting of all these accomplishments. [24]

No one in Andover pretended that the benefit earned by "diligence and good conduct" was the same as salvation; no one accused Justin Edwards of preaching a "gospel of works." And yet, this scheme of linking religious instruction with competition in earning money for missionary work was a compelling mechanism that came close to encouraging children to see religion as a set of finite tasks.

The entire activity of the religious society was transformed into a chain of mechanically linked devices. The children memorized, but not for their own sake or even primarily to assist their own religious development; rather, their work contributed to a symbolic earning of money to buy Bibles for such far-off lands as Persia and Ceylon, aiding missionaries to establish religious services and eventually perhaps bringing heathens to Christ. Although the vision of the final end—the conversion of the whole world to the Word of God— was used to entice parishioners to enter upon this obstacle course of charitable effort, it was also true that these hurdles provided a set of intermediate achievements all along the way. The parish and the child could take pride in the number of verses mastered, the amount of money raised, the number of Bibles sent, the number of religious missions assisted, and the number of Oriental natives converted. [25]

The quantitative representation of religious progress assisted parishioners continually to see and be gratified by their contributions. For moralism, this approach supplanted that of the "gospel scheme" favored by their doctrinalist forebears. The latter, we recall, had promised sinners that their personal journey on the way to regeneration could be accompanied by a clear and logical arrangement of the signs of grace. Ultimately, the rebuffs that sinners encountered made them understand their entire dependence upon the Lord for this "great change." In the moralist scheme, exactly the opposite was true. At every stage, one could see where and how one's steady progress had gone.

Rather than being frustrated continually, however, he could feel that only his own weakness in pushing forward could keep him from achieving the final reward. The example of Benjamin Franklin, whose autobiography had similarly charted his behavioral progress toward "moral perfection," not that of Jonathan Edwards, underlay the moralist strategy. The demand for a total, life-altering, dramatic change was quenched by the moralists, and more stable sources of assurance were offered.[26]

The result of these encouragements to personal consecration clearly diminished the importance of man's encounter with the divine. The pledge to total abstinence, the essential act of the temperance crusade, was an example. "Teetotalism," says Charles Foster, "was a romantic affair: it required the same type of emotional upheaval as religious conversion, resulting in a decision to lead a new life." But it was not a religious conversion, in fact, and the new life to which one was now committed involved only (relatively small) behavioral changes in most people. Similarly, the expansion of Sabbath schools everywhere in the northern states in the 1820s and 1830s lowered the level of religious commitment by simplifying the message of Christianity for both children and their parents. The technique of developing special aids for special audiences divided the congregation, but invariably it lowered the level of religious literacy. Theology became the province only of the seminarian; for most parishioners, the insipid little tales that filled Sabbath school tracts and the simple-minded moralistic lessons they pressed unsinewed the "tough muscle" of the minds that Horace Bushnell remembered among his childhood neighbors. Of course, the eventual benefit of the Sabbath school materials, of the tracts that went with them, of the Sabbath Manual, Temperance Manual, and even Bible Manual that were edited to structure one's observance of these religious duties—the benefit of all was surely attracting larger and larger numbers into the evangelical church world. But it was an invitation to a much more intellectually modest religious community.[27]

All this institutional inventiveness was devoted to the goal of achieving confidence. The dilemma of moralism was that mediate successes only reinforced the need for further exercises of will. Assurance was never entirely possible so long as each moment was a new test; small deviations from propriety might loosen the hold of good habits altogether. So the moralists continued to invent new tests, in order to achieve a continuing series of new gratifications. Each one in turn became the "one thing needful," as they liked to say, for the victory of Christianity over the world. The enthusiasm of the evangelical community was ceaselessly exploited as these challenges were posed, met, and then overwhelmed by succeeding ones.[28]

The alternative for the evangelical moralists was to rest in their confidence, to fall back into the relaxed expenditure of their accumulated virtue. Here was the crux of their differences with the Unitarians, who shared many of their moralist precepts. An excellent illustration of this divergence was published in the New Haven religious paper, the *Christian Spectator*, in 1819.

It is believed, that very few christians will question the propriety of imploring a blessing, and returning thanks at the table. Many professors of religion, however, live in the daily, or partial neglect of these duties. The excuse of some of those, who thus live, is, that they have not the *confidence* necessary to the performance of the duties; though, perhaps, they can rise with the greatest composure, in a town meeting, at the bar, or in a legislative assembly.—Surely, such men, and indeed all others, who would shelter themselves under the plea of *diffidence*, would do well to inquire, whether this plea will exculpate them in the eye of God.

The word *diffidence* helps us place this passage historically, for the term was often used by Unitarians themselves to explain why some men could not bring themselves to expose their personal religious experience before others. For example, Aaron Bancroft complained about the typical religious enthusiast who "too often in an unchristian manner censures those who from *diffidence* are restrained from rising to his lofty pretensions." To which the evangelical might reply, as the *Christian Spectator* said, that such men had enough confidence to act in public spheres but were diffident only about religion.[29]

For the evangelical moralist, the test was to put more and more of one's will and one's confidence or faith into sanctified activities. Alternately, one could declare that such occasions as dining were sacred and consecrate them with special ceremonies like saying grace before meals. In this way, the whole texture of everyday life could become a seamless religious cloak. The Unitarians feared the excessive pickiness of the evangelical model of moral action; setting up tests for everything only inhibited, they thought, the realm of private judgment and human freedom. "The propensity in our fellow-creatures, which we have most to dread," said William Ellery Channing, is "the propensity to rule, to tyrannize, to war with the freedom of their equals, to make themselves standards for other minds, to be lawgivers, instead of brethren and friends, to their race." Channing's "Remarks on Associations," from which this complaint comes, made clear his view that such tyranny was the real work of the evangelically dominated benevolent societies of the day.[30]

The evangelicals, for their part, had to fear another sort of tyranny; when they remarked on the way in which diffident men could dominate the political and judicial forums in New England, they showed their fright at the Unitarian eminence in public life. Channing preached his famous "heretical" sermon, "Unitarian Christianity," in 1819. The loss of all but one of Boston's churches to Channing's liberal allies was profoundly threatening to the evangelicals within Congregationalism. Heirs of the Puritan theocracy, they had seen the Standing Order in Connecticut collapse the year before, and in 1820 they heard the awful news that the Unitarian-dominated Supreme Judicial Court of Massachusetts had ruled that the property of the First Church of

Dedham resided with the liberal *parish* rather than the evangelical *church* members. The evangelicals' ability to influence religious matters seemed to be fading. Religion itself was at stake, and it could only be saved by insisting on the dedication to religious ends as the central act of a man's life.[31]

In conclusion, the liberals felt that secular habits of steady conscientiousness could be applied to sacred and profane affairs alike; in fact, the difference between sacred and profane would then disappear completely. The evangelicals, in their moralistic rhetoric, instead took the habits and skills of secular life and applied them to an ever more rigidly defined sphere of religious experience. Such a strategy was an effort, ultimately, to harness the energy of millions of American wills to the goal of the conversion of the world to Christianity. The exuberance of the nineteenth century could then be channeled into activity sanctioned by the evangelicals and poured into vials of their own making. This union of the religious and the secular was a bold stroke, worthy of the age, and destined to promote powerfully the moralistic intentions of American government and the repressiveness of middle-class manners. But its impact on lessening religious piety as an end in itself cannot be overestimated.[32]

Chapter Eleven

Enlisting Character in the Moral Community

IT IS APPROPRIATE that we conclude our study of moralism where we began it, redefining the *social* experience of religion. From start to finish, the moralists' image of a new sort of religious consciousness was a picture of people assembled in groups, glancing at one another and competing to be the finest exemplars of propriety. Joining a league of moralists, by either conversion or personal consecration, was never a passive affair like one's *espousal* to the orthodox church. No scowling deacons sought to pinion one's arms into an expression of bewilderment at the complexities of Calvinist doctrine.

Instead, as Lyman Beecher told his listeners in East Hampton, "in societies of the description we are considering, every member is a soldier, every soldier a sentinel." In the thousands of benevolent and moral improvement societies formed in the northern states between 1800 and 1860, and indeed in the churches themselves as they adjusted to disestablishment and were reorganized on the "voluntary principle" of support, membership involved signing up, *enlisting,* for service in the battles of the Lord. Whenever one enlisted in the moral army, the characteristic procedure was an act of one's will—swearing to an oath, taking a pledge, signing a petition, subscribing to an expression of sentiments.[1]

But if personal exertion was preeminent, it was more the witnessing of one's willfulness, and less the willfulness itself, that was to be the central tenet of the movement. As Beecher's phrase indicated, moral soldiering was generally reduced to serving as a sentinel.

Such restraint was a part of the aesthetic of moralist faith, akin to defining that faith as "confidence." And in other crucial ways, the social life of evangelical religion resembled the aesthetic we discovered in the self's relation to God or in the particular event's relation to habits. In both cases the lesser body, the human self or the individual event, was connected by a modestly assertive commitment to the larger body, God or steady habits. The larger then sustained the smaller by providing a stable field for the exercise of continuing and consistent acts of faith.

In social terms, this meant that moralists demanded that individuals submit their activity to the judgment and sanction of the group. The vigor of the community as a whole, then, would validate individual expressions of moral behavior. Proper behavior was action in behalf of the community's standards, not action to benefit one's self-interest.

The inclusivist impulse within moralism gathered within the moral society and the church many who could not evidence the strenuous soul-shattering conversion experience required by the orthodox. In this chapter, we shall look at the way that impulse drove the moralists toward a national and indeed universal expansiveness. The moral consensus of active Christians in New England villages would be the model, they thought, for social and religious transformation of the entire nation. This would usher in a millennium of American proportions: the entire globe could become imbued with their enormous energy.

The early nineteenth century was the age, preeminently, of the rural *village.* The *town,* in New England a unit of geography and administration, not of settlement, now came to have a population clustered in distinct villages within its boundaries. In the early eighteenth century, population growth, the weakening of Puritan authority, and the end of the Indian threat had encouraged a disposal of settlements. With the new century, this trend was reversed. New Englanders began to cluster, in village centers, around the intersections of new roads, and near larger commercial and industrial establishments; that movement can still be seen in the nineteenth-century Federal and Greek Revival architectural styles in such villages today. The adoption of district schools, too, meant that there were facilities near every such collection of houses for educating the young.[2]

The new textile manufacturing villages, founded after 1812 in any place in southern New England where water ran swiftly (and that was almost everywhere), demonstrated this new model of community building best. Mill owners frequently included company stores, churches, and schools in their plans, along with the mills themselves and boardinghouses and tenements for the workers' families. Similar conglomerations of buildings also grew up, though less coherently, in hundreds of rural village centers.[3]

In the capacious old town of Woodstock, Connecticut, for example, the old common and graveyard on Woodstock Hill were now ringed by houses, churches, a post office, a law office, taverns, shops, and a local academy. But there were also village centers in South and West Woodstock, in Woodstock Valley, Harrisville, Kenyonville, and North and East Woodstock; the last four were manufacturing villages.[4]

This era of community building was also perforce a great period of church building. No one expected all the faithful to climb Woodstock Hill for every Sabbath service. The proliferation of Congregational churches within a single town, and of the ever more numerous Universalist, Methodist, Episcopal, and Baptist societies that competed with them, dissolved the ancient association of the first church with the town. There were two fundamental results of this change, both of which shaped the social and political strategy of evangelical moralism.

First, the religious community became more visibly coherent. One shared worship and meetings with one's neighbors, people whom one might see on a much more regular basis in the other aspects of everyday life. They were more often one's trading partners, especially now as commercial opportunities expanded and more New Englanders worked for cash income. They were one's childhood friends, schoolmates, and possible spouses. One could see them at political rallies, lyceum lectures, reading and social circles, and Masonic lodge meetings. Indeed they were virtually inescapable. Everyone noticed when one purchased the newest styles of English printed cottons at the store, and everyone saw the dress made from it at temperance meetings. Life in a New England village became a constant display of one's taste and one's virtue.[5]

Moralism could build a sense of community out of such relatively trivial pieces, in the process identifying one's taste in cottons and economic standing with one's moral fervor. An inevitable advantage fell to those with the most refined tastes and disposable cash, as well as the best speaking manner and personal "carriage," so long as none of these violated local norms.

Second, the causes for which one contended could no longer be contained inside the boundaries of one's hometown. Just as the goods purchased and the styles applied came from elsewhere, so too would one's participation in moral reform gain status by being played out on a larger stage. Voluntarism put a premium on achievement, and over the years each community was challenged to do more and more for ultimate rather than proximate goals. The variety of benevolent enterprises, as we shall see, attracted wider and wider participation; for example, if Mr. Williams was not interested in contributing to the education of young ministerial students, perhaps he would give something to save the souls of seamen or heathens. Success was always just over the next hurdle, the "one thing needful" to bring the world to Christ. It was unworthy to devote oneself to creating a single holy village in rural Connecticut when the whole world thirsted for help. Conversely, neighbors had to cork the bottles of local tipplers and scowl fiercely at Sunday skylarkers lest the reputation of the entire community be tarnished.

These twin impulses, toward greater intimacy in social life and wider identification with distant causes, transformed the orthodox understanding of the local church. In comparing nineteenth-century evangelicalism with the covenant ideology of the Puritans, Perry Miller writes that the religious "were forced to recognize that in fact they now dealt with the Deity only as particular individuals gathered for historical, capricious reasons into this or that communion. They had to realize, at first painfully, that as a united people they had no contractual relationship with the Creator, and that consequently a national controversy with Him could no longer exist."[6]

The "Church of Christ in ——" no longer had special, inherent status because it incarnated God's ancient covenant with New England. Its claim would now rest on activity and effectiveness, not on prerogative. This turn of events was drawn in sharp relief by the disestablishment of the Standing Order churches. The evangelicals had been terrified of separating church and state, eliminating for the first time in New England religious teaching as a public responsibility. But separation came formally to Connecticut in 1818, New Hampshire the following year, and Massachusetts in 1833 (after a near miss in 1820).

The result confounded the evangelical clergy. Forced to rely now upon voluntary contributions rather than tax support, they found themselves even better off than before. Now commitment to the church, rather than status in the community, would dictate key roles in religious life, and ministers discovered that they were more comfortable associating with those who wanted to work with them than they had been with the elite social leaders of the previous generation.

Disestablishment forced the Congregationalists to compete with other denominations. Now every conversion, every moral reform, was a great achievement. The churches ceased to think defensively, fearing the loss of their rightful position in the community. Now they could be aggressive, seeing every unchurched person as a possible adherent and every vice as an opportunity to reform. Each achievement was a milestone on the path to something much grander if more distant—the reformation of the entire world, the millennium.

Following disestablishment, local religious societies became more embedded in larger networks, and parish life became more and more standardized. The training of ministers through the new theological seminaries and their licensing only after two or more years of study brought a uniformity to their qualifications. It became extremely rare for a minister to remain with one congregation all his professional life, and only then, as with Joel Hawes in Hartford, by resisting countless blandishments and invitations to assume higher offices. Parishioners, too, were moving about more in the 1820s and after; the tenure of church members was sharply reduced when it could so frequently be terminated by "dismission" to another congregation rather than death. Religious society clerks now struck long torpid members from the church rolls, without the bother about church trials for "absenting oneself from gospel privileges" that were usual around the turn of the nineteenth century.[7]

A new national consciousness emerged within the moralist persuasion. Newspapers were crucial in nurturing this consciousness. As Charles Roy Keller observes, "the years 1815–1816 saw many revivals, while the inauguration of the *Religious Intelligencer* [in Connecticut] and the beginning of religious news columns in secular newspapers in 1816 testified to the public interest in the subject of religion." It did more. By emphasizing events, newspapers discounted the value of introspection and theological reading. "Religious intelligence," wrote the anxious Alvan Hyde in 1821,

> is diffused in every part of the State, and by almost every newspaper; but after all, I greatly fear, many, by reading these papers weekly, as they would some interesting novel, are rapidly losing their relish for more solid reading, and that the distinguishing doctrines of the cross, so ably defended by Edwards, Bellamy, Hopkins, and many others now no more, are beginning to be crowded into the background.

As the theological giants faded, so too did the preeminence of the clergy in local religious affairs. The newspapers overturned the hierarchy of learning in a town just as surely as the charitable society overturned the hierarchy of social leadership; they forced an obedience to national norms that undercut local peculiarities, and this effectively standardized and flattened the quality of religious knowledge and action everywhere in New England.[8]

In purely religious terms, denominationalism posed theoretical problems for Congregationalists. How could they insist on their most ancient credo, the independence of each church, when their pastors were trained by professional academics, supplied by a central office for short periods, and increasingly alien from the social life of their temporary installations? No such worries applied to the "benevolent empire," the enormous bureaucracy of social and moral reform that grew up between 1812 and 1860. Here moralism could exercise its magic mix of local initiative, and state, regional, and national leadership without constraint. Again let us turn to Lyman Beecher as a prime innovative spirit.

In 1808, Beecher's ambition overcame his allegiance to the traditional practice of lifetime tenure in clerical office and took him to Litchfield, an active and affluent shire town in northwestern Connecticut. Litchfield was a propitious base. From here, Beecher threw himself into clerical politics, particularly propagandizing for his pet scheme of establishing moral societies. In the next decade, dozens of such groups were planted all over New England, even in remote villages where vice could hardly have brought sinners much pleasure. They were advertised, so to speak, in religious periodicals like the *Connecticut Evangelical Magazine* and at ministerial conferences, legislative sessions, and college commencements. At the Yale Commencement in

1812, Beecher persuaded leaders of the evangelical clergy and their lay allies to establish a statewide body, the Connecticut Society for the Reformation of Morals, to urge enforcement of state laws against immorality. It also would be, Beecher hoped, "the parent and patron of local auxiliary societies."[9]

This word "auxiliary" was a leap ahead for the evangelicals. Did Beecher mean that local societies would be merely the assistants, the servants, of the state society? He would not have admitted as much. But he did know that the battle for moral reformation needed stronger rhetorical weapons than the disapproving frowns of next-door neighbors. Beecher set the proper tone for the new society in his keynote sermon, "A Reformation of Morals Practicable and Indispensable." All the passion of the traditional New England jeremiad came through the Litchfield parson. "Our fathers established, and for a great while preserved," he wrote, "the most perfect state of society, probably, that has ever existed in this fallen world. . . . New-England can retain her pre-eminence, only by upholding those institutions and habits which produced it." This was the stuff of a typical election sermon, in which ministers instructed legislators and state leaders each year to trust to the pious past as a guide into the future. But now the rhetoric served an organization designed to apply its lessons energetically. What issued from the capital was no longer simply a dispassionate account of what transpired in the state. The state society wrote reports, appealed for contributions, rented offices, and hired staff. It was a lobbying group, not a prophetic voice of condemnation.[10]

Connecticut, and to a lesser extent Massachusetts, had always had associations of ministers, joined together to examine candidates and approve ecclesiastical practice. The clergy had always had a statewide (or colonywide) presence in the tradition of election sermons before the governor and legislature. And the Second Awakening, as we have seen, had already spurred the creation of new publications and seminaries. But the organizations of the 1810s were different; their work was no longer the product of settled local ministers. Church bureaucrats, professional academics, and missionaries sponsored by these associations—all without local pastoral responsibilities—were coming to play a larger and larger role in the intellectual and organizational life of the Congregational Church. Above parishioners, deacons, and clergy, another tier was being added to the church as it became a denomination.

On the local level, reform efforts were soon dominated by the energies of Christian women. New England had long inhibited the participation of women in the public life of the community—in voting and office holding, in speaking in public and discoursing in such "public" languages as theology, law, or political theory, even (except for widows and spinsters) in many aspects of economic life. The turn toward the reform of individual moral behavior, always a province of female concern, was an opening for female leadership and organization on the local level. In town after town, female charitable societies took the lead in the 1810s, creating virtually another church alongside that of the ministers and deacons. The state and national organizations were still led by men, but as their local auxiliaries were more clearly in the control of female Christians they issued fewer appeals for a return to the "New England of our fathers." Increasingly they called upon Christians to exemplify in their religious life the same exuberance and industry they were so boldly demonstrating in other aspects of their current lives.[11]

Although the real work of reform, shaming the sinful and inhibiting the tempted, was still the responsibility of the local society, it was being urged to such efforts by reformist energies emanating from elsewhere. The activity of local benevolent and charitable organizations became harmonized with the regional and national societies housed in second-story offices in old Hartford, Boston, New York, or London. These in turn sent evangelical reform into heathen territories around the globe. For more than twenty-five years after establishing the first moral societies, this union of rural communities with the enthusiastic world-reforming energies of urban centers dominated New England religious life.

There were societies for every conceivable charitable or reformist intention, but they can be divided roughly into two types: some tried to make rural New Englanders act like mannerly city folk; the others tried to make unmannerly heathens, some of them in cities, act like Yankee villagers. In the former we may include the "cent" or education societies that collected pennies (later dollars), used clothing, and volumes of classical literature to assist young men with empty purses in their ambitions for a clerical education. This was vital to maintain the supply of ministers for New England pulpits. Other examples of such local benevolence were the newly instituted Sabbath schools instructing youth in Christian morality, rather than forcing them to sit through largely unintelligible doctrinal sermons; maternal associations, which confirmed the mutual responsibility of townswomen for their children's upbringing and evangelical conversion; and prayer and inquiry meetings organized specifically for young or old, for men or women. By the 1820s, the most important schemes were temperance and Sabbath observance societies. These began by claiming that reform would improve the community, but progressively they focused on the benefits to Christians themselves of such improvement.

The second type of benevolent endeavor, those charged with broadcasting the message of small town Congregationalist reformism, focused on the domestic and foreign mission societies. To these were added in the decade after 1815 major efforts to translate, publish, and distribute Bibles and religious tracts. Finally, in this class of organizations we may collect the diverse associations to protect young men in the cities from Satan, to save the Satanic women of the waterfront streets from ensnaring these young men in their vices, to convert the Jews in preparation for the millennium, and to resettle American blacks in Africa. The American Colonization Society, charged with this last undertaking, could have been the collective name for all these voluntary associations. They each proposed to universalize the social patterns and behavioral norms of prosperous New England villages. Evangelism implied the nationally sponsored transformation by missionaries of distinct local cultures anywhere in the world into replications of their auxiliary societies.

Every New England town supported a number of these organizations. Despite their variety, these societies often began the same way, in an appeal for the church to rally itself on behalf of some pressing need, some common ideal, some higher goal, ultimately "the one thing needful to bring the world to Christ." At first, this appeal was often delivered from the pulpit at the conclusion of the Sunday afternoon sermon. Harboring in his breast the enthusiasm of his fellow ministers for this idea since his last meeting with the county association, the pastor had been waiting for the propitious moment to propose a new association. In later years, the role of instigator might be played by a visiting preacher, a lyceum lecturer, or even a paid agent of a regional or national organization. Those most thoroughly convinced, perhaps the same folks who offered the speaker home hospitality during his visit, would then take responsibility for the organizational work itself. Or, alternately, some respected citizen would draw a copy of the latest *Panoplist* from the capacious pockets of his cloak and read aloud the report of some equally respected citizen in another town about the founding of a local union for some specific benevolent purpose.

Each week or month, the recording secretary would carefully count the attendance for the regular meetings of these societies and enter it in new ledger books bought for this purpose. Next to the names were the columns of regular contributions. Below, the secretary inscribed the minutes of each meeting—the resolutions adopted, the officers elected, and incidental expenditures accounted for. An honored person was entrusted to convey the group's collection to the eminences in the capital. In the front or the back of the book, the constitution and by-laws of the society were often copied with care from the models provided in evangelical magazines.[12]

But the ledger book was chiefly a record of activity. Every entry was a sentence whose subject was a Christian and whose predicate was a step toward millennium. How different this was from the church records of the eighteenth century, with their scratchy lists of births, baptisms, members, and deaths. There the church seemed to be acting in place of its people, reproducing, educating, dying as they did. Now the moral society, or the church, was only an accommodation, an avenue, for the actions of energetic, world-changing Christians.

What had begun as a warm gathering of neighbors to discuss their moral failings in East Hampton and other remote places was thus becoming a way of identifying with events on the larger stage—not, as during the revival seasons, because God's grace showered down all over New England and because the gospel plan was universally applicable, but because of human organizational effort.

Heretofore, the Congregational Church had rested in a specific, clearly bounded landscape. With the moral society movement and its successors, the environment for religious activity became more abstract and distant. The church lost its primary rootedness in its local terrain and became absorbed in some mental construction, "the friends of order," "the partisans of faith," "the good and wise people of Connecticut." By institutionalizing the moral consensus outside the realm of formal religious and political authority, "community" became a sensation, an abstraction, no longer equivalent to "locality." The moralists were among the first Americans to identify a hometown primarily by its "sense of community."

The new moralist associations never have precise physical form; there is no way to picture them standing together in a particular place or speaking in the same voice. Nor are they tied together, like "the Kingdom of God," by an invisible spiritual tie even stronger than physical proximity. Like the state and federal governments, the regional and national associations do meet. But these are gatherings of representatives of local groups, each one charged with confirming by nod and by vote the chapter's agreement with the larger body's action and returning home to confirm the local society's activity with a blessing from the central headquarters.

The moral society was an important milestone in the history of evangelical religion. Organizationally, it had many innovative qualities. Its membership was open to all those of respectable intentions, whether or not they had undergone an intense conversion experience. Its group unity came from commonsense judgments about behavior, rather than complex doctrinal tenets, and it relied upon mutual adherence to the evolving customs of agricultural communities increasingly enmeshed in a regional economy.

For the next decade, until the late 1820s, the evangelicals continued to believe that morality was an attribute of communities as well as of individuals and that a person could not sustain his rectitude unless surrounded by the baleful glare of others in his town. The moralists were successful in widening and intensifying the activity of the religious community. In his forty-four years in the Hartford pulpit, beginning in 1818, Joel Hawes reckoned that he had added more than six hundred members to the church. But this represented, he conceded, only an increase from 20 to 30 percent in the proportion of parish adults who attained full communion. Even with such great success in leading religious revivals and incorporating new members into church life, Hawes (and others of his ilk) must have realized that there was no hope of winning all to the standard of the Lord. The conversion of the whole world was hardly nearer because of such incremental and local success.[13]

In the 1820s, when this recognition began to dawn on the evangelicals, it called forth a variety of responses. The first was to plunge ahead anyway and measure one's success another way. Moralism could be the dominant, even if only implicit, ethos of the best people. Joel Hawes observed that the middle and upper classes were much better behaved in the 1860s than they had been fifty years earlier, although the life of the lower classes showed little or no improvement during that period. Even for those who never graced the doorways of the new Greek and Gothic Revival churches, middle-class standing could be associated with the values espoused by moralist ministers—work, self-control, individual moral responsibility, social progress, the link of reputation and social standing, and family discipline. All who wanted to join the group had to pass the scrutiny of those already admitted. And what happened to the rest?[14]

Over the years, a new and haughtier attitude developed. As religion came more and more to facilitate the achievement of social status through behavioral reform, many moralists turned inward. One might as well set adrift those unfortunates who did not subscribe to their code of propriety. A modern student of the movement summarizes, "That Temperance was one part of improving status was evident in several changes in the movement during the 1830s and 1840s. In this period it changed from one in which the rich aimed at reforming the poor into one in which members aimed at their own reformation." In 1826, for example, when the American Society for the Promotion of Temperance was being founded, its leading supporters announced that "Our main object is, not to reform inebriates, but to induce all temperate people to continue temperate by practicing total abstinence: the drunkards, if not reformed, will die, and the land be free."[15]

This cockiness relied upon a well-tried evangelical tactic. By requiring a higher level of consecrating self-commitment, the virtuous could be drawn to the moralist camp without a difficult and introspective conversion experience. In addition, moralists could thus evidence their trust in God's blessing of their cause. Drunkenness in the lowly was their own fault; it would be punished in due course. Using the same argument, it might be said that the churches should not attend to the conversion of sinners at all but simply confer their holiness on those already within the fold (and on their children), letting the sinful die off. In fact, as the cities in which they preached became filled with immigrants of ethnic, religious, and economic backgrounds different from the majority of church congregants, many mainline Protestant denominations would turn inward toward their own members. Not surprisingly, then, urban ministers like the older Lyman Beecher or Horace Bushnell of Hartford could begin to imagine a "race war," in which Anglo-Saxon Protestants were besieged by untamed Catholics in a contest for dominance. As moralism became a tribal ethos for New Englanders, it laid the groundwork for its own form of nativism.

Still, such self-confidence had to contend with older conventions of stewardship. With the rapid development in the 1820s of industrial capitalism, that is, of the concentration of ownership of the resources of production—land for mill villages, machinery, and control of distribution networks—evangelical moralism began to play a major role in American economic conflicts. Among the class of factory owners, many appear to have been ardent evangelicals, and not a few began to insist that their workmen subscribe not merely to a new regimen of regular hours of work but to proper behavior even in their time away from work. The contest over drink in flour mills, foundries, and textile factories spilled over into a ceaseless battle between two distinct cultures: one capitalist, evangelical Calvinist, and Whig, bitterly opposed to labor unions; and the other freethinking or low church (usually Methodist or Universalist, but eventually Roman Catholic), Democratic, antireform, and built on the foundations of workingmen's associations.[16]

But the most powerful response of moralism was politics. From his first sermons, Lyman Beecher had envisioned a way for moralists to move from the vigorous local community.

> But, it may be asked, What can we do to preserve the nation; a small town, and one only among thousands? We can do our part. The nation is formed by the addition of such small districts; it is preserved by their purity, and destroyed by their vices. Every town is a member of the body politic, and, if a healthful member, is a great national blessing; let every town reform, and the reformation will be national. Who can tell how far the influence of our example may extend? How great a matter a little fire may kindle? Who can tell how much kindness God has for us?[17]

But as the years went by, it became harder to assume that communities as well as individuals might have moral characters, might be themselves units of the body politic. By 1812, Beecher was complaining that local officials were too lax, perhaps because they feared political retribution for applying laws against immorality. "To secure, then, the execution of the laws against immorality in a time of prevailing moral declension," he said, "an influence is needed distinct from that of the government, independent of popular suffrage, superior in potency to individual efforts, and competent to enlist and preserve the public opinion on the side of law and order."[18]

By the mid-1820s, evangelicals were ready to give up the struggle to add East Hampton to New Haven to Litchfield and produce a millennium. As Beecher wrote in 1826, "Voluntary associations to support the magistrate in the execution of the law are useful, but, after all, are ineffectual; for though in a single town or state they may effect a temporary reformation, it requires an effort to make them universal, and to keep up their energy, which never has and never will be made." By 1826, he preferred the legislative prohibition of all ardent spirits to the work of small groups of like-minded vigilantes as a method for ridding the country of drunkenness.[19]

In fact, it had not taken Beecher as long as twenty years to discover such a relationship of local morality to changes in the national life. Much earlier, he had recognized that small groups in each town could not rally sufficient energy to transform the nation without a suitable *national* target. Even the "hardened, open champion of vice," who could be found skulking around the nearby cider mill, did not inspire enough fear to call forth a continuing moralistic fury at home, much less to sustain a national crusade against vice.

Beecher's first national target was Aaron Burr, the vice-president of the United States, who had killed Alexander Hamilton in a duel in 1804. The duellist, said the East Hampton parson, violated not only the sixth commandment but a more mundane political principle, "Equal laws are essential to civil liberty." For Beecher, the duellist's claim to exemption from equal laws was, as we have seen, a cardinal (and representative) offense against local public opinion. Furthermore, because norms of personal conduct inspired by the local evangelicals were to dominate such public opinion, the offense against the republican ethos of equal laws was equivalent to an opposition to the moralists' code. Through a canny set of associations, Beecher had linked evangelical morality and republican citizenship and made them mutually interdependent. The "remedy for duelling," then was to deny duellists the *political* support, that is, votes, of those committed to *moral* purity.[20]

This intention to achieve religious ends through political means was, furthermore, amplified by Beecher's suggestion that all the local moral societies in the United States could focus their antagonisms at the same time and that the entire nation could then be mobilized. By the mid-1820s, with the establishment of an interdenominational "Evangelical United Front" of benevolent agencies on a state and national level, the moralists were ready to translate their opinions into true political power. In 1828, when the General Union for Promoting the Observance of the Christian Sabbath was established, therefore, it aimed at more than encouraging greater consecration of the Lord's day. It aimed to abolish, by legislation and executive action, the federal requirement that the mails arriving on a Sunday had to be sorted and handed out that day.

Beginning with a campaign to petition Congress, the Sabbatarians came eventually to throw in their weight with Andrew Jackson's opponents, the National Republicans, on this issue, but they were soundly defeated by an electoral backlash and congressional inaction. Bertram Wyatt-Brown describes the movement's results:

> It is ironic that so restrictive a cause as Sabbatarianism should lead so many pious dissenters to a deepened sense of the meaning of democracy and equal rights, but so it was. The Tappan Brothers, [William] Jay, Joshua Leavitt, [Theodore Dwight] Weld, and Garrison—and many other young, energetic reformers—took up the call for immediate eman-

cipation within a year or two of the fall of the Sabbath Union. In time, their religious prohibitions became secondary to a grander vision of a revitalized America. In the process, they learned that a Christian and a tranquil society had to rest upon morally defensible foundations or suffer ruin. Although frequently criticized for this indictment of national civil life, the religious abolitionists were not seeking to destroy government, but to expand its functions in behalf of those outside existing legal arrangements.[21]

The failure of the Sabbatarian campaign was a crucial crossroads for evangelical moralism. As Wyatt-Brown says, it led in a few years to the emergence of radical abolitionism with the call by Garrison and others for the immediate emancipation of the slaves. Garrison and many of his closest associates were not from evangelical backgrounds. Their antinomian antagonism to religious creed and ritual flowed more logically from Boston Unitarianism. But the call of immediatism was felt intensely by younger evangelicals as well, especially those who had been converted in the "new measures" revivalism of Charles G. Finney in western New York and Ohio. They had come of age within the moralist camp, and their conviction of the utter sinfulness of slavery as a violation of elemental human dignity stemmed from the teachings of Beecher and Taylor. They scorned the claims that southern society was built on honor and traditions of deference.[22]

When most older evangelicals, Beecher included, resisted immediatism, either by continuing to work for the American Colonization Society or by gradually moving toward a more moderate, *political* antislavery position, the strains within evangelical moralism came to the breaking point. Theodore Dwight Weld, the son of an orthodox Connecticut evangelical, led a secession of radical students from Lane Seminary in Cincinnati, where Beecher had recently been installed as president. Beecher, now nearly sixty, claimed to be both a colonizationist and an abolitionist, preferring the former, he said, because it did not "row upstream" against public opinion. "True wisdom," counseled the old champion, "consists in advocating a cause only so far as the community will sustain the reformer."[23]

The conflict was waged for a quarter-century longer. Abolitionism drove a wedge through evangelical moralism, pulling it toward both a greater abhorrence for slavery and for slaveholders, but also toward a conservative fear of the public and political disorder engendered by abolitionist protest. In many ways, the immediatists—with their perfectionist encouragement of the secession of small-group sectaries from established churches, openness to the woman's rights and peace movements, and sense of mystical purposiveness—resembled the devotionalists we shall explore in Part Three more than their moralist colleagues in the antislavery struggle.

Finally, in the 1860s, the evangelical crusade against slavery—understood as the application of the social aesthetic of moralism on the highest level—reached its most logical and apposite culmination in the election of Lincoln, the decision to force the South back into the Union by war, and finally the Emancipation Proclamation. At last, in the spring of 1861, the moralists could call men to the most perfect and most awesome sort of enlistment, the call to arms to defend the Christian principles of the United States. And the record of their success is to be found not merely in the reunion of the states or the freedom of the African-Americans but in the monuments that list the dozens of local youths killed in the war. These statues and obelisks, standing quietly in the centers of a thousand northern towns, are a silent reminder of the era when religion became active, when the New England village came alive as a model of a morally assertive community.[24]

PART THREE

PERSONALITY
The Economy of Devotional Experience

Chapter Twelve

Edward Payson and the Prayers of Portland

BORN IN 1783, the year of American Independence, Edward Payson was a precocious son for the Rev. Seth Payson of Rindge, New Hampshire, and his wife. He was so well tutored in the church doctrines by his father that, as his biographer recounts, young Edward "was often known to weep under the preaching of the gospel, when only three years old." He was reading a year later. Even in childhood, he hauled and hewed, cultivated and gathered in the seasons of manly work on the stony farm fields of southwestern New Hampshire. But one significant achievement, the saving experience of grace for which his parents earnestly prayed, eluded him into his late teens. And so, though he had completed his preparatory studies for college at his father's desk and at the nearby academy in New Ipswich, he was held back from college. "To give you a liberal education, while destitute of religion," Rev. Payson is said to have chided his son, "would be like putting a sword into the hands of a mad man."[1]

As for many other children of his generation, an orthodox conversion experience never did come to Edward Payson, and his father's opposition relented. Payson entered Harvard as a sophomore at age seventeen, completed his undergraduate work in 1803, and then assumed a schoolmaster's post at Portland, Maine. For three years, he tested the social waters of the seaport town, refining his manners and his skill at Federalist declamations against intemperate vice and political faction.

Payson's diary for his schoolmaster years shows deepening religious feelings. On a visit home in 1805, he professed his faith and was admitted to the Rindge church; a year later, he resigned his position in Portland and returned home to study for the ministry with his father. He was examined and licensed to preach, contemplated a missionary career, and tried his prowess as a preacher in several Massachusetts and New Hampshire pulpits, all without success. Finally, in the fall of 1807, he was recalled to Portland by the Rev. Elijah Kellogg of the Second Church to serve as a colleague pastor. "Under this accession of ministerial power," says a historian of Portland, "the society increased very rapidly, and Mr. Payson showed that he possessed the elements of a powerful and persuasive minister; his society and church became by far the largest in the State, and himself the most popular preacher of his day."[2]

Such success was fitting for the booming city growing up along Casco Bay. Payson was only one of many emigrants from the New Hampshire, Vermont, and Maine hinterland who were swelling Portland's population to more than 7,000 in 1810, about twice what it had been a decade before. Portland was half the size of Portsmouth, New Hampshire, in the 1790 census, but it had passed its coastal rival by 1810. In the year of Payson's ordination, Timothy Dwight revisited Portland for the first time in ten years. "No place in our route, hitherto," he noted, "could for its improvements be compared with Portland. We found the buildings extended quite to the cove, doubled in their number, and still more increased in their appearance. Few towns in New England are equally beautiful and brilliant. Its wealth and business are probably quadrupled."[3]

Even so, commercial prosperity was an uncertain phenomenon, and only weeks after entering his new station as colleague pastor Payson wrote home that "the prospect of war has produced here such a scene of wretchedness as I never before witnessed."

> A large number of the most wealthy merchants have already failed, and numbers more are daily following, so that we are threatened with universal bankruptcy. Two failures alone have thrown at least three hundred persons, besides sailors, out of employ; and you may hence conceive, in some measure, the distress which the whole number must occasion. The poor-house is already full, and hundreds are yet to be provided for, who have depended upon their own labor for daily bread, and who have neither the means of supporting themselves here, nor of removing into the country. Many, who have been brought up in affluence, are now dependent upon the cold courtesy of creditors for a protection from the inclemency of the season.

The frequency of such cycles of confidence and panic must have bewildered those who grew up in the relatively stable economic world of the countryside. Payson's prospects suddenly were clouded, for in the city crisis was contagious. "I have scarcely a hope of receiving more than enough to pay my board, if I should stay till next spring," he wrote; and speaking of his senior pastor, he noted that "Mr. K. will want all his salary to support himself, as he fears that all his property is swallowed up in the general destruction."[4]

But worst of all, the panic threatened to unglue the social ties of Portland altogether. In Payson's words, "These failures have brought to light many instances of dishonesty among those in whose integrity unbounded confidence was placed. And now all confidence is lost; no man will trust his neighbor; but every one takes even his brother by the throat, saying, 'Pay me that thou owest.' But I cannot describe, and I doubt whether you can conceive, of the distress we are in." For a moralist, such a wholesale loss of confidence would have been a disastrous portent, a crippling of religious as well as social order, but Payson was no moralist. Instead, he saw the economic blight as a spiritual opportunity. In January 1808, Payson wrote home again that "the tumult in town has subsided into a dead calm; the embargo has put a stop to every thing like business, and people have now nothing to do but attend to religion; and we endeavor to give them meetings enough, since they have leisure to attend them. Next week, we purpose to keep a town fast, on account of our distressed situation. I am not without hopes that these things may be overruled to bring about a more extensive reformation. The attention appears to continue, and we hear of new instances of persons under concern." To accomplish this, of course, Kellogg and Payson had to sever the gospel message from the troubles of the commercial traffic. Though the customs duties collected in Portland declined from $342,909 in 1806 to one-tenth of that in 1808, religious activity increased correspondingly; twenty-nine sinners were brought to Christ in the first year of Payson's ministry.[5]

Of course, successful economic years brought their own trials. "You can scarcely form an idea," Payson wrote in 1823, "how soporific the air of a seaport is, nor of the irresistible force with which the world assails Christians in such a place as this. The moment they step out of doors it rushes in at their eyes and ears, in ten thousand shapes; so that, unless their hearts are pre-occupied with better things, they are filled with it in a moment." Religious life, in this view, was delicately counterpoised to secular activity. In fact, by the tone of Payson's words, one might infer that the secular sphere was the immaterial one, transversed by darting phantasms that distracted men from the truer sphere of "better things."[6]

When Payson, ignoring the common sense of Portland, viewed business life as the less real world, he was rejecting as well the effort of evangelical moralists to adjust religion to that world. Payson's mode of religious consciousness was just as dependent as Lyman Beecher's upon the development of American commerce and industry, but he refused to model his faith on the economy of business ledgers. Religion was for him on a see-saw with business, bound together to the ground but going in opposite directions.

For Payson, religion was different from such ordinary life tasks as making, buying, and selling. Still, it was a way of occupying one's ordinary time, not a metaphysical experience extending in significance before and beyond the cradle and the grave. Religion was, in short, a thing to do—not the only thing to do, but the best. Furthermore, it was worth doing for its own sake, not— as the moralists would claim—because piety had any beneficial effect on the rest of one's life.

Such an idea of religion was, as Payson's letters show, built upon an antagonism to the worldly concerns of ordinary life. Whether in prosperous or declining times, secular activity was to Payson "dead" or "soporific." To withdraw from the world, then, was not to seek for stillness, according to the orthodox formula. The realm of activity for Payson was the sphere of religion, the arena for the deepest sort of excitement.

In these ways, Payson's religion was best suited for those on the fringes of the economy, dependent upon mercantile fortunes but not directly involved in calculating profit and loss. In times of stress, such people needed the security and "engagedness" of personal religion. So, when Payson was so gloomy about his temporal prospects, he told his relatives, "do not feel one emotion of sorrow on my account, but rather join with me in blessing God that he keeps me quiet, resigned, and even happy, in the midst of these troubles." The experience of worldly trials only confirmed the superiority of the spiritual life: "I thought I knew, before, that this world was treacherous, and its enjoyments transitory; but these things have taught me this truth so much plainer, and weaned me so much more from creature dependencies, that I desire to consider them among my chief mercies."[7]

Aside from professional men like ministers, those most likely to adopt this form of religiosity were women, and Payson's preaching was exceptionally popular with Portland's better classes of females. When Sarah Connell Ayer arrived in Portland in 1811, she was "much gratified to learn the flourishing state of religion in this town." Joining Payson's church, her diary records frequently that she "experienced the salutary effect of religious society." And, one evening, when she stopped to pick up her friend Mrs. Willis on the way to one of Payson's evening lectures, she heard an irreligious husband complain that the minister was "the author of what he term'd his wife's superstition and enthusiasm." Mr. Willis "looks on evening meetings," said Mrs. Ayers, "as the bane of order and morality. However, he consented that Mrs. Willis should go with us. I never enjoyed a meeting more." Mrs. Ayer copied down Payson's words and carried them with her everywhere, and when she missed a meeting because of indisposition she eagerly queried her friends about what "that worthy man" had said of the progress of grace in Portland.[8]

Poor Mr. Willis did not know what to make of his wife's devotionalism, and he could well be confused by Rev. Payson's unwillingness to support order. In his personal experience of religion, and later in his pastoral labors, Edward Payson piloted a form of evangelical spirituality distinguishable from both doctrinalism and moralism, a third stream in the early nineteenth century. It was an urban phenomenon, and as American cities grew during the century such devotionalism outstripped its rivals in Protestant churches, especially among female parishioners.

I will call this movement either devotionalism, because it focused religious activity on regular performances of personal devotions to God, or sentimentalism, because it stressed so powerfully the role of the emotions in one's religious consciousness. More abstractly, it might be known as technical religion; for, in making religious feelings into goals worthy in themselves, devotionalists were preoccupied with finding the best technical means for producing such feelings. In another sense, their religion was technical because it limited the relatedness of religion to other aspects of life; one was religious not for the sake of morality, or because it was true, but simply to be and feel religious. In its own day, such spirituality was often called "heart religion."

Many clues to the character of evangelical devotionalism can be found in examining Payson's own religious experience; what happened to him and the way he understood it influenced and modeled the experience of his parishioners, his students, and the thousands who read his memoir when it appeared as Volume 12 in the set of best-selling classics published by the American Tract Society under the rubric of the Evangelical Family Library.

The first question we might propose was one asked by Payson's biographer and many others, "When did Dr. Payson become religious?" The origins of Payson's gospel hope lay shrouded in mystery, apparently with some purpose. "No solicitations by others," the mystified memorialist confessed, "could draw from him a particular history of that process." But despite inklings of encounters with the divine in early youth, or during college, it is clear that Payson never underwent a conversion experience. Evidently this was so embarrassing to the Tract Society editor that the lengthy discussion of possible episodes of youthful religiosity was excluded from its version altogether.[9]

Instead, Payson came to religion gradually. He did not, however, choose the path of moralists like William Hallock who devoted themselves practically to Christian work in lieu of a conversion moment. For Payson, withdrawal was the key to his emerging piety. The first statement of his personal religion came in a letter responding to the news of a brother's death in 1804, and it shows the importance to him of being a provincial amidst the glitter of Portland society. "Infatuated by the pleasures and amusements which this place affords," he complained,

> and which took the more powerful hold on my senses from being
> adorned with a refinement to which I had before been a stranger, I

gradually grew cold and indifferent to religion; and, though I still made attempts to reform, they were too transient to be effectual.

From this careless frame, nothing but a shock like that I have received could have roused me; and though my deceitful heart will, I fear, draw me back again into the snare, as soon as the first impression is worn off, yet I hope, by the assistance of divine grace, that this dispensation will prove of eternal benefit.

As if to insure, though, that he did not easily slip back "into the snare" of vice and vanity, Payson apparently confined himself in bereavement to his chamber for three days. When he emerged, he forswore an intended career in the law and devoted himself thenceforward to a pitched battle with the highest spiritual aspirations.[10]

Withdrawing from society to achieve communion with God became the key religious stimulant for the parson's son in Portland. He excelled in isolation, noting that "it does appear a duty to shun all communication with the world, when there is no well-grounded reason to hope to do good." The price of sociality was constantly inflated. "Now, I shall hardly see a person in a week, except our own family," he exulted; "and I have no doubt of being much happier for it." Only the divine presence was worthy company, and Payson established "two or three plain rules" by which all participation in society could be understood to militate against enjoying that higher presence. "One is, to do nothing of which I doubt, in any degree, the lawfulness; the second, to consider every thing as unlawful which indisposes me to prayer, and interrupts communion with God; and the third is, never to go into any company, business, or situation, in which I cannot conscientiously ask and expect the divine presence. By the help of these three rules, I settle all my doubts in a trice."[11]

Payson's melancholy temperament and his need to demur from the worldly prospects of social mobility clearly exacerbated this tendency to retire from company, but still he found continued refreshment from these seasons of intimacy with God. In 1806, for example, his diary recorded the following entries within one week:

> JULY 2. Still harassed and perplexed about my oration. Could not have believed, that the desire of applause had gained such power over me.
>
> JULY 4. Was enabled to ask for assistance to perform the services of the day. In the evening, felt in a most sweet, humble, thankful frame. How shall I praise the Lord for all his goodness!
>
> JULY 5. Felt much of the same temper I experienced yesterday. In the evening, was favored with much of the divine presence and blessing in prayer.—*Mem.* Applause cannot confer happiness!

> JULY 6. Sabbath. My infinitely gracious God is still present, to make
> his goodness pass before me. He has been with me this morning in
> prayer, and enabled me sweetly to say, *My Father, my God* . . . At the
> sacrament, my gracious Saviour favored me with some tokens of his
> presence.

Note how the antagonism in Payson between social acceptance and divine
presence forced him to associate the latter with an entirely private experience, secluded from the eyes of the world. Even the sacrament was not a
shared experience but one of perfect communion only with the Lord. And
when Payson read narratives of the experiences of others, he was generally
alarmed and disheartened by his unlikeness to them.[12]

In a way, Payson resembled those orthodox contemporaries who found solace and stability by adopting biblical descriptions for their personal distress.
But his use of scriptural language was altogether different in intent and effect. At one point, he "felt," as he wrote, "for the first time in my life, what
the apostle meant by 'groanings which cannot be uttered'; and my desires
after holiness were so strong, that I was in bodily pain, and my soul seemed
as if it would burst the bands which confined it to the body." Here Payson
needed, apparently, to *dramatize* the biblical metaphor in concrete, physical
terms. The end was not thereby to feel oneself adequately placed within the
gospel plan; instead, the enlivened reading of the Bible would generate real
pain and thus prove the truth of Payson's spiritual condition.[13]

This was, after all, exactly the same instinct that had informed his earlier
physical retreat to his room to grieve for his lost brother. Only by such gestures of self-dramatization could the devotionalist's thrill at the real presence
of God be realized. In the privacy of one's room, the "bands which confined
the soul to the body" could become *physically* painful and suggest the immediacy of God's interest in a young man's eternal condition. Without suffering
through a conversion experience, Payson repeatedly induced—for the whole
of his life—ever more painful tortures upon himself. A powerful example
appeared in a letter home early in 1806:

> In one of the classics, which form part of my daily occupation, there is
> an account of a tyrant, who used to torture his subjects, by binding
> them to dead bodies, and leaving them to perish by an unnatural and
> painful death. I have often thought the situation of a Christian is, in
> some respects, like that of the poor wretches. Bound to a loathsome
> body of sin, from which death alone can free him, and obliged daily to
> experience effects from it not much less painful and displeasing to him,
> than the stench of a putrefying carcass was to those who were united to
> it, he must suffer almost continual torment.

Among the orthodox, verbal formulas aimed to stabilize and comfort a sinner's tantrum of painful experiences; for Payson, such imaginative exercises had the opposite effect. They worked to initiate a sequence of religious emotions that was alternatively settling and unsettling but always engaging. As one Boston woman described such a sequence, "Tribulation has worked patience, and patience experience, and experience hope." The feelings were both the medium and the end of such devotional religion. When Payson told his sister in 1810 of his preaching, what came to mind were "the agonies, the unutterable, the inconceivable agonies which must be endured by those who attempt, with such a state as mine, to perform this work!"[14]

Impressive as was his preaching, though, Payson's prayers were the expression that became legendary—"a thousand forms, of his prayers even," says his biographer, "could never teach another to pray like him." In this, Payson was a forerunner of the nineteenth-century movement within American religion to emphasize prayer; the movement included Charles G. Finney's stress on the self-fulfilling efficacy of the "prayer of faith" and culminated in the gigantic prayer meetings of the Great Revival of 1858. About the latter, one commentator wrote that "it was a revival characterized not by preaching but by prayer, by an intense desire on the part of a great multitude of people for personal communion with Him who is invisible and eternal."[15]

Payson was proud of his skills in public prayer and wrote extensively on the proper "performance" of devotional exercises. "The design of public prayer," he stressed, "is to honor the being to whom it is addressed, and to excite and direct the devotional feelings of his worshippers." Because these two objects were "inseparably connected," the psychological effect of the prayer upon its participants achieved equal status with the worship of divinity. Devotionalism offered devotees a splendidly self-contained religious universe, in which devotional performances excited devotional feelings that, presumably, must then be poured into further devotions to God, and so on. This self-propagating quality exemplifies the *technical* aspect of Payson's religion, in that he found the end of his religious exercises in the means he employed, and vice versa. Such indulgence of personal feelings was clearly antithetical to the orthodox dictum that only the complete neglect of the self could be commensurate with honoring God. Payson, who had grown up in a doctrinalist household, was treading on dangerous ground.[16]

But the Portland minister did not stop there. The whole epistemological scheme of the orthodox evangelicals and all their talk of the primacy of the understanding were also subjected to a blistering attack from the protoromantic preacher. "I conceive that our devotional performances," he wrote, "are too often the language of the understanding, rather than of the heart." As such they excite nothing.

> They too often consist almost entirely of passages of Scripture—not always judiciously chosen or well arranged—and common-place phrases,

which have been transmitted down for ages, from one generation of ministers to another, selected and put together just as we would compose a sermon or essay, while the heart is allowed no share in the performance; so that we may more properly be said to make a prayer, than to pray. The consequence is, that our devotional performances are too often cold and spiritless: as the heart did not assist in composing, it disdains to aid in uttering them. They have almost as much of a form, as if we made use of a liturgy; while the peculiar excellences of a liturgy are wanting. Our hearers soon became familiarized to our expressions, and not unfrequently learn to anticipate them; and though they may possibly be instructed, their devotional feelings are not excited.[17]

Far from fearing "the movements of animal emotion," as Edward Griffin did, Payson turned the orthodox priority and superiority of the understanding on its head. Where did prayers come from, he asked. "From the fulness of a heart overflowing with holy affections, as from a copious fountain, we should pour forth a torrent of pious, humble, and ardently affectionate feelings while our understandings only shape the channel, and teach the gushing streams of devotion where to flow, and when to stop." Like any partisan of the "religion of the heart," Payson did not stop to consider where or how these holy affections were to arise. His main interest was in rescuing the heart from the remote corner where the intellectualist clergy had hidden it. For the orthodox, we recall, emotions could only be addressed through the understanding; for Payson and other romantics, the heart's foundation of emotion needed only to be unstopped, and devotion to the divine would follow.[18]

The orthodox used the commonplace phrases of the Bible to provide sinners with the security of knowing when their thoughts were properly impersonal, when they had become sufficiently divorced from self-interest. To Payson, prayer was by contrast "a kind of devout poetry," and the more original it was the better. Hence he disdained writing down his prayers. Not only did he compose prayers spontaneously, allowing the "effusions of the heart" to furnish "the whole subject matter" of the prayer, but his tone would be suffused with personal emotion. In this way, devotional performances would never be monotonous and stilted, and his innermost feelings would be revealed accurately in his prayers.[19]

In one further way did Payson's devotionalism break away from the orthodox models of mind and religious exercise. Where the doctrinalist loved abstraction in itself, Payson criticized most prayers for "the want of sufficient particularity."

Indeed, most of our public prayers, are too general. They bring so much into view, that nothing is seen distinctly. . . . We should, therefore, aim at as great a degree of particularity, as the time allotted us, and the variety of topics on which we must touch, will allow. Especially it is important, that we enter deeply and particularly into every part of Christian experience, and lay open all the minute ramifications, and almost imperceptible workings of the pious heart, in its various situations, and thus show our hearers to themselves in every point of view.

To show oneself in prayer, to see oneself in performance, became central to the devotionalist enterprise. The public experience of prayer became vital. "In a word," Payson concluded, "our public prayers should resemble, as nearly as propriety will allow, the breathings of a humble, judicious, and fervently-pious Christian, in his private devotions." But in public the skills attained in private devotion became recognizable; one could see oneself, or one's mirror image, by performing the rhapsodic worship of divinity.[20]

Prayer was the exact opposite, then, of the public examination of one's doctrinal background, for here the encouragement was to aim higher, to see oneself in ecstatic intimacy with God. Payson complained that too many people prayed as though they were "awakened, but still impenitent" sinners. Why were they so reserved? "Some are apparently led to it by doubts respecting their own character. They often suspect that they are not truly pious and therefore fear to utter the language of a pious heart. Others seem to adopt it in consequence of false humility. They fear it would be thought indicative of pride, should they use expressions which intimate that they think themselves to be the real disciples of Christ." With all such caution, laudable among the orthodox as the most elemental form of Christian discretion, Payson would have nothing. Instead, he wanted congregants to assume the role of the pious in their prayers and to take on, for the purposes of performance, the character of "eminent Christians." As for the minister, his role, too, was to exemplify this emboldened devotion.

> As an eagle tempts her young to soar higher than they would dare to do were they not encouraged by her example, so the minister of Christ should, occasionally at least, allure his people to the higher region of devotion, by taking a bolder flight than usual, and uttering the language of strong faith, ardent love, unshaken confidence, assured hope, and rapturous gratitude, admiration, and joy. Some of his hearers can, probably, at all times, follow him, and many others who at first tremble and hesitate; many, who would scarcely dare adopt the same language in their closets, will gradually catch the sacred flame; their hearts will burn within them. While their pastor leads the way, they will mount up, as on eagles' wings, toward heaven, and return from the house of prayer, not cold and languid, as they entered, but glowing with the fires of devotion.

Here, in an early use of the iconography of the "soaring eagle," so significant in nineteenth-century America, Payson made clear how self-dramatization could have spiritual consequences. His words breathed a fiery willfulness that was missing from musty doctrinalists and repressed moralists. Here, finally, retreat from the social pressures of Portland could be vindicated by leading the populace to heights of aspirations that shamed mere commercial ambition.[21]

Edward Payson was not an original thinker, but at an extraordinarily early date in our history he caught the sense of what religion would be if it were understood chiefly as a psychological experience. Thirty years later, Horace Bushnell brilliantly outlined a theology systematically embodying Payson's insights. Seventy-five years later, William James produced a masterpiece of analysis that also pictured religion as essentially experiential. But in the most peculiar way, as a provincial youth in a flourishing port town, with a delicate frame and a disposition to be gloomy, Payson provided clues to what "modern" religion would be like.

Payson understood religion as personal and private; he found the proof of God only in his own feelings of intimacy with him. He saw that religious exercises "filled needs" and that they could be both staged and spontaneous. He described a religious world in which one's authenticity lay in some mysterious inner region that could never be fathomed sufficiently, where the originality and uniqueness of each person (his "personality") made it harder and harder to be sure that anyone else was similar or even comprehensible. If we find ourselves tempted to cluck knowingly at Payson's account of his own experiences or his intentions, as if to say, "I know what he really meant," that may be because we, too, live in a world where "performance" needs always to be measured against some truer or more ideal personal "expression" that we can never quite achieve.[22]

Neither Payson nor any other ministers who shared his enthusiasm for personal feeling could be accused of doctrinal deviations. The sympathies of Payson lay with orthodox Calvinism, though he expressed some skepticism about the extreme positions of the Hopkinsians. In general, though, Payson cared little about systematic theology. In 1828, when Reverend Bennet Tyler, the conservative opponent of the New Haven moralists, succeeded to Payson's pulpit in Portland, he found no official confession of faith in the Second Church. Tyler's biographer recorded the key difference between the new Portland minister and the late Rev. Payson.

> Dr. Tyler came to Portland in the right time. While he remained, he was the right man in the right place. His clear and logical mind was needed to systematize the truth which had been so faithfully and pungently preached by his beloved and almost adored predecessor. No man that ever preached in this city could set before the minds of his hearers more clearly the controverted and mysterious doctrines of the gospel. He was at home in a doctrinal discussion. There is no doubt that he loved

to preach on the doctrines; and he was, by doing it, made the occasion of great and lasting benefit to this community.

Despite such historical regressions, however, the cause of religious sentimentalism went forward in subtle ways over the course of the second third of the nineteenth century. But, even if we were seeking the theological landmarks of a group of thinkers who labeled themselves devotionalists or sentimentalists or partisans of romantic religion, we could not find them. Even more than moralism, devotionalism was a change in the structure of personal experience, not a premeditated attack on orthodoxy.[23]

Although not all the sentimentalism of the 1830s, 1840s, and 1850s was religious in nature, evangelicism itself was highly sentimentalized during these decades. The evidence for that change is found not in treatises but in dozens of private diaries, recording devotional exercises that brought Christians into greater intimacy with God, especially Christ. Many of these diary entries were made by men and women whose outward lives bore the signs of a moralist organization but whose inward yearnings were for experiences more intense than those provided by benevolent committees. And many, if not most, of these diaries were kept by urban middle-class women, for whom devotionalism offered a flowering of one's internal spirituality that compensated for a woman's declining role in social and economic spheres. Virtually the only outward sign of this transformation of American religion was the emergence of the perfectionist and "holiness" movements in the years before the Civil War. Still, without a single trial for heresy, devotionalism had by 1860 become one pole of American evangelicism, sharing with moralism in picking up the pieces from the collapse of orthodoxy.

The complex relations between moralists and devotionalists will occupy much of our attention in the next four chapters. Certainly they lived in an alliance against both vice and paralysis and shared a growing faith in the activity of the mind and the importance of religious affections. But the tie between them was uneasy; they needed each other too much to be able to dominate the other completely, and often within families as within a single person's mind there were swings from one form of religiosity to another.

A homely example of such an alliance was the marriage of Lyman Beecher to his second wife, Harriet Porter. Into that moralist household moved a women whose religious experience sounded rather different from the Beecher model. After her conversion she wrote,

> Never was any creature so blessed, so filled with joy and consolation. "Come, all ye that fear the Lord, and I will declare what He hath done for my soul." This is the language of my heart. Such freedom and perfect liberty, as though emancipated from the most goading and oppressive shackles. I rejoice, yet with excessive trembling. To support such

elevation is impossible. Corruption must return; it is not yet extinguished; but it is written "My grace is sufficient for thee."

It should come as no surprise that Harriet Porter had been converted under the ministrations of Edward Payson in Portland. A little aloof for the convivial Beecher clan, Harriet Porter's influence on the youngest children of Roxana—Henry Ward and Harriet—and on her own offspring—Thomas, James, and Isabella—was considerable. Like her, these younger Beechers heavily favored a devotionalist understanding of the key aspects of religious experience.[24]

In the next four chapters, I will explore the devotionalist experience by studying its emphasis upon the cultivation of the inner life; its urgent searching for holiness as a repeated encounter with the divine spirit; its way of enjoying intimacy with God; and the effect all this had, in sum, on weakening the social bonds of the Christian church.

This restructuring of Christian experience cannot, of course, be laid to the influence of Payson or any other single figure. But as a representative of the new mood in American evangelicism, he was a key figure. He was so overwhelmingly successful in his preaching that Rev. Kellogg, who had brought him to Portland, left the scene in 1811 with Payson in full command of the church. Until 1827, when he died at the age of forty-four, he established a remarkable reputation for personal piety. In 1830, when a Boston minister was saying his own prayers, for example, he demonstrated the power of this reputation in pleading, "Lord, make me more like Payson; more like Paul; nay, more like Jesus."[25]

Chapter Thirteen

Inner Worlds: Reverie as a Religious Exercise

A SPIRITUAL MOVEMENT always springs from a spiritual crisis, and a spiritual crisis from the slowly perceived inadequacies of a spirituality itself once invented with enthusiasm. So it was that moralism, which had arisen from the disenchantment of evangelicals with the empty orderliness of orthodoxy, soon was plagued with its own discontents. Among the most ardent devotionalists were those men who feared that the organizing impulses of moralism, in particular, would destroy the experiential intensity of evangelical religion altogether. Such a warning was expressed, for example, by Henry Clay Fish in his 1855 prize essay, "Primitive Piety Revived":

> The number of benevolent enterprises which have recently sprung into being, and which are the glory of the age, increase this danger of neglecting the *heart-work*, upon which these very enterprises are dependent for success. There are so many "Societies," and "Boards," and "Conventions," the importance of whose efficient operations and liberal support, must of necessity be often urged upon the churches, that we are in danger of imbibing the sentiment that these are the *only* things of importance; and that, when we have done our proportion for their adequate support and encouragement, we may rest satisfied as if all were attained. Thus the *inner work* of the closet, and the individual's own bosom, is left undone.

How could the efficient operations of bureaucratized charity, Fish and others wondered, produce the inner "heart-work" of religion? Indeed, all that laboring in the vineyard of reform could bring a Christian perilously near an interior deadness that would gainsay having undergone a saving change at all.[1]

Busy and active people could suddenly discover this painful loss of their spiritual feelings. When Baron Stow reread a portion of his 1838 diary thirteen years later, he complained that "I do not feel as I did then."

I fear I have deteriorated in my piety. . . . I have not a lively sense of divine things. I have very little of the spirit of prayer. I am not so concerned for souls as formerly. I do not so deeply realize my responsibilities as a Christian and a minister of the gospel. I am more sluggish in my affections, and less energetic in my efforts. O God, help me, by thy Spirit, to examine my case, and review the process by which I have so greatly declined.

But Stow already had a presentiment of where the cause lay, and he wrote,

I know that my mind has been too much distracted by a diversity of objects, many of which are extraneous to my particular charge. I am connected with too many boards and committees. My time is cut into fragments, and I am driven rapidly from one thing to another, so that I do nothing well, and have little fixedness of attention to my one paramount class of duties.

But the solution to Stow's crisis was not better organization of his time. More than that he wanted an opportunity for richer private experiences:

I do not read the Scriptures, or meditate, or pray so much as I ought; I do not live for eternity as I should; consequently I am backslidden in heart. . . . Lord, help me now to repent and turn to thee with my whole heart.

Stow's world was not confusing or boring; rather, he had lost his way, having "not a lively sense of divine things." "Whole-heartedness" was not easily scheduled into a busy week.[2]

Stow's complaint, familiar as it is to us today, indicated a widening disparity between organization and social experience, on the one hand, and private experience on the other. As long as one could feel one's activity bound up with the goals of those drawn out committee meetings on Beacon Hill, as long as one's identity somehow merged with the moral community that shaped those goals, one could dedicate oneself to longer and more regular hours of laboring for temperance, tract distribution, and missionary endeavors. But there came a moment when all such work seemed only a surface undertaking, unrelated to personal piety, a regimen that could be performed with empty gestures and motions.

When this sentiment was realized, devotionalists recognized that ordinary life could apparently have two distinct levels. Unlike their doctrinalist grandparents, the devotionalists in mid-nineteenth-century America did not believe that a single event took place on two entirely separate metaphysical planes at once: that is, as both a spiritual occurrence affecting one's eternal destiny and a psychological happening that marked one's ordinary life on earth. Like their moralist acquaintances, devotionalists measured every experience by the same clock. But for moralists like Taylor and Beecher, as we have seen, all experiences were similarly products of a smoothly functioning mental apparatus. All perceptions were received by the understanding, judged by the moral sense, and acted upon by the will. Whether the perceptions were of the shortage in French silk imports, the propriety of chaperoning the young, or the passion of Paul's epistles, all could be treated the same way. Religion was simply the proper action of the mind.

This far the devotionalists would not go. Did not such a flattened, mechanistic mentality preclude the special qualities that made religion different from mere prudence or morality? The old orthodox solution was not acceptable. Believing that the Holy Spirit could change the rules of its action on the occasion of regeneration seemed both implausible and inadequate to the repeated religious intensity that devotionalists, following the example of people like Edward Payson, favored. In sum, whatever distinguished religious experiences for the sentimentalists had to be as much a part of the natural functioning of the mind as it was in the moralist scheme and as special and dramatic as it was in the orthodox evangelical view.

Devotionalists like Baron Stow solved this problem by inventing and developing a new sort of mental experience, an act of profound devotion that occurred in natural time like any moralist event but was deeper and more personal than others. For devotionalists, proper religious experience had to be *profound*. Only deep experiences could be accorded the name of religion henceforth. To express this zeal for depth, devotionalist writers redrew their diagram of the mind, turning its faculties ninety degrees. Thomas C. Upham, an ardent defender of the moralists' tripartite division of the mind, placed the intellect, the emotions, and the will "behind" one another. Dissatisfaction with any particular experience could now be explained by its evident failure to "reach" as deeply as the will.

Let us say, Upham proposed, that a person "experiences, to a considerable extent, new views of his own situation, of his need of a Savior, and of the restoration of his soul to God in spiritual union." For Upham, this much is still purely intellectual. But to continue further, suppose that "the perception of new truth, as we should naturally expect, gives him happiness; and the perception of its relation to his salvation gives him still more happiness. We are willing to admit," Upham judges of this much, "that he has a valuable experience—an experience which is naturally preparatory to religion, and is closely connected with it, and looks very much like it. But if the experience stops here, in such a manner as to constitute a merely emotional experience, and without reaching and affecting a still more inward and important part of the mind, . . . we cannot with good reasons regard it as a truly religious experience." The "still more inward and important part of the mind" was, of course, the affections and the will, where an intense experience had to go. "Any religion, or rather *pretence* of religion," Upham concluded, "which is not powerful enough to penetrate into this region of the mind, and to bring the affections and will into subjection of God, is in vain."[3]

Upham's analysis was extremely important because it made the degree of participation by the self in an idea more significant than the power of the idea itself. Only when our affections and our wills were deeply imbued with a particular notion could it be understood to be ours, no matter how morally pure or doctrinally correct it was. "The moral quality of an idea or object," Theodore Spencer wrote in 1854, "is not impressed upon the mind as a signet produces its likeness upon the wax; but is imparted to the agent by his own voluntary adoption of it as a motive influence, or principle of action." In other words, those ideas that deeply affected us were motives for our actions. The motive idea and the will became, through this face-to-face confrontation, one with the other. The idea, Spencer continued, "thereby becomes his own, a real moral unity with himself; he and his principles become one in morals, one in approvableness, or the contrary; so that, if his motive is right, *he* is right, and if that is wrong, he is wrong also."[4]

In this way of thinking, the mind was no longer a mechanism perfectly keyed into the motions of the world, a machine for morally testing and capably responding to the stimuli from the environment. The devotionalist could not assume, with Nathaniel William Taylor and other moralists, that a moral idea would compel obedience, that something actually in the idea and outside the mind would force itself to be accepted and make a person behave properly. From the mid-nineteenth century onward, motives were internal drives, pushing themselves outward upon the world, not external ideas that spurred the mind to action as they had been since Edwards's passionate advocacy of Lockean psychology. The devotionalists were taking only the first step, but it was a step toward empowering the mind to create its own world.

It had still to be a rather modest step in that direction, for a number of dangers lurked in identifying deeply moving experiences with the life of faith. Most basic, of course, was the implication that the innermostness of an experience was somehow equivalent to its divine origin. How, in other words, did the devotionalists know that they were not substituting their own private fantasies for legitimate religious experiences? Although the moralists sat through hundreds of merely surface contacts with religious matters, they could at least believe that such attendance evidenced the ruling principles of their minds and subscribed to behavioral rectitude. Inevitably the devotionalist had to question whether the merely powerful penetration of intense affections was the same thing as faith.

The devotionalist answer to this dilemma was generally to emphasize that the crucial voluntary act was not an open-ended sort of creativity, but a more limiting "subjection to God." Theodore Spencer and Thomas C. Upham and others of their way of thinking presumed that the act of will was, ipso facto, an act of submitting to some law. As Spencer wrote,

> The character of our external actions depends exclusively upon their being in fulfillment or in violation of some law which is authoritative over us, or of some obligation which we are under to others. In determining the character of the *agent,* we refer, as has been said, to that of the motive or intention which produced his outward conduct; but in determining that of such *conduct* we ask, was its legitimate tendency (whether so designed by him, or not), to fulfill a law or obligation resting upon him? If it was, we pronounce the action good; if it was not, we pronounce it evil.

Our actions were moral because they subordinated the self to some law or obligation, something higher than one's own self-interest. If the will accepted the authoritativeness of some law when it enacted a particular idea, it was moral.[5]

Moralists had done nearly the same thing. The inherent moral sense or conscience would insure that the will bent to the dictates of the moral law, if the latter was allowed to operate freely. In this view, the conscience acted as an on-off switch; the mind could choose only between virtue and vice. This already displayed considerable development from the orthodox notion of conscience as the internal register of one's divergence from the gospel truth. Slowly the conscience was changing from a cognitive to a volitional organ, from one that belonged to God to one that was uniquely personal. The devotionalists went further than the moralists by enabling the conscience to select *any* higher law; they prized voluntary obedience more than the precise moral law being obeyed.

By adopting this idea of the conscience, the evangelical devotionalists used a principle that had great importance in the eventual secularization of morality. For, if the will could morally follow any law, then conscientious action could be in the service of many ideals other than that of Christian love. Interestingly, 1854, the year in which Spencer outlined this devotionalist definition of the conscience, was also the year in which Thoreau's *Walden* appeared. Nowhere is the new conscience more fundamentally expressed than in Thoreau's familiar call, "If a man does not keep pace with his companions, perhaps it is because he hears a different drummer. Let him step to the music which he hears, however measured or far away." And by that definition, John Brown and a million other Americans have acted "conscientiously."[6]

Thoreau, if not an evangelical, was very much a devotionalist, and his sort of conscientious action was decidedly antimoralist in so strenuously opposing the norms of his local community. The implication, of course, was that only the will set against those norms had the possibility of being true to divine law. To the idea of local antagonism, Thoreau added a point of companionship. Inevitably, all acts of conscientious devotion seemed, like his, to mean listening to, or accompanying someone. One heeded a drummer, neither a drum nor a drumbeat. Subscribing to the law, then, was not deciding in favor of some abstract principle but rather joining forces with some personal incarnation of the good. For evangelicals, this usually meant the figure of Jesus Christ. The need for a more profound personal experience could not be satisfied by shaping one's thoughts to the form of orthodox doctrine. Instead, a kind of internal "society" or perfect companionship had to replace the dull obligations of one's role in moralist organizations and families.

Escaping from the boredom and impersonality of everyday social life, even when that life was dedicated to moral ends, could thus be achieved by imagining the interior consciousness in the midst of a difficult dialogue. On the one side stood one's natural self, squirming with the recognition that it was inadequate to perform the expected formalities, that it could not exert itself sufficiently for worthy ends, and so on. On the other side a better self called one to conscientious devotion to some higher principle and offered to replace a social role with the perfect communion with a righteous figure. When the mind could wholly turn away from its self-interest and subordinate itself to the divine law, it was thereupon swelled with images of Christ. "The old life perishes," Thomas C. Upham promised, "in order that there may be a new creation in Christ. The deformity of the ancient nature passes away, and the image of Christ in the soul takes its place." The immediate presence of the Saviour rewarded the inner drama of willfulness.[7]

That the exercise of one's will could result in feeling the nearness of Jesus is evident in this episode recorded in Baron Stow's diary:

> March 1 [1852]. At twelve M. a young lady called, borne down
> under a heavy burden of conscious guilt, seeming to need nothing but
> the direction given to the jailer, "Believe in the Lord Jesus Christ, and
> thou shalt be saved." I presented before her Christ as a Saviour of sin-
> ners, and submitted the question, "Will you *now* renounce the world
> and sin, and consecrate yourself to Christ, depending on him for ac-
> ceptance with God, and serving him while life lasts?" She reflected a
> moment, then burst into tears, and said, "I will; I have done it! Christ
> is mine, and I am his!" O, what a thrill shot through my soul! I felt that
> Christ was near, receiving a new-born soul.

Linking the "decision for Christ" with the felt physical presence of the Saviour was an important development for evangelical religion. The same model continues today to provide the central focus of revival and devotional meetings among evangelicals everywhere. The epistemology of this model is based upon the equation of *decision* with both the unity of the entire mind in favor of a particular course of action and the overcoming of certain restraining environmental concerns—the feared jibes of one's associates, for example. Henceforth, to decide for something was to be "in favor of it no matter what." Rather than seek the validation of others' approval, for the decision maker the right thing was more often done in opposition to what others were supposed to think. In the end, one's emotions would fall into line.[8]

Therefore, the crucial factors in making a decision were neither the doctrinal nor the moral arguments in favor of either option but the degree of willfulness available for implementing each. Evangelicals now puzzled long and hard over whether they were "entirely sure," or "prepared to be entirely dedicated," or "committed to their entire consecration to Christ." There was no question they wanted to be close to Jesus, only whether they could commit their will sufficiently to that vision.

Passing the autonomy for decisions to the mind made such sentimentalists feel that their own wills were the key elements in their becoming Christians. To find eternal truth at the core of one's own being, not in the alien world outside us, was a remarkable discovery. The devotionalists, in their own way, were approximating the division customarily made by contemporaneous romantics between the faculties of the understanding and the reason. When the will subjected itself to the divine law by replicating the figure of Christ in the mind, it acted as the independent mind's connection to universal truth, exactly the function of the romantic reason. Like reason, the devotionalist will was defined as the entire mind acting as one and acting from within. Such higher faculties were capable of leading the self to encounter the truths of the noumenal sphere, the meaning beneath appearances. And yet, both the will and the reason (at least in the Coleridgean version of the latter which reigned in American forms of transcendentalism and romantic religion) were immediately accessible in subjective experience. They were subjective in both the modern sense of an interior and individually biased way of knowing and the older sense of the self's being obedient to a law outside itself.[9]

The understanding, by contrast, was a shallower instrument, capable of assessing and responding to the surface phenomena of the world. In fact, its mechanism was commonly understood to be triggered by and plugged into the motions of the external world. So much revered by doctrinalists and moralists for its skillful receptivity to the presentation of truth from the environment, the understanding was scorned by romantics for failing to unify its perceptions. Living close to the surface of the world, the understanding seemed a smoothly operating device for absorbing a constant jumble of miscellaneous facts and images. The reason, in comparison, had the power to seize the truth by a single, willful stroke, shaking oneself to the core.

Rejecting the primacy of the understanding was the epistemological equivalent of the devotionalists' rejecting the social world. Just as that organ of perception seemed to traffic so conveniently with the doings of the external world, so did it seem to preclude the richer wisdom of both the more profound will and the private world in which the will resided.

Finally, it must be asked, of what significance were such philosophical revolutions in the daily lives of Christians? How was their experiential history transformed by these alterations in the definition of understanding, conscience, and will?

For one thing, devotionalism seemed to suggest a rather profound loss of legitimacy for both church institutions and their public discourse. The dramas of interior consciousness in the musings of the saints—fantasies, as will be seen, of more and more intimate companionship with God—continually nourished the impulses of Christians to contest for their faith. So the inwardness of the devotionalist was anything but a retreat into stillness and paralysis; it was not a turn away from action toward thought, but rather a substitution of imagined action on the highest levels of faith for more ordinary efforts at improving and testing personal behavior.

Devotionalism was the transposition to a more accessible arena of a struggle that had lost its plausible setting in the cosmological and social images of its day. That is, both the world-ordering comprehensiveness of orthodoxy and the integrating social pressures of moralism offered little room for doubt, for triumph, for drama. When God could not be felt immediately and personally in shaping the order of the entire universe, and when the activities of benevolence seemed, after years of labor, to be only human endeavors after all and scarcely productive of the world transformations originally intended, the inner life became a more likely place to witness the contest with truth. The richness of this inner drama is evident to any reader of Emily Dickinson, arguably the finest playwright of this restaging. Going to church and signifying one's assent to church doctrines seemed to have little to do with Dickinson's religiosity, and she and many of her contemporaries were the first Americans to pronounce what has since become a commonplace, the sentiment that one might be religious without being at all interested in institutional religion.

Moralism had so strenuously insisted upon the importance of playing one's social role properly that it led pious young people to claim a sense of their own inner mystery. Elizabeth Payson, the daughter of the Portland minister, sounded a common note about such lonely reaches in her journal entry for Christmas Day, 1840:

> I've been "our Lizzy" all my life and have not had to display my own private feelings and opinions before folks, but have sat still and listened and mused and lived within myself, and shut myself up in my corner of the house and speculated on life and things thereof till I've got a set of notions of my own which don't fit into the notions of anybody I know. I don't open myself to anybody on earth; I can not; there is a world of

something in me which is not known to those about me and perhaps never will be.

In orthodox times, she would have been asked to "open" herself with embarrassing frequency. Among moralists, Miss Payson would have felt most comfortable as "our Lizzy." But now she had to foster a secret realm of belief within her.[10]

Such a gesture of private defiance did not give Elizabeth Payson much pleasure. In the same diary entry, in language I shall cite later in examining devotionalist friendship, she went on to dream of finding friendship and love compatible with such interiority. Her retreat, then, was not an act of self-absorption and self-indulgence. Like other devotionalists, she employed a technique of mental projection to escape the bounds of the inner world she had created. This fulfilled the purpose, of course, of requiring that her will be subjected to the divine law discovered deep within. By projecting one's inner feelings as an extreme otherness, a perfect purity, and then subjecting oneself to *its* authoritativeness, selfishness and all other sins were overcome.

This emphasis upon the dramatic interaction with the divinity inside consciousness led devotionalists to revolt against the centuries-old disdain for the visual among pious New Englanders. As the next chapter will show, this revolt resulted in increasing interest in the physical representations of the Godhead, particularly of Jesus, but also of less personal biblical metaphors, as when Edward Payson felt so *physically* constrained by the bondage of sin. In the corners of their houses, to which devotionalists repaired to muse about coming closer to the Saviour, the use of the imagination became a legitimate religious activity. The imaginative faculty of the mind had been denounced from the earliest days of the Puritan migration, with repeated fervor after the excesses of the Salem witch trials and the First Great Awakening; finally, the didactic moral philosophers who dominated nineteenth-century American colleges again denounced imagination, precisely for the reasons that now lent it luster among devotionalists. Always the moralists feared that the mind, responding to the leadings of its own physical images, would become absorbed in pursuing these little pantomimes everywhere, at the cost of alertly recognizing what was really going on in the world. Ultimately, so the traditional argument went, if one did not test one's ideas against either established dogmatic interpretation or local opinion, one would unavoidably set one's own judgment higher than anything, including God's word.[11]

Despite devotionalist claims that God's word was exactly what the imagination discovered at the nether reaches of the mind, without some external standard to use as a check such subjective probings at truth could not claim to be rooted in the truth or the nature of all things. When reason became a subjective faculty of the mind, tested only by its ability to generate emotions perceptibly religious (that is, perceived by one's own subjective consciousness), an important change had occurred. Whether imagining oneself strolling across the fields in eager conversation with Jesus or sharing secrets with a chosen friend while others strained to hear, it was all permissible; the best test, when one had to choose between such fantasies, was which one brought the most delight to one's heart. What felt best *was* best.

We have no way of knowing whether mid-nineteenth-century Americans daydreamed more than their grandparents did, but their diaries suggest that frequent reverie was a more substantial part of their lives. And now that the religious culture seemed to authorize these inner episodes of projecting oneself into imaginary situations, reverie became the perfect antidote for those long boring meetings of the local self-improvement league and the perfect medicine for a hundred other social disappointments. The enormous interest in Freud's analysis of night dreaming as a way into the world of the unconscious has obscured the importance of daydreaming in the intellectual history of the West since Rousseau's *Rêveries d'un Promeneur Solitaire* (1778). The undercurrent in our minds, varying between vague scenes of pleasure and towering expressions of rage, is an important product of a culture in which strangers are thrown together so commonly. To communicate among such strangers, it became necessary to project physical alternatives to the here and now. Because we meet on no shared ground, we find affinities in shared reveries of other places.

Can we understand reverie as an historical phenomenon? Obviously as a solitary activity, reverie demands a certain amount of privacy. But it seems more likely to occur amid scenes where the environment is more complex than the attentive mind can handle easily, and where elements in that environment must be "tuned out" to preserve an internal order.

Much contemporary industrial labor and much modern urban interaction, of course, are of this quality. On the farm or at the village store one had seen familiar people doing diverse but familiar things. All such activity made sense as a comprehensive whole. In the factory, or walking along State Street, one encountered strangers apparently doing the same things but only abstractly interconnected. It was puzzling, and ultimately unnecessary, to conjecture what was going on inside their heads. Daydreaming, or the stream of one's consciousness, is noticeable once one avoids expressing and then even shaping responses to such an environment—when the events of our public, articulated mental life (thinking in full sentences or saying things aloud) seem tiny by contrast with the submerged rush of sensations beneath them. The city, then, is where the mind is most likely to dart in and out of these mental alleys and dooryards. Urban life transforms observant souls into passersby and hawk-eyed countinghouse men into strolling daydreamers.[12]

But the other important feature of the phenomenology of reverie is that we must catch ourselves at it by missing our attention elsewhere. "Daydreaming," writes one scholar, "represents a shift of attention *away* from some primary physical or mental task we have set for ourselves, or *away* from directly looking at or listening to something in the external environment, *toward* an unfolding sequence of private responses made to some internal stimulus." It seems likely, therefore, that reverie is more noticeable when the pressure to pay attention to the "primary physical or mental task we have set for ourselves" is greatest. The more, in other words, that moralism inveighed nineteenth-century Christians to be present-minded, to focus their energies on useful tasks, and to apply themselves with greater and greater exertion, the more alluring and passionate became the impulse to drift away to intense private fantasies. Particularly because the tasks organized by moralist endeavors were themselves only means toward greater ends—for example, by sewing shirts that would be sold to gather funds for a young man's theological training, he might aid the salvation of souls in a parish or mission station many years hence—one might understandably seek more precious beauties to contemplate in the stead of such stitches.[13]

The exercise of reverie was available for every moralist's son and daughter who would or could escape from such social pressure. "I have no more of society than I had last summer," Mary Hawes, the child of Hartford's minister, wrote in 1841, "but I have learned to look for happiness in another channel." Mary Hawes, however, cautioned herself about traveling in that channel.

> And *here* I am in danger—I feel it. I am in danger on many accounts: and first, of being *self-satisfied*—of thinking *I have something within that lives without the world's breath.* This is being puffed up. I may thank God that he gives me grace to do so, but any thing like pride will ruin all peace. I am thankful that I have sources within my heart, of happiness. But *here* another trouble meets me. I ask myself whence is this happiness? Comes it from doing God's will? Does it proceed from a consecration to the Saviour? Or is it from a feeling within, which is merely a kind of poetic religion? A meditative pleasant communion with natural beauties? If this be the case, then my peace rests on no safe foundation. Lately I have been troubled about this; and it requires my serious attention. I do not think that my religion is mere poetry, but I fear it may all run away in feeling, without producing any or but little good effect. I must guard against this.

These were wise reservations against the potential self-indulgence of the devotionalists' cultivation of private feeling as a religious activity. How would the sentimentalist be able to tell about the godliness of her feelings, after all, when feelings in themselves had become the proofs of her godliness?[14]

So Mary Hawes, in the style of many of her contemporaries, sought other proof, namely that her religion would produce some "good effect." Afraid of the self-deluding snares implicit in the devotionalist's turn inward, she could only swing back to the moralist's accounting of positive effects. Just as devotionalist mind wanderings were the product of boredom with moralist benevolence, so moralist activity could be a safe haven for the self recovering from such voyages. The nineteenth-century evangelical thus shaped a world for himself, which all of us today inhabit, in which one flies back and forth between moralist commitments to external improvement and devotionalist adventures in private feeling.

The mutual dependence of moralism and devotionalism upon each other was not so easily noticeable to nineteenth-century evangelicals. One flew from one to the other with great hope and scarcely recognized the trap that the two—by dividing private experience so radically from social interaction—created. Each mode of religious sensibility was progressive, not static, and there were ever new causes to work for and new fantasies to dream of. Most evangelicals could intermingle their moralism and their devotionalism into a single day, although any single act was clearly definable as one or the other.

Devotionalists faced a particularly important challenge in advising young businessmen. Principled rectitude was no longer sufficient, as it was for moralists, to guarantee a proper degree of personal responsibility. The answer was periodic withdrawal. Truly pious businessmen cannot, suggested Henry A. Boardman, "live only in the crowd. . . . If our Saviour found it needful to retire frequently for prayer, how essential must secret meditation and devotion be to us! The very circumstance of withdrawing for this purpose—the consciousness of being alone with God—is peculiarly adapted to foster that feeling of personal responsibility."[15]

The withdrawal into the rich inner drama of the mind's quest for Christian perfection was not, therefore, a total reversal of the moralist's disdain for epistemology and preference for fixing on behavior as the key to Christian life. Devotionalists did not choose to scrutinize how the inner workings of the mind affected one's conduct. They looked inward only because the behavior there, not its connection with social activity, was more pleasant to contemplate than what happened in full view of the crowd. Every religious sensibility, as we have seen, includes some experience of one's mind; in devotionalism, that became the key experience. Religion was becoming a psychological phenomenon above all else. There was a world of difference, then, between Jonathan Edwards's sense of piety as the activity of religious affections and the devotionalists' sense of affections as religious activities in themselves.

With this in mind, we can proceed to explore the behavior of the inner self taken as a whole and look at the way the central fantasy of devotionalist faith, "an intimate walk with Jesus," formed an aesthetic by which all the rest of the self's experience could be understood.

Chapter Fourteen

Closeness to God

NEAR THE END of his life, a half century after his conversion in 1815, the Rev. Nathaniel Bouton of Concord, New Hampshire, recalled that he "passed through a painful experience of what was termed the 'law-work' on my heart" during that momentous change. "In contrast with all this," he reflected,

> very little is said at the present day of the condemning power of the law. God's mercy is magnified, while his adorable justice is kept out of view. Sinners were called upon to "submit to God." Now "Come to Jesus" is the song—"Come just now, Jesus loves you." Little or nothing is said of the danger of self-deception or a false hope. The Christian's life is represented as strewn all the way with flowers, while the Christian's cross-bearing and yoke are ignored. Then conversion was thought to be a great change wrought by the power of the Spirit of God. Now it is as easy as to turn your hand over or to walk across a room. Then "Questions and Counsel" were applied to young converts for self-examination. Now only "believe and trust in Jesus, and all well." I note these differences because they mark a change in the current thought and style of preaching, and the views entertained then and now of certain great doctrines of the Gospel.

Bouton clearly disapproved of the changes he had witnessed, and his vexation stirred warm memories of the doctrinalist setting of the church of his youth, with all its emphasis upon God's judgmental role, its excruciating testing of the knowledge and experience of young converts, and its unceasing presumption of their guilt. By the time Bouton retired from the pulpit, all that glumness had given way to a gentler and more loving spirit in religion, or at least (Bouton hinted) an easier one.[1]

What sort of change was this? Bouton noted that it occurred "in the current thought and style of preaching, and the views entertained then and now of certain great doctrines of the Gospel." But his description says little specifically about either preaching or doctrines. Instead, he points to the altered experiential situation of young Christians. Religious experience in each age was guided by the key phrases of invitation: "submit to God" was the message of Bouton's doctrinalist youth; "come to Jesus" was the plea of his devotionalist maturity. These phrases, almost clichés, were far more important than theological or ecclesiastical concepts in organizing the daily lives of Christians— how they felt and expressed themselves, how they acted and interacted with others. In the earlier age, the language of religion was deliberately formal and stilted, as befit its doctrinal rigor: "conversion was thought to be a great change wrought by the power of the Spirit of God." But in the present, he seemed to say, all such museum pieces of diction are banished, and the language could be as blunt as possible: "it is as easy as to turn your hand over or to walk across a room."

"Submit to God," of course, was an invitation to sinners to enter the kingdom of God by understanding it through the aesthetic of stillness; the emphasis was upon getting oneself correctly located within the logic of the gospel plan. The plan, entirely outside man, encompassed him totally.

In this chapter, we will explore the aesthetic of a religious experience built upon the invitation to "come to Jesus." For devotionalists such an invitation had important implications for answering several questions: Where was God? How was he represented? What did being in his presence mean? And how did approaching him approximate becoming like him? We will see how sentimentalism relied upon an aesthetic notion of a "one-to-one" correspondence between the self and its deity, its friends, and the events of its daily life.

First, one must find God. The invitation to approach Jesus implied, of course, that he was in a particular place. Recall that for the orthodox it was simply not possible to locate the specific place of God. Sinners found relief when they could discover their own precise distance from the complete order of the universe and thereby their own places in it. By the mid-nineteenth century, the problem was less geographical. Rather than map their distance from God, devotionalists cried out, "I cannot live so far away from thee." They wanted to be in the same place as God.[2]

To be in God's place, to share his place with him, seemed to demand closing one's eyes on the outer world. Abbie A. Dickerman's journal, says her biographer, "shows that she maintained unbroken her habits of private devotion, the daily hour of retirement, of reading and prayer; evincing that, though so young, she had learned that rare lesson of subordinating the most pressing worldly care to the cultivation of her heart, and an intimate walk with God." The divine could be discovered in the recesses of her mind through the most arduous sort of private concentration.[3]

The devotionalists did not mean, of course, that God was physically present in some remote suburb of our consciousness. They did mean that his spirit was accessible only by going down this inward path. As evangelicals, the devotionalists maintained ardently that faith was a subjective experience of the divine, heightened by a greater mindfulness.

In some ways this resembled the orthodox command to look inward for confirmation of gospel truth. Devotionalists, though, were looking for livelier emotions, not scriptural language. For example, Abbie Dickerman talked about being near to God: "I feel that Christ has been near to me. If I know my own heart, I do desire to have more enlarged views of him and of heaven, to drink more freely of the wells of salvation, and to take up my cross daily and follow Christ." As with Edward Payson, the devotionalist strategy was to use scriptural language—here "the wells of salvation"—but not as a final resting point for one's introspections. Instead, the episode of inward glancing is stimulating. By dramatizing such conventional language, Abbie Dickerman could feel as though she were in the midst of an intense interaction with God. The act of locating God within could set off profound emotional tremors.[4]

Furthermore, Dickerman's language tells us something about what God looked like once he was discovered deep inside one's mind. When she was near to God, she reported having "enlarged views" of Christ and of heaven. In fact, the sentimentalist mind was always attracted to the most concrete, even physical, images of the divine. When God was imagined as another human figure, one's interaction with him seemed more intensely psychological, more personal. Such relationships made possible the self-dramatization that devotionalists sought. It was thus quite natural that the figure of Jesus became more significant than the Father in such visions, for the Son seemed much more likely to reassume an earthly presence than would the metaphysical judge of earlier Calvinist dogmatists. The latter, we recall, was basically understood through verbal form; with all these new visualizations of divinity came an emphasis upon Christ.

The contrast with moralism is instructive. The behavioral reformers in New England, as has been seen, thought of Christ as a model. But they meant that Jesus' obedience taught certain precepts still applicable to Christians. And beyond that, their humanization of the Father had been limited to the idea that he might be trusted as one would trust a parent or friend. That was analogy, but the sentimentalists wanted the real thing. So Elizabeth H. Dickerman, Abbie's sister, celebrated a particularly triumphant moment of intimacy with God by exclaiming, "I feel as if God was really my reconciled Father and Friend, and Christ my elder brother indeed!"[5]

Such literalness about close relations with the divine led devotionalists to think of Jesus in the most human forms. Even though these ideas were discovered in the mind's furthest recesses, the picture needed to be acceptable to the culture at large. For the first time in Protestant America, there was a healthy market for engravings of Renaissance paintings of Christ, the Madonna and Child, and the Annunciation. For their orthodox grandparents, such images would have been an affront to lingering Puritan suspicions of Papist idolatry. In one Woodstock, Connecticut, house, occupied by members of Henry Ward Beecher's congregation during their summers away from Brooklyn, an engraving of a Raphael Madonna shared the walls with an English pastoral scene, a painting of George Washington, a compilation of tiny portraits under the heading of "Friends of Freedom" (which included dozens of noted abolitionists), and an oil painting, done posthumously, of a child whose death in infancy also led family members to memorialize his passing with pages of sentimentalist verse. This pictorial aggregation—idealized nature, moral reform, national loyalty, innocent childhood, and the haloed Virgin and Child—almost constitutes in itself a catalogue raisonné of the confluence of moralist and sentimentalist aesthetic taste.[6]

The middle of the nineteenth century, everywhere in Western culture, witnessed an increasing emphasis on Christological elements in worship. This was the era, also, where biblical criticism and extensive research in the historical veracity of the New Testament accounts emerged. In America, the most powerful intellectual expression of this interest in Jesus was the revival of the reformed doctrine of the "spiritual real presence" of Christ in the Eucharist. As this doctrine was articulated most vigorously—in the Mercersburg theology of John Williamson Nevin—it was coupled with an attack on the way Americans had thought of God and Christ in merely metaphysical or symbolic ways. Nevin charged that American theologians considered the Lord's Supper only a commemorative ordinance, an event reminding Christians of their reliance upon divine grace. As the chief spokesman for the German Reformed Churches in America, he countered that Calvin had taught Christ as objectively present in the offering and the ceremony as a sacrament, "by definition the conjunction of grace with an outward ordinance."[7]

In their renewed fascination with communion, New England devotionalists shared Nevin's high sacramental position. They also tended to favor his view that the presence of Christ in the Eucharist meant something more than the activity of the Holy Spirit; and unlike Nevin's major opponent, Charles Hodge of the Princeton Theological Seminary, the devotionalists liked to imagine Christ in bodily as well as spiritual ways.

On the whole, however, New England devotionalists would have subscribed more to Hodge's theology, given its familiar evangelicalism and individualism, than to Nevin's mystical corporatism and high-church ritualism. Hodge, an archdoctrinalist fond of denying that Princeton had entertained an original idea during his tenure, believed that the sacrament—like other religious events—worked along two tracks. First, it was an ordinary exercise of religious psychology in which the self was stimulated to reverence; second, it was the scene of a metaphysical transaction, the operation of the Holy Spirit. The Lord's Supper was not in and of itself a sure means for the offering of divine grace to parishioners, but only as men and women were "affected" by it. Moreover, Hodge could not understand what Nevin meant in saying that Christ's body was actually incorporated in the Eucharist and that the Supper was offered to the entire body of Christians collectively.[8]

Devotionalists would have agreed with Hodge on these points, that is, were they at all interested in doctrinal matters. Instead, they were intent upon viewing the Eucharist and the human encounter with the divine as thoroughgoing experiences of personal psychology, not as theological events. They shared Nevin's sense of the bodily presence of Jesus rather than Hodge's emphasis upon the mysterious workings of the Spirit because the former was easier to imagine and more powerfully stimulating. But they balked at the notion that Christ was physically incorporated by the communing believer because that, too, did not seem a likely occurrence in the world of one's subjective consciousness. If the imagination was now legitimated, it was certainly not farfetched.

Here the history of theology diverged from the history of religious experience. Concepts like the indwelling of the Holy Spirit, regeneration through participation in the sacrament, even the distinction between the spiritual and mundane spheres—all seemed outlandish to the devotionalist, or at best only metaphorically true. Only subjective experience counted, and so the notion of divine majesty, omnipotence, immutability, or even infinitude, was irrelevant. The beauty of God, because it could be felt, was more vital to New England saints than his power. And when the devotionalists spoke of God's beauty it was not the order and the symmetry of the divine plan that impressed them, for these would have to be seen from afar. They wanted God's beauty close to them, close enough to be personally engaging. The image of Christ, one minister wrote, is "a conception, perhaps dim, of something absolutely perfect,—a form of matchless beauty floating before their imaginations, towards which they could not help but strive, though conscious that they should never grasp it." The image had to be real enough to draw us to him and then so surpassingly perfect that full communion with him would be humanly impossible. Above all, though, the image had to be experientially believable.[9]

So while they could find themselves agreeing with Nevin's Christology, the devotionalists avoided his theological categories altogether. They wanted Christ's companionship, not his indwelling. They prayed for Christ's support, not for his interpenetration of their substance. The relationship with God was to be splendid, but it had to be between two autonomous personalities. If we use the phrase "closeness to God" for this relationship, we should also understand that there was still a divide between the human self and the divine character.

Perhaps Abbie Dickerman's phrase, "an intimate walk with God," is more accurate in any case. The devotionalist, we see, objected to the "distant logic of the gospel plan" on two counts. First, the orthodox scheme put God too far away, making him too abstract for human feelings of companionship. And second, it was too static, assuming that once the sinner found himself precisely located in the plan he could stay there forever. By the mid-nineteenth century, the perfection of God was no longer contingent upon man's passivity or stasis; it was not a reminder of man's frailty, but quite the opposite. As Bela Bates Edwards wrote, "the absolute perfection of the Saviour comes in as a refreshment to the spirit. It does not operate as a discouragement because unattainable by man; because the garland is on a height to which no mortal has reached. Such is the nature of the human soul, that it needs to have absolute perfection before it. In the struggle to gain what it cannot gain fully, it grows, rises, and is happy.[10]

God's perfection was no longer seen as a metaphysical status against which to judge man's finitude. The chief value of the divine loveliness was now to serve as a psychological inducement for man's rise into his own personal perfection. To be a Christian was thus to abandon one's weakness, to strive for godlikeness oneself. This precept informed the mid-century holiness movement by which converted Christians in all the mainline Protestant denominations were encouraged to devote themselves to continued and "perfect sanctification."

At least for those already within the Christian fold, the Reformation ideal of a personal progression through sin and redemption was giving way to an older, Catholic pattern of grace through "the imitation of Christ." Certainly the moralists also believed in imitation, even using Christ as a model for man's industriousness in the service of the Lord. But for them industriousness and similar virtues were the main points, and the figure of the exemplar meant less than the lesson he taught. That worthy citizen, Mr. Morality Smith, who worked on behalf of temperance, was much to be admired, but temperance, not Mr. Smith, deserved copying. Devotionalists, on the other hand, found the human figure more precious than any abstract principle, even a moral one they could hardly oppose. They cared little about general principles of any kind, of either theology or morality; they wanted particularity. Hence, having pictured Jesus in his mortal frame as the embodiment of absolute perfection, these romantics thought that nothing could express one's spiritual longings better than modeling oneself on the Saviour.

So we find Elizabeth H. Dickerman, Abbie's sister, writing to her students, "Do not follow the unworthy example of your teacher, who daily mourns her shortcomings in duty, but remember that you have in Jesus a perfect pattern. Be like him, 'meek and lowly,' and you shall find rest to your souls." Coming closer to Jesus was becoming more like him: that was the central truth of devotionalist religion.[11]

Of course, one's failure to achieve a likeness with Christ could also disqualify one from taking any comfort in one's life as a Christian. Such was the poignant case of Deborah Porter, whose diary for February 12, 1838, records this entry:

> Were it not for my great unlikeness to Christ, [I] would delight to talk of benefits received and pleasure enjoyed from communion with him; but as it is, would it not be a libel on his character? If a person is known by the company he keeps, he exhibits to the world something of those peculiar traits which characterize that company, whether virtuous and elevated, or otherwise; and do I exhibit those graces which adorned the Savior? Do I possess any of that decision of character, that Christian independence, which moves forward, regardless of flatteries and frowns; any of that willingness to suffer, which he manifested? Alas, how wanting in every requisite to portray his lovely character! and how many judge of the king, by the poverty of his subjects!

How alien this might have sounded to the orthodox! Their sense of God's power depended upon the very quality of unlikeness that made Mrs. Porter so despondent. Nor would they have understood how any mortal could seek to mirror the most personal traits of Jesus' character and temperament. By saying that she wanted to possess Christ's "decision of character" or "willingness to suffer," Mrs. Porter seemed to want to be just like him, even perhaps to be him.[12]

When religion turned, as Deborah Porter's did, to focus on the most intimate details of the human personality, the effect was to consecrate those details. Because the desirable qualities in the Saviour were aspects of his personal manner, and because these personal qualities were seemingly within the grasp of his disciples, the human and the divine became more difficult to distinguish. Although the persons of Christ and the Christian could be separated, as we have seen, the characteristics of each were qualitatively similar. Now feelings, temperaments, manners became the very stuff of religious life, and men or women had no place in the world other than the psychological and physical condition of their ordinary lives. A human being was no longer an actor on the metaphysical stage.

Devotionalism, in making so much of personality, went even further than moralism in consecrating everyday life. The moralists had simply assumed that God acted by routinizing the way things proceeded for his ends and that one's life could similarly be consecrated by devoting one's activities to religious ends. They argued against the orthodox requirement of the intervention of the Holy Spirit at irregular moments. Devotionalism wanted to make things sacred by witnessing the divine presence in everything, at all times. One's feelings of generosity, for example, could now be understood in reference to Christ's gentle temperament. Where the orthodox had always denigrated natural generosity by comparing it to the magisterial love by which God ruled the universe, the devotionalist emphasized the potential likeness between human and divine dispositions.

Still, the sentimentalist evangelical, even in his most passionate perfectionist moods, did not believe that man was likely to replicate Christ's character here on earth. The injunction to model oneself on the Lord, and the process by which one was encouraged to do so, were more important to devotionalists than examining proofs of saintliness. But there was another, far more significant, result from this emphasis upon the similarities between humanity and God. Whenever one failed, whenever one could not match the holy standard, the deficiency was not so much a sin as a "need," a certain emptiness and inadequacy that could be rectified in only one way—by appealing for Christ's love.

The devotionalists, by visually emphasizing the human personality in human-divine relations and in subtly redefining humanity's errors as needs, were transforming religion into a psychological phenomenon. Look, for example, at the way the idea of Christ's sufficiency had changed in the century after 1750. Since the time of Bellamy, New England evangelicals had argued that Christ's atonement was sufficient to redeem all, though as Calvinists they averred that in fact not all would take advantage of the terms of salvation. The object of Christ's atonement, as Edward Griffin and others discovered, was to win pardon for humanity from the offended Lord. Jesus was not to do everything for men and women, only to exercise his power on their behalf. What he did, it was well understood, he did for his own sake because that was his peculiar cosmological role. His struggle to appease the Father's anger was entirely a metaphysical event, occurring between two divine beings. People were to look upon the outcome of the struggle, no matter how important it was to their own internal destinies, with a cool disinterestedness because they had to respect the vast metaphysical divide between themselves and the divine. Thus, though the significant act of redemption happened within the human lifetime, it was not somehow an event of that lifetime. It required a wholly special operation of the Holy Spirit, thereby distinguishing it from the rest of one's ordinary life (assisted by the Spirit's "common" operations).

But now, for devotionalists, the atoning sacrifice of Christ was only one such expression of his sufficiency for humanity's need. In much more common ways, in whatever ailed a man or a woman, Christ would be there to help. So to Christ's aid in securing regeneration for humanity was added the Saviour's willingness to assuage our physical, psychological, social needs—every need. Men and women were no longer to "fit" into the entire gospel plan of the universe; Christ, instead, was now "fitting" for all that one sought.

The degree of one's disparity from divine perfection thus became the extent of one's needfulness. Christ always remained a cornucopia of perfect satisfactions, and the passion of the meeting of need and satisfaction became an intense and frequent personal experience, as this sermon of Payson's makes clear:

> So when persons come to Christ, their hearts leave the objects with which they have been occupied, fly to him with affectionate desire, and cling to him as the supreme object of their confidence and love. They see that he is just such a Saviour as they need; they are sweetly, but powerfully drawn to him by the attractions of his moral glory and beauty, and feel bound to him by bonds which they have no wish to break.

The attraction of the sinner to the Saviour resulted in a mutual compatibility. The perfect "fittingness" of the devotionalist, then, was in pinpointing the match between humanity and Christ, rather than in discovering humanity's place in the temple of God's universe.[13]

From the simple correspondence between people's deficiency and Christ's supply, several further developments ensued. Devotional manuals, like Thomas C. Upham's important work, *Principles of the Interior or Hidden Life; Designed Particularly for the Consideration of Those Who are Seeking Assurance of Faith and Perfect Love* (1843), trained the devout to rid themselves of any remedy other than Christ for their difficulties.

> Such is the nature of God, and such are our relations with him, that he cannot possibly admit of a rival in our affections. It is reasonable, there-fore, that he should expect us in our troubles to make the first applica-tions to himself, and to lay our trials and wants before him with that readiness and confidence which we notice in little children, who natu-rally seek the advice and assistance of their parents, before looking to other sources of support; and we shall always find this course safest for ourselves, as well as most pleasing and honorable to God.

The result of all this was that the Christian would be left quite alone with Christ, progressively prevented from creating any possible rivalry by turning to parents or friends for advice.[14]

The distinctions between the moralist and the devotionalist in this regard are significant. The moralist emphasized that the individual person was joined to society, God, or "errands of mercy" by placing confidence in the underlying principles of moral character. So a good Christian citizen em-barked upon service to God by performing all the tasks necessary to everyday life and by dedicating those tasks to the ends of religion; making money and cleaning house were equally capable of being consecrated, if each could be understood as exemplifying a commitment to moral principles like order and charity and cleanliness.

Devotionalists were equally committed to the consecration of everyday life. As one of them, Henry Clay Fish, complained in 1855, "the pew is consecrated to God, but not the counting-room." Businessmen "must be shown," said Fish, "that secular pursuits may be made sacred." But the devotionalists did not find the remedy simply in turning secular tasks to sacred ends. Instead, they again resorted to the figure of Christ. "Christ himself," said Fish, "stands forth to all time, as the finest model, the grandest illustration of this devotedness to life's *one work.*" The wording is important. For moralists "there is a day allotted us to do *all* our work in," but for devotionalists there was but *one* work, modeling oneself on Christ. [15]

So the moralist, with a "one-to-many" aesthetic, had to arrange all tasks to conform to the proper order of religious ends. Devotionalists understood their work in a strictly one-to-one way; the work was as large and as integrated as the self engaged in it. Devotionalists cared nothing for a job's duration; the entire frame in which the work existed was dropped from their consciousness. Devotion to work was not, then, the same as productivity; it did not depend upon increasing the ratio of output for effort. Even the orthodox had understood life as a "short winter's day" in which conversion as a single event had to be achieved; the sentimentalist cared little about such major changes and ignored the bounds of human life. Work, in sum, was not service *to* the Lord but an emulation *of* him.

If we were to make an analogy with the way work was reinterpreted in the process of industrialization, we could say that the moralist impulse was to systematize all the details of the work process and to connect them with as much mechanical smoothness as possible. Devotionalism thought of work in rather different ways. It wanted to distinguish each task, investing each with a tremendous significance by deliberating intently upon it and perfecting it. Moralist husbands were incorporating all the stages of textile production in the thriving factories along New England's rivers; their sentimentalist wives were turning with as much passion to reading, needlepoint, and charity to fill their hours.

Or maybe it is fairer to say that the sentimentalist women were making an industrial model of personal experience, in which the product was a heightened emotional communion with Christ. As we will see, their aim was for a continuous, unceasing holiness, rather than the regular and continual (but intermittent) activity of the moralists. As with any technical process, it soon became hard for devotionalists to separate themselves from the demand for a greater and greater efficiency in the production of religious sentiments. But at least initially, the impulse to devotionalism was an effort to look at life's moments face-to-face, to see God directly. In that sense, devotionalism is exactly the right word, for it expresses well the way this mode of religious sensibility was based on devoting oneself to God.

Excellence in coming to Christ was an achievement of pure devotion.

Though it may have cost much in terms of shining in worldly society, devotionalism offered its initiates an enormously satisfying infusion of religious excitement. As Phoebe Palmer, a leading light of the movement, wrote, "The standard of Christian excellence being thus fixed by the ratio of approximation to the image of Christ, wherever she saw the characteristics of his loveliness most clearly described, the more abundant was her love."[16]

Love was an ever more important aim and standard of religious life as the devotionalists restructured it during the middle decades of the nineteenth century. And the love they spoke of so frequently was increasingly identical in all its manifestations—in the love between spouses, between parent and child, between friends, and between Christ and Christian. In each case, the dominant aesthetic, the main concern, of the devotionalist was establishing a one-to-one relationship. The passion always was directed at pinpointing the matching characteristics of the pair, and these correspondences were dramatized further by their pointed exclusion of other, lesser relationships.

This does not imply that devotionalists sought only to stabilize the interaction between two loved ones. By positing the notion of needs and satisfactions, the relationships could be seen as evolving into perfect mutuality. In all such encounters was heard the "I-thou" dialogue that expressed both needs and gratifications.

But not only in interpersonal connections did devotionalism employ an aesthetic of one-to-one correspondence. In viewing his work, the devotionalist eagerly set to matching himself against it, "becoming equal to the task." In assessing life experiences, as we shall see, the aim was to replicate particularly joyful moments, to relive one's most exciting memories. Devotionalism delighted in these momentary feelings of "rightness." Theirs was not the eternal righteousness searched for by doctrinalists but a more intense, personal epiphany: a world perfectly centered around one's personality.

Chapter Fifteen

Life History and the Repetition of Holiness

DEVOTIONALISTS were making evangelical religion "portable." By uprooting religious life from its place in a specific geography of faith or in a particular community of public opinion, the midcentury sentimentalists hoped that one could seek an inward drama of the will and achieve nearness to God wherever one was. The techniques they taught, like the manuals of piety and devotional prayers they printed, could be useful anywhere, perhaps most especially amid the anonymity of the booming American cities in which devotionalism thrived.

Each person's religion, it was often said, was entirely his or her own. Common complaints were heard during the 1850s of an unnecessary insistence upon uniformity in religious exercises; the day of orthodoxy was clearly over. Bela Bates Edwards, for example, lamented that "we sometimes err in not making sufficient allowance for diversities of natural character. We erect a standard, and determine that all men shall conform to it. . . . But distinguished holiness is consistent with countless varieties of innocent natural temperament."[1]

Henry Ward Beecher similarly advised young people "not to try themselves by other people's evidences":

> It is supposed that if religion is of God, it will, of course, be just the same in all men. But, in fact, religion is the right using of the whole mind and life. Men are different from one another. They were meant to be. The strength of some lies in the feelings, of others in their intellect, of others in their stability and will. Some men are calm, others excitable. Some are imaginative, and others literal and practical. Some are nervous and quick, others phlegmatic and slow. Besides these constitutional differences, men have had widely different teaching and training, and all these circumstances conspire to make their religious developments personal and peculiar! God leads every soul according to what that soul is, and what its history has been.

189

Beecher's enumeration of the variations in religious temperaments was like a nineteenth-century inventory of personality characteristics. No single quality was itself virtuous or vicious; religion could be accommodated to each of them equally. Though man's personality was morally neutral, it did shape his spirituality. We are religious in the way our personalities determine us to be, Beecher said.[2]

Note, too, that Beecher concluded his description of temperamental types with a nod to what shaped that personality—in short, to a person's life history. When religion could be carried inside one's head, the proper context for understanding it was no longer one's place of worship but one's memory of prior experiences. Determining the direction of one's religious life could compensate for the loss of its precise location.

This chapter will trace the emerging significance of the idea of life history in the shaping of religious experience. The notion that each event was determined and explained by its antecedents in one's previous experience was a significant contribution of the nineteenth century to the analysis of human behavior. In our Eriksonian age, in which life is almost synonymous in our minds with life history, we often fail to understand how recent this notion is. The word "life," of course, had always referred to the entirety of a person's time between birth and death and to the written accounts thereof. But the intense new interest in life history early in the last century was reflected by the assumption of their modern meanings of such key words as "biography" and "autobiography," "career" and "memoir."[3]

This zeal for life history found its most familiar expression, of course, in the nineteenth-century novel, particularly the *Bildungsroman;* in this novel of education, the conflicts between traditional moral values and the skills needed for commercial success were dramatized within the developmental unfolding of one young man's life. The entire social history of the century, Dickens and Balzac seemed to be saying, could be focused on the life history of a young man who began with great expectations and ended with lost illusions.

Among devotionalists, history was also valued for its powerful aesthetic and dramatic interpretation of religious issues. "The history of the development of each faculty of the human Soul," Henry Ward Beecher promised in 1858, "will be the highest ground of true history, and the last to be occupied. When that day shall arrive, the most profoundly affecting chapter will be the history of man's Religious nature." Then Beecher elaborated on the possible outlines of such a history:

> The blind outreaching of the human soul toward purity, toward rest, toward strength; the aspirations of earnest men for divine life, their conflicts with fear, with doubt, with passions, will constitute a history in the presence of which all outward events, all changes of kingdoms, or movements of commerce, of art, of diplomacy, will be both coarse and

tame. The single record of the struggles of great souls with a legitimate doubt, will be a history of itself. In every church, in every age, there have been men who made their way out of error, formalism, or death, as seeds do, lifting up the dirt and forcing their way to the light by the irresistible might of growth. The conflicts of such, usually accompanied by reproach without, and by pains and deep sufferings within, would be more profoundly affecting than the most touching history of disappointed love, or of any of those passions of which Dramas are made.

Religious biography, Beecher was saying, would be more dramatically engaging than the histories of political and economic institutions or the fanciful tales of romantic fiction. It would even best such narratives on their own ground—as gripping entertainments. Though Beecher scoffed, with the normal mien of devotionalists, against secular happenings, he also seemed to be adopting secular standards by which to judge religious events.[4]

In fact, each religious saga he imagined as a metaphor for the process of salvation—purification, rest after tension, strength after weakness, confidence after fear, faith after doubt, the control of passion, and most important, the blooming of the seed—could be understood as an entirely temporal occurrence. Each was a this-worldly sequence of crisis and resolution, with many analogues in the natural (physical or psychological) world. A half century earlier, religious conversion was also understood as a *relief*—in the psychological sense—from the pains of conviction, but such a meaning was always coupled with more significant metaphysical terms like *reconciliation* and *pardon;* regeneration was both a natural event and a metaphysical change, yoked uneasily together. Now, the change was just like what might happen to one's economic life (reward after hard work) or to one's health (recovery after illness). Salvation was a natural, human process.

Process is a key word. Beecher was obviously delighted by the way the religious crisis moved toward its most fitting resolution. He certainly did not want to exclude any path to holiness. Far from setting any particular standards, for him it was splendid that there were such various approaches to an inward walk with God. The sinner did not, after all, need to have the logical stages of his progression available for constant checking; he would know, internally, if he were on the right track and how near he felt his own will to a perfect submission to God's will. Religion was becoming the process by which one lived one's life most fully, most closely in touch with the power of God.

The dynamic of a life history counted for more, then, than did its frame. Both the moralist and the orthodox evangelicals had spoken of one's life span as "the time in which" one either acquired religion or performed God's work. Looking at the duration of a lifetime as a "short winter's day," the orthodox had pressed the claims of conversion as the solely valuable experience. Similarly, the duration of one's stay on earth challenged moralists to organize their days effectively to serve God best. For both, life was an outline that needed filling in; to understand what a good person did, one had to see his activity against the frame of his time on earth. A holy person "improved his time"; that time, though, was a given.

For the devotionalist, all that was changed. Life was an ongoing process, an organic "playing-out" of certain mysterious but powerful laws. For Henry Ward Beecher the moving force of man's regeneration was "the irresistible might of growth." This internal thrust toward its own right end contrasts sharply with the orthodox Calvinist equivalent, the "irresistible grace" of God. For the orthodox, man's life was the scene in which God acted out an extraordinarily significant drama by visiting his glorious grace on mortals. For the devotionalist, God had provided the arena whereby man's fundamental yearnings toward a heightened spirituality could be fulfilled. Charles Backus had warned evangelicals against the organic analogy as smacking of the heresy of progressive regeneration. Fifty years later, the trelliswork of Backus's Calvinism was fast disappearing beneath the luxuriant vines of Henry Ward Beecher's loving and most romantic Arminianism. Now, it appeared, every man carried within himself the seeds of his own fruition as a holy being.

The nineteenth century, in religion as much as in physics, was an era in which motion triumphed over stasis. In Hegelianism, Marxism, Darwinism, and physical mechanics, the direction of history overwhelmed the classification of the stages through which it passed. Yet, though no stage was perfectly still any longer, it was important to demark the species types through which development or evolution passed. No less was this true for devotionalist evangelicals as they inaugurated an era in which religious life was understood as dynamic. They needed to know the rules by which such changes occurred.

One such rule was *the continuity of life experiences.* Simply stated, this meant that the resolution of one's religious concerns was found in one's prior experiences, not in an external guide like Scripture or local norms. The incidents in one's past life became, like a phrenological chart, indicators of one's future way of spirituality. In memoirs of this period, we find pious souls like Mary E. Clapp pining endlessly about a falsehood spoken when she was twelve years old; she finally found the courage to confess her sin to the entire family a dozen years later. Only this relieved her pain and allowed her to enjoy her religion.[5]

This pattern is followed repeatedly in the hundreds of conversion accounts compiled by William C. Conant for his *Narratives of Remarkable Conversions and Revival Incidents: Including an account . . . of the Great Awakening of 1857–'8* (1858). The actual duration of the conversion experience was now much shorter than ever, as sinners described how they were awakened and almost instantly brought to throw themselves on the mercy of Christ's love. But the event was usually predicated upon the convert's prior life history. So the young man who was hounded from his sailor's life by the tyranny of the ship's captain, in one account, returns as a Christian to convert the gruff old man. A distiller, in another case, after leading hundreds to debauchery, was converted and brought thousands to grace by enlisting in tract distribution. Always the circle of a life was closed when salvation was achieved.[6]

In this very simplest form of biographical irony, Conant aimed to stress the rather wonderful quality of such reversals. Such thaumaturgical displays of the Spirit's working provided good evidence for the devotionalist's belief in "particular providences," that is, God's willingness to answer specifically the prayers of a single person. And these divine interventions surely precluded a totally naturalistic, "secular" view of life history, in which events followed one another with a predictable consistency. But the crudeness of the 1858 accounts should not blind us to the new emphasis on the incidents of early life as forming the structure of personal religion. God's responsiveness to man's prayers came by connecting one's personal memory with a present experience of grace. Embarking on a new life in Christ was not, therefore, totally rejecting one's past. Like the sentimentalist mothers who carried their pianos to new homes in frontier Michigan and Iowa, the elements of an old life were retained as the material for the new.[7]

What, then, was the purpose of conversion? Unlike the doctrinalists, proponents of devotionalism did not believe that conversion was a sinner's accommodation to a plan of life set forth in Scripture. Now it seemed more like a profound life change, one that made sense of both past and future as a coherent story of a developing religious consciousness. Conversion, in other words, *set one's religious life in motion.* To feel the presence of God with all one's will and one's heart was to escape the jumble of events that led this way and that without meaning; it was to learn how the direction of one's life fit the laws of Divine Reason.

For Baron Stow, as a minister, seeing the power of Christ at work with individual parishioners renewed his own piety. "O, what a thrill shot through my soul! I felt that Christ was near, receiving a new-born soul. . . . It was easy to see her soul was letting go its hold on everything else, and coming to him as her only hope. The Saviour seemed near." And the nearness of Christ sparked both visions of him and impulses toward imitation.[8]

The momentum of religiosity, then, was increased by the sudden decision of the mind to follow Christ. In devotionalist discussions of conversion, a new stage emerged in midprocess. This was called "obtaining a hope." An account of a pastor's conversation with a potential convert illustrates how the concept worked:

> P. [Pastor] And was not this pleasure so new and eventually so
> strong, as to induce the full belief that you had succeeded, and that the

Spirit had given these feelings as a witness of your pardon, and acceptance, and title to hope in Christ; and did you not then hope in him for
pardon and happiness?

I. [Inquirer] Such were precisely my views and feelings. After some
hesitation, lest my good prospects might prove deceptive, I could no
longer resist the force of such evidences, but embraced a hope in the
pardoning mercy of Christ.

As it was used here and elsewhere during this period, acquiring a hope (or a
"title to hope") meant reaching a point in one's spiritual life where one could
reasonably expect to succeed in winning grace. Without moving all the way
to the notion of becoming assured of one's salvation, a title to hope was a fairly
tangible possession. The probability of success it offered became a logical and
psychological inducement to further efforts. The anticipated fruits of one's
endeavors, then, became more secure grounds for continuing in them than
either their essential philosophical correctness (according to one's prevailing
world view, e.g., "the gospel plan") or moral propriety (according to local
norms). It was worth pursuing Christ, therefore, because pursuit would
likely be successful, not because it was mandated by Scripture or by the opinion of one's community.[9]

In short, it paid to do what worked. If it worked, do it. Such clichés express the new dominance of basically technical criteria for one's behavior.
Doing something with primary reference to the anticipated consequences of
the action seems such an ordinary way of proceeding that we may forget how
doctrinalists and moralists would have found it wanting. Obtaining a hope in
Christ was a conceptual leap into a new religious universe, for having the
hope was inherently only of instrumental value. Hope did not describe a distinct religious condition, but used properly it was helpful in setting one's
religion in motion, bringing one to a full appreciation of Christ's love.

The same idea, applied to the secular sphere, is familiar to us as "the dream
of success." The Protestant Ethic, as Max Weber described it, the faithful
pursuit of a calling pleasant to God and contributing to his glory, was rapidly
changing in the nineteenth century. Economic success was becoming an end
in itself, a sport (in Weber's terms), its own reward and target. Success bred
success, and success only. Having a hope of success was a prime qualification
for participating in this social world. Devotionalists, for whom faith was its
own reward and the hope of it their essential prod, were mirroring that social
world even as they withdrew from it.

The title to hope brought converts to focus their attention on the future; it
was a way of getting through the conversion experience as quickly as possible.
The key religious experience, among devotionalists, was not conversion but
the intimate walk with God, and there was little point in encouraging new
adherents to dawdle on their approach to that walk. Why should they puzzle

over their genuine spirituality? If they acted as though they were Christians, parishioners were told by devotionalist pastors from Payson's time forward, they would grow into true Christians.

Conversion could not, however, be abandoned. There were still many outside the fold for whom the intense experience of reordering their life histories was an extremely valuable technique. In that sense, conversion had become transformed. No longer the goal of religion, it was now a therapeutic technique to prepare saints for religion; it rectified their confusion and unpreparedness for a life with Christ.

But if conversion had such a narrow function as a psychological device, what had happened to its original theological meaning as the experience of one's redemption from sin? In the effort to enforce the notion of the continuity of one's life experiences, were not evangelicals abandoning the crucial idea of the saving change, without which one would be doomed to the hellish destiny implicit in one's original sinfulness?

There were some ingenious, even bizarre, endeavors to reconcile the *evangelical* mode of a disjunctive life history with the newer *devotionalist* concept of a continuous life pattern. For example, Edward Beecher, another son of Lyman's, blamed the original sin for which we must atone in this life on the preexistence of our souls. As Robert Meredith has summarized Beecher's argument, "souls are born into this world, not newly created and corrupt, but as spirits who fell from innocence in a free and previous existence." Thus God could be absolved for all blame in our sinfulness, as our own previous voluntary disobedience caused this blameworthy state. Prenatal sin mandated both the need for a converting experience and, in Beecher's prescription, a commitment to social reform. By putting the moment of our sinfulness at a point before our birth in this life, Beecher was able to defend the evangelical insistence upon conversion without rejecting the emerging consensus in his society that one's redemption had to compensate for one's own misdeeds. Thus Beecher could "make," he wrote, "a supernatural development rational."[10]

In a revealing phrase, Beecher proclaimed "the true end of this world as a moral hospital." Others spoke of religion as filling the needs and wants of the personality. "There was still a want rising more and more in his soul," said W. E. Boardman of a case in point. "The want—the sense of want, from a sense of his lack of—*holiness*. He had not yet learned to find in Jesus, by faith, the supply of this want." The entire evangelical drama of sin and redemption could, with this precept in mind, be remade into a course of therapy, in which our spiritual ailments would be fittingly cured by dredging up our past, even prenatal, lives for analysis and various this-worldly remedies like confession and repentance. Our episodes of distress would "naturally," then, be cured by a clear view of the consistency of our psychological lives. Philip Rieff, who has written about the "triumph of the therapeutic," notes that "the hospital is succeeding the church and the parliament as the archetypal institution of Western culture." By understanding religion as curative, Edward Beecher was, from the pulpit of the church itself, enacting a transformation like the one Rieff describes.[11]

Here was the fate of nineteenth-century evangelicism: to see its classic description of the winning of one's individual pardon for the shared sinfulness of the human condition translated into the wholly secular, and rather different, story of how psychological health can follow confronting and overcoming one's interior "dividedness." When William James psychologized the religious experience of the "twice-born" in his *Varieties of Religious Experience* (1902), Edward Beecher's work was completed. Inevitably, the skill of James's analysis has made his description of the psychological drama seem generalizable to entirely nonreligious contexts, and so the evangelical model has been merged in the contemporary American mind with the parallel ideas of Freudian depth psychology.

Philip Rieff would label all of devotionalism, with its interest in liberating one's interior thoughts from the limits of traditional "interdictions" and encouraging the mind to achieve harmony in itself, as part of the "emergence of psychological man." Such religion, for Rieff, is inherently therapeutic, based in an illness/cure model rather than one of sin/redemption. But, for our purposes, it is worth preserving William James's distinction between the "once-" and "twice-born" forms of religious psychology, limiting "therapeutic" to the latter group. Within devotionalism, those once-born types avoided the crisis experience and, by growing their faith gradually from small seeds, might better be termed "liturgical." Their interest was in expanding and revivifying elements of religious consciousness until religion became a total environment in which to live each day and a substitute for the secular world outside the mind.[12]

For "therapeutic" or twice-born devotionalists, as we have seen, the continuity of life experiences linked crisis events with early episodes of distress; these sinful remnants in one's memory were purged by the conversion experience. Their liturgical brethren simply thought this was not necessary. Why could not children simply act as Christians and exemplify their faith without a severe crisis? Clearly, the earlier that children were initiated into church life, the less likely they would be to indulge in sinful excess needing later expurgation.

The decline of doctrinal tests for faith facilitated the process of admittance considerably. And so, while therapeutic devotionalists were quickly inducting adults into the church through sudden conversions, there was also a growing pressure to convert children at the earliest possible age. One mother confessed that if her large brood of children had "not [been] converted before seven or eight years of age, they would probably be lost." This was perhaps a little extreme, but the midcentury church rolls do show children acceding to membership in their early teens.[13]

The next step for devotionalists was questioning the whole premise of conversion. The milestone in this movement was the publication of Horace Bushnell's first book, *Views of Christian Nurture*, in 1846. As Barbara M. Cross has shown, Bushnell capitalized on the sentimentalism of Hartford's mercantile middle classes to attack the "ostrich nurture" of evangelical families, who tended to leave children uninstructed and outside the faith community until their late adolescent or adult hearts were converted to Christ. Instead, Bushnell put forward his famous proposition, "That the child is to grow up a Christian, and never know himself as being otherwise." By identifying the training of a Christian with the loving nurturance offered by sentimentalist mothers, Bushnell rejected the need for a life-altering conversion experience altogether. In the place of orthodox conversions, Bushnell offered a devotionalist strategy for the education of Christian children. As Cross explains, "The parents taught religion not by doctrine but by the reality of the impressions given in their lives. The love of the mother revealed the love of Christ. Parents were given by God 'to personate and finite Himself, and gather to such human motherhood and fatherhood, a piety transferable to Himself.' Since parents enforced moral laws upon the child, they became for him the 'natural and moral image' of God." Once Christian faith, in other words, became the approximation of believers to the image of Christ, children could begin their faith by modeling themselves, point-for-point, on the moral image of their Christian parents. "The Christian parent has, in his character," Bushnell said, "a germ which has power, presumptively, to produce its like in his children."[14]

Bushnell's antirevivalism certainly made him a controversial figure, but these excerpts from *Christian Nurture* show how integral to the devotionalist enterprise he really was. Bushnell's most severe criticism came not, as it turned out, from a revivalist of the Taylor-Beecher-Finney school but from old Bennet Tyler, the archdoctrinalist and regional curator of the memories of the 1800 revivals. Bushnell had indeed been innovative and provocative in broaching a radically different Congregationalist ecclesiology; his theory of the church incorporated the notions of a gradual growth in grace, of child membership in the church under the baptismal covenant, and of family and church as "organic" bodies. But, in using terms like the "image of Christ" and "the germ of Christian character," he pinned those innovations to the way many ministers and parishioners had already sentimentalized religious experience. And his demand for an ongoing parental responsibility for Christian education not only appealed to the sentimental images of little children flourishing in American culture, but it also made sense to a newly entrenched middle class engaged in stable businesses like the insurance enterprises of Hartford. In such a community, children did not need to undergo the shocks of urbanization and commercialization as their parents had. Their secular life histories were becoming more stable and predictable, their formal education and fixed life experiences locked ever more into a regular pattern. Bushnell brought them a religious life history every bit as reliable and continuous.[15]

For Bushnell, it was not that conversion was too hard for his parishioners; by diminishing the need for a sharply disjunctive experience, he was not lowering the standards of Christian piety one bit. Here was a major aspect of the distinction between the moralist and the (liturgical) devotionalist alternatives to conversion; while the former wanted to substitute commitments to Christian service for the evangelical crisis of self-doubt and regeneration, the latter wanted something deeper. "I believed," wrote Bushnell, "from reading, especially the New Testament, and from other testimony, that there is a higher, fuller life that can be lived, and set myself to attain it." For the Hartford minister, such a faith was even more demanding than that of doctrinalism. "Christian faith," he wrote, "is the faith of a transaction. It is not the committing of one's thought in assent to any proposition, but the trusting of one's being to *a being*, there to be rested, kept, guided, moulded, governed, and possessed forever. . . . It gives you God, fills you with God in immediate, experimental knowledge, puts you in possession of all there is in him, and allows you to be invested with his character itself." Such a commitment to a higher religiosity was the most important characteristic of devotionalist religion, and it also shifted evangelicals decisively away from merely amassing larger numbers to their cause.[16]

The perfectionist impulse was variously called, as its best historian, Timothy L. Smith, notes, "entire sanctification" or "holiness" or "Christian perfection" or "the baptism of the Holy Ghost." In any case, proponents argued that the convert could consecrate himself to live in perfect obedience to God's will. For some, this "second blessing" accompanied the attainment of saving faith itself; for others, sanctification was still a gradual process of a willful growth in grace after the initial encounter with the Holy Spirit. But the fundamental principle was that one's energy was focused forward, on living Christ more intently, rather than backward, in seeking to expurgate ruinous heretical tendencies or immoral impulses. "'Perfection,'" Smith writes, "meant perfect trust and consecration, the experience of 'the fullness of the love of Christ,' not freedom from troublesome physical and mental appetites or from error and prejudice." One young woman, in coming to believe in "perfect righteousness" or "entire sanctification," announced that her religious life was shifting "from a state whose predominant element was a scrupulous and exacting conscientiousness, to a condition of peace and joy through faith." Perfectionism released one from the intellectualist confines of doctrinal orthodoxy and from the censuriousness of moralism. Given its expansive air, perfectionism would feed upon its own triumphs as long as one did not retreat into a more nervous self-doubting.[17]

Perfectionists, believing in the continuity of life history, could not accept the notion that one's sole encounter with the intimacy of God occurred during the conversion experience. Elizabeth Payson, for example, was shocked when another young female teacher in her school at Richmond, Virginia, "said she did not think continued acts of faith in Christ necessary; she had believed on Him once, and now He would save her whatever she did; and she was not going to torment herself trying to live so very holy a life, since, after all, she should get to heaven just as well through Him as if she had been particularly good (as she termed it)." This may have been good orthodox Calvinism, but to Elizabeth's mind it was horrifying:

> Who can believe himself thus chosen of God, who can think of and hold communion with Infinite Holiness, and not long for the Divine image in his own soul? It is a mystery to me—these strange doctrines. Is not the fruit of love aspiration after the holy? Is not the act of the new-born soul when it passes from death unto life, that of desire for assimilation to and oneness with Him who is its all in all? How can love and faith be *one act* and then cease?

Elizabeth could not understand the static quality of her colleague's religion. Why, if this was the same kind of faith as her own, did it not stimulate rhythmic acts of piety? Why was there no progression in it?[18]

To devotionalists, the singularity of the conversion experience could hardly be proof of its divine origin. How could any individual moment of joy be a reliable test of one's piety? Phoebe Palmer, a Methodist pietist, argued for a passionate continuousness in one's religious life. As she wrote in 1847,

> She also found one act of faith not sufficient to insure a continuance in the "way of holiness," but that a *continuous* act was requisite. "As ye have received Christ Jesus the Lord, so walk ye in him," was an admonition greatly blessed to her soul. Assured that there was no grace but by the exercise of the same resoluteness of character, presenting all and keeping all upon the hallowed altar, and also in the exercise of the same faith, she was enabled, through the teachings of the Spirit, "to walk by the same rule, and mind the same thing," and for years continued an onward walk in the "way of holiness."

This key word for Palmer, used four times here, was "same." The test of a good experience of holiness was that it perfectly resembled a prior one. If the will exercised a kind of "resoluteness of character" that recalled an exactly similar exercise in the past, then one's grace was retained. If the rule followed in two different cases was the same, then it would be verified as "the teachings of the Spirit." One's memory was a perfect and perpetual reference book for testing the truth.[19]

Events were holy, then, if they resembled one another perfectly. Here the devotionalist aesthetic of one-to-one correspondences was employed in determining the continuousness of our life histories. A significant change had been made in the moralist view of habitual conscientiousness. For the moralists, events had to represent the same moral principles; this allowed them to be formed into steady habits and consequently proofs of virtue. For devotionalists, the acts themselves had to be as repetitive as possible, indistinguishable from one another, in order to fulfill the divine law completely.

Of course, the ultimate repetitiveness in religious life comes in the ritual application of symbol and sacramental act. The French sociologist of religion, Hervé Carrier, observes that the most advanced people in the faith commonly seek for rituals or symbols in their observance rather than such discursive elements as sermons. We have already seen how Edward Payson made the prayer, rather than the sermon, the prime act of religious life for his congregation.[20]

Devotionalists spoke freely and frequently of their dismay with theological language. Doctrine seemed a persistent distraction. Ada Parker was "glad that I have always been inclined to read the Bible so much as a devotional book, in quest of practical doctrines of godliness. . . . I am not always free from misgivings on doctrinal points, but the thought that they need not be settled in a minute keeps me calm." Ministers soon caught the drift of this antagonism. E. P. Powell, a Michigan Congregationalist, wrote that "the days yearn for a platform and organs of simple piety, instead of dogmas; less of Calvin, and Beza, and Edwards, and everybody else, and more of Christ." The great names of the past were now reinterpreted as exemplary devotionalists. Samuel Wolcott, for example, despite his doctor of divinity degree, noted that he cited Edwards only for "his rich and beautiful religious experience, his holy resolutions, his solitary walks and devotions in the meadows and groves of the Connecticut valley, and among the Berkshire hills, his constant communion with the Master, or his lofty and glowing discourse on the great theme of Redemption."[21]

The most sophisticated argument in this vein was made by Edwards A. Park before the annual convention of the Congregational ministers of Massachusetts in 1850. *The Theology of the Intellect and of the Feelings* offered no explicit challenge to evangelical orthodoxy. Indeed, as professor of theology at Andover, the leading theologian in Congregationalism, and editor of the works of Emmons and Hopkins, Park did more than anyone to preserve and sanctify the New Divinity's intellectual rigor. But now Park argued that these doctrines were true not because of their consistency with revelation or their congruence with observable data. "If the Bible could be proved to be a myth," he went so far as to say, "it would still be a divine myth; for a narrative so wonderfully fitted for penetrating through all the different avenues to the different sensibilities of the soul, must have a moral if not a literal truth."

Theological acceptability was a function of personality traits. "In unnumbered cases, the real faith of Christians has been purer than their written statements of it." No longer was the soul to put on the armature of the gospel plan. Now gospel truth was what appealed most to the soul.[22]

Park evoked the stillness of the communion service as an illustration of his "theology of the feelings." The liturgical incantation—"This is my body, this is my blood"—was, he said, "demanded" by the occasion, "as more pertinent and fit than any other. . . . But no sooner are these phrases transmuted from hearty utterances into intellectual judgments, then they merge their beautiful rhetoric into an absurd logic, and are at once repulsed by a sound mind into their pristine sphere." As Austin Phelps, Park's colleague, said ten years later, "We think more than we believe. We believe more than we have faith in. Our faith is too calm, too cool, too sluggish." But activity and organization were not the remedies. " 'It is trusting, not working,' " announced W. E. Boardman, " 'by which God has ordained to save sinners.' " Ritual, devotion, continuous and repeated prayer would lead one to a higher Christian life.[23]

This intensified "liturgicalism" led devotionalists to construe particular religious events as examples of heavenly models. As Maria Elizabeth Clapp of Boston wrote, "There is a difference, a rich variety, in our sabbaths: and yet all sabbaths are alike; for they remind us of the eternal sabbath of rest prepared for all who love God." But even more suggestive of this was the great care she took in elaborating a description of one Sabbath into an act of sacred commemoration:

> May 30.—Sweet, sacred sabbath! welcome have been thy hours of worship and of communion. This anniversary is dearer to me than all others, dearer than my birthday and than any festival, because it marks and recalls the day of my sweet and solemn covenant with Jesus, of perpetual love and trust. Often, often, has my soul been revived and refreshed, and more ardent desires after holiness been awakened, as I have sat in the stillness and quiet of the sabbath afternoon at the table of the dear Lord, to whom I have joined and committed myself, my all. How gently has he led me by the silken cords of love! how abundantly has he fulfilled his promise to me,—to keep and to restore my soul, and lead me in green pastures!
>
> Today I again enter "my Father's house." As I advance towards my accustomed seat, I see the old and the young assembled to worship God. Silence reigns. What thoughts fill the mind! what emotions swell in the heart! As I look around upon faces over which reverence spreads its calm and cultivated expression, methinks, here and there, true hearts are disposing themselves to worship in spirit and in truth, and silently are praying for the presence and blessing of God upon the sacred duties about to be performed. Soon the silence is sweetly broken by the tune-

ful peal of the organ, as the earthly shepherd of the assembled flock as-
cends the sacred desk, causing our hearts to swell with gratitude and
praise. A portion of God's holy word is then read. The minister is
seated. The voice of the organ is again heard, in soft and subdued
tones, inviting and helping the mind to meditate on the divine truths
which have been uttered, and preparing it to engage in the succeeding
act of devotion, when our pastor shall stand up, and say, in reverential
and persuasive tones, "Let us pray." The hymn of praise is then sung.
And now the words of the text are heard,—"*I came not to condemn the
world, but to save the world.*" Our hearts are then led to the Saviour, and
fastened on him. Another brief prayer, a doxology, and a benediction, a
sweet invitation is given from the pulpit to a participation at the table of
our common Lord, to the dear and sacred rite in commemoration of the
Saviour who died for us. But why, why does any one go away? Why do
not all remain? Is not that Saviour dear to all?

They [those not members in full communion] have departed. Sadly
have we seen them rise, and go away. . . . The door is shut; and we are
left, a little band of Christ's disciples, faint ourselves, but pursuing;
. . . coming near and clinging fast to our Lord and Master, because we
have felt how weak we are, how kind and strong he is, and that, separated from him, we cannot stand nor rest.

Lo, Christ is here! Thoughts of the world, begone! this is no place
for you. Cares and pleasures of earth, be far from the mind! This
ground is holy. Disciple of Jesus, thou are drawing near in spirit to thy
Saviour. . . .

Now we have sung our parting hymn, and, covered with a heavenly
benediction, leave the sanctuary.

Each incident could, for the young devotee, be connected with previous memories of similar beauties or its present loveliness augmented and suspended in
midair by emotional overtones. By the careful use of the present tense, the
dramatic moment of a particular Sabbath in May was made not only more
immediate but also more representative of other communion days. In the
diary entry, the immediacy of the date, for example, was quickly followed by
the memory of previous Sabbaths; the specialness of this month and day, as
the anniversary of Maria Clapp's first communion, commingled with the satisfactions that followed that first tasting. Even when Maria's account finally
turned, in the second paragraph, to the description of the communion Sabbath worship—in much greater detail, incidentally, than one finds in earlier
diaries—she could not point out the kinds of happenings, colors and sounds
that would have marked this day off from others. Except for the text of the
minister's sermon, nothing about Sunday, May 30, 1847, was distinguishable
from any other Sabbath. Most of Maria Clapp's narrative was occupied with

her own sentimental reactions to the service. The facts of the Boston morning meant less than the consistent way she responded to them; and, according to Phoebe Palmer's formula, the similarity between her response now and her response before verified the godliness of her communion experience.[24]

By taking so seriously the need to present the entirety of a church service and then by emphasizing the interior emotional effects of the service, Maria Clapp satisfied both conditions for ritualization. The sacrament had to be precisely performed so that its regular repetition would be possible; then it needed to have a calculable effect on church members that would be repeatedly recognizable. Both the outward gestures of the minister and his congregation and the inward affections needed to be systematized to produce the perfect "act of devotion."

Finally, the young woman's narrative was such a remarkable revisualization of the communion service. To have written as she did, she needed to abstract herself a bit from immediate participation and look at herself only as a part of this portrait of preacher, parishioners, and communicants. This eye for the visual aesthetics of the service was, as we have seen, rather new for New Englanders but in keeping with their ever more exact images of Christ. And it fit comfortably in the many highly ornamented Gothic Revival churches built by devotionalist congregations.[25]

An attempt to visualize, construct, and maintain a physical environment designed for holiness concretely expressed the liturgical spirit among evangelicals in the 1840s and 1850s. In such spaces, the perfect consistency of cause and effect could be realized in the devotionalist ritual. Here, one's life history would achieve its most perfect consistency. Each act of devotion would then be a reliving of every other one, an exact replication of that perfect intimacy with Christ toward which all of one's life was directed. Life history, ideally, reached its apotheosis when development became repetition.

Chapter Sixteen

The Religion of Friendship

EVERY TYPE OF RELIGIOUS SENSIBILITY, even one that emerges in a withdrawal from society, is predicated upon a particular social setting. For its devotees it must provide, no matter how highly individualized its promise of grace is, some manner of social communion. We conclude our study of devotionalism, then, by asking, what was its effect on the social experience of religion? If we were to stand with Maria Clapp, looking down at the fashionably dressed parishioners parading into the ornate edifices of mid-nineteenth-century American religion, what kind of community would we see? How would such a throng of people experience one another, and how would they relate to those who did not attend their churches?

A careful analysis of Maria Clapp's rapt account of the communion service can provide a good initial answer to this question (see the extract at the end of chapter 15). The whole passage breathes with the spirit of an intensely private experience. Maria Clapp began, one sees, with a paragraph of personal feeling and memory before she entered the church itself. Then she surveyed the assembled congregation and insisted upon projecting her own hallowed feelings—reverence, calmness, gratitude, and praise—into the minds of those present. The movement of the service was transacted only within individual minds; no interaction among the parishioners was suggested. And each was brought to feel that he was approaching Jesus personally in the Eucharist: "Disciple," the singular is stressed, "of Jesus, thou are drawing near in spirit to thy Saviour."

Although the consciousness of the congregants was highly individuated, their experience was anything but lonely. The feelings Clapp projected into each mind are, after all, shared feelings. They could only have arisen in a social experience, and, because all are said to be weak and dependent, the entire group can be called a "band of Christ's disciples." And while each parishioner had an independent and personal relationship to the minister and to Jesus, both "the earthly shepherd of the assembled flock" and "our common

Lord" are emphatically shared objects of the group's attention. Finally, when the attenders have left the room, Maria noted, "*we* are left."[1]

For devotionalists, then, coming nearer to Jesus was an individual responsibility and a personal achievement. One never lost oneself in the collective worship. But coming to Christ worked best when accomplished in the company of other Christians. The perfect religious mood could be replicated within each person and shared sympathetically with others. This method of cohesion differs from the stronger group sense of moralism. In moralist congregations, the group cohered by excluding others from their shared principles. Unity was a defensive gesture, a way, for example, of warding off vice. Among devotionalists the positive attachment to Christ's fellowship created a powerful mutuality. The evangelical impulse to test lost its social bite in this generation; devotionalists were reluctant to invalidate the qualifications of others.

Gradually, the requirement for a public testimony of one's faith and doctrinal knowledge was being eliminated in churches of the 1830s and 1840s. In 1836, the Hampton, Connecticut, Congregationalists reversed their 1799 vote to examine candidates for church membership publicly. The decision was prefaced by the following explanation: "As the prosperity of every church depends more upon its graces than upon its numbers, and as great responsibility is involved in the admission of members; and believing that the practice of first propounding candidates, and then publicly examining them before a promiscuous assembly [i.e., including nonmembers] in order to judge of the propriety of their being received into the church is not most likely to promote the interests of Christ's Kingdom." Once an increased membership was abandoned as the goal of every church, it seemed better to think of religion in a more inward way. And though the resolution did not say so outright, it seemed somewhat indelicate now to expose one's personal experience before everyone in the community, especially in front of those who had not themselves been vulnerable to cross-examination by the diaconate.[2]

For devotionalists, religion was a mysterious affair, hidden from the world's purview and not worn outwardly. Devotionalism separated the experience of religion from its institutional arrangements, apologizing for the latter as a convenience at best. The conversion narratives of the Dickerman family, for example, encompassing hundreds of pages from the diaries of three sisters and a brother, mentioned church attendance only in passing and prayer meetings only as occasional stimulants to piety. The contest, as we see in this excerpt from the writings of the youngest sister, was between the "closet" (where she conducted private devotions) and the "world":

> The commencement of my religious impressions I owe, under God, to
> my mother's prayers. Often, when I was quite small, and slept in her

room, I would be awakened by her voice; and as I listened to her and my father in eager prayer for their children, I wept in silence, and felt that I ought to love God. Alas! when morning came, I forgot those feelings in play, and was as thoughtless as ever. Yet those impressions have never been wholly effaced. About three years ago it pleased God to pour out his Holy Spirit upon this community, and I then hoped that I obtained an interest in Christ. I believe that the weekly inquiry meetings which were held at the house of our pastor, and the little afternoon prayer meetings with Mrs. W. [Warren, the pastor's wife], were blessed to my soul. I felt then a new life within me, and longed to do something for the cause of my Saviour. But as the interest subsided I was, in a measure, drawn back to the world, and I grieve to say that I can recall seasons spent in the closet in which I had no enjoyment, but prayer was a cold and heartless exercise. Thanks be to God that he did not cut me off from his favor, but has, I hope, led me by my failures to see my own weakness, and trust alone in him. God grant that I may never more go astray.

So gradual and internal was Fannie Dickerman's conversion, at the tender age of eleven, that she could scarcely identify a particular crisis or any real obstacle to her assumption of piety. Her faith came with the support of parents, siblings, the church, the pastor and his wife, and neighbors. The process comprised only the ebb and flow of religious emotion within her own mind. When she could finally will her trust in God deeply enough, she was evidently saved.[3]

This internalized progress of the soul profoundly rejected the institutional traditions of New England evangelicism. More immediately, the moralist enterprise seemed particularly challenged by the way Baron Stow and other men tired of the endless committee work that evangelical reform demanded. As we have seen, they turned to sentimentalism to recover the depth of spirituality missing for them in everyday organizational life. Henry Clay Fish, for one, disputed the central premise of the moralist's focus on the act of Christian enlistment. Nothing was "more common," Fish wrote, "both in civil and sacred things, than for membership to weaken the sense of responsibility. But, was it the design of Christ," he asked pugnaciously, "that the church should absorb the individual? For what are any combinations formed? Not to neutralize the personal element, but to render it more effective."[4]

Clearly, devotionalists like Fish did not wish to dispense with the institutional structures of the churches altogether but rather to use them for other ends. It was still dangerous, for example, for young Christians to live outside the church, where temptations abounded. When she was fifteen, Fannie Dickerman reflected that her church membership "has been a shield to me many times, to remember that the vows of God are upon me, and that I am compassed about with a great cloud of witnesses, who are looking to see if there is really any love of Jesus in my heart." The defensive power of moralism worked for young devotionalists as well, to protect themselves most pertinently from those neighbors who expected better behavior from a "disciple of Jesus."[5]

This was hardly the stuff of real piety, but membership could also at least make richer experiences like communion available to the pious. "Could you but know the happiness I have felt," one young woman wrote, "since I united with that band (though there is no virtue in the *mere outward act*); the inward strength I have received; the calm, subduing influences of those seasons of communion." By and large, however, those who yearned for an ever more perfect intimacy with God felt somewhat supercilious and superior toward the elementary commitments that actuated moralist religion. "Retirement and self-communion do more for the soul than social intercourse," one typical comment went, "but then we must come down from the mount that we may win others."[6]

If, then, moralism was defensive against the sinful impulses of Christians, and occasionally haughty in pointing fingers at offenders, devotionalism was potentially even more exclusivist and elitist. Even certified Christians, if they had not the special saintliness that true disciples could recognize intuitively in one another, might be scorned. "I am always ready," Maria Clapp wrote in this vein, "to join in converse with Christian friends, but more especially with the chosen, the beloved of those friends." The church of the beloved, she hinted, was an invisible body. The worship of such a communion was as private as it was holy. Moralism, especially in the early Beecherite days of winning all to the banner of evangelical propriety, had stressed the individual's adherence to a collectivity of believers and could never have sanctioned such a division of the congregation as Maria Clapp and other devotionalists were prepared to discover.[7]

As we have seen, devotionalism tended to retract from ordinary social situations. Believing in a face-to-face encounter with divinity, the devotionalists were quick to withdraw from social tensions to the rich communion with Christ promised to the faithful heart. In 1851, for instance, Horace Bushnell wrote to a friend that "I seem to be now very much cut off from access to the public; not so, I trust from access to God. God is left, and he is the best public to me," Bushnell consoled himself, "the only public in which I have any satisfaction; and I think with the highest delight of going apart with him into a desert place to rest awhile."[8]

But, significantly, devotionalists did not confine their efforts at intimacy only to such fantasies of perfect communion with God. Instead, their abundant love could apply the same fundamental model—again, of one-to-one relationships, becoming ever more perfect—to interpersonal concerns. The ideal Christian society thus became the friendship between two souls. Christopher Lasch discovered the following sentiment in a letter between two New England women in 1839: "Life is short, and kindred spirits are few, the chances of their meeting are fewer still, and poor human nature has so many jarring strings, that, after all, friendship is something more to be worshipped as an ideal good, than a real, and possible thing, something that *may be,* rather than something that *is."* Before the 1830s, evangelicals had generally scorned friendship as distracting from the single, larger, and mandatory commitment to the church or to the moral community. Now it had become the essence of religion itself, the surest and most accessible metaphor to *secular* sentimentalists, for the life of faith.[9]

By 1859, when Maria Clapp's memoir was published, her biographer could claim that "almost every Christian has a bosom-friend." About her closest friend, he wrote,

> With her she held almost daily communion; to her she revealed the inmost feelings of her heart. This friend she had first been led to love by her efforts to lead her to Christ. In these endeavors she had been successful; and the result was that close intimacy which continued for many years, without a moment's interruption or the slightest jar, till her death. The friendship that subsisted between them was like that between Naomi and Ruth, with the addition of still another element,—a mutual devotion to the Saviour; a mutual daily draught, as out of one cup, of the living water which he giveth; that "agreement as to what they should ask of the Father in his name" to which he encouraged his disciples, two and two, by precious promises.
>
> It was the custom of these friends, both of whom were teachers in primary schools, and whose paths crossed on the way to their separate posts of duty, to exchange notes as they passed each other, containing a few morning thoughts, or a word of Christian salutation and encouragement.

There is something more here than a sharing of new and exciting experiences among acquaintances, who thereby build up a set of common memories from which to draw sustenance for their development. Maria and Lucy are said to minister to each other, to provide even the precious fluid of divine love for each other. This, then, was a friendship that appropriated the world of religion for itself; the friends did not simply share a Saviour; they adopted Jesus' role for each other's immediate benefit. To be a friend was, in that sense, to consecrate oneself, to assume the mantle of the sacred on behalf of another person. A friend substituted for both the revealed wisdom that the orthodox found in Scripture and the common sense that the moralist found in the local community. And in the process of assuming that role, the Christian friend presumably also made progress toward a fuller replication of the Christ-figure in her own mind. Acting as a friend was, thus, an act that brought oneself nearer to God.[10]

There is further evidence for this in the fact that Maria and Lucy, and dozens of other pairs of women friends, bothered to write to each other. Rather than live together and converse endlessly, they found themselves spending enough time alone to gather and reflect upon their religious emotions. To express these feelings in writing was to go beyond nodding agreement with other people's sentiments; as the letters included in Maria's memoir show, it meant taking responsibility for a measure of originality. Each day, as in a dance, they would converge on the way to school, exchange their messages, and separate once again. What an unnecessary formality, unless of course one wanted to accentuate one's privacy by making something grand about its revelation to another person. But the rhythm of establishing and then bridging their aloneness was a significant element in the relationship; so, too, was their extravagant insistence upon "secrecy," which isolated them from others and intensified their communion. "I don't often open my secret heart to my friends," Maria confided in one note, "but it has always been pleasant to commune with *you*. None other knows the secret workings of my soul. Sympathy of spirit unites us to one common Father and Saviour. May we be drawn yet nearer, nearer, nearer!"[11]

Those last words boldly imply that the friend, who "knows the secret workings of my soul," is also an alter ego and the devotionalist divinity. Coming nearer to the core of one's own being, approaching the image of Jesus, and now pleading for more intimacy with one's bosom friend—all seem the same act. Introspection, worship, and communion could be one and the same thing for devotionalists.

Why should the decades around 1850 have been such important seasons for this upsurge of friendship? Men, except for writers and clergymen, seemed relatively immune from this passion for mutuality, but almost every Christian woman's memoir speaks of bosom friendship. (Of course, the theme of "kindred spirits" was a significant one in American art and literature of the day, viz., Ishmael and Queequeg.) Friendship among women had been an important element in the social context of evangelical religion since the First Great Awakening, but, as the famous case of Esther Edwards Burr and Sarah Prince shows, it was often in the service of mutual encouragement in accepting subordination to an orthodox deity and, sometimes, the authority of husbands. As historian Nancy F. Cott suggests, the word "friend" in the eighteenth century still might connote "kin" as much as "peer."[12]

In moralist congregations and reform societies, women shared a new public voice, offering them very specific assistance in clarifying their new social roles. Through female societies and maternal associations, published manuals and benevolent enterprises like sewing circles and reading groups, young wives and mothers learned techniques and manners that compensated for leaving the superintendence of their parents. As women moved from farm work to domestic management, from farms to villages, and from villages to cities, their "sphere" of life became more distinct from that of husbands and brothers. Heroic teachers like Catharine Beecher instructed women on how to glory in the domestic accomplishments of their newer and cleaner (and also smaller) households and household roles.[13]

Moralism proffered a platform for women's voices in its admiration for shared, commonsense wisdom, as it could emerge in the course of habitual gathering with one's neighbors. Female society records repeatedly note the pleasure women took in "conversation" with one another. In a society rife with enthusiasm for rule making, it legitimated the ability of women to shape the refinements of dress, manner, and sensibility that would mark their families' subscription to middle-class norms. Women could note their progress every bit as concretely as their ledger-keeping male associates.

But voice was not enough. Once one had joined the church and become expert in the ways of moralist religion, women glimpsed spiritual possibilities that exceeded the group's expectations. Subordination to the gospel plan was easily verifiable. Correct personal carriage and a deference to locally established opinion could be noted quickly. But an openness to an "intimate walk with God," such as devotionalist women enjoyed, could never be a universal achievement, measurable and recordable. Inevitably, an embarrassment crept in; to reveal oneself to the whole company might subject one to ridicule. Subjectivity was a dangerous snare, self-flattery was a nasty indictment, and scorning domestic virtues was impossible. Under the watchful eyes of older women, emotionally charged seekers after sanctification might meet such remonstrances with a blush. In the place of social voice, devotionalism substituted the hushed whisper or the secret letter between intimate friends.[14]

Where young men might test the limits of moralism in business competition, the ambition of their sisters and wives was potentially more transgressive. Emily Dickinson, for example, could not bring herself to attend the Amherst Sewing Society, "notwithstanding my high approbation." "Somehow or other," she wrote to her friend Jane Humphrey ("my friend encourager, and sincere counciller, my rock, and strong assister"), "I incline to other things. Satan covers them up with flowers, and I reach out to pick them. The path of duty looks very ugly indeed." Fortunately for most New England women, the choice was not simply between the path of moralist duty and picking the flowers of Satan. Devotionalism offered an escape, a way to attenuate the social pressures of playing one's assigned role with great scrupulosity without leaving the religious sphere.[15]

To exemplify this, we can look once again at the diary of Elizabeth Payson. The young woman was actuated by the highest moralist intentions, noting once that "I have not a very extensive sphere of action, but I want my conduct, my every word and look and motion, to be fully under the influence of this desire for the honor of God." But standing in Elizabeth's way was her anxiety in being watched by others. "You can have no idea of the constant observation to which I am exposed here." In December 1841, she wrote, "I went to the sewing-circle this afternoon and had such a stupid time! Enough gossip and nonsense was talked to make one sick, and I'm sure it wasn't the fault of my head that my hair didn't stand on end. Now my mother is a very sensible mother," she conceded, "but when she urges me into company and exhorts me to be more social, she runs the risk of having me become as silly as the rest of 'em." [16]

Against all this pushing into a clearer social role, Elizabeth Payson wanted, "Oh, what is it I *do* want? Somebody who feels as I feel and thinks as I think; but where shall I find the somebody?" Withdrawing from society, then, promised a retreat into a deeper and richer company. "There is a world of something in me which is not known to those about me and perhaps never will be," she had written earlier, and then broached the real object of her quest, "but sometimes I think it would be *delicious* to love a mind like mine in some things, only better, wiser, nobler. I do not quite understand life. People don't live as they were made to live, I'm sure. . . . I want *soul*. I want the gracious, glad spirit that finds the good and the beautiful in everything, joined to the manly, exalted intellect—rare unions, I am sure, yet possible ones." [17]

It was communion she prayed for, even in marriage, not following an elderly and respected model or observing a code book of proprieties. Elizabeth was frank enough to acknowledge, as many devotionalists were not, how much she wanted to have communion with someone just like her. But "better, wiser, nobler," of course, for in sharing intimacy with such a person she would herself grow in grace. To her great friend, Anna S. Prentiss, she wrote in 1843, "I have found a certain something in you that I have been wanting all my life. . . . While I wish you to know me just as I am," she continued, "faults and all, I can't bear to think of ever seeing anything but the good and the beautiful in your character, dear Anna, and I believe my heart would break outright should I find you to be otherwise than just that which I imagine you are." Though this has to be taken with some lightness, Elizabeth's devotion was clearly to an object of her imagination. Or, at the very least, she felt herself capable and correct in reaching within for the soul she wanted to love: first, it was Anna Prentiss; ultimately, it was Anna's brother, George, who became Elizabeth's husband. In either case, she found in the devotionalist rhetoric a way of dramatizing her quest for a perfect communion. The drama of her life, then, was not played according to the standard and approved script. She had taken responsibility for writing it herself. [18]

Think of what it meant to write one's own life history in this way; think of the sensation of personal freedom that came with the ability to consider oneself in different biographical guises. To accomplish this, Elizabeth Payson and other devotionalists had to rely upon the newly developed sense of the history of one's life as a work of art. And, too, the notion of a full biographical development was by definition an object of reverie. To write one's history, one had therefore to *imagine* the possibility of others.

Simply to read the memoirs of saints who had passed before, taking solace or inspiration from the acts of their lives or the insights of their minds, was not sufficient. Devotionalists did not want to transfer bits of others' lives into their own, but to displace themselves entirely into another's life. Friendship was the easiest and best way to achieve such a displacement. "The very ground and gist of a noble friendship," a book on *The Friendships of Women* assumed, "is the cultivation in common of the personal inner lives of those who partake in it, their mutual reflection of souls and joint sharing of experience inciting them to a constant betterment of their being and their happiness." People who allowed these sorts of exchanges were prime candidates for devotionalist religion; in turn, lesser relationships, which did not offer such intimacy, were scarcely admitted to the honor of true friendship.[19]

Of course projection into another personality also allowed one to glimpse shared spiritual conditions. Ada R. Parker awoke one night, the moonlight streaming through her window, and her "thoughts wandered to my dear sister. . . . with her I seemed to go up to our Father in heaven; soul in soul went we up together for a word and smile of love. . . . Our different personalities seemed melted into one, and when I came to a kind of self-consciousness, it surprised me to find that my eyes were filled with tears." For the self that had given up both doctrine and moral norms as anchors, friendship could be the best confirmation of the essential rightness of one's individual course. The "shock of recognition," seeing one's deepest mysteries mirrored in the interior personality of a friend, became an experience of righteousness, as close as modern people were likely to get to the infusion of divine harmony in their souls.[20]

Such acts of imaginative projection achieved redemptive significance in the great fiction of the mid-nineteenth century, as in Ishmael's sympathy for Queequeg and for Ahab and in Huck Finn's love for Jim (at the explicit cost of both social ostracism and orthodox damnation). Imaginative projection is the prime act of *Leaves of Grass,* and the failure to achieve it is a sign of moral failure in a dozen of Hawthorne's tales.[21]

One by-product of this devotionalist zest for projection was an intensified charitable impulse. The standard of compassion, particularly compassion for complete strangers, was raised as the Christian obligation to feel oneself suffering in the place of others was repeatedly articulated. As Timothy L. Smith writes, "The nineteenth-century quest for holiness was turned into avenues of service, instead of the byways of mystic contemplation." And, clearly, as Smith's description of their social service work shows, the enterprises of devotionalist women differed significantly from the reform endeavors of the earlier generation of moralists. The latter had usually focused upon issues of individual moral uplift—combating drunkenness, Sabbath violations, prostitution—in which the chief technique was to reorganize the converts' lives on the lines of community morality. Or, some moralists had devoted themselves to organizing the expansion of Christian communities—by missionary work, subsidizing indigent ministerial candidates, tract and Bible distribution. Finally, through antislavery and peace crusades, moralists hoped that a commitment to righteousness would have powerful effects on the whole society. Devotionalists like Phoebe Palmer, Smith says, worked hard to maintain many of these efforts. But their special contribution was in direct service to the poor and helpless: establishing agencies like the Young Men's Christian Association to tend to the needs of strangers in the midcentury city and caring for orphans, unwed mothers, and prisoners through urban missions. Although both devotionalists and moralists shared the evangelical belief in an individual experience of regeneration, the devotionalists seemed more attuned to the alleviation of suffering than the reformation of behavior, more conscious of the need than the sin of their clientele. In fact, well before the Civil War, devotionalist social services were shaping the models for the Social Gospel movement of the late nineteenth century.[22]

In addressing the needs of the poor so directly, rather than upholding and attracting adherents to the standards of evangelical moralism, devotionalists were activated by a passionate feeling that Christian love could best be expressed in tending another's body and soul. These "angels of mercy," with hearts overflowing with love for the unfortunate, had a therapeutic impulse similar in nature to that concern Maria Clapp shared with her friend. They would devote themselves to this work as fully as Christ had dedicated himself to the task of redeeming human sinfulness. The larger the need, the more they felt themselves engaged in the work.

It is hard to set limits to such charitable feelings. The Victorians were thrilled to shed a tear for the sufferings they read about in novels as well as newspapers, and with the expansion of the mass media—penny papers, ladies' magazines, and telegraphs in the nineteenth century, radio, television, and photojournalism in the twentieth—the opportunity for such sympathizing has steadily increased. "Generosity," says the theologian Richard Reinhold Niebuhr about the condition of modern man, "has become the fate of every man. . . . With our communications technology," he explains, "we have extended our senses and our sensibilities in making the scope of our eyes and ears coterminous with the inhabited earth and its solar environment. . . . The common human passions pass along the earth's channels of intersubjectivity with speed and ease. Such unremitting and extensive emotional sharing as this has multiplied by a ratio not yet calculated the susceptibility of the individual to emotional infection by his generation." How are we to answer all these demands for our sympathy? The ease with which the plight of others is communicated to us has no analogue in our ability to alleviate that plight; we cannot solve the problems by talking back to our radios or newspapers.

Furthermore, by understanding the difficulties of others through the method of a devotionalist's projection into a friend's mind, we tend to concentrate on the symptoms of mental anguish among victims of natural disaster, war, and poverty and to downplay the impersonal causes of such distress. Pictures of starving children are more telling than explanations of social, economic, and political conflict. Of course, "moralist" governments and bureaucratic agencies tend to work in the opposite way, substituting organizational strategies for emotional and/or political sympathy.[23]

Paradoxically, the mental process by which we achieve the greatest freedom of self-identification also leads to profound disappointment and pain. By the same projection of our selves into the hearts of others, we can pretend to be a daring young flyer, a movie star, or the president of the United States; or we can feel ourselves inhabiting a European village torn by war and living among Asian farmers ravaged by earthquakes and floods.

Moralism had provided a defense against such promiscuous projections, and it continues to do so whenever we emphasize the bounds of a community tied by origin or sentiment. The cost of moralism, of course, is the way it delimits our identity to our place in such a community. If we escape such limits, it is only into ourselves or a projected identity.

One result of this pattern of mental experience has been the collapse of alternatives to friendship among our relationships with others. When we can think of others only as ourselves, we become incapable of the myriad shades of otherness that were known in the past, and every relationship—formerly filial, or conjugal, or deferential to one's social betters, or condescending to one's inferiors, or loyal to the rules, or alien from strangers—can now only be legitimately fraternal. Slowly, over the last century, a gigantic democratization of relatedness has occurred, and personal authority has diminished everywhere. The only connection we can admit is a one-to-one correspondence between the parties.[24]

This was felt most strongly, perhaps, within the devotionalist household. Urging parents to rear their children by using themselves as model Christians, Horace Bushnell was hoping that the effects of such one-to-one correspondences between parent and child would be as beneficial to the older member of the pair as to the younger; parents would themselves be improved in piety by assuming the role of ideals for their offspring. In itself, this was not exceptional; repeatedly since the days of Cotton Mather, American parents had been pressed to institute family prayers and to inquire about the spiritual welfare of their wards. But Mather's paternalism demanded that children subordinate themselves to the magistracy of their fathers just as they would the majesty of the universe in God. He would never have expected parents, as Bushnell did, to imagine being a childlike Christian. Mather demanded that children quickly emulate their parents; he would have scoffed at the notion of projecting oneself into the lives of his children. For Bushnell, the parent-child relationship, like all those between the Christian and God, was fraternal. Filial authority had devolved into mutual support and respect.[25]

Not surprisingly, the middle-class mother became the focal point of the new childrearing in the mid-nineteenth century. Devotionalist women shared a key characteristic with their well-nurtured children in the Victorian household. Neither were expected to play significant economic roles in the commercial world outside. Instead, both could convert their dependence on the father's cash income into a spiritually strong "refuge" from the world's corruption. A mother's authority in this setting was less significant than her modeling of loving kindness and showing ways to use leisure time profitably, in educationally and recreationally rewarding activities. Just as mothers were expected to gather their sense of participation in the political and productive economic world vicariously through their husbands, so their husbands could take vicarious pleasure in the ways wives exercised their taste as consumers and housekeepers. And for both parents, children provided considerable gratification as the family's "representatives in enjoyment," whether in scholastic, athletic, or social spheres or later in getting themselves financially settled and well-married.[26]

It has taken more than a century for the revolution in private life to run its course, but gradually the symmetrical relationships among family members have become more and more acceptable. Ultimately, in our own day, diminishing sexual differences between partners and an emerging interest in adult development on the model of child development studies, have made the family a more thoroughly fraternal organization. The momentum for this transformation has been fueled by the gradual disappearance of entrepreneurship and economically independent roles for either men or women, as the proportion of salaried workers has climbed steadily. By the mid-twentieth century, men too were chiefly identified as consumers and participants in vicarious enjoyments. Under these circumstances, spouses can also demand to be intimate friends, and the family has focused its collective energy on various consumer decisions, including life planning for parents and children alike.[27]

In short, devotionalism provided models by which all experiences have come to be understood in the last century and a quarter, and middle-class women, as the pioneers in this way of understanding themselves, have blazed the trails for almost all of the population. Cultivating one's inner life has become the major defense for all of us against the confines of an overly organized bureaucratic society. But to be masters within ourselves, first women and now men have had to become dependents in what has since come to be called the "real world." It is not odd, then, to find women like Elizabeth Payson, after claiming a demesne of private freedom for herself, to blurt out, "I wish I could always live, as I have hitherto done, under the shelter of my mother's wing." The widowed Mrs. Payson, like most of the husbands and fathers of her generation, had to provide a stable environment for her dependents. For men still facing the uncertainties of an emerging capitalist economy, moralism could help in establishing such a haven; it could be a reliable guide to proper conduct. There was enough drama for commercial men in the boom-and-bust cycle of American business, without needing the inward intensities of mood that their wives sought in devotionalism.[28]

But moralism must also be seen as the intrusion of the social realm into our private lives. It insisted upon giving publicity to a man's private character; it demanded that he submit the education of his children to the society at large; it internalized proper social norms as the regulative principles of personal activity. Perhaps most important, moralism made his ability to earn a living contingent upon subscribing to certain norms of business practice, ultimately involving him in an enormous, impersonal commercial network.

In response, seemingly to save a semblance of privacy in the modern world, devotionalism posited a new, deeper, sense of intimacy. Its key experiences were entirely subjective, unique exercises of reverie, protected from the snooping of society. Its definition of the relationship with God emphasized personal receptivity to divine companionship, at the cost of social interactions. Its way of dealing with other people similarly sealed them off from community interference. As long as the parent-child, husband-wife, or friend-friend relationship remained private, its heated intimacy was freed from moralist restraints.

Devotionalism allowed one, as we have seen, to become another person's vicar, even when that person was thousands of miles away. In this way, personal experience became increasingly vicarious; one lived through one's fantasies of other people's lives, even one's children's lives. One could, at the end, not even be sure of one's own identity, for in making the self capable of being projected into so many new circumstances of life, one's own life history became problematic. Even though it was engaged in diving deeper in one's own subjective consciousness, devotionalism had the awful effect of making one a stranger to oneself, a detached observer of one's biographical possibilities. In turning to the inner self as the only safe refuge from the disappointments and frustrations of social life, the alarming discovery was made that no self was there. From that spiritual crisis we have not yet found an escape.

Conclusion

It was the same God, and it may have been in the same places and the same buildings. But the religious experience of New Englanders had been transformed in the first century of American independence and had been reorganized according to the successive experiential economies of doctrinalism, moralism, and devotionalism. At least six different elements of personal experience constitute such an economy:

- the closeness of the religious person to God;
- the locus of authority for regarding oneself as religious;
- the aspects of mental life most significantly involved in religious experience;
- the relationship of single spiritual events to a life history;
- the comparison of the religious sphere of life to other, nonsacred activities;
- the connection of the individual believer to a specific religious community.

I can make six generalizations about how religious experience changed from 1790 to 1860:

First, God was increasingly experienced intimately rather than distantly and ever more clearly as a personal (anthropomorphized) figure. The orthodox divinity was a metaphysical power, presumed to enact his own ordered plan for the universe, which it was then man's responsibility to discover. By impressing upon sinners the need to trust such a power, moralists reinterpreted God as a figure with whom one could have a relationship as one could with one's parent or trusted guardian. Gradually, by midcentury, the divine figure became more precisely recognizable in the human image, and was enjoyed for its companionable qualities. Christ rather than the Father became the focal point of this attention to God as a friend.

Second, the criterion for regarding oneself as a Christian moved away from well-understood "objective" standards and toward more interpersonal and personal judgments. While the orthodox enjoined sinners to test themselves by introspection, they were to measure themselves against the "fixed standard" of the "gospel plan," which was to be found in both biblical language and the logic of Calvinist argument. The turn toward behavioral standards was, in some ways, an externalizing of religious life, but assurance still rested upon internal evidence of one's faithful following of local proprieties. Conscience, in other words, was transformed from the orthodox saint's guide to eternal truth into the moralist's internalization of virtuous principles. Finally, the best evidence for a devotionalist's faith was an intense and wholehearted communion with the divine, cultivated through repeated exercises of inner self-dramatization.

Third, the process of becoming and living as a Christian gradually involved the cognitive faculties of the mind less and the affective and volitional faculties more. For the orthodox, discovering one's consistency with the gospel plan was so important that the intellect or understanding was treasured for its faultless discernment. Over time, one's willful commitment to religion seemed to furnish the mind with the requisite perceptions of religious truth. Converts were taught to will rather than to doubt. The religious feelings that had been conceived by the orthodox as the secondary products of intellectual insight became the core of true religion.

Fourth, the life history of the Christian was more often seen as a continuing, developmental process by which moral activity and personal devotion were stabilized as routine ways of life. Although conversion was always an important part of evangelical religion, the success of nineteenth-century revivals—as well as the desire of religionists to be part of a commercial civilization—added significance to the gradual process of sanctification (i.e., the growth of Christians after their conversion). Spectacularly distinctive events like conversion crises, which had formerly provided the entire meaning to a person's life, were downgraded in favor of consistent acts. Both moralists and sentimentalists believed that piety could be systematically developed by exercise over time, leading moralists to firmly establish habits of virtue or provoking sentimentalists continually to repeat moments of communion with Christ. Gradually, earthly life came to be thought a time for living in grace, not merely attaining it. And the course of whole life far outweighed—in the writings of Christians—the special significance of individual incidents.

Fifth, religious life came more and more to occupy a sphere of ordinary life, marked off from the secular by its attention to different objects but sharing the same patterns by which secular time and space were organized. The doctrinalists tended to view all events as transpiring on two levels: (1) within the order of grace, in which divine intervention might be felt to alter the course of events; and (2) within the order of nature wherein God was assumed to govern the world on consistent Newtonian principles. When the confusions of interpreting every event in two ways became too much for evangelicals, they began to depict religion as simply another sphere of natural life. Religion was conducted on the same plane of life as commerce, childrearing, or politics—that is, with no miraculous intermissions. Moralists wanted to apply the lessons of an increasingly bureaucratized and commercial society to the religious sphere in order to achieve greater consistency and order, but devotionalists opted for considering religion apart from society, as a way of intensifying a personal "engagedness" impossible in social and economic life.

And lastly, joining the society of religious men and women was increasingly a matter of associating with specific people and less adhering to the institutional incarnation of a metaphysical principle. Loyalty to the church of the orthodox was equivalent to the enactment—but in human, physical terms—of one's eternal connection to God's kingdom. The church itself embodied truth. Interactions among church members were more important by the second quarter of the nineteenth century. Loyalty was now to the church members rather than to the institutional church itself. This suspicion about institutions was carried further by the devotionalists; by midcentury, they believed that Christians were bound to one another only by personal feelings of sympathy. The most appropriate form of Christian social expression became friendship and fellow discipleship.

Although they did not see these changes as we do, nineteenth-century evangelicals were hardly oblivious to the transformations of religious experience. Sometimes, as indicated in the passage from Nathaniel Bouton's autobiography with which I began the exploration of "Closeness to God," the weakening of orthodoxy augured a loss of experiential nourishment for which the sweet diet of midcentury devotionalism was not ample compensation. Occasionally, the purpose of such comparisons was more avowedly polemical, as when Bennet Tyler, writing in 1846, brandished the revivals of the early nineteenth century as a weapon against contemporary declension. Speaking of those early days, Tyler observed that "the converts in these revivals, were not made in that easy way, in which many professed converts in more recent times have been made, without any struggle in their minds, and without feeling any sensible opposition to God and the claims of the gospel; but they endured great conflicts." That language, of course, had been quite familiar in New England since the mid-seventeenth-century Puritans began complaining about the degeneration of their children.[1]

A more interesting, because more balanced, outline of changes in the form of religious experience appeared in Joseph Tracy's 1841 volume commemorating the centennial of the First Great Awakening. After long excerpts from revival narratives of the 1740s, Tracy compared the religiosity of his own day.

> Many, who can understand how sinners should be overcome by a sense of danger, will be staggered at these accounts of intense, overpowering emotion in Christians, in view of purely spiritual objects,—of God, and the glorious truths that relate to him. But the fact that they did thus feel, and were thus overcome by their feelings, is undeniable.

And the testimony is abundant, that such beholdings of the glory of the Lord did exert a transforming influence upon them, making them more humble, more kind, more patient, more ready for every good work, more entirely amiable in the eyes of all who love true goodness. It would scarce be possible to produce such effects on one of the congregations of the present day. The pulpit has labored so long, and so powerfully, to give all our religious thoughts a practical direction, to engage us in plans for accomplishing appreciable good here on earth, and we have been so thoroughly taught to expend our sensibilities in action for the good of others, that we should need a long and laborious training, to make us capable of such engrossing contemplation of objects purely spiritual. Whether we are, on the whole, the worse or the better Christians for the change, is a question not to be answered hastily. There can be no doubt that we are better than they for certain uses; and perhaps we should be better still, if we had occasional seasons of contemplation and feeling, more like theirs.

Although his 1841 readers, Tracy assumed, could still "understand how sinners should be overcome by a sense of danger," they did need to be reminded that such powerful emotionality could be a legitimate part of religious life. When this was written, after all, New England evangelicals were living through the halcyon days of moralist restraint, and, as secretary of the American Board of Commissioners for Foreign Missions, Joseph Tracy was a viceroy of the "benevolent empire." But like those moralists whose diaries have been cited here, Tracy seemed ready to acknowledge that the "practical direction" of evangelical reformism might be improved by "occasional seasons" of a more intense contemplativeness and religious feeling.[2]

Tracy's lament was more than a tear shed for ancient religious heroes. As the next decade was to show, this quest for feeling was part of the new economy of devotionalist religious experience. Although mid-nineteenth-century devotionalism differed substantially from the emotional exuberance of the First Great Awakening—in inclining, for example, to private withdrawal rather than intense sociality—to bored moralists the two might seem quite similar. Both offered an inner experience of divinity sorely lacking among those whose religion established steady habits.

I hope this book demonstrates that economies of religious experience are both specific social systems for organizing the personal encounter with God and also forms of language and meaning that continually arise in cultural history to challenge one another. Given the late eighteenth- and early nineteenth-century "liberal" dilemma, a world that had a coherent meaning and yet was also composed of individuals capable of discovering that meaning for themselves, New England evangelicals posed three alternative economies for bridging the gulf between human beings and their God. Doctrinalism connected the "one" to the "all" by ridding the self of activity; its gospel plan could totally incorporate all the details of an individual's life. Moralism reduced the all into the "many" and encouraged individuals to model themselves on the collectivity, uniting them in their moral endeavors. Devotionalism incarnated the all within the one, as a perfect but entirely self-contained "other," and emphasized the importance of "one-to-one" relatedness in all things. To accomplish these bridging acts, each economy regularly examined individual experience in the light of distinct "levels of moral discourse," as the philosopher Henry David Aiken puts it. Doctrinalists tested experience by its conformity to theological principles, moralists by its adherence to moral norms, and devotionalists by its anticipated and remembered consequences.[3]

I have by no means intended to suggest that similar shifts in the economy of religious experience did not occur in other cultures and at other times in history, perhaps in others where the gulf between the individual and the world was not so great. The historian Peter Brown has written recently about these kinds of changes in spirituality in the Near East during the period of Late Antiquity. Anthropologists like Clifford Geertz and Mary Douglas have insisted that the full range of modern religious temperaments and social structures can be found among what used to be slightingly called "primitive" peoples. But if atheism or the intense religious excitement of private fantasies can be discovered in sixth-century Syria or twentieth-century Polynesia, then they cannot be special characteristics of modern or postmodern religion. If we can find devotionalism in thirteenth-century France and again in nineteenth-century New England, though the Virgin-worship of one had given way to the idolatry of the Dynamo in the other, then modernization or secularization hypotheses are considerably strained. These theories suggest that religion and other forms of experience are moving in all cultures in the same direction, toward technical rationality and freethinking and away from ritual and a belief in divine presence. Instead, it may be that a form of religious experience on the model of doctrinalism arises repeatedly when coherence is valued more than intimacy in a person's relationship to the universe, when emotionality has to be suppressed, and when the social order wants to exclude a few outsiders by posing a standard of orthodoxy for all. Moralism, devotionalism, and possibly other economies of religious experience are similarly parts of patterns of cultural change, not simply stages on the path to today's most "advanced" social state.[4]

To conclude this study, then, it would seem best to locate the connections between these economies of religious experience and other aspects of New England culture and society during these years. Can the praxes of religious life be compared with those that underlay other cultural acts—like the adjudication of disputes, the rearing and educating of children, commercial life, and so on—which also involve ordinary assumptions about human behavior and efforts to channel it in particular directions? Can the economies of doctrinalism, moralism, and devotionalism help explain changes in these experiences as well as those of religion? Fortunately, recent scholarship in the histories of law, education and family life, commerce and industry, has increasingly turned toward accounting for the ordinary practice of these fields, and so can help develop such analogies.

For example, late eighteenth-century lawyers conceived of the English Common Law as a static and unchanging register of truth, as much an authority in legal practice as the Scriptures were for evangelical clergymen. "The equation of common law with a fixed, customary standard," historian Morton J. Horwitz observes, "meant that judges conceived of their role as merely that of discovering and applying preexisting legal rules." Legal argument tried to align particular cases with the exacting language of precedent rather than to determine the underlying principles of the law. In this sense common law practitioners might be said to be as much orthodox or doctrinalist in following Coke and Blackstone, especially in private rather than public law, as evangelical ministers were in adhering to Calvin and Edwards.[5]

The life of the law was meant to exemplify the truth of the whole system, and each member of the bar was expected by his careful attention to precedent to signify his allegiance to the total order set down in those venerable compilations and commentaries. Nor was this obedience to custom for its own sake. Orthodox lawyers and clergymen went at their work with considerable intellectual energy. By assuming the fundamental rationality and consistency of the body of doctrines they followed, exegetical research had the quality of scientific discovery for them. The more painstakingly one collected information from daily experience, and the more intently one studied the wisdom of the received truths, then the more one could see exact correspondence between the two. The Christian whose religious pilgrimage most exactly copied the verbal usages of the New Testament was the best Christian and the best proof of the Bible's veracity. This effort to treat Scripture or common law as scientific statements, not merely as tenets of belief, and to test them by experience made the immediate postrevolutionary generation unusual. The legal and religious orthodox were traditionalists, to be sure, but not blind believers.

In fact, orthodoxy inherited all the intellectual ambitiousness of the eighteenth-century Enlightenment, all its zest for discovery and taxonomy. But "for the Christian thinker, for all right-thinking Americans," Donald H. Meyer explains, for all "who were concerned about infidelity and skepticism, this meant that the Enlightenment had to be appropriated to the cause of faith and morals. Enlightenment thinking had to be used as a weapon against its own extremes." As Meyer suggests, this conservative and defensive rationalism was inextricably tied to an emerging American nationalism. Conservative nationalists assumed that the ideological debates of the era of the American Revolution had established once and for all the essential character of the new republic. The news of the Reign of Terror in France only made the new American order even more distinctive to its loyal citizens.[6]

In the 1780s and 1790s, it became necessary to identify all aspects of the culture as properly republican. Commentaries and guides to architecture, education, and childrearing insisted that the proper practice was distinctly American. For example, when Noah Webster wrote "On the Education of Youth in America" in 1790, he conceded that "our constitutions of civil government are not yet firmly established; our national character is not yet formed." But still Webster insisted that beyond diffusing "a knowledge of the sciences," American education should also "implant in the minds of American youth the principles of virtue and of liberty and inspire them with just and liberal ideas of government and with an inviolable attachment to their own country." His imprecision about the American polity did not, thus, soften his plea that education should be answerable to it. In that, Webster's essay fits the orthodoxy of his generation, in which the highest goal of any element of culture was not its moral character or its instrumental effectiveness but rather its consistency with the established world view.[7]

Defenders of orthodoxy placed their faith in the operations of the understanding, that cherished instrument of an Enlightenment faith in science, and were quick to accuse their opponents of succumbing to irrational prejudice. The aim of their mental lives was to be disinterested, impartial, capable of distinguishing the transitory from the eternally correct. Customary institutions like churches and law courts were understood to embody the wisdom of centuries of enlightenment, and attachments to established institutions were defended as the most reasonable. This explains why opposition to authority in church, court, or legislature was so often accused of being both irrational and foreign. Adversaries within the political system could not grant the legitimacy of opposition to one another. "Faction" itself was the enemy, and each party accused the other of harboring corrupt European (either radical French or royalist English) ideas and interests.

Given the doctrinalists' emphasis on uniformity, the law was not expected to take heed of the interests involved in a case, the teacher was not expected to focus on a particular student's aptitude, and the minister was not expected to redraw the plan of salvation anew for each sinner. The details of the subject (law, education, theology) were tremendously important—a student had to know the intricacies of geography flawlessly, and his parents needed to know the precise stages of conversion on the Calvinist plan. But the personal characteristics of the student, client, or parishioner did not enter into the matter.

Many of the same patterns of thought operated in the economic order that came to New England after the shocks of postwar inflation had diminished. In the predominantly rural communities where as much as 90 percent of the population lived, a man's labor was worth fifty cents for a day, whether it was winter (when many men were available) or summer (when even one was hard to find). Bushels of grain, ordinary tools, and supplies of staple goods like salt continued to bring the same price despite modest fluctuations in scarcity. This was not because commercial transactions were rare; they were not. Almost no farm households or communities in New England were self-sufficient, and contemporary account books record as income-producing activities some things we might share or give away: helping a neighbor plow his land, selling an old coat to a poor man, carting another person's produce to an urban market, instructing a sister's children in a craft or domestic skill.

There was nothing primitive about this economic world, even though it lacked the distinctions we commonly make between occupations (few people could support themselves by only one form of labor), between employers and employees (most people who hired also were hired at some point, often reciprocally), or between producer and consumer.[8]

It was, then, a commercial world in which customary prices and traditional values limited the possibilities for risk and profit. Because everyone acknowledged the temptation to greed, honestly subscribing to the economic rules— paying what was expected and receiving no more than that—was an act of allegiance to the system as a whole. It was considered more important for fairness to prevail in commercial transactions than for each party to achieve his maximum advantage.

Such restraint was not simply rooted in informal custom and conscience. "In both England and America," Morton Horwitz notes, "when the selling price was greater than the supposed objective value of the thing bought, juries were permitted to reduce the damages in an action by the seller, and courts would enforce an implied warranty in actions by the buyer." Courts thus had the powers to investigate and to insist upon equal exchange. Not only were buyer and seller equal before the law, but their transaction had to exemplify the substantive justice implicit in the legal order itself. In this sense, the law served the same function as the gospel plan, demanding an eternal standard against which merely human considerations could be ignored.[9]

This may sound like the precapitalist world of the "just price," with guilds and the prohibition of usury, but the political economy of late eighteenth-century New England was an altogether different universe. Each family was economically independent from every other; as Timothy Dwight rhapsodized in his 1794 paean, *Greenfield Hill*, "every farmer reigns a little king." No corporate bonds or special obligations bound members of the community together into any economic collectivity. "Much virtue's found in fencing well," Dwight advised. A "competency" was what a farmer sought, all agreed, and in most country towns such a stable economic position was well within the reach of four fifths of the male heads of households. But men could hardly grow rich by their farming; until the market for foodstuffs and technical improvements flourished in the second quarter of the nineteenth century, few farmers cultivated more than ten or twelve acres of corn and oats. "Till little; and that little well," the old farmer told his neighbors in *Greenfield Hill.*[10]

There were, of course, opportunities for wealth in the New England of 1800—in land speculation, in transportation and banking ventures, and most especially in shipping—but these were rarely available to ordinary farming folk. Resisting the allure of luxury and European manners was not, then, very difficult for most New Englanders. Nor was it wise to overemphasize economic activity in proclaiming one's identity. Work was only uncomfortably yoked to economic ambition. As J. E. Crowley concludes, in a study of the conceptualization of economic life by eighteenth-century Americans, "The most obvious feature of their ideas about work was their persistent moralizing about it. They thought of society as a moral realm in which men's actions were accountable for their justice. Selfishness could not be excused as the unavoidable response to social and economic imperatives; such moral neutrality would have destroyed their sense of community and undercut their self-esteem." In the New England town, too much concern for wealth might lead to a dangerous separation from the common condition of life. A "competence" or sufficiency was more praiseworthy, and a plodding faithfulness toward such modest ends was more virtuous. All bent to the work of the seasons and limited their ambitions, shaping common values among independent yeomen.[11]

Such men did not even need to see one another very often to know that they belonged to the same universe. The society was bound together by common fealty to the established order, by equality of all within that order. New England's stable economy, like its law and religion, did not deserve obedience simply because it was the established way. Things actually were as they should be. "A thorough and impartial developement of the state of society, in Connecticut, and a complete investigation of the sources of its happiness," promised Timothy Dwight, "would probably throw more light on the true methods of promoting the interests of mankind, than all the volumes of philosophy, which have been written."[12]

But Dwight's society, happy as it was, had within it the seeds of its own demise; its economic individualism and the attractions of commercial trade could hardly be frozen forever in the wintry orderliness of the Federalist solstice. In any case, order to one man was pure void to another, and moralism emerged as a strategy to control ordinary experience rather than to overcome it.

The impulse of commercialism was assisted by the marked improvements in New England's roads during the first two decades of the nineteenth century and by the organization of small factories that produced hundreds of objects for daily use—cut nails, axes, shoes, spades, tinware, cordage, candles—which had once been made at home or in a neighbor's shed. Newly imported commodities—English printed cottons, Swedish and German steel, English and Chinese dishes, French silks, and Spanish wines—brought the glow of fashion to compete with homespun goods, thus stratifying the community by how far commercial trade "penetrated" into particular households. To pay for this merchandise, on both a family and a regional economic basis, New Englanders needed to develop exports; and few southern New England farm families missed the chance to earn extra cash by weaving or braiding palm leaf hats.[13]

The reign of traditional prices could hardly be long sustained in this expanded mercantile climate. A bushel of rye was clearly understood to be worth just so much, and maybe the value of New Bedford spermaceti candles could be compared with locally dipped tallow ones, but what was one to make of Castile soap, Havana cigars, oranges and lemons? Such commodities, isolated from any clear and familiar process of labor, were, in Marx's terms, "mysterious things." Opportunities for chicanery appeared to every merchant who plied such trade, and *caveat emptor* became the customer's slogan.[14]

This new moral crisis in economic life was immensely complicated by the development in the decades after 1815 of a regional and national commodities market in which goods (including perishable ones) were sold for delivery months ahead, creating obvious risks with changing conditions of supply and demand. Contract law, in its traditional form (permitting courts to verify the equality of a transaction), worked well enough when merchandise was sold and delivered immediately. But the law faced new burdens to ensure the return on a buyer's investment months or years later.

Horwitz cites an 1825 legal treatise in describing this dilemma and its significant resolution:

> Where "there is no fixed or unchangeable comparative value between one price of property and another" and all value "depends on the wants and opinions of men," it becomes impossible to measure damages by reference to customary value. The only basis for measuring contractual obligation, then, derives from the "will" of parties, and the crucial legal issue shifts to whether there has been a "meeting of minds."

Formerly, every transaction partook of the assumed fairness of the total economic order. Each could be judged by how well it represented the equity of that order. Now there was no standard of objective value. The economic system was simply composed of distinct transactions; it had no transcendent identity beyond all transactions. It was not a lawless system, and if the authority for enforcing the performance of a contract could not be derived from the order itself, it had to be found elsewhere. The answer was to make the will of the transacting parties accountable. A man was held responsible for what he had agreed to, no less and no more. If he made a bad deal, so much the worse for him. A court would intervene and release a contractor from his side of the bargain only if he had been defrauded. The law would insure, thus, only the equality of the parties, not of the business they transacted.[15]

As a form of religious experience, moralism was almost exactly analogous to this commercial economic world. Escaping from the still void of Calvinist metaphysics, moralists viewed religion as the activity of men and women, not as their place in the divine order. God had provided, instead of a plan for comprehending themselves, the human mechanisms (the conscience and the will) for people to act morally. A person's responsibility, thought Nathaniel William Taylor and Lyman Beecher, *began* with the act of will. There was no prior responsibility to will, as Jonathan Edwards had taught, based on man's or woman's infinite and unconditional obligation to love God and godliness. A moral being had the power to act morally or not, just as he had the power to accept or reject an offering in the marketplace.

By emphasizing personal responsibility in this way, the new moral intelligence was attempting both to encourage and to limit activity at the same time. People might feel free, now, to do whatever they wanted. They need not check themselves against the example of established precedent. But they had to assume total responsibility for their actions and could not exempt themselves by subscribing to the ancient uniformities.

In legal circles, this impulse to take responsibility spurred "an attack on the colonial subservience to precedent." Stop all these appeals to ancient certitudes, lawyers told one another; their only effect was to restrain one's ability to act in the modern world. How could one safely lease riverfront property when its use was hindered by age-old riparian rules? Needed were simple, clear, commonsense principles, against which everyone's action could be measured. No longer, therefore, did reason inhere in the revealed wisdom of the ages. As Horwitz writes, " 'reason' and 'principle' came to be understood not as rules or doctrines to be discovered, not as customary norms to be applied through precedent, but as a body of prudential regulations framed, as [Zephaniah] Swift himself saw, from the perspective of 'enlarged and liberal views of policy.' "[16]

In this context, Swift and his allies meant "policy" to be the potential good of the society. His law, like Beecher's religion, would be an instrument for improving or even reforming the condition of society. But in a crucial move the good of society was more specifically defined as unhindered commercial development by private entrepreneurs, for their own financial advantage. For example, as Horwitz shows, "the idea of property underwent a fundamental transformation" in the early years of the nineteenth century, "from a static agrarian conception entitling an owner to undisturbed enjoyment, to a dynamic, instrumental, and more abstract view of property that emphasized the newly paramount virtues of productive use." Through this, he argues, the centuries-old precedents of English common law regarding riparian rights, the access to water power privileges, were torn asunder by American judges eager to encourage the development of such sites for manufacturing purposes. Now a man who enjoyed enough water to serve his cattle, wash his clothing, even to run a little carding mill, might one day find his flow sharply reduced (or his land flooded) to enhance the productivity (and profitability) of a woolen factory on the same river. By the middle of the century judges who ruled on property rights claims came to depend upon "an explicit consideration of the relative efficiencies of conflicting property uses."[17]

Such language would have been familiar to Unitarians and Calvinists from their debates over whose interpretation of the Scriptures produced greater virtue. In fact, Americans now insisted, generally, that the instrumental use of something was more important than its static enjoyment. Grace, itself the highest end of life for the orthodox, was now valued for its ability to produce more morally active Christians. Holiness became a means for the moralist community, a sort of investment fund for reform. The purpose of property and grace, as valued commodities, was to "return" something else, which might again be invested for future gain. Like any commodities, their chief characteristic was their ultimate exchangeability for anything else; grace might make one successful in business, while business fortunes could earn a reward in one's spiritual affairs.

Was the moralist perspective thus simply a response to the demands of commercial life? Commerce supplied key metaphors to enrich the language of moral experience—terms like investment, contract, and credit. And the mental discipline of commerce was a new model for other areas of life, insisting upon planning, regularity, calculation, and the like in everything one did. But the fact that both legal instrumentalism and religious moralism were somewhat equivocal about full-scale economic ambition, that both sought to make one actively pursue wealth, yet careful of overstretching one's interests, tells us that unrestrained commercialism was not their true meaning. There was a deeper change under way, in which economic development played a key role, to be sure; but it was larger than that.

The interchangeability of means (like order and regularity) and ends (like grace or wealth) in the minds of moralists provides a clue. With the demise of orthodoxy also crumbled the idea that some activities are more important, even holier, than others. Hannah Arendt, in *The Human Condition*, posits that in classical Greece and for two millennia thereafter, the public realm (politics, philosophy, action) was distinguished from and superior to the private realm (economy, family, work, and personal matters). By the nineteenth century, Arendt argues, these distinctions had collapsed before the rise of a new, "social" realm, in which all these areas of life were shared by citizens who viewed themselves as a family writ large, as a national household. With this collapse, the ancient hierarchy of life worlds was squashed. All activities were implicitly equal.[18]

When the objective standards of economic justice were no longer mandatory for traders in American markets, each transaction became a free negotiation. The backdrop that had formerly given order and meaning to these dealings could now be entirely ignored. The same process occurred in the transformation of religious life under moralism. The orthodox had argued that the experience of conversion simultaneously occurred on two stages—as a metaphysical event signifying one's eternal salvation and as an episode in mundane life history wherein the self achieved great joy after suffering excruciating pain. Moralism, by eliminating the special operations of the Holy Spirit, reduced all experiences to the same plane of meaning.

Before this, the ordinary experiences of work and family had counted for little in a man's life; the true measure of a man lay elsewhere, in his spiritual condition, perhaps in the exercise of his political freedom. The tasks of moralism were to inflate, even to consecrate, the value of everyday life and to make religion as much a part of that ordinary social realm of life as commerce, education, childrearing, or anything else. One sign was that religion now shared a set of operating assumptions with other aspects of life. For example, the emphasis upon one's eternal religious condition was dropped in favor of concern with the here and now—this was the time to do one's holy work. One had to "do good," then, on the same schedule as one "did well." Even more suggestive was the way religion became simply another obligation in one's week, to be entered in one's weekly appointment calendars.

By providing the basis for these operating assumptions commerce worked its will upon the society. The commercial week and the fiscal year became the organizing pattern for every activity. The commercial ledger now provided the model for understanding all experiences as expenses and receipts, investments and returns, output and income. The new economic order also taught people how to specialize roles and spaces.

When orthodoxy could no longer command respect as a way of interpreting experience and a new social realm emerged in which all experiences could have the same status and share the same assumptions, the ideas that bound members of society together were no longer doctrinal tenets but moral principles. Because a dynamic economic expansiveness was underway in America during this period many of these moral norms were identical to the tacit assumptions of commercial men. Predictability in one's affairs thus became a virtue to the whole society, even for those not commercially active.

The new virtues were essential for those who wanted to be part of the new society, the new way of doing things. These moral principles were prized more for their socially cohesive power than for their functional benefits to particular individuals. That is, accepting these principles, which we would call middle-class norms, helped integrate a person into the new order of commercial/moralist society. In fact, accommodating oneself to these organizing assumptions of everyday life became a ticket of admission to a social role. The new society demanded that citizens make a strong and conscious decision, to earn their ticket, to enter the community of trusted men and women. The orthodox had assumed that anyone with sense would realize that he or she was already a part of the total world order they represented; that was why orthodoxy could not tolerate opposition. Now moralists were prepared to embrace all who assented to their ideals and to exclude and penalize all others. Failure became a fault. They were making a voluntary association out of the social world.[19]

The central ideal, the norm around which the new society was to be shaped and by which all the commercial virtues were encompassed, was the notion of individual moral character. Every agency in the society was obliged to focus on encouraging moral character. About the schools, historian Paul H. Mattingly concludes that "from the 1820s to the end of the century, the fundamental goal of educational improvement was, in their terms, the inculcation of character."[20]

Both educational moralism and religious moralism depended upon imitation as a major technique for inculcating character in the young. Providing models for imitation was a major goal of professional development in education. "The rhetoric of the time," Mattingly reports, "attributed any change of mind, any alteration of moral conviction, any development of social consciousness in a student, or, in a word, any educational experience, primarily to the moral and personal qualities of the instructor." In order to train teachers for this demanding role, educational reformers under the leadership of Henry Barnard hit upon the "teacher institute," an itinerant "'educational revival agency'" (in Barnard's words), which would set up brief demonstration classes and inspirational meetings in different towns. Commenting on this application of revivalistic techniques, Mattingly notes, "For the first generation of professional educators, this institution made explicit, more than any other educational agency, how determined schoolmen were to equate professionalization with 'awakening' of moral character rather than with the training in communicable skills and the standard techniques of teaching."[21]

More important than developing specific technical skills was arousing a powerful commitment to the goals of moralism. Barnard found, as Beecher had, that conversion experiences might be more effective in creating stable moral exemplars than were training and discipline, although conversions themselves were unsettling. Thus, the nineteenth century commonly turned to intensely surprising or painful moments, like the Horatio Alger episodes where poor boys stumbled over bags of gold, in order to initiate new members in the steady habits of the routinized business society. Conversion was increasingly understood as a profound but not difficult process; it readied an untidy self for full-fledged membership in modern society.[22]

These striking parallels between educational reformers and evangelical moralists, including their exact duplication of methods and goals, help reveal the character of the new order. It was now possible to focus on almost any aspect of ordinary life, from housecleaning to certifying teachers, and to scrutinize it with a seriousness formerly reserved for the sacred aspects of life, as long as it ultimately encouraged morality. The proliferation of manuals and instruction books for hundreds of diverse activities, in the half century after 1815, suggests the mental energy directed to the analysis of everyday life. For the most part, these manuals neither developed new knowledge nor suggested new techniques to their readers. Instead they codified traditional practice, previously passed along orally within families and local communities. Measurements were rather hazy (standard measures were often not yet available in most places, certainly not in the kitchen), and "rules of thumb" provided guidance where scientific grounding did not exist. Following a recipe in the new cookbooks was hardly the same as making a dish according to childhood memories. The traditional manner became ordered, rationalized, and regularized to guarantee predictable results. But progressing step-by-step did not, however, attach one to the traditional order, as following a parent's advice would.[23]

Still, following the published recipe did attach one to a world in which both information was passed along literate pathways and consistent practice was highly valued. Furthermore, the first generation of manuals often carried explicit moral messages, and even made the attainment of moral excellence a goal of their titles. Lydia Maria Child's 1829 cookbook was called *The Frugal Housewife;* the subtitle directed it "to those who are not ashamed of economy." Frugality, not deliciousness, was its chief goal. By paying such close attention to the practices of ordinary life, then, moralists did not want to worship technique. Every activity of life, buying and selling and making and maintaining and worshipping and learning, was meant to serve other ends, to tie one to an integrated moral community of like-minded people.[24]

Moralism assumed that if a person of character exercised his will he would take responsibility for his actions. Moralists could therefore leave much of the traditional world intact and expect that men would now feel that it was theirs simply because they consented to it. So parents could be respected as deeply as before because "morally free" children obliged themselves willingly. Much the same reasoning underlay the growing acceptability of the liberal theory that social good would be produced best by the untrammeled exercise of individual wills. This idea, spread through the writings of the Scottish philosophers like Adam Smith and Frances Hutcheson, required the moralist link of will and responsibility. Through the ideal of moral character, which made such a link, the world was thus made safe for enterprise.[25]

Finding analogies for the moralist form of religious experience is relatively easy; moralism was, after all, an integrative device whereby religion came to resemble other experiences in cherishing moral character. Devotionalism was another story altogether; in its withdrawal from the social world in order to achieve "an intimate walk with Christ," devotional experience was disintegrative. It pulled religion away from the rest of one's life.

A similar concern with inner experience can be found in contemporary fiction, visual art, and advice on love and childrearing. But "innerness" was not the feature of devotionalist religion that it most significantly shared with other elements of the culture. No, its disintegrative tendency was, paradoxically, most characteristic of the movement. The impulse of religious intensity to seek its own ends and detach itself from other forms of experience also occurred in other fields like economy and family life. This tendency enables us to place devotionalism in a historical perspective.

I must return to moralism for a moment. In compressing the orthodox hierarchy of activities, moralism channeled the application of intelligence to such ordinary problems as children's health or bridge building or recreation. Such subjects now felt as important and probably more interesting than "God's wisdom in the permission of sin," a central controversy among the orthodox generation. At first, as we have seen, moralist manuals were essentially compilations of traditional wisdom, with frequent nods to the community's cherished values of individual responsibility, reverence, present-mindedness, and the like. Gradually, the level of sophistication and expertise rose, and manuals became more specialized by nature. For example, Andrew Jackson Downing's popular *Architecture of Country Houses* (1850) emphasized the moral values in house design, insisting that the architect's client's character would be proclaimed by his rural villa or his cottage. Other books taught designers and carpenters to construct these same buildings, just as new guides for women showed them how to furnish and maintain them. By the Civil War years, many of these guides spoke largely to professional practitioners, in technical language increasingly reliant upon special symbol systems: draftsmen's symbols in architects' and builders' guides, chemical formulas, differential calculus rather than simple proportion in engineering practice. Even for teachers, says Paul H. Mattingly, "professional aids like the anecdotal manuals of 'hints' and 'suggestions,' such as Samuel Read Hall's *Lectures on School-Keeping* (1829), were replaced by highly simplified and systematic guides like Norman Calkins' *Object Lessons* (1860)." [26]

Moralism found itself, as this process of specialization developed, in danger of losing its stable and integrating qualities. Initially, for example, Lyman Beecher's moral society was designed to include almost everyone in the community, pointedly excluding only a few sinners. Twenty years later, during the heyday of the "New Measures" revivalism associated with Charles G. Finney, the distinction between saint and sinner, and between each stage of the transit from one to the other, was hammered home to the congregation. Despite an essential agreement on what constituted moral character, the competition between religious liberals and evangelicals led to the secession of the

Unitarians from Congregationalism during the 1820s. And after twenty years of interdenominational cooperation in Bible and tract distribution and various other reform endeavors, the Evangelical United Front collapsed in 1837, leaving each denomination to compete thenceforward as agents for the shared ideal of moral character. The moralist tendency to split and split again was seen also in the sectarian divisiveness that befell temperance and antislavery societies throughout their history.[27]

The moralist scheme of things, perhaps because it so dearly prized the sense of specific community with like-minded people, soon led to a world where the most fundamental distinction was between insiders and outsiders. Within one's own field of proficiency, and among those who shared one's norms, one felt like an insider; anywhere else one stood the chance of being humiliated and excluded. In the early years of the nineteenth century, a shared commitment to virtue might mitigate these divisions. By 1860, the common denominator between two different specialists was less likely to be their mutual adherence to the ideal of character than their agreement to provide services to each other for cold cash.

This situation was the moral crossroads where the devotionalist journey began; as insiders they went one way, and as outsiders another. It is important to trace these different paths, seeing how both employed similar strategies to organize experience. Within religious communities, devotionalists felt that the intensity of their personal experience set them apart from those Christians whose claims resided only in proper behavior and active exertion in benevolent enterprises. The devotionalist insider was sure that others, equally engaged in religious feelings, would be instantly recognizable and ready to form a community of ardent souls in the midst of duller, merely moral, types. Therefore, they celebrated religious emotion as an end in itself and preferred an intimate experience of communion with the Lord to the prospects of social integration through moral character.

The same impulse was felt throughout American society, by men and women who chose to celebrate the pursuit of wealth, excellence in housekeeping, proficiency in legal argument, education of the young, or development of technology, or any such field, as its own end. Men and women saw only dubious merit in bending every course to a moral harbor; it was more exhilarating sailing freely in one's own chosen direction. The more specialized manuals of the 1850s and after seldom insisted on directing every improvement toward social ends. Architects and builders were instructed to erect stronger and cheaper structures, not ones that expressed moral virtues. Housewives were taught how to cook more delicious meals, even if they were less nutritious and less economical.[28]

In this concern with technique, insiders broke free of moralist restraints. In fact, they completely reversed the place of ordinary experience and moral norms. For moralists, any activity could be consecrated to serve the end of promoting a fixed virtuous character. In the technical society, character became instead an instrument. In the "completely secular marketplace," the historian Rush Welter observes, "character itself appeared to be an asset to a career but not a moral title to wealth." Habits of order and regularity, then, could assist one in pursuing one's business. Devotionalists, though, conceded that such virtues might not be effective and could be abandoned if necessary.[29]

In describing the new society, we have to distinguish what we mean by a concern with technique. The old operating assumptions of the moral, commercial world, emphasizing habits of foresight and restraint, lost their special status and became equivalent to the technical skills required in the labor process—tending a child's ailments, twisting steel wire, balloon framing a house. They were all valuable skills. Moral habits had no special merit because of their unique relationship to the bonds of social life.

The process of labor, or of any other activity, was thus being severed from the social world. Each aspect of life seemed now to have its own inherent rules. The end of each activity was clarified, becoming much more vividly perceptible to the insider. Moralists aimed at converting the whole world to Christianity, a remote and abstract goal. But devotionalists could easily imagine God's loving companionship and feel his presence nearby. Parents and teachers had more concrete if limited objectives: well-groomed children who could read and write. "More and more teaching," one scholar notes, "coincided with the transfer of technological knowledge, which had been but one component of the earlier ideal, the inculcation of character."[30]

Furthermore, such goals seemed rooted in the essential nature of the activity. Just as the soul was now understood to have the seeds of grace within itself, needing only loving nurturance to blossom into full-flowering Christian perfection, so a mother was only obeying her "natural" instincts in her mothering. David N. Camp, a leader of the second generation of professional educators, "preferred," says Mattingly, "to stress natural, rather than volitional qualities as the prerequisites of professional teaching. If one possessed a natural disposition to teach, one could easily be instructed in technical skills, become imbued with professional ardor, and entrusted with a classroom assignment." In the same way, houses, bridges, and ships could be built better according to their own laws. It was less important that they reflect the character of the society that sponsored them.[31]

This new teleology obeyed the tightly bound self-determination presumed to be a part of any technical activity. The origins and the ends of any particular activity could now be derived from the process itself. If a business was to make cloth, its only purpose was to make that cloth efficiently, that is, with as little interference from the environment as possible. To obtain a charter of incorporation from state legislatures (and hence protection from unlimited liability), for example, businesses no longer had to defend their worthiness to the commonwealth. Courts overturned the privileges of monopolies in order to secure "the benefit," as the New York Supreme Court wrote, "which always attends competition and rivalry." Profit, not the benefit to society, proved the value of any enterprise.[32]

The moralizing curtain parted, and now there was no society, no environment, no authority beyond the implied rules of the activity itself. The workings of the system became the whole meaning of the system. Such a change is reflected in the comparison Rush Welter offers between two business manuals, one written by Freeman Hunt, an old moralist, and one by Edwin T. Freedley, a member of the more technically oriented younger generation.

> Although both authors' handbooks were potpourris of anecdote, advice, and "philosophy," Freedley's stressed the actual workings of the world of business (albeit in rather general terms) whereas Hunt's was "a collection of maxims, morals and miscellanies for merchants and men of business." Freedley did incorporate a good deal of hortatory advice, some of it highly traditional, but he also described how to make money in a variety of undertakings, which included both speculation and banking, and he expressed a striking ambivalence toward the traditional moral code of success. Although he paid homage to agriculture and the prudential virtues, he complained that traditional moralists had devoted too much time to admonitions respecting the getting of wealth and too little to its spending, and he argued that business was the real test and therefore the real source of morality.

Welter notes that Freedley was an apologist for industry rather than commerce, and, in this narrow focus on business practice, there is something of an industrial model for experience whereby products—or profits—could be turned out repetitively and routinely. The merchant, engaged in connecting suppliers and consumers, needed the common mediating language of moral character in order to create the confidence that made transactions go smoothly. The manufacturing model of experience freed itself from these demands, just as industrial producers tried to protect themselves from the uncertainties of the environment by insuring a steady flow of raw materials and a steady demand for goods through regular channels of distribution. In suggesting that the empirical nature of "business was the real test and therefore the real source of morality," Freedley was arguing that "what is, ought to be"; no other external tests could be applied to judge the intrinsic morality of the marketplace. In participating as an insider in this world, one had to subscribe to its code of practice. If one were engaged in making cotton cloth, one had to accept the system that provided that fiber, including (to the consternation of many moralists) the slave labor system that supplied the raw cotton and the wage labor system that operated the textile-making machines.[33]

The insider could now bring only technical, not moral, authority to bear on any production activity. The insider's personality became completely inter-twined in the discipline of his specialty; decisions were informed only by the anticipated and remembered consequences of the body of knowledge that un-derlay practice. The insider's ideal, like those of the evangelical devotional-ists, was to grow more perfect in enacting those imagined goals. This was the exuberance, and the danger, of the technical era.

That was the experience of insiders. As outsiders, however, Americans felt the greater effects of specialization. If the clothing manufacturer felt bound to adopt the prevailing morality of the textile business, then how much less free was the industrial worker to judge how things were done. And when no other cotton shirts were available to the consumer, how little could the out-sider question the ties of technical activity to the social good. In the abolition-ist crusade, this feeling of complicity in the slave economy spurred the first thoughtful challenge to the morality of industrial capitalism among its middle-class beneficiaries. To be sure, moralist advertising (even in the nineteenth century) tried to secure the identification of workers and consumers with the interest of insiders (owners and managers).[34]

In any case, one now had to divide one's time among a large number of distinct activities, and each role—spouse, parent, breadwinner, teacher, friend, worker, colleague, citizen, spectator, player, learner, consumer, be-liever, and so on—had to compete with the others on many grounds. Each activity was based upon its own particular technique with its own ethical demands. Work skills and the ethos of the work world, particularly, had little to do with the rest of one's life. Each activity could be taken with great seri-ousness, and there were instruction guides for each one. But professionali-zation meant that few could hope to emulate the new experts. Few home owners knew how to install the heating equipment that replaced coal stoves; fewer commuters knew how the streetcars operated. No one in the kitchen could quite match the Fannie Farmers of this world, no matter how closely one followed the recipes in the new cookbooks. Such inadequacy was partic-ularly bothersome when experienced in such realms of life as parenthood, where authority was itself part of the activity. Urban parents, unlike their farming forebears, could not inculcate moral lessons in their children by going to work in offices and factories.

Each part of one's life brought with it a distinct code of behavior and dif-ferent kinds of companionship. Consumers were taught to be suspicious, be-lievers to be trusting; colleagues had to cooperate, breadwinners to compete, and so on. The people one knew at work were not necessarily those one wanted to see socially. So little of one's life overlapped; there was little coher-ence in it all. The division was sharpest between those acts relating to work and those relating to family life, so that a parent was capable, as time went on, of instructing his child only in activities that were economically trivial or peripheral to work. Leisure time pursuits became the focus of parent-child interaction; middle-class parents began to teach children to fish rather than to calculate actuarial rates, to bake holiday cakes rather than to catalogue books, to play the piano instead of buying cheap and selling dear.

Some confident middle-class adults, especially in small-town America after the Civil War, felt like insiders most of the time. Their religion was untroubled, their income stable, their social circle unbroken. Like William James's "once-born souls," the concelebrants of the "genteel tradition" felt at one with the world. They passed moral maxims back and forth as if they were articulating the commonsense wisdom of the whole society. But their ethos had less and less authority in an economy of huge industrial corporations, a politics of competing interest groups, and an art and literature in ever more strident revolt against the "village."

For the others, becoming a myriad-faced fellow was the more likely alternative, like the "cosmopolitan" in Melville's The Confidence-Man who announces that "'Life is a picnic en costume; one must play a part, assume a character, stand ready in a sensible way to play the fool.'" Adroitly playing the fool well expressed the duplicitous quality of social roles for many people. In Melville, the confidence man was still the exception; by the Gilded Age, even the heroes were a heap of contradictions. With the collapse of orthodoxy, no one could authentically wrap all of one's life in a single thread of meaning.[35]

Devotionalism was a strategy whereby divided souls could invent a private realm of experience beneath ordinary life, behind the facade of social life. In this deeper world, the true self, the locus of one's personal authenticity, could enjoy perfect peace unharmed by the conflicting demands of others. Now every event seemed to transpire on two stages. On the surface, one performed sincerely in the routines of the social world; from beneath, these "empty rituals" were shadowed by a more personal, hence more authentic, meaning.

Truth now lived only in these lower reaches. The more clearly one's inner experience diverged from the outward signs, the truer it was. A sacrament lost its double role as an outward experience and an inward, objective conveyer of grace; it became an outwardly objective ceremony accompanied by mysterious, but more significant, subjective experiences. In the "real world," the real story was always hidden. Politics was a screen for the shenanigans of politicians, commerce the mask of untold machinations. The public realm was ever more cynically distrusted. Whatever veracity one found was within—only a subjective and personal truth.[36]

Because one's outward behavior was ruled more and more by technical rationality, the contrasting life within appeared correspondingly emotional. While the surface life moved to the clock of the commercial work week, inner experience could either compress an entire life history into a moment's reflection or expand a fleeting reverie into an eternal pleasure. Against the attentiveness of work consciousness was posed, as we have seen, the daydream of feeling in closer touch with oneself and with God.

These two avenues of technical life, the insider's worship of expertise and the outsider's retreat into a private world, occasionally crossed into each other's territory. There were attempts to develop the inner life technically, as in spiritualism and other forms of mind cure; on the other side, outsiders who felt themselves cut off from exercising their wills in the technical process could appropriate aspects of ordinary life, as Thoreau most eminently did at Walden Pond (and as did thousands of urban Americans who hunted and fished and otherwise exercised their "primitivist impulses"), and conduct them as deliberately antimodern acts of private life. Both these admixtures of the technical and the subjective could be described as "getting control of one's life."[37]

But when we look at the technical and the subjective in light of what had preceded them, the qualities they shared stand out more sharply than the areas in which they disagreed. Both were products of the progressive closing of the distance between a person's mind and his ultimate authority, his God. As divinity came to be a more inward experience and as the human mind came increasingly to center on its volitional faculties, its most godlike powers, there arose a magical intimacy between mindfulness and godliness. The decline of orthodoxy in New England did not mean, therefore, a weakening of religion. On the contrary, the 1850s were an intensely more religious decade than the 1790s, whether one measures that by the numbers of believers, the hectic activity of the churches and benevolent societies, or the frequency with which one might encounter pious people and pious sentiments. But the religious experience of the mid-nineteenth century was more subjective, more psychological, and less theological and abstract than that of the earlier period. Though more Americans felt God within, they had less assurance of the God out there, in the world.

By internalizing divinity, there was nothing to hinder the expression of man's will in the outer world; no thing could resist his desire to build his own world. To dispel the world's givenness and resistance was as strong an encouragement to the technical imagination of Americans as to their inner fantasies. The explosive development of American technology in the mid-nineteenth century and after has much to do with this shift in emphasis toward the future, the unfilled, the open character of the external world, the way it invited man's energy and inventiveness. The traditional carpenter, or even a farmer nimble with hand tools, had measured by eye, "letting the board nearest at hand determine subsequent widths and heights," but the new technician saw things in his mind that had never been. His "visual intuition," as one historian calls it, could see a bridge rising high above a river never bridged before, and he could imagine how deep the piers must be sunk for such a bridge to stand. Then he could draw what he imagined or make a model of it, and finally he could build it. By definition, the work of the society began to focus on the unprecedented and the undeveloped; the task of technique was to convert problems from obstacles into opportunities, just as devotionalists had construed needs as leading directly to satisfactions. In the metallurgical and chemical researches of this period, the nature of materials began to reveal how they might be better used. It was in the nature of steel, then, to be twisted into cable of remarkable strength. Using the same rhetoric, "discoveries" of the nature of women, men, and children provided guidance for new forms of childrearing and family life.[38]

Visual acuity and imagination had to be made legitimate. The transition from an orthodox to a technical world was accompanied by a shift in the culture's cognitive abilities. "A real verbal ability and audience, such as was revealed in some eighteenth-century sermons," writes Daniel Calhoun, "was giving way before a generally spatial or visual turn of thought." Even more significant and certainly more paradoxical was that this envisioning power implied such a radical devaluing of the world as it was. The power to transform this world, in other words, was purchased by granting greater respect to another world, elsewhere, only imagined.[39]

Such power would have been unthinkable as late as the eighteenth century, when all power or willfulness was derived from God and allowed to happen only because of God's loving support. A man's free willing, thought Jonathan Edwards, should make him feel all the more dependent on the Being that so enabled him to act. The orthodox evangelicals, at the end of the century, sensed that willful men were most often ungodly, and so they stressed that God's order was most noticeable when men were powerless. Hating this void between the supreme order and passive humanity, evangelical moralists began to offer men the chance to act as they wished but only within the channels of a regulated, God-given moral character. Moralists looked more toward the future than toward the past but always with an air of *expectation,* as though the present and future were mortgaged totally to each other. They tried to make the future predictable by establishing consistent routines and habits and to encumber present enjoyment with heedfulness or foresight. In a world of expectation, nothing happened that could not be greeted with a knowing air of vindication or disappointment.[40]

If expectation is the apt word for the moralist scheme, projection was the key characteristic of the technical society that challenged it. Man's actions now came from deep within himself, where his "motives" resided. People projected their personalities in each of their acts; nothing was done that did not bear the characteristic stamp of a particular person, and each person's acts could be justified as internally determined and hence personally correct. One could project into the future, or into the not here and the not now, because the imagination had become the perfect tool for the expression of this autonomous perspective. Thinking about one's life became an exercise in projecting alternative biographies. Empathetically projecting oneself into another's self became the chief link to others. Projection promised to transcend all limits of nature, all constraints of society, all experience of the past. It made man godlike in his own domain by marvelously foreshortening the distance between his mind and the edge of his power. Even death, the final point of resistance, could be transcended. While sentimentalist writers described heaven with astonishing detail and resemblance to the purest New England places, only corrosive intellects like Melville's could announce the terrible truth, as he did in *Mardi*, that "we die, because we live." Devotionalists spoke instead of a life without bounds, and in their flood of sentimentalizing about death they tried to give it every meaning but that of finality, of "annihilation" (another favorite word of Melville's).[41]

In sum, the transformation of religious experience, as the evangelicals in New England understood it, was part of a far-ranging change in the understanding of ordinary life in the culture as a whole. The way problems were encountered and solved, the way one thought and acted, the way authority was defined and obeyed, the order by which an individual life was enmeshed in others: all these praxes were transformed together, and the example of the Calvinists is instructive even for their most secularized countrymen. This transformation was, of course, part of reorganizing the economic relations of Americans, but it is too limiting to say that the development of a capitalist dominated, technologically developed, individualistic, commercial economy "caused" such changes. More fairly we can say that these forms of life and the changes in them were the ways in which Americans experienced the coming of an urban industrial society.

Much of this process of transformation still rings, contemporaneously, in our ears, although the orthodox doctrines, the moral codes, and the technical achievements of the early nineteenth century are dead and buried. It was difficult, even by 1850, for Melville to find a credible "something, somehow like Original Sin," to account for Hawthorne's "power of blackness." Hester Prynne, Redburn, and the recluse at Walden Pond had discovered the sham of the moral norms by which Americans wanted to live. Already the dangers of Hollingsworth's visionary experiments at Blithedale or Ahab's projections behind the "pasteboard mask" of reality were being described with chilling effect.[42]

The beliefs of the doctrinalist, the habits of the moralist, the techniques of the devotionalist have not survived. But we still are caught thinking about our experience in the modern-day successors of these forms. As we come to the end of this work, the reader should see that the experience of orthodoxy, for example, does not mean any particular set of established dogmas, or world views, but rather living primarily as though we exemplify doctrinal truth. In light of this definition, the twentieth century in America has always had powerful dogmas, but in relatively rare episodes has doctrine been of unchallenged importance. Perhaps the best example of such a time was the decade following the Second World War, when both liberals and conservatives made a dogmatic test out of anticommunism and tried to confirm their own activities and beliefs as loyal to the "American way of life." Orthodoxy of this sort seems to emerge in the wake of war or revolutionary upheaval.[43]

The competing claims of moral and technical criteria for shaping an understanding of experience have been more persistent in the last century. As American society became more organized, the specific moral norms of the village society—emphasizing individual will and personal responsibility, segregating behavioral deviants—have been superseded. With the emergence of the corporate-welfare society, will has devolved into participation and responsibility into accountability. For propriety we now substitute matching a particular statistical category or social stereotype—yuppie, redneck, egghead. This devolution stems from the success of statistical knowledge in the rational organization of society. Our richest sense of community is now often shared with those nameless and faceless others, participants in what the historian Daniel Boorstin has called "statistical communities," who buy what we buy, watch what we watch, think—according to pollsters—as we do.[44]

But while our lives are ever more bureaucratically regimented, this modern moralism has had to contend with its own increasingly sophisticated technical dynamism. Technical criteria generally prevail these days, especially in times of economic stagnation or uncertainty. The argument of experts that something will work better usually is stronger, even in discussing personal life, than whether it is morally or theoretically correct. By technique we mean much more than the technology of machines, rather the willingness to accord to a particular process the ability to set its own goals. As the technical process requires more and more specialized forms of expertise, and as the introduction of "feedback loops" and "smart" (self-correcting) computers shortcircuits human decision making in the midst of the process, there are fewer chances to be an insider. Gradually the work of technique has involved less of a projection outward of anyone's imagination—the word "project" has come to mean any undertaking, not merely those based on a previous design—and more the filling in of "gaps" dictated by the logic of earlier work or of the discipline. Technique is therefore experienced by most people as an alien force. It is less common, then, to make technology accountable, by posing moralist claims against it, than to withdraw to a private realm where the self can be free of the "depersonalizing" effects of both bureaucracy and technocracy. We spend an immense amount of cultural energy (and money) in cultivating and marketing materials for private fantasies. Numerous magazines hawking methods of inner liberation could be aptly titled "Popular Mechanics of the Self."[45]

This conflict between moralism and devotionalism, though in our own era's terms, makes us recognize our kinship to the world of mid-nineteenth-century America. Our world is not so individualistic and our communities not so neatly bounded, but we still feel the dilemma of choosing between playing a substantial, if duplicitous, role in social life or enjoying inner harmony by becoming social ciphers. The first course, says the contemporary moral philosopher Roberto Mangabeira Unger, leads to "resignation, . . . a despairing submission to a social order whose claims are inwardly despised." The second, the devotionalist alternative, leads, he predicts, to "disintegration, . . . the falling apart of different elements of the self, and revulsion against the external world, especially against the social world."[46]

Intellectuals may clamor or pine for a new orthodoxy, but, except among fundamentalists, none seems likely to have any lasting power. Moralism and devotionalism are, in the absence of an orthodoxy, both necessary for our survival, providing the cause and the antidote of the other's pain. We must live with this contradiction as long as we want to take ordinary life as intensely personal and divinely significant at the same time. For our dilemma comes from nothing less than appropriating divinity to ourselves and eliminating the humility by which people had enchained themselves in a subordinate realm in the past. But that humble acceptance of our simple humanity, it is now clear, also provided a stage for the drama of recognizing and reconciling us to God. So, while we thought to feel God with more power and more freedom by having him so close, all our motion has left us alone and immobilized in our quandary. Ironically, now our "hope," as the theologian Peter Homans says, "is the result of gaining distance on the past, on one's age, on the social other, and on oneself." We pray that history, although an approach to the past, may also be a way of gaining distance from the past and from ourselves.[47]

Notes

REFERENCES are generally grouped at the end of each paragraph in the text. Unless otherwise indicated, emphases in the text are taken from the original. Fuller titles can be found in the Select Bibliography. References to articles in nineteenth-century religious journals are not listed separately in the Bibliography. More extensive references, especially to secondary literature, can be found in the notes to corresponding sections of Richard Rabinowitz, "Soul, Character, and Personality: The Transformation of Personal Religious Experience in New England, 1790–1860 (Ph.D. diss., Harvard University, 1977) [cited as "Rabinowitz, Ph.D. diss."].

CEM refers to the *Connecticut Evangelical Magazine; MMM* refers to the *Massachusetts Missionary Magazine.*

Notes to the Introduction

1. Among studies of the ages of religious converts, see J. M. Bumsted, "Religion, Finance, and Democracy in Massachusetts: The Town of Norton as a Case Study," *Journal of American History* 57 (1971), 817–831; Philip J. Greven, Jr., "Youth, Maturity, and Religious Conversion: A Note on the Ages of Converts in Andover, Massachusetts, 1711–1749, *Essex Institute Historical Collections* 108 (1972), 119–134.

2. Erik H. Erikson, *Young Man Luther: A Study in Psychoanalysis and History* (New York: Norton, 1958); Erikson is, to be sure, well aware of such historical changes and the way they make certain psychological events more noteworthy. "In some young people," he notes, "in some classes, at some periods of history, the personal identity crisis will be noiseless and contained within the rituals of passage marking a second birth; while in other people, classes, and periods, the crisis will be clearly marked off as a critical period intensified by collective strife or epidemic tension" (*Life History and the Historical Moment* [New York: Norton, 1975], 21). The study of the distinctions between such historical moments might better be termed "historical psychology." See Zevedei Barbu, *Problems of Historical Psychology* (New York: Grove Press, 1960), and Lucien Febvre, *A New Kind of History: From the Writings of Febvre,* ed. Peter Burke (London: Routledge & Kegan Paul, 1973). Philip Greven's *The Protestant Temperament: Patterns of Child-Rearing, Religious Experience, and the Self in Early America* (New York: Knopf, 1977) is an ambitious and suggestive study of the historical psychology of seventeenth- and eighteenth-century America; I have profited greatly, in small ways and large, from Greven's reading of "The Evangelicals: The Self Sup-

243

pressed," one of his three basic character types. But I disagree with his central assumption that evangelicals shared a single personality structure (or a single mode of personal expression) over such a long period, and I am troubled by the author's reluctance to expound a relationship between these aspects of personal life and social change.

3. William James, *The Varieties of Religious Experience: A Study in Human Nature* (New York: Longmans, Green, 1902); an excellent guide is Wayne Proudfoot, *Religious Experience* (Berkeley: University of California Press, 1985).

4. See *Vital Records of Sturbridge, Mass. to the Year 1850* (Boston: New England Historic Genealogical Society, 1906). Town records are in the possession of the town clerk; religious society records are held similarly by their clerks, although the Baptists, Congregationalists, and Unitarians combined to form the Sturbridge Federated Church in 1922; many other records, including the papers of several Sturbridge ministers, have been collected in the Research Library of Old Sturbridge Village, an outdoor history museum in the town. With Nancy Osterud, Polly Price, and former students and staff at the museum, I participated in a number of Sturbridge community history studies in 1967–1975. One product of that work is Nancy Osterud and John Fulton, "Family Limitation and Age at Marriage: Fertility Decline in Sturbridge, Massachusetts, 1730–1850, *Population Studies* 30 (1976), 481–494. Other published sources on the town include George Davis, *A Historical Sketch of Sturbridge and Southbridge* (West Brookfield, Mass.: O. S. Cooke, 1856); Holmes Ammidown, *Historical Collections* (New York: privately pub., 1874); and George H. Haynes, *Historical Sketch of the First Congregational Church, Sturbridge, Massachusetts* (Worcester, Mass.: Davis, 1910). Many of my observations on everyday life in nineteenth-century communities are derived from my work at the museum. See Jack Larkin, "The View from New England: Notes on Everyday Life in Rural America to 1850," *American Quarterly* 34 (1982), 244–261.

5. F. W. Emmons et al., *The Biography and Phrenological Character of Deacon John Phillips: With the Addresses, Poem, and Original Hymns, of the Celebration of his C [One-Hundredth] Birthday* (Southbridge, Mass.: O. D. Haven, 1860).

6. Mary Douglas, *Natural Symbols: Explorations in Cosmology* (New York: Pantheon, 1970), 144.

7. A useful contrast is to Marc Bloch's chapter, "Modes of Feeling and Thought," in *Feudal Society* (London: Routledge & Kegan Paul, 1961), 72–87.

8. An excellent illustration of the notion of a competence appears in an 1827 letter from Zadoc Long, a Maine country storekeeper, to his brother-in-law:

> I have made inquiries respecting Turner [Maine] as being an eligible place for another shoemaker, but cannot ascertain as you would find sufficient encouragement there. You must be aware that no town in the country will afford a man much of an income who relies solely upon his trade. In the country he must unite with it other advantages such as speculation or cultivating the soil to render his gains ample. As your wife is willing and anxious to live on a farm and to assist you all in her power by the labor of her hands, it might be well for you to procure a snug little place where you can till the ground, raise some stock, have a small dairy, do something at your trade, and try if you cannot make several things work together to produce a competence.

Long complains, in concluding, that he should still have to give advice to a grown man about such matters (Pierce Long, ed., *From the Journal of Zadoc Long* [Caldwell, Idaho: Caxton, 1943], 82.)

9. See Sidney Lanier, *The English Novel and Essays on Literature* (Baltimore: Johns Hopkins University Press, 1945); these 1881 lectures were revised in 1897 under the title "A Study in the Development of Personality." Herman Melville, *Moby-Dick, or the Whale*, ed. Luther S. Mansfield and Howard P. Vincent (New York: Hendricks House, 1952), 345 (chap. 79).

10. On the rise of a statistical frame of mind, see, among many other works, John Theodore Merz, *A History of European Scientific Thought in the Nineteenth Century* (1904; rpt. New York: Dover, 1965), 2:548–626; J. Bronowski, *The Common Sense of Science* (New York: Random House, 1959), 80–96; Max Weber, "Bureaucracy," in *From Max Weber: Essays in Sociology*, trans. and ed. H. H. Gerth and C. Wright Mills (New York: Oxford University Press, 1946), 196–244; Anton Zijdervald, *The Abstract Society: A Cultural Analysis of our Time* (Garden City, N.Y.: Doubleday, 1970).

11. On these questions, see Osterud and Fulton, "Family Limitation and Age at Marriage"; William G. McLoughlin, *New England Dissent, 1630–1833: The Baptists and the Separation of Church and State* (Cambridge: Harvard University Press, 1971), 2:1063–1185; James M. McPherson, *Battle Cry of Freedom: The Civil War Era* (New York: Oxford University Press, 1988), 162; Eric Foner, *Free Soil, Free Labor, Free Men: The Ideology of the Republican Party Before the Civil War* (New York: Oxford University Press, 1970), 149–185.

12. See Darwin P. Kelsey, *Farming and Field Crops: Agriculture in New England, 1790–1840* (Sturbridge, Mass.: Old Sturbridge Village, 1967); Howard S. Russell, *A Long, Deep Furrow: Three Centuries of Farming in New England* (Hanover, N.H.: University Press of New England, 1976); Abbott Lowell Cummings, *Architecture in Early New England* (Sturbridge, Mass.: Old Sturbridge Village, 1958). George Moore, a schoolmaster in Acton, Massachusetts, noted in his diary for Thursday, December 25, 1828, "Happened to think that to day is Christmas, but saw no one take any notice of it, and thought, if I did, I should appear odd, and so let it pass" (Diaries, 1, Harvard University Archives).

13. See, for example, Kenneth Kilby, *The Cooper and His Trade* (London: Baker, 1971); and *The Cooper* (London: Houlston and Stoneman, n.d.), 16–19; Richard J. Bernstein, *Praxis and Action: Contemporary Philosophies of Human Activity* (Philadelphia: University of Pennsylvania Press, 1971).

14. See Clifford Geertz, *The Interpretation of Cultures* (New York: Basic Books, 1973), esp. 3–30, 87–125, 126–141; Mary Douglas, *Natural Symbols;* Douglas, *Purity and Danger: An Analysis of Concepts of Pollution and Taboo* (London: Routledge & Kegan Paul, 1966); Douglas, ed., *Rules and Meanings: The Anthropology of Everyday Life* (Harmondsworth, Eng.: Penguin, 1973).

15. See the outline Perry Miller had prepared for a chapter entitled "The Religion of Geology," in *The Life of the Mind in America from the Revolution to the Civil War* (New York: Harcourt, Brace and World, 1965), 316–317. The key contemporary source is Edward Hitchcock, *The Religion of Geology and its Connected Sciences* (Boston: Phillips, Sampson, 1851).

16. On quality control, see Daniel J. Boorstin, *The Americans: The Democratic Experience* (New York: Random House, 1973), 195–200.

17. Alfred Schutz, "On Multiple Realities," in *Collected Papers, I: The Problem of Social Reality*, ed. Maurice Natanson (The Hague: Martinus Nijhoff, 1962), 229–233.

18. Kenneth Burke, *A Grammar of Motives* (1945; rpt. Berkeley: University of California Press, 1969); also see Burke, *The Rhetoric of Religion: Studies in Logology* (1961; rpt. Berkeley: University of California Press, 1970).

19. The conventional account is given, for example, by Clarence H. Faust, "The Decline of Puritanism," in *Transitions in American Literary History*, ed. Harry Hayden Clark (Durham, N.C.: Duke University Press, 1953), 3–47; Frank H. Foster, *A Genetic History of the New England Theology* (1907; rpt. New York: Russell and Russell, 1963); Joseph Haroutunian, *Piety versus Moralism: The Passing of the New England Theology* (1932; rpt. New York: Harper & Row, 1970); Conrad Wright, *The Beginnings of Unitarianism in America* (Boston: Beacon Press, 1966); Daniel Walker Howe, *The Unitarian Conscience: Harvard Moral Philosophy, 1805–1861* (Cambridge: Harvard University Press, 1970); William G. McLoughlin, ed., *The American Evangelicals, 1800–1900: An Anthology* (New York: Harper & Row, 1968); McLoughlin, ed., *Lectures on Revivals of Religion*, by Charles G. Finney (Cambridge: Harvard University Press, 1960), vii–lii; Sidney Mead, *Nathaniel William Taylor, 1786–1858: A Connecticut Liberal* (1942; rpt. Hamden, Conn.: Archon Books, 1967). Among more recent scholarship in this area, see William Kern Breitenbach, "New Divinity Theology and the Idea of Moral Accountability" (Ph.D. diss., Yale University, 1978); Bruce Kuklick, *Churchmen and Philosophers: From Jonathan Edwards to John Dewey* (New Haven: Yale University Press, 1985); Ann Douglas, *The Feminization of American Culture* (New York: Knopf, 1977); Daniel Walker Howe, "The Decline of Calvinism: An Approach to its Study," *Comparative Studies in Society and History* 14 (1972), 306–327; Norman S. Fiering, "Will and Intellect in the New England Mind," *William and Mary Quarterly*, 3d ser., 29 (1972), 306–327.

20. Sydney E. Ahlstrom, *A Religious History of the American People* (New Haven: Yale University Press, 1972), 385–509; Whitney R. Cross, *The Burned-Over District: The Social and Intellectual History of Enthusiastic Religion in Western New York* (Ithaca, N.Y.: Cornell University Press, 1950); Charles Roy Keller, *The Second Great Awakening in Connecticut* (New Haven: Yale University Press, 1942); John B. Boles, *The Great Revival, 1787–1805: The Origins of the Southern Evangelical Mind* (Lexington: University Press of Kentucky, 1972); Timothy L. Smith, "Congregation, State, and Denomination: The Forming of the American Religious Structure," *William and Mary Quarterly*, 3d ser., 25 (1968), 155–176; still helpful is George Leon Walker, *Some Aspects of the Religious Life of New England with Special Reference to Congregationalists* (New York: Silver, Burdett, 1897), 126–199.

In two areas, the history of women and of the abolitionist challenge to New England orthodoxy, recent scholarship has begun to disassemble this picture of "social control." On the former, see Nancy F. Cott, *The Bonds of Womanhood: "Woman's Sphere" in New England, 1780–1835* (New Haven: Yale University Press, 1977); Barbara Leslie Epstein, *The Politics of Domesticity: Woman, Evangelism, and Temperance in Nineteenth-Century America* (Middletown: Wesleyan University Press, 1981). On abolitionism, see Bertram Wyatt-Brown, *Lewis Tappan and the Evangelical War against Slavery* (New York: Atheneum, 1971); Donald M. Scott, *From Office to Profession: The New England Ministry, 1750–1850* (Philadelphia: University of Pennsylvania Press, 1978), 76–111; and

Lawrence J. Friedman, *Gregarious Saints: Self and Community in American Abolitionism,* *1830–1870* (New York: Cambridge University Press, 1982).

21. Among the flood of books on American Puritanism, several have attempted to explore personal religious experience. See Charles Lloyd Cohen, *God's Caress: The Psychology of Puritan Religious Experience* (New York: Oxford University Press, 1986); Charles E. Hambrick-Stowe, *The Practice of Piety: Puritan Devotional Disciplines in Seventeenth-Century New England* (Chapel Hill: University of North Carolina Press, 1982); Daniel B. Shea, Jr., *Spiritual Autobiography in Early America* (Princeton: Princeton University Press, 1968); Patricia Caldwell, *The Puritan Conversion Narrative: The Beginnings of American Expression* (Cambridge, Eng.: Cambridge University Press, 1983); John Owen King III, *The Iron of Melancholy: Structures of Spiritual Conversion in America from the Puritan Conscience to Victorian Neurosis* (Middletown: Wesleyan University Press, 1983); and Greven, *The Protestant Temperament.*

22. C. B. Macpherson, *The Political Theory of Possessive Individualism: Hobbes to Locke* (London: Oxford University Press, 1962).

23. See *Oxford English Dictionary,* s.v. "experience."

24. Perry Miller, "Jonathan Edwards on the Sense of the Heart," *Harvard Theological Review* 41 (1948), 123–145; Miller, *Jonathan Edwards* (New York: Sloane, 1949); Norman Fiering, *Jonathan Edwards's Moral Thought and Its British Context* (Chapel Hill: University of North Carolina Press, 1981).

25. Perry Miller, *The New England Mind: The Seventeenth Century* (Cambridge: Harvard University Press, 1954), 365–491; Miller, "From the Covenant to the Revival," in *Nature's Nation* (Cambridge: Harvard University Press, 1967), 90–120; Sacvan Bercovitch, *The Puritan Origins of the American Self* (New Haven: Yale University Press, 1975); a "total criticism" of the liberal antinomy between parts and wholes, both in psychological and political theory, is Roberto Mangabeira Unger, *Knowledge and Politics* (New York: Free Press, 1975). Each of the three variants of liberalism that define the three parts of this study can be seen as efforts to reconcile this dilemma.

26. On my use of the terms *soul, character,* and *personality,* and other issues involved in developing these as ideal types, see Rabinowitz, Ph.D. diss., 402–404.

Notes to Chapter One

1. Charles Backus, *The Faithful Ministers of Jesus Christ Rewarded* (Litchfield, Conn.: Collier & Buel, [1792]), 5–6.

2. The best assessment of ministerial life is Donald M. Scott, *From Office to Profession;* a wonderfully rich compendium of individual biographies of New England ministers is William B. Sprague, comp., *Annals of the American Pulpit,* 9 vols. (New York: Carter, 1856–1869) (hereinafter cited as *Annals*), esp. vols. 1 and 2. On one minister's role as a sage in worldly matters, see *Annals,* 2:270, q.v. "Elijah Parish." On balancing farm and clerical obligations, see *Annals,* 2:261, q.v. "Jacob Catlin." On politics in the pulpit, there are many examples; see *Annals,* 2:54, 83, 180. The mid-eighteenth-century ministry is illuminated in Christopher M. Jedrey, *The World of John Cleaveland: Family and Community in Eighteenth-Century New England* (New York: Norton, 1979).

3. Nathanael Emmons, "Faithful Ministers Seek the Salvation of Their People," *Works,* ed. Jacob Ide (Boston: Crocker & Brewster, 1842), 1:203; on Puritan conversions, see Charles Lloyd Cohen, *God's Caress: The Psychology of Puritan Religious*

Experience; Jerald C. Brauer, "Conversion: From Puritanism to Revivalism," *Journal of Religion* 58 (1978), 227–243.

4. On Bellamy, see the sketch in *Annals*, 1:404–412.

5. On Whitefield and the Awakening, see Alan Heimert and Perry Miller, eds., *The Great Awakening: Documents Illustrating the Crisis and its Consequences* (Indianapolis: Bobbs, Merrill, 1967); Richard L. Bushman, ed., *The Great Awakening: Documents on the Revival of Religion, 1740–1745* (New York: Atheneum, 1970); still useful is Joseph Tracy, *The Great Awakening: A History of the Revival of Religion in the Time of Edwards and Whitefield* (Boston: Tappan, 1841); a vivid recent account is Stephen A. Marini, *Radical Sects of Revolutionary New England* (Cambridge: Harvard University Press, 1982), 11–24.

6. Tryon Edwards, ed., "Memoir," *The Works of Joseph Bellamy, D.D.* (Boston: Doctrinal Tract and Book Society, 1853), 1:ix.

7. Stiles, cited in Harry S. Stout, *The New England Soul: Preaching and Religious Culture in Colonial New England* (New York: Oxford University Press, 1986), 260; also see Nathan O. Hatch, *The Sacred Cause of Liberty: Republican Thought and the Millennium in Revolutionary New England* (New Haven: Yale University Press, 1977); Alan Heimert, *Religion and the American Mind from the Great Awakening to the Revolution* (Cambridge: Harvard University Press, 1966).

8. In addition to the works just cited, see William Breitenbach, "The Consistent Calvinism of the New Divinity Movement," *William and Mary Quarterly*, 3rd ser., 41 (1984), 241–274; Breitenbach, "Unregenerate Doings: Selflessness and Selfishness in New Divinity Theology," *American Quarterly* 34 (1982), 479–502; C. C. Goen, *Revivalism and Separatism in New England, 1740–1800* (New Haven: Yale University Press, 1962); Wright, *The Beginnings of Unitarianism in America*.

9. Charles Royster, *A Revolutionary People at War: The Continental Army and American Character, 1775–1783* (Chapel Hill: University of North Carolina Press, 1979).

10. Joseph Bellamy, "The Millennium," in Heimert and Miller, eds., *The Great Awakening*, 614.

11. Ibid., 613.

12. Ibid., 610.

13. Levi Hart, *Liberty Described and Recommended; in a Sermon, Preached to the corporation of Freemen in Farmington, at Their Meeting on Tuesday, September 20, 1774* (Hartford: Watson, 1775), 13.

14. Ibid., 11, 12–13.

15. Ibid., 20–21.

16. Ibid., 22.

17. Emmons, "Autobiography," in Ide, ed., *Works*, 1:xxvii.

18. Edwards A. Park, *Memoir of the Life and Character of Samuel Hopkins, D.D.*, 2nd ed. (Boston: Doctrinal Tract and Book Society, 1854), 89 ff.; Robert Clark Morris, ed., *Memoirs of James Morris of South Farms in Litchfield* (New Haven: Yale University Press, 1933), 46.

19. Richard M. Rollins, *The Long Journey of Noah Webster* (Philadelphia: University of Pennsylvania Press, 1980), 80.

20. David P. Szatmary, *Shays' Rebellion: The Making of an Agrarian Insurrection* (Amherst: University of Massachusetts Press, 1980).

21. Heimert, *Religion and the American Mind*, 535.

22. "Extracts from the Journal of Charles Backus," *CEM* 4 (1804), 358; also see *Annals*, 2:61–68.

23. All references to the Somers revival, except otherwise noted, are to Backus, "Revival of Religion in Somers," *CEM* 1 (1800), 19–21.

24. Griffin, cited in Richard D. Birdsall, "The Second Great Awakening and the New England Social Order," *Church History* 39 (1970), 353.

25. *CEM* 1 (1800), 6; I have generally cited the original publications of such revival accounts. Many of the *CEM* narratives were compiled by Bennet Tyler, *New England Revivals* (Boston: Massachusetts Sabbath School Society, 1846); and by Heman Humphrey, *Revival Sketches and Manual* (New York: American Tract Society, 1859). A valuable article is Richard D. Shiels, "The Second Great Awakening in Connecticut: Critique of the Traditional Interpretation," *Church History* 49 (1980), 401–415.

26. Somers Congregational Church Records, Connecticut State Library. Vital records for the town (and others) are also available in the state library.

27. *Annals*, 2:63.

28. Ibid., 64.

Notes to Chapter Two

1. Phrases are from Edward D. Griffin, "Revival of Religion in New Hartford," *CEM* 1 (1800), 219, 220, 222, 266.

2. See Norman Pettit, *The Heart Prepared: Grace and Conversion in Puritan Spiritual Life* (New Haven: Yale University Press, 1966).

3. Jonathan Edwards, *Religious Affections*, ed. John E. Smith (New Haven: Yale University Press, 1959), 383–461; Miller, "Jonathan Edwards on the Sense of the Heart," 123–145.

4. Samuel Hopkins, *The System of Doctrines* (Boston: Thomas and Andrews, 1793), 1:xxx.

5. On the Hopkinsians, see Kuklick, *Churchmen and Philosophers*, 43–65; Joseph A. Conforti, *Samuel Hopkins and the New Divinity Movement: Calvinism, the Congregational Ministry, and Reform in New England between the Great Awakenings* (Grand Rapids, Mich.: Christian University Press, 1981); still valuable is Haroutunian, *Piety versus Moralism*.

6. Charles Backus, *The Scripture Doctrine of Regeneration Considered* (Hartford: Hudson and Goodwin, 1800), 67.

7. Hopkins, *System of Doctrines*, 1:537.

8. On Fitzwilliam, see Edward W. Gilman, "Confessions of Faith," *Congregational Quarterly* 4 (1862), 181; Ebenezer Porter, *Letters on the Religious Revivals* (Boston: Congregational Board of Publication, 1858), 93; Edwin F. Hatfield, *Memoir of Elihu W. Baldwin, D.D.* (New York: Leavitt, 1843), 31–32.

9. William B. Sprague, *Memoir of the Rev. Edward D. Griffin, D.D.* (New York: Taylor & Dodd, 1839), 16; Lyman Beecher, *The Autobiography of Lyman Beecher*, ed. Barbara M. Cross (Cambridge: Harvard University Press, 1961), 1:55–57.

10. William A. Hallock, *Memoir of Harlan Page* (New York: American Tract Society, 1835), 42; Beecher, *Autobiography*, 1:48.

11. Edward Griffin, "A letter on religious revival in about forty adjacent

parishes," 1 August 1799, Connecticut State Library; William B. Sprague, *Lectures on Revivals of Religion* (Albany: Webster & Skinners, 1832), 20; Timothy Dwight, *Theology Explained and Defended*, 12th ed. (New York: Harper, 1850), 2:314.

12. Edwards, *Religious Affections*, 95–96.

13. Backus, *Scripture Doctrine of Regeneration*, 17.

14. Humphrey, *Revival Sketches and Manual*, 106; Sprague, *Lectures on Revivals*, 100.

15. Sheldon S. Wolin, *Politics and Vision: Continuity and Innovation in Western Political Thought* (Boston: Little, Brown, 1960), 339–340; Jonathan Edwards, "A Dissertation on the Nature of Virtue," *Works* (Worcester: Thomas, 1808), 2:437–447 (chap. 5).

16. McLoughlin, *New England Dissent*; John D. Cushing, "Notes on Disestablishment in Massachusetts, 1780–1833," *William and Mary Quarterly*, 3d ser., 26 (1969), 169–190; Cushing Strout, *The New Heavens and the New Earth: Political Religion in America* (New York: Harper & Row, 1974), 91–101.

17. *Annals*, 2:64.

18. Samuel Buell, *A Faithful Narrative of the Remarkable Revival of Religion, in the Congregation of Easthampton, on Long-Island, in the year of our Lord*, 1764 (Sag Harbor, N.Y.: Spooner, 1808), 3–4.

19. Ibid., 55–56.

20. Miller, *Jonathan Edwards*.

21. Gladys Bryson, *Man and Society: The Scottish Inquiry of the Eighteenth Century* (Princeton: Princeton University Press, 1945); Donald H. Meyer, *The Democratic Enlightenment* (New York: Putnam's, 1976); Meyer, *The Instructed Conscience: The Shaping of the American National Ethic* (Philadelphia: University of Pennsylvania Press, 1972); Henry F. May, *The Enlightenment in America* (New York: Oxford University Press, 1976), esp. 342–350.

22. Kuklick, *Churchmen and Philosophers*, 128–145; Sydney E. Ahlstrom, "The Scottish Philosophy and American Theology," *Church History* 24 (1955), 257–272.

23. Ralph Waldo Emerson, "The Transcendentalist," in *Nature, Addresses, and Lectures*, rev. ed. (Boston: Houghton Mifflin, 1883), 333.

24. The Scottish texts in moral philosophy had not yet entered the Hopkinsian-influenced college curriculum in the 1790s. Hopkins's *System of Doctrines* was used as a text for seniors at Williams College until it was "expunged" by the anti-Hopkinsian forces in 1796. See *Diary of Thomas Robbins, D.D., 1796–1854*, ed. Increase N. Tarbox (Boston: Beacon, 1886), 1:18.

25. Griffin's diary entry, considered over the next few paragraphs, is from Sprague, *Memoir of Griffin*, 25–27; on evangelicals and the doctrine of the atonement, see Claude Welch, *Protestant Thought in the Nineteenth Century: Volume I, 1799–1870* (New Haven: Yale University Press, 1972), 25.

26. Griffin, "An Humble Attempt to Reconcile the Differences of Christians Respecting the Extent of the Atonement," in Edwards A. Park, ed., *The Atonement: Discourses and Treatises* (Boston: Congregational Board of Publication, 1859), 137–427.

27. Gillett, "Revival of Religion in Torrington, Connecticut," *CEM* 1 (1800), 133.

28. Porter, *Letters on Revivals*, 64; "On Self-Examination," *CEM* 5 (1805), 414–415; but cf. Edwards: "Assurance is not to be obtained so much by self-examination as by action" (*Religious Affections*, 195).

29. Until 1819, the Bible was never read during Sabbath services without interpretive commentary, "'giving the sense,'" in Danvers, Massachusetts. To read it so was called "'dumb reading'" (Charles B. Rice, "History of the First Parish in Danvers," *Proceedings at the Celebration of the Two Hundredth Anniversary of the First Parish at Salem Village, now Danvers, October 8, 1872* [Boston: Congregational Publication Society, 1874], 118–119); the phrases in the text appear, respectively, in Tyler, *Memoir of Nettleton*, 66; Humphrey, *Revival Sketches*, 126; Backus, "Revival of Religion in Somers," *CEM* 1 (1800), 19.

30. Sprague, *Memoir of Griffin*, 65–66; "secret" (i.e., private) prayer also had its heuristic purpose as "perhaps the best criterion by which we can judge of our state before God" (John Codman, *A Sermon, on Prayer, Preached at Dorchester, December 12 . . . , 1813* [Boston: Armstrong, 1814], 9).

31. Porter, *Letters on Revivals*, 99.

32. William F. Miller, "Revival of Religion in Wintonbury [Windsor, Connecticut]," *CEM* 1 (1801), 306.

33. "Letter to Miss N—," *CEM* 1 (1800), 108; Henry Clarke Wright, *Human Life: Illustrated in My Individual Experience* (Boston: Marsh, 1849), 97.

34. Calvin Colton, *Thoughts on the Religious State of the Country*, 2d ed. (New York: Harper, 1836), 47; cf. Ammi R. Robbins, "Revival of Religion in Norfolk, Connecticut," *CEM* 1 (1801), 311–312; Nathan Perkins, *Two Discourses on the Grounds of the Christian's Hope* (Hartford: Hudson and Goodwin, 1800), 26.

35. Gillett, "Revival in Torrington," 134; Edwards, *Religious Affections*, 156–157, 210–217; cf. Francis Bowen, *The Metaphysics of Sir William Hamilton* (Cambridge, Mass.: Sever and Francis, 1868), 145, passim; Timothy M. Cooley, *Sketches of the Life and Character of the Rev. Lemuel Haynes* (New York: Taylor, 1839), 109.

36. "On Dreams," *CEM* 1 (1801), 397.

37. Nathanael Emmons, *Sermons, on Various Important Subjects of Christian Doctrine and Practice* (Boston: Armstrong, 1812), 71.

38. Locke noted, "This wrong connexion in our minds of ideas in themselves loose and independent of one another, has such an influence, and is of so great force to set us awry in our actions, as well moral as natural, passions, reasonings, and notions themselves, that perhaps there is not any one thing that deserves more to be looked after" (*Essay*, ed. Alexander Campbell Fraser [New York: Dover, 1959], 1:531 [Book II, chap. 33, sec. 9]); Locke distinguished between a "natural correspondence and connexion" of ideas, to be developed in reasoning, and such "wrong connection" (ibid., 529, editor's note). On Locke's followers, see Ernest Lee Tuveson, *The Imagination as a Means of Grace: Locke and the Aesthetics of Romanticism* (Berkeley: University of California Press, 1960); Michel Foucault, *History of Sexuality, Volume I: An Introduction* (New York: Pantheon, 1978), 156.

39. "On Dreams," 396–397.

40. "The Bible the Only Revelation to Man," *CEM* 5 (1805), 349; also see Joseph Bellamy, *True Religion Delineated; or Experimental Religion* (Boston: Kneeland, 1750), 92; Hopkins, *System of Doctrines*, 1:603–604.

41. The description of baptism is from William W. Woodward, comp.,

Surprising Accounts of the Revival of Religion in the United States (Philadelphia: Woodward, 1802), 19.

42. *The Autobiography and Journal of Rev. Heman Bangs* (New York: Tibbals, 1872), 12; *The Life, Experience and Travels of John Colby*, 3d ed., rev. (Cornish: Me.: Cole, 1829), 11, emphasis added; [Letitia J. S. Brown], *Memoir of Elder Elijah Shaw*, 3d ed. (Boston: Shaw, 1852), 18.

43. See Dean C. Jessee, "The Early Accounts of Joseph Smith's First Vision," *Brigham Young University Studies* 9 (1969), 275–294; Marini, *Radical Sects;* Richard L. Bushman, *Joseph Smith and the Beginnings of Mormonism* (Urbana: University of Illinois Press, 1984).

44. The discussion of Nancy Pomeroy's experience in the next several paragraphs comes from "Character and Experiences of Mrs. Nancy Bishop," *CEM* 1 (1800), 186–187. Nancy Pomeroy, daughter of Adino Pomeroy, was born in Northampton, Mass., in 1764, lived in Middletown until her marriage to Nathaniel Bishop of Richmond, Mass., in 1797. She died in childbirth nine months later. She was converted and joined the Middletown church in 1790; her "difficult" Sabbath is dated October 20, 1793.

45. On church architecture, see Peter Benes, ed., *New England Meeting House and Church: 1630–1850,* Annual Proceedings for 1979 of the Dublin Seminar for New England Folklife (Boston: Boston University, n.d.), esp. Jane C. Nylander, "Toward Comfort and Uniformity in New England Meeting Houses, 1750–1850," 86–100; Benes and Philip D. Zimmerman, *New England Meeting House and Church: 1630–1850: A Loan Exhibition held at the Currier Gallery of Art, Manchester, New Hampshire* (Boston: Boston University and the Currier Gallery for the Dublin Seminar for New England Folklife, 1979); J. Frederick Kelly, *Early Connecticut Meetinghouses* (New York: Columbia University Press, 1948); Arthur B. Mazmanian, *The Structure of Praise: A Design Study, Architecture for Religion from the 17th Century to the Present* (Barre, Mass.: Barre Publishers, 1973); and Marian Card Donnelly, *The New England Meeting Houses of the Seventeenth Century* (Middletown: Wesleyan University Press, 1968); on sound and sight in religion, see Paul W. Pruyser, *A Dynamic Psychology of Religion* (New York: Harper & Row, 1968), 21–46.

46. Harry S. Stout, "The Great Awakening in New England Reconsidered: The New England Clergy," *Journal of Social History* 8 (Fall 1974), 21–41; Stout, *The New England Soul,* 316.

47. Backus, *Scripture Doctrine of Regeneration,* 66–67.

48. Sturbridge Congregational Church Records, in the possession of the clerk of the Sturbridge Congregational Society.

49. By midcentury, as this book will show, much had changed in this regard. A splendid brief memoir is Joseph S. Clark, "A Lesson from the Past: Catechising," *Congregational Quarterly* 1 (1859), 393–396. An even more adroitly expressed summary is from Allen Tate, "Emily Dickinson," *Essays of Four Decades* (1928; rpt. Chicago: Swallow, 1959), 281–298.

50. Porter, *Letters on Revivals,* 17; the letters were first published in *The Spirit of the Pilgrims,* 5 and 6 (1832–1833).

51. Wright, *Human Life,* 225.

52. Bushnell, "The Age of Homespun," in *Work and Play: or Literary Varieties* (New York: Scribner, 1864), 389.

Notes to Chapter Three

1. Missionaries frequently commented on the resemblance of new settlements to New England villages and even their superiority, e.g., "The meetinghouses [in Paris, N.Y.] are thronged on the sabbath. . . . Their gravity and morality are worthy the esteem and imitation of the old settlements in the New England states" ("Missing Intelligence," *MMM* 1 [1803], 70).

2. "Lines Addressed to a Person," *MMM* 2 (Jan. 1805), 325–326; Alvan Hyde, "The Purpose of God Displayed in Abasing the Pride of Nation," in *Sermons on Important Subjects* (Hartford: Hudson and Goodwin, 1797), 276; for example, the 1814 drought in Fryeburg, Me., according to Rev. Nathaniel Porter, "vindicat[ed] God in the exercise of his sovereignty" (*Annals*, 2:55).

3. "Literary Taste," *MMM* 3 (1806), 407.

4. Porter, *Letters on Revivals*, 8.

5. Alvan Hyde, in Sprague, *Lectures on Revivals of Religion*, Appendix, 46; Simon Waterman, "Revival of Religion in Plymouth, Connecticut," *CEM* 2 (1801), 25.

6. Hooker, "Revival of Religion in Goshen," *CEM* 1 (1801), 342.

7. "Letter from a Young Woman," *CEM* 1 (1800), 34; the Coventry woman's letter is in Hallock, *Memoir of Harlan Page*, 42; the note to Nettleton is in the Nettleton Papers, Case Memorial Library, Hartford Seminary Foundation, Doc. Box 177, Folder No. 2831, Item No. 78289.

8. Sprague, *Memoir of Griffin*, 64, 59.

9. Waterman, "Revival in Plymouth," 25; Griffin, "Revival of Religion in New-Hartford," *CEM* 1 (1800), 218; Bennet Tyler, *Memoir of the Life and Character of Rev. Asahel Nettleton*, 3d ed. (Boston: Doctrinal Tract and Book Society, 1850), 156.

10. Josiah B. Andrews, "A Narrative of a Work of Divine Grace in Killingworth, Second Society," *CEM* 5 (1804), 32; also see Giles H. Cowles, "Revival of Religion in New-Cambridge [Bristol]," *CEM* 1 (1800), 56.

11. Edward Griffin, "A letter on religious revival"; Waterman, "Revival in Plymouth," 25.

12. "Admonitions," *CEM* 2 (1801), 68.

13. Jacob Catlin, "The Wicked, on Account of Worldly Prosperity, and the Unbelief of a Future State, Openly Reject and Despise the Almighty," in *Sermons on Important Subjects* (Hartford: Hudson and Goodwin, 1797), 505.

14. So prayer, said the *MMM* in 1803, is as necessary to salvation as the sun is to harvest: "It may just as well be said, that as God had decreed that the year 1803 should produce its annual harvest, it would as certainly be produced, without the heat of the sun, and the fertilizing showers of rain, as with them" ("On Solitary Devotion," 1 [1803], 249).

15. Tyler, *Memoir of Nettleton*, 156; Backus, *Scripture Doctrine of Regeneration*, 23.

16. Joseph Emerson, ed., *Writings of Miss Fanny Woodbury*, 4th ed. (Boston: Armstrong, 1819), 170; also see "Letter to a Friend," *CEM* 1 (1801), 337.

17. Samuel Hopkins, *A Treatise on the Millennium . . .* (Boston: Thomas and Andrews, 1793), 83 [bound with his *System of Doctrines*, vol. 2].

18. *Annals*, 2:82.

19. Timothy Dwight, *Greenfield Hill: A Poem* (New York: Childs and Swaine, 1794), 169.

20. Rollins, *The Long Journey of Noah Webster*, 126.

21. *Noah Webster's First Edition of an American Dictionary of the English Language* (1828; rpt. Anaheim, Calif.: Foundation for American Christian Education, 1967), s.v. "nature," "peace," "reconciliation," "soul," "sovereign," "submission."

22. Kuklick, *Churchmen and Philosophers*, 61.

23. William James, "The Sentiment of Rationality," in *The Will to Believe and Other Essays on Popular Philosophy* (New York: Dover, 1956), 77.

24. Ralph Waldo Emerson, "Historic Notes of Life and Letters in New England," in *Lectures and Biographical Sketches, Works* (Boston: Houghton Mifflin, 1883), 10:311.

Notes to Chapter Four

1. Timothy M. Cooley, "Revival of Religion in Granville, Massachusetts," *CEM* 2 (1802), 271.

2. Tyler, *Memoir of Nettleton*, 66.

3. Griffin, "Revival of Religion in New-Hartford," *CEM* 1 (1800), 218.

4. Ibid., 219.

5. John E. Todd, ed., *John Todd: The Story of His Life* (New York: Harper, 1876), 62; Beecher, *Autobiography*, 1:74–75.

6. See the discussion of "The Distance of God from Man" and "The Distance of Man from God," in James M'Cosh, *The Method of the Divine Government, Physical and Moral* (New York: Carter, 1852), 47–55.

7. Timothy M. Cooley, in Humphrey, *Revival Sketches and Manual*, 141.

8. "On Submission to God," *CEM* 5 (1804), 127.

9. Backus, *Scripture Doctrine of Regeneration*, 148.

10. Excerpts from these conversion narratives were reprinted in Tyler, *Memoir of Nettleton*, 62–68. I have not been able to locate the original accounts. Barbara Leslie Epstein has studied women's conversion narratives in *The Politics of Domesticity*, 55–62. Epstein finds women expressing a great deal more anger and self-hatred in these accounts of conversion than I have. Nancy F. Cott's excellent *Bonds of Womanhood*, 126–159, focuses chiefly on women's activity in religious and moral societies.

11. Backus, *Scripture Doctrine of Regeneration*, 86.

12. J. Hillis Miller, *The Disappearance of God: Five Nineteenth-Century Writers* (Cambridge: Harvard University Press, 1963), 5.

13. "On Prayer," *CEM* 1 (1800), 170.

14. Backus, *Scripture Doctrine of Regeneration*, 15–16.

15. Porter, *Letters on the Revivals*, 17.

16. On Burke, see Basil Willey, *The Eighteenth Century Background: Studies on the Idea of Nature in the Thought of the Period* (1939; rpt. Boston: Beacon, 1961), 240–252.

17. Cowles, "Revival of Religion in New-Cambridge [Bristol]," *CEM* 1 (1800), 56; Cyrus Yale, *Life of Rev. Jeremiah Hallock* (New York: Haven, 1828), 99.

18. Sprague, *Memoir of Griffin*, 168.

19. Beecher, *Autobiography*, 1:48.

20. See Morris, ed., *Memoirs;* Morris recorded the conversion narratives referred to in n. 10 above.

21. Ibid., 51–52.

22. See Jonathan Edwards, "Dissertation Concerning the End for Which God Created the World," in *Works* (Worcester: Thomas, 1808), 6:9–124; a key to the centrality of aesthetic thought in Edwards is Roland André Delattre, *Beauty and Sensibility in the Thought of Jonathan Edwards: An Essay in Aesthetics and Theological Ethics* (New Haven: Yale University Press, 1968).

23. Foster, *A Genetic History of the New England Theology,* 113–117; John Stanley Mattson, "Charles Grandison Finney and the Emerging Tradition of 'New Measures' Revivalism" (Ph.D. diss., University of North Carolina at Chapel Hill, 1970), 123.

24. Mattson, "Finney," 129; Hopkins, *System of Doctrines,* 1:561; cf. Edwards, "A Dissertation on the Nature of Virtue," *Works,* 2:395–471.

25. Hopkins, *System of Doctrines,* 1:561.

26. Daniel Day Williams, *The Andover Liberals: A Study in American Theology* (New York: King's Crown, 1941), 7.

27. Wright, *Human Life,* 161; for a contrasting view of the Hopkinsians, see Kuklick, *Churchmen and Philosophers,* 53: "Disinterested benevolence showed the movement of Congregationalists away from a mysterious divine cosmos to a human-centered one, just as the theology itself relied less on mystery and more on what appeared to be reasonable for divines to believe." The paradox of orthodox Hopkinsianism, as I show in chapter 2, is that a "reasonable" (highly appreciative) view of the mind could be combined with an acknowledgment of the mystery of the "special operations of the Holy Spirit."

Notes to Chapter Five

1. Samuel Shephard, "Revival of Religion in Lenox, Massachusetts," *CEM* 2 (1801), 140.

2. Colton, *Thoughts on the Religious State,* 47; cf. Ammi R. Robbins, "Revival of Religion in Norfolk, Connecticut," *CEM* 1 (1801), 311–312.

3. Wright, *Human Life,* 97.

4. "Letter to Miss N——," *CEM* 1 (1800), 108–109; Sarah Connell Ayer, *Diary* (Portland, Me.: Lefavor-Tower, 1910), 162, 165.

5. Miron Winslow, *Memoir of Mrs. Harriet L. Winslow, Thirteen Years a Member of the American Mission in Ceylon* (New York: American Tract Society, 1840), 15.

6. "Friendship is but a partial, and ease a temporary, pleasure" ("Mrs. Sarah Gill: Extracts from her Diary," *MMM* 1 [1803], 201).

7. The Hughes-Brewster imbroglio occurred in 1820–1821. Seventeen years later, incidentally, Dr. Brewster—by then treasurer-librarian of the Sunday School, a Tract Society distributor, and a leading church member—was totally excluded for "having . . . administered medicine . . . with the intention of producing an abortion." Hampton Congregational Church Records, Connecticut State Library, 1:144–145 and 2:78; Bristol Congregational Church Records, Connecticut State Library, 2:38–45, 60–63.

8. General Association of Connecticut, *An Address . . . to the Congrega-*

tional Ministers and Churches of the State on the Importance of United Endeavors to Revive Gospel Discipline (Litchfield, Conn.: Hosmer and Goodwin, 1808), 12. The address was signed by Azel Backus as moderator of the General Association.

9. On "visiting," see *Annals*, 2:218; the summary of church discipline is based upon a careful reading, not a quantitative analysis, of the cases in the records of the following churches: Baptist and Congregational churches in Sturbridge, Mass., each in the possession of the societies' clerks (with my notes deposited at the Old Sturbridge Village Research Library), and Congregational churches in Bristol, Hampton, New Hartford, and Somers, Conn., Connecticut State Library.

10. Samuel M. Worcester, *The Life and Labors of Rev. Samuel Worcester, D. D.* (Boston: Crocker and Brewster, 1852), 1:249.

11. *A Narrative of the Religious Controversy in Fitchburg* (Worcester: Thomas, 1804), 9, 49; also see Doris Kirkpatrick, *The City and the River*, 1 (Fitchburg: Fitchburg Historical Society, 1971), 128–130; and Rufus C. Torrey, *History of the Town of Fitchburg, Massachusetts* (Fitchburg: Fitchburg Centennial Committee, 1865), 122–124; Rev. Worcester was inducted into an already contentious situation in Fitchburg, but his tenure saw the division form on doctrinal lines. After his dismissal in 1802, Worcester and fifty-four allies established a new Calvinistic Congregational Church, which was incorporated in 1805. The town did not again "settle" a minister. Its meetinghouse was thereafter used by diverse groups, and town meetings ceased to have any role in managing religious affairs. Similar breaks occurred in many Massachusetts towns. Worcester's whole career was characterized by efforts to sharpen the conflict with liberals along doctrinal lines. See *Dictionary of American Biography*, s.v. "Worcester, Samuel." Worcester wrote, "In this day of abounding error it is of the highest importance that the churches of Christ should make a firm and decided stand for truth" (Kirkpatrick, *City and River*, 1:129). Nineteenth-century church historians attributed the spread of required confessions of faith to Worcester's influence; see Edward W. Gilman, "Confessions of Faith," *Congregational Quarterly* 4 (1862), 186.

12. Worcester, *Life and Labors*, 1:337, 355.

13. Backus, "Revival of Religion in Somers," *CEM* 1 (1800), 20.

14. Wright, *Human Life*, 145–146.

15. Alvan Hyde, "The Purpose of God Displayed in Abasing the Pride of Nation," in *Sermons on Important Subjects*, 276.

16. Scott, *From Office to Profession*, 16; *Annals*, 2:268–272; see *A Statistical Account of the Towns and Parishes in the State of Connecticut*, 1, no. 1 (New Haven: Connecticut Academy of Arts and Sciences, 1811); the Acorn Club of Connecticut has republished others of the original responses, e.g., Samuel Nott, *Franklin in 1800*, ed. Thompson R. Harlow (Hartford: Acorn Club, 1949); and Azel Backus and Chauncey Prindle, *Bethlem in 1812 & Watertown 1801* (Hartford: Acorn Club, 1961).

17. Timothy Dwight, *Travels in New England and New York*, ed. Barbara M. Solomon (Cambridge: Harvard University Press, 1969), 1:169, 302–303; also see Porter, *Letters on Revivals*, 114 ff.

18. Dwight, *Theology Explained and Defended*, 2:415, 478.

19. Hopkins, *System of Doctrines*, 1:555, 544–545.

20. Edwards, "A Dissertation on the Nature of Virtue," 2:407 (chap. 2).

21. Jacob E. Cooke, ed., *The Federalist* (Middletown: Wesleyan University Press, 1961), 57.

22. Worcester, *Life and Labors*, 1:184–185.

23. "Concerning the Duty of a Church to Censure its Members for the Sin of Heresy," *MMM* 1 (1803), 165; Rollins, *The Long Journey of Noah Webster*, 99.

24. Anna Roosevelt Cowles and Laura Hadley Mosley, eds., *The Diaries of Julia Cowles: A Connecticut Record*, 1797–1803 (New Haven: Yale University Press, 1931), 68–69.

25. Boles, *The Great Revival*, suggests that a similar strategy of heightened discipline in Southern churches "produced a large body of churchless people who desired reconciliation and renewal of religious fellowship" (11). But Boles is speaking more of behavioral discipline here, and less of doctrinal orthodoxy; Cowles, "Revival of Religion in New-Cambridge [Bristol]," *CEM* 1 (1800), reported "that the converts are chiefly from families where one or both of the parents were professors or hopefully friendly to religion, and where some serious regard has been paid to divine things" (59); Porter, *Letter on Revivals*, 9, estimated the proportion of children of religious parents (one parent a church member) as "not far from two thirds," but higher in some places; on James Morris, see Morris, ed., *Memoirs*, and his obituary in the *Christian Spectator* 2 (1820), 447–448.

26. See Robert A. Gross, *The Minutemen and Their World* (New York: Hill & Wang, 1976), 173–174, passim; David Hackett Fischer, *The Revolution of American Conservatism: The Federalist Party in the Era of Jeffersonian Democracy* (New York: Harper & Row, 1965).

27. On dissidents in Somers, see Fred C. Davis and Richard W. Davis, *Somers: The History of a Connecticut Town* (Somers: Somers Historical Society, 1973), 35–38.

Notes to Chapter Six

1. Beecher, *Autobiography*, 1:46; Beecher, *The Practicability of Suppressing Vice, By Means of Societies Instituted for that Purpose* (New London, Conn.: Green, 1804), 7; the key source for Beecher's experience in East Hampton is the *Autobiography*, 1:60–130; also see chap. 3 of Stuart C. Henry's biography, *Unvanquished Puritan: A Portrait of Lyman Beecher* (Grand Rapids, Mich.: Eerdmans, 1973), and of chap. 1 in Milton Rugoff, *The Beechers: An American Family in the Nineteenth Century* (New York: Harper & Row, 1981). The best study of the entire Beecher clan is Marie Caskey, *Chariot of Fire: Religion and the Beecher Family* (New Haven: Yale University Press, 1978). Lyman has inspired other splendid historical sketches, among them Constance Mayfield Rourke, *Trumpets of Jubilee* (New York: Harcourt, Brace, 1927), 3–86, and Edward Wagenknecht, *Ambassadors for Christ: Seven American Preachers* (New York: Oxford University Press, 1972), 1–39. Also see Kathryn Kish Sklar, *Catharine Beecher: A Study in American Domesticity* (New Haven: Yale University Press, 1973), 3–14. On East Hampton and Long Island, there are many local histories. But readers should not miss Dwight, *Travels*, 3:218–222.

2. Beecher, *Autobiography*, 1:97.

3. Ibid., 93.

4. Beecher, *Practicability of Suppressing Vice*, Appendix.

5. Ibid., 13.

6. Dwight, *Travels*, 3:219–220.

7. Nathanael Emmons, *A Discourse, Delivered, September 3,*

MCDDXCII, to the Society for the Reformation of Morals in Franklin (Worcester: Worcester, 1793), 20.

8. Beecher, *Practicability of Suppressing Vice*, 8.

9. Ibid., 7.

10. Lyman Beecher, "The Remedy for Duelling," *Works* (Boston: Jewett, 1852), 2:71.

11. Eventually, when the moralists had finally codified their consistent credo in the New Haven or New Divinity or New School Presbyterian theology (as it was variously known), the implications of their thinking struck terror in the hearts of such orthodox stalwarts as Bennet Tyler and the professors at the Princeton Theological Seminary. To the charges of heresy from these conservatives, the New School party replied by "drawing a distinction between doctrine and what it called the 'philosophy' of the doctrine. No New School Leaders," says Charles I. Foster, "ever went astray in doctrine; they were as solid there as Jonathan Edwards could wish. But the philosophical implications of doctrine they considered wide open to speculation, and it was there that the revolution took place" (*An Errand of Mercy: The Evangelical United Front, 1790–1837* [Chapel Hill: University of North Carolina Press, 1960], 264). The "philosophy" of the doctrine was, of course, the mental philosophy by which the implications of the theology could be applied to a parishioner's life. Also see George M. Marsden, *The Evangelical Mind and the New School Presbyterian Experience: A Case Study of Thought and Theology in Nineteenth-Century America* (New Haven: Yale University Press, 1970), 1–87.

12. See Mead, *Taylor,* 179, for an analysis of the "moral tendency" dispute. Also see Howe, *The Unitarian Conscience.*

13. *A Sermon, entitled "The Remedy for Dueling," by Rev. Lyman Beecher, D.D., Applied to the Crime of Slaveholding* (Boston: Knapp, 1838), 4.

Notes to Chapter Seven

1. William Ellery Channing, "The Moral Argument Against Calvinism," *Works* (Boston: Channing, 1849), 1:224, 235–236; Wright, *Human Life,* 46, cf.115; Orville Dewey, *Autobiography and Letters,* ed. Mary E. Dewey (Boston: Roberts, 1883), 16, 35. A fascinating study which looks at the problem of the void in a much larger cultural context is Robert Martin Adams, *Nil: Episodes in the Literary Conquest of Void During the Nineteenth Century* (New York: Oxford University Press, 1966).

2. Dwight, *Theology,* 2:326 (the italicization of the entire passage has been deleted), 333.

3. Ibid., 335; see Leon Howard, *The Connecticut Wits* (Chicago: University of Chicago Press, 1943), 342–401; *Noah Webster's First Edition of An American Dictionary of the English Language,* s.v. "honor."

4. Dwight, *Theology,* 2:334.

5. Samuel Hopkins, *Memoirs of the Life of Mrs. Sarah Osborn* (Worcester: Worcester, 1799), 357.

6. Dwight, *Theology,* 2:336.

7. Ibid., 332.

8. The early nineteenth century witnessed a general movement among American Protestants against theological contextualizing of biblical passages and toward a reliance on *sola scriptura,* the Bible and only the Bible (or even the New Tes-

tament) as the fount of truth. The denomination of "Christians," later called the Disciples of Christ, made this a cardinal principle of its secession from Calvinism in the West and in New England. Of course, the New England Calvinist evangelicals, heirs to the richest tradition of dogmatic interpretation among all Americans, would not go this far. But the New Haven Theology did make important concessions to this wider movement, as in the gradual shift toward the distribution of Bibles rather than tracts. See William A. Hallock, *A Sketch of the Life and Labors of Rev. Justin Edwards* (New York: American Tract Society, 1855), 482. The best summary of the trend is Nathan O. Hatch, "*Sola Scriptura* and *Novus Ordo Seclorum*," in Hatch and Mark A. Noll, eds., *The Bible in America: Essays in Cultural History* (New York: Oxford University Press, 1982), 59–78.

9. According to Joseph Haroutunian, the process of "the waning glory of God" had pretty much been completed in the transition from Edward to Hopkins (*Piety versus Moralism*, chap. 4), that is, in the transmutation of the Calvinist divinity from a metaphysical center of Being into a Law-Giver. Still, the moralists were making important constitutional amendments by forcing so clear a human image on God.

10. Mead, *Taylor*, 120.

11. Ultimately, Taylor's son-in-law and successor at Yale Divinity School, Noah Porter, completed this transition by publishing *Human Intellect* in 1868. Porter's book begins with the sentence, "Psychology is the science of the human soul," and attempts, at enormous length, to reconcile the new study of mental phenomena with the claims of spiritual experience (*The Human Intellect: With an Introduction upon Psychology and the Soul*, 4th ed. [New York: Scribner, 1872], 5); Beecher, "A Reformation of Morals Practicable and Indispensable" (1812), *Works*, 2:84.

12. Rush Welter cites the following example: "William Ladd, the founder of the American Peace Society, articulated the fundamental faith common to most reformers when he wrote in 1840, 'It is an incontrovertible axiom, that every thing of a moral nature which ought to be done, can be done'" (*The Mind of America, 1820–1860* [New York: Columbia University Press, 1975], 334).

13. Beecher, "The Bible a Code of Laws" (1817), *Works*, 2:155.

14. Ibid.

15. Mead, *Taylor*, 95–127.

16. "*The motive to obedience*," Beecher wrote, "*is as the opinion concerning it is*: if that be correct, the true motive is presented to the mind; if incorrect, the true motive is thrust aside, and another substituted" ("The Bible a Code of Laws" [1817], *Works*, 2:191). Even for Emerson, only the self's communion with "Reason" permits this kind of creative willfulness; and while the individual self is thereby willful, such willfulness is circumscribed by the identification of Reason with the universal. See Merrell R. Davis, "Emerson's 'Reason' and the Scottish Philosophers," *New England Quarterly* 27 (1944), 209–228; Stephen E. Whicher, *Freedom and Fate: An Inner Life of Ralph Waldo Emerson* (Philadelphia: University of Pennsylvania Press, 1953), chaps. 1–5; Joel Porte, *Emerson and Thoreau: Transcendentalists in Conflict* (Middletown: Wesleyan University Press, 1966), chap. 4; and Sidney E. Mead, *The Lively Experiment: The Shaping of Christianity in America* (New York: Harper & Row, 1963), 94.

17. Often the appeal was to Romans 7:23, in which Paul speaks of the "law in my members, warring against the law of my mind, and bringing me into captivity to the law of sin which is in my members." See the discussion in "On the Nature

of the Saint's Perseverance," *CEM* 1 (1801), 325–330. The moralist position was in general a retreat from the applicability of theological and metaphysical categories to everyday life experience.

18. Aaron Bancroft, *A Discourse on Conversion* (Worcester: Manning, 1816), 34–35.

19. Beecher, "The Design, Rights and Duties, of Local Churches" (1819), *Works*, 2:220.

20. Daniel Webster, "The Sub-Treasury," *Works* (Boston: Little and Brown, 1851), 4:407.

21. Georg Simmel, *The Sociology of Georg Simmel*, trans. and ed. Kurt H. Wolff (Glencoe, Ill.: Free Press, 1950), 318.

22. Karen Halttunen, *Confidence Men and Painted Women: A Study of Middle-class Culture in America, 1830–1870* (New Haven: Yale University Press, 1982).

23. Ibid., 8.

Notes to Chapter Eight

1. The evangelical moralists did not, generally, write long and detailed revival narratives. For an explanation, see John Keep, *A Narrative of the Origin and Progress of the Congregational Church in Homer, Cortland County, N.Y., With Remarks* (Homer, N.Y.: Kinney & Aikin, 1833), 5. The progress of individual sinners through the revival process occupied less attention, but more emphasis was placed upon the methods of revivalism. The classic expression of this, of course, was Charles G. Finney's 1835 manual, *Lectures on Revivals of Religion*. Other sources for revival practice are Charles G. Finney, *Memoirs* (New York: Barnes, 1876); Sprague, *Lectures on Revivals*; and such hostile commentaries on the "New Measures" as Calvin Colton, *Thoughts on the Religious State*; *Letters of the Rev. Dr. Beecher and Rev. Mr. Nettleton on the "New Measures" in Conducting Revivals of Religion* (New York: Carvill, 1828); [Orville Dewey], *Letters of an English Traveller to His Friend in England, on the "Revivals of Religion," in America* (Boston: Bowles and Dearborn, 1828). A concise summary is in Foster, *An Errand of Mercy*, 259–265, most of it drawn from a contemporary sketch of a revival led by Lyman Beecher at Hartford in 1828.

There continued, of course, to be both orthodox revivals and orthodox revival accounts. One is Charles Prentice, *A Sermon, delivered September 20, 1829, at the Twenty-Fifth Anniversary of his Ordination. To which is added, a Brief Narrative of a Revival of Religion* (Litchfield, Conn.: Adams, 1830). But the long revival accounts that had been so significant in the heyday of orthodoxy—around the year 1800—had usually been replaced by perfunctory reports of instances of God's favor, mentioning only the places affected and the numbers of "hopeful converts."

2. "The inquiry room," wrote John Keep, "was the place for the most heavy and successful labor, because here the *attention* could be *fixed*. We did not invite into this room *Visiters* [sic], lest the attention should be diverted" (*Narrative in Homer, N.Y.*, 8).

3. Quoted in Foster, *Errand of Mercy*, 261–262. Plainly such a conversion experience, culminating in the task of spreading the word, was more conducive to obtaining commitments to work than commitments to worship.

4. Cross, *The Burned-Over District*; see also McLoughlin's introduction

to Finney, *Lectures on Revivals; Letters of Beecher and Nettleton*; Beecher, *Autobiography*, 2:66–80.

5. Again, from John Keep: "Whenever, and to the same extent in which the church will bestow *special labor* for the conversion of sinners, God will bless. . . . God helps those who help themselves. . . . [He rewards such] confidence" (*Narrative in Homer*, N.Y., 3–4). And Calvin Colton, who had been converted in an orthodox revival himself, complained about the new measures as a mechanistic and disruptive form of religion:

> The theory assumes, that no religious training can be good and right—that all is wrong—so long as the sinner remains unconverted. To dislodge him, therefore, by whatever means, entirely from his accustomed position, from all his habits of thinking, at whatever anxious and conscientious pains they may have been acquired and established under the best religious guardians and teachers, and to bring his mind under the influence and control of this new moral machinery, is conversion (*Thoughts on the Religious State of the Country*, 173–174).

6. A brilliant exposition of the changed process of conversion is in Scott, *From Office to Profession*, 76–94. On the crisis of youth, see Joseph F. Kett, *Rites of Passage: Adolescence in America, 1790 to the Present* (New York: Basic Books, 1977), 11–108.

7. Porter, *Letters on Revivals*, 144; John Keep reordered the orthodox sequence in his revivals, offering instruction "into the nature of the Christian religion: what is expected of him as a disciple of Christ; and what he can and ought to do," but only *after* the sinner had professed his submission (*Narrative in Homer*, N.Y., 7).

8. E. Goodrich Smith, *Memoir of Charles Henry Porter* (New York: n.p., 1849), 112.

9. Ibid., 112–113.

10. Ibid., 113–114.

11. Cooley, *Sketches of Lemuel Haynes*, 94–95.

Notes to Chapter Nine

1. For example, Joseph Haroutunian shows how "Channing struck a new note" in the chaos of issues surrounding the emergence of Unitarianism,

> thereby completing the alliance between *Unitarianism* and that *secular humanitarianism* which had been growing in New England half a century since. His *Unitarian Christianity*, preached in 1819, was a clear and comprehensive statement of the faith in human power, in human dignity, in human reason, and in human rectitude. It was a brilliant discourse, setting forth the principles of a theology congenial to the interests and the ideas of the new age.
> [Then Haroutunian cites some of Channing's sermon, and concludes,] This ethical note was the real burden of Channing's message. It soon became the center of his controversy with the orthodox and the foundation of his arguments against their doctrines (*Piety versus Moralism*, 206).

See also ibid., chaps. 6 and 8; and Mead, *Taylor*, 128–146.

2. An important distinction, commonly made by moralists, appears in Channing's "Moral Argument against Calvinism": "Men's characters are determined, not by the opinions which they profess, but by those on which their thoughts habitually fasten, which recur to them most forcibly, and which color their ordinary views of God and duty" (*Works*, 1:239).

3. Haroutunian, *Piety versus Moralism*, chap. 5; Foster, A *Genetic History of the New England Theology*, 189–223.

4. The most famous evangelist of the Methodist camp was Lorenzo Dow, whose breathless adventures in facing down the "cannot-ism" of the Calvinists were chronicled in his autobiography, *The Dealings of God, Man, and the Devil, as Exemplified in the Life, Experience, and Travels of Lorenzo Dow in a Period of More than a Half Century; With Reflections on Various Subjects, Religious, Moral, Political, and Prophetic*, 4th ed., rev. (Norwich, Conn.: Faulkner, 1833), and that of his wife, *Vicissitudes in the Wilderness; Exemplified, in the Journal of Peggy Dow, to which is added, An Appendix of Her Death, and also, Reflections on Matrimony*, by Lorenzo Dow, 5th ed. (Norwich, Conn.: Faulkner, 1833). An almost equally emphatic, but more convenient, biography is Charles Coleman Sellers, *Lorenzo Dow: The Bearer of the Word* (New York: Minton, Balch, 1928). See also n. 35, below.

5. See Sklar, *Catharine Beecher*, 28–55; Beecher, *Autobiography*, 1:277–280, 288–289, 310–313, 316–317, 319–322, 355–384; Edward A. Lawrence, *Life of Rev. Joel Hawes, D.D.* (Hartford: Hammersley, 1871), 250; Alvan Hyde, *Memoir of Rev. Alvan Hyde, D.D. of Lee, Massachusetts* (Boston: Perkins, Marvin, 1835), 171, 178–179, 192–193, 223, 282–284; Asa Cummings, comp., *Memoir, Select Thoughts and Sermons of the Late Reverend Edward Payson, D.D.* (Portland, Me.: Hyde, Lord and Duren, 1846), 1:20–22; Benjamin B. Wisner, *Memoirs of Mrs. Susan Huntington*, 2d ed. (Boston: Crocker & Brewster, 1826), 3; H. C. Knight, *Memorial of Rev. Wm. A. Hallock, D.D., First Secretary of the American Tract Society* (New York: American Tract Society [1882]), 11–12.

6. Knight, *Hallock*, 11–12.

7. Ibid., passim; see *Dictionary of American Biography*, s.v. "Hallock, William Allen."

8. Knight, *Hallock*, 100.

9. See chap. 2, above.

10. See Miller, *Life of the Mind in America*, 3–35; also, Richard Hofstadter, *Anti-Intellectualism in American Life* (New York: Knopf, 1963), chap. 4.

11. Joel Hawes, *Lectures Addressed to the Young Men of Hartford and New Haven*, 2d ed. (Hartford: Cooke, 1828), 36; another important example is from the pen of Aaron Bancroft. "Conversion, or regeneration," he wrote, "in the New Testament means a change of the affections from vicious to virtuous objects, altering the course of one's life, the formation of Christian habits. The man who has given an uncontrolled indulgence to irregular passions, and formed habits of vice, under divine influence corrects the disordered affections of his mind, and subdues the correct propensities of his heart" (A *Discourse on Conversion*, 12). Here the positive moral actions were indicated by a change in the "objects" of one's affections, "from vicious to virtuous objects," that is, outside the mind itself; negative moral results came instead from an internal force and merely needed the man's "indulgence." Mental images constructed of notions

of indulgence would imply that the conscience was an "on-off" switch; those which spoke of changes in orientation would construe the conscience as a "pointer." But, in either case, moralism, as these passages indicate, saw only two choices—virtue or vice.

    12. William A. Hallock, *Life and Labors of Edwards*, 353–354.

    13. Mead, *Taylor*, 160; Beecher, "The Bible a Code of Laws" (1817), *Works*, 2:162.

    14. See Meyer, *The Instructed Conscience*, 51–59.

    15. Tyler, *Nettleton*; Tyler, *Lectures on Theology, with a Memoir by Rev. Nahum Gale, D.D.* (Boston: Tilton, 1859); Porter, *Letters*, 152–156; Edward D. Griffin, *The Doctrine of Divine Efficiency, Defended against Certain Modern Speculations* (New York: Leavitt, 1833); a distinct position from that of the Taylorites or Tylerites, but ultimately equally important in the history of American philosophy, came with the introduction of Coleridgean idealism. See James Marsh's "Preliminary Essay" to the first American edition of Coleridge's *Aids to Reflection* (Burlington, Vt.: Goodrich, 1829), vii–liv. For the compilations of and commentaries on revival narratives which were stimulated by the New Haven schism, see n. 25 for chap. 1, above.

    16. See especially Beecher, "The Bible a Code of Laws" (1817), *Works*, 2:154–203, and "The Faith Once Delivered to the Saints" (1823), and his reply to a review of that sermon (1825), ibid., 243–413.

    17. Beecher, *Autobiography*, 1:48.

    18. Henry Ward Beecher, intro. to William C. Conant, *Narratives of Remarkable Conversions and Revival Incidents: Including . . . an account . . . of the Great Awakening of 1857–'8* (New York: Derby & Jackson, 1858), xvi–xvii.

    19. On Edwards and Locke, see Miller, *Jonathan Edwards*; on overt and covert behavior, see Schutz, "On Multiple Realities," in *Collected Papers, I*, 211–212; many of the conventions of "sentimental drama" in the eighteenth and the nineteenth centuries depended upon the reign of the "epistemological self."

    20. Beecher, *Autobiography*, 1:264, emphasis added.

    21. *Oxford English Dictionary*, s.v., "character."

    22. Edwards, in his *Religious Affections*, wrote,

> This new spiritual sense, and the new dispositions that attend it, are no new faculties, but are new principles of nature. I use the word "principles" for want of a word of more determinate signification. By a principle of nature in this place, I mean that foundation which is laid in nature, either old or new, for any particular manner or kind of exercise of the faculties of the soul; or a natural habit or foundation for action, giving a person ability and disposition to exert the faculties in exercises of a certain kind; so that to exert the faculties in that kind of exercises, may be said to be his nature (206).

Also see *Oxford English Dictionary*, s.v., "principle."

    23. Hawes, *Lectures*, 66–74, 75–76 (for cited passage).

    24. Ibid., 82.

    25. Ibid., 88; on the responsibility of morality both to revelation and to enlightened conscience, see Conrad Wright, "Rational Religion in Eighteenth-Century America," in *The Liberal Christians: Essays on American Unitarian History* (Bos-

ton: Beacon, 1970), 1–21; Wright uses the term "supernatural rationalists" to describe those indebted to these two sources of moral principle.

26. An increase in the number of cases of church discipline for intoxication or intemperance among Massachusetts parishes is shown by Emil Oberholzer, Jr., *Delinquent Saints: Disciplinary Action in the Early Congregational Churches of Massachusetts* (New York: Columbia University Press, 1956), 240, but the significance of these figures is difficult to assess.

27. Hawes, *Lectures*, 88–89, 116 (cited sentence). Cf. Henry Clarke Wright, who felt himself reformed from Calvinism when he "learned to associate my destiny in the unending future with personal character, and not with any thing out of myself" (*Human Life*, 208).

28. Hawes, *Lectures*, 16.

29. See Hyde, *Memoir*, 284.

30. Hawes, *Lectures*, 17.

31. Beecher, *Autobiography*, 1:47.

32. In the First Awakening, it was the "effectual lasting change" (as Jonathan Dickinson put it) or the "habitual change" (as it was called by Edwards) in sinners' lives that most precisely testified to the presence of God in their conversion. See Dickinson, "A Display of God's Special Grace," in Heimert and Miller, eds., *The Great Awakening*, 179–181; Jonathan Edwards, "A Faithful Narrative of the Surprising Work of God," in *The Great Awakening*, ed. C. C. Goen (New Haven: Yale University Press, 1972), 185; also see Edwards's discussion of the twelfth sign of gracious affections, "holy practice," in *Religious Affections*, 383–461.

33. Backus, "Revival of Religion in Somers," *CEM* 1 (1800), 20.

34. Williams, *The Andover Liberals*, 9.

35. See, for example, the splendid story Samuel Griswold Goodrich tells about Lorenzo Dow's visit to Ridgefield, Connecticut, where Goodrich's father was the Congregational minister, in *Recollections of a Lifetime* (1857; rpt. Detroit: Gale, 1967), 1:212–214.

36. Bancroft, *Conversion*, 12.

37. Backus, *Scripture Doctrine of Regeneration*, 23.

38. See Emmons's sermons on "The Nature of Regeneration" and "It is the Duty of Sinners to Make Them a New Heart," in *Sermons, on Various Important Subjects*, 153–184; Dwight, *Theology*, 2:519, emphasis added.

39. Todd, ed., *John Todd*, 64; [Brown], *Memoir of Elder Elijah Shaw*, 195.

40. John C. Stockbridge, *A Memoir of the Life and Correspondence of Rev. Baron Stow, D.D.* (Boston: Lee and Shepard, 1871), 296; "'Every man,' says [Nathaniel William] Taylor, 'has some object of supreme regard. . . . This supreme affection, or governing purpose is that which constitutes character. Nor do we ever properly speak of character, as belonging to single or occasional subordinate acts, but solely to the governing principle or purpose of the man as developed in his actions'" (*The Congregationalist*, 2, no. 47 [Nov. 22, 1850], 185).

41. Wisner, *Susan Huntington*, 159.

42. The process was aided by the introduction of heating stoves into meetinghouses, which permitted the high walls of the eighteenth-century box pews to be lowered, and by the development of formal and regular church interiors, in which

standardized seating arrangements accentuated the differences among those inhabiting them.

43. "On Religious Conferences," *Panoplist* 9 (1813), 74.

44. Hawes, *Lectures*, 42.

45. And further, there were constant efforts to recruit ministers for the urban battle against "barbarism." See Lawrence, *Joel Hawes*, 134–163, for a description of the offers made to the Hartford minister to remove. The Tappan brothers wrote Hawes that 6,000 merchant clerks in New York awaited his shepherding (ibid., 143).

46. See David J. Rothman, *The Discovery of the Asylum: Social Order and Disorder in the New Republic* (Boston: Little, Brown, 1971); Christopher Lasch, "The Origins of the Asylum," in *The World of Nations: Reflections on American History, Politics, and Culture* (New York: Knopf, 1973), 3–17; Henry Barnard, *School Architecture, or Contributions to the Improvement of Schoolhouses in the United States*, 6th ed. (Cincinnati: Derby, 1854); Richard Rabinowitz, "The Crisis of the Classroom: Architecture and Education," *History of Education Quarterly* 14 (1974), 115–123; Catharine E. Beecher, *A Treatise on Domestic Economy*, rev. ed. (New York: Harper, 1851).

47. Foster, *An Errand of Mercy*, 116, 117; when moralists engaged in self-examination, they might ask, "Suppose all Christians were just like me?" The importance of imitation made one fear one's own poor example for others more than (as for doctrinalists) one's lost fate. ("Self-Examination," *The Congregationalist* 2, no. 32 [Aug. 9, 1850], 125).

48. Sprague, *Memoir of Griffin*, 82.

49. Nathaniel Bouton, *Autobiography*, ed. John Bell Bouton (New York: Randolph, 1879), 14; cf. Todd, *John Todd*, 63–64.

50. Winslow, *Memoir of Mrs. Harriet L. Winslow*, 38.

51. [Brown], *Elijah Shaw*, 225; see "Life Long Enough," *The Congregationalist* 1, no. 15 (Aug. 31, 1849), 60: "[Life] is long enough for the *benevolent and useful*. Such might wish to live for the world's good—to dry up yet more of its sorrows and wipe away other tears. But yet the close of their short day will find them with their work done, their task finished, their reward ready, and what they would gain by serving longer in the flesh."

52. [Brown], *Elijah Shaw*, 225–226.

53. Hawes, *Lectures*, 96.

54. [Dewey], *Letters of an English Traveller*, 71.

55. Bancroft, *Conversion*, 10.

56. Smith, *Charles Henry Porter*, 65.

57. Hawes, *Lectures*, 101.

Notes to Chapter Ten

1. Alvan Bond, "A Pastor's Review of His Life at 80," Alvan Bond Collection, Old Sturbridge Village Research Library.

2. See, for example, *Annals*, 2:566–572, on Samuel J. Mills, Jr., a missionary to the South and West and to Africa, on behalf of the American Colonization Society; *Annals*, 2:596–601, on James Richards, who worked with the poor in Boston; *Annals*, 2:609–615, on Thomas H. Gallaudet, the pioneer in the education of the deaf; *Annals*, 2:617–622, on Daniel Poor, missionary to Ceylon; *Annals*, 2:622–629, on Pliny

Fisk (Alvan Bond's roommate at Andover), and 2:644–648, on Levi Parsons, both missionaries to the Levant. See Alvan Bond's *Memoir of Rev. Pliny Fisk* (Edinburgh: Waugh & Innes, 1829), for an excellent example of a missionary's diary.

3. This and the following paragraphs are based on the diaries and letters of Alvan Bond in the Old Sturbridge Village Research Library.

4. See Austin Phelps's memoir of his father Rev. Eliakim Phelps's crusade for night meetings, in *My Portfolio: A Collection of Essays* (New York: Scribner's, 1882), 15; the formal debate is witnessed in Aaron Bancroft, *The Duties Enjoined by the Fourth Commandment*, 2d ed. (Worcester: Manning, 1817), and Enoch Pond, *Apology for Religious Conferences; Letter to Rev. Aaron Bancroft, D.D. on his Discourse on the Fourth Commandment* (Worcester: n.p., 1817).

5. See Susan Geib, "Changing Works: Agriculture and Society in Brookfield, Massachusetts, 1785–1820" (Ph.D. diss., Boston University, 1981); Francis H. Underwood, *Quabbin: The Story of a Small Town* (1893; rpt. Boston: Northeastern University Press, 1986), 107–127; Goodrich, *Recollections of a Lifetime*, 1:75.

6. W. J. Rorabaugh, *The Alcoholic Republic: An American Tradition* (New York: Oxford University Press, 1979); Epstein, *The Politics of Domesticity*, 89–151.

7. Jacob Ide, *The Nature and Tendency of Balls, . . . Preached in . . . 1818* (Dedham, Mass.: Mann, n.d.), 12.

8. Ibid.; "On Dancing," *Christian Spectator* 1 (1819), 185–187.

9. Joan M. Jensen, *Loosening the Bonds: Mid-Atlantic Farm Women, 1750–1850* (New Haven: Yale University Press, 1986), 54–55; Hambrick-Stowe, *Practice of Piety*, 96–103; Winton U. Solberg, *Redeem the Time: The Puritan Sabbath in Early America* (Cambridge: Harvard University Press, 1977).

10. Hawes, *Lectures to Young Men*, 56.

11. Beecher, *Treatise on Domestic Economy*, 159–160; similarly, Beecher advised, the regimen of the Lord as Creator could also be applied to the rhythm of domestic housekeeping tasks themselves and the chores apportioned on a weekly (and hence more rational) basis (162).

12. Bancroft, *The Duties Enjoined by the Fourth Commandment*, 12, 10.

13. Ibid., 14.

14. Ibid., 36.

15. "Review of Dr. Bancroft's Disourse," *Panoplist and Missionary Magazine* 13 (1817), 117–131, quotation at 128.

16. Hawes, *Lectures to Young Men*, 57–58; "The Sabbath a Test of Character," *Spirit of the Pilgrims* 6 (1833), 175.

17. Lyman Mathews, *Memoir of Ebenezer Porter* (Boston: Perkins & Marvin, 1837), 168.

18. Near the end of the eighteenth century, the Congregational Society in Acushnet, Massachusetts, warned, "'If the town do not restrain its voters at town meetings from standing on pews and seats and going into the pulpit the Precinct [the religious society] will not admit them into there [sic] Meeting house'" (Franklyn Howland, *A History of the Town of Acushnet* [New Bedford, Mass.: privately pub., 1907], 149); and in 1830, Major S. B. Phinney wrote to the Barnstable [Mass.] *Patriot* to ask, "what consistency can there be in using a building dedicated to the exclusive purpose of the worship of the Almighty, to assemble men to furnish business, where all the worst passions of human nature are called into action, where all reverence for the

house cannot but be forgotten in the noisy and passionate language which not infrequently disgraces town meetings'" (Donald G. Trayser, ed., *Barnstable: Three Centuries of a Cape Cod Town* [Hyannis, Mass.: Goss, 1939], 221). On graveyards, see Stanley French, "The Cemetery as Cultural Institution: The Establishment of Mount Auburn and the 'Rural Cemetery' Movement," *American Quarterly* 26 (1974), 37–59; on domestic architecture, note this passage from Andrew Jackson Downing, *The Architecture of Country Houses,*

> If it [the house] plainly shows by its various apartments, that it is intended not only for the physical wants of man, but for his moral, social, and intellectual existence; if hospitality smiles in ample parlors; if home virtues dwell in cosy, fireside family-rooms; if the love of the beautiful is seen in picture or statue galleries; intellectuality, in well-stocked libraries; and even a dignified love of leisure and repose, in cool and spacious verandas; we feel, at a glance, that here we have reached the highest beauty of which Domestic Architecture is capable—that of individual expression ([New York: Appleton, 1850], 23).

The association of individualism with the conformity to normative virtues is characteristic of moralism, as is the link of the moral integrity of the house to its array of specialized spaces.

19. Sprague, *Memoir of Griffin*, 56.

20. Hallock, *Justin Edwards*, 282.

21. On the link between means and ends as aspects of modern consciousness, and especially in regard to the implications for consciousness of technological production and bureaucracy, see Peter Berger, Brigitte Berger, and Hansfried Kellner, *The Homeless Mind: Modernization and Consciousness* (New York: Random House, 1973), 28, 53.

22. Hallock, *Justin Edwards*, 69–70.

23. See the *Extracts from the Minutes* (sometimes called *Acts, Proceedings,* etc.) of the General Association of Connecticut, the General Association of Massachusetts, the General Association of New Hampshire, and the General Convention of Congregational and Presbyterian Ministers in Vermont, published annually after 1801. Narrative descriptions of the "state of religion" in individual churches and in county-level associations or consociations prevailed until 1815 or so; tables of parishes and ministers were introduced in all four states over the following decade. After 1816, New Hampshire included, after its narrative, "A Compendious View of the Associations and Churches," listing the numbers of churches; ministers; communicants (male/female); additions (by profession/letter); removals (dismissed/excluded/died); and baptisms (adults/infants). Connecticut finally followed this example seventeen years later, and by 1834 was counting all churches as of a particular time of the year. By 1840 its "Report on the State of Religion" was now called "Statistics of the Churches: Report of the Agent on Statistics," and among its inquiries it sought to determine the average age of ministers and their average term in office to date. See Alonzo H. Quint, "The Numbering of the Churches and their Members," *Congregational Quarterly* 1 (1859), 135–141.

24. Hallock, *Justin Edwards*, 70–71.

25. Ibid., 68–72; the process has been described as "goal displacement" by Berger, Berger, and Kellner, *The Homeless Mind*, 53.

26. Of course, the name of Edwards, as the exemplary creative mind in American evangelicism, stood higher in the moralist pantheon than Franklin's. On the moralist's pleasure in steady progress; see "Difference of Degree in the Rewards of Heaven," *The Congregationalist* 1, no. 7 (July 6, 1849), 25, and no. 8 (July 13, 1849), 29.

27. The proliferation of benevolent acts was worthy in itself. "When Lewis and Arthur Tappan, the New York philanthropists," Lois W. Banner notes, "were criticized by their brother Benjamin, an Ohio politician and religious skeptic, for supporting senseless causes like Bible and tract distribution in addition to their more worthwhile ventures into education and anti-slavery, they retorted that in God's sight all humanitarian endeavors were of equal importance. What was needed for the divine favor, they explained, was simply that the 'benevolent principle' be in operation" ("Religious Benevolence as Social Control," *Journal of American History* 60 [1973], 36).

Justin Edwards, as he was outlining a biblical manual (he had already written ones for temperance and Sabbath observance), wrote,

> I sometimes please myself with the hope, that somebody at some time may be enabled to prepare a Biblical Manual, to go with the Bible, which shall contain what its common readers may need to know about the nature of the book, the proper mode of treating it, and the effects of treating it in this way; all needful tables of weights, measures, distances, coins, titles, offices, etc., together with history, chronology, geography, etc.; in a word, whatever is needful to enable the people to understand the Lord's meaning in all the words which he uses (Hallock, *Justin Edwards*, 515).

On the intellectual decline wrought by moralism in the edifice of evangelicism, see also Foster, *An Errand of Mercy*, 166–167; Mead, *The Lively Experiment*, 127–129; Daniel H. Calhoun, *Professional Lives in America: Structure and Aspiration*, 1750–1850 (Cambridge: Harvard University Press, 1965), 170–171, 182–183; a contemporary review, often cited by historians, is Bela Bates Edwards, "The Influence of Eminent Piety on the Intellectual Powers," in *Writings* (Boston: Jewett, 1853), 2:472–500.

28. For example, Justin Edwards wrote in 1826 that "Thousands and thousands are now perishing, for the want of tracts, on the island of Ceylon" (Hallock, *Justin Edwards*, 209). Three years later, it was intoxicating drinks which were "one of the most terrific obstacles to the spread of the gospel" (ibid., 312), and so on.

29. "On the Duties of the Table," *Christian Spectator* 1 (1819), 241; Bancroft, *A Discourse on Conversion*, 7–8, emphasis added.

30. Channing, "Remarks on Associations," *Works*, 1:291–292.

31. See William E. Nelson, *Americanization of the Common Law: The Impact of Legal Change on Massachusetts Society, 1760–1830* (Cambridge: Harvard University Press, 1975), 127–129; and Leonard W. Levy, *The Law of the Commonwealth and Chief Justice Shaw* (Cambridge: Harvard University Press, 1957), 29–42.

32. See Marty, *Righteous Empire*, 69.

Notes to Chapter Eleven

1. Beecher, *The Practicability of Suppressing Vice*, 7.
2. See George Rogers Taylor, *The Transportation Revolution, 1815–1860* (New York: Holt, Rinehart and Winston, 1951); Roger N. Parks, *Roads and Travel in New England, 1790–1840* (Sturbridge, Mass.: Old Sturbridge Village, 1967); on town commons, see John D. Cushing, "Town Commons of New England, 1640–1840," *Old-Time New England* 51 (1961), 86–94; Herbert J. Levine, "In Pursuit of the Nucleated Village" (Research report, Old Sturbridge Village Research Library, 1971); the new aesthetic of village centers is best seen in the engravings John Warner Barber did for his *Connecticut Historical Collections*, 2d ed. (New Haven: Durrie & Peck, 1836), and *Massachusetts Historical Collections* (Worcester: Dorr, Howland, 1839); on schools, see Catherine Fennelly, *Town Schooling in New England, 1790–1840* (Sturbridge, Mass.: Old Sturbridge Village, 1962); Harland Updegraff, *The Origin of the Moving School in Massachusetts* (1907; rpt. New York: Arno Press, 1969).
3. See Gary Kulik, Roger Parks, and Theodore Z. Penn, eds., *The New England Mill Village, 1790–1860* (Cambridge: MIT Press, 1982); John B. Armstrong, *Factory Under the Elms: A History of Harrisville, New Hampshire, 1774–1969* (Cambridge: MIT Press, 1969); John R. Stilgoe, *Common Landscape of America, 1580 to 1845* (New Haven: Yale University Press, 1982), 256–262, 324–333; Richard M. Candee, "The Early New England Textile Village in Art," *Antiques* 98 (1970), 910–915.
4. See Clarence Winthrop Bowen, *The History of Woodstock, Connecticut* (1926; rpt. Woodstock: Woodstock Libraries, 1973), esp. chaps. 17–18.
5. Richard D. Brown, "The Emergence of Urban Society in Rural Massachusetts, 1760–1820," *Journal of American History* 61 (1974), 29–51.
6. Perry Miller, "From the Covenant to the Revival," in *Nature's Nation*, 113.
7. Among Congregationalist seminaries, Andover was established in 1807, Bangor (Maine) in 1814, Yale in 1822, and the Theological Institute of Connecticut at East Windsor (later Hartford Theological Seminary) in 1834. Harvard had a separate theology faculty after 1819. Among other groups, the Baptists organized Newton (Mass.) Theological Institution in 1825; the Methodists founded the School of Theology at Boston University in 1839; the Universalists a school at Tufts University in 1852; the Episcopalians formed the Berkeley Divinity School at Middletown, Connecticut, in 1854, and the Episcopal Theological School at Cambridge, Massachusetts, in 1867. On the calls of ministers to other posts, see Lawrence, *Joel Hawes*, 134–163; Stockbridge, *Baron Stow*, 82–86, tells an interesting story of how a thriving Boston Baptist church prevailed upon the young minister of a small Portsmouth, New Hampshire, church to join them, in exchange for $1,000 which paid off the building debts of the smaller congregation. The question of clerical tenure is the main subject of Calhoun, *Professional Lives in America*, chaps. 4 and 5.
8. Keller, *The Second Great Awakening*, 55; Hyde, *Memoir*, 93.
9. Cited by Mead, *Taylor*, 80.
10. Beecher, "A Reformation of Morals Practicable and Indispensable" (1812), *Works*, 2:93.
11. Keith E. Melder, *Beginnings of Sisterhood: The American Woman's*

Rights Movement, 1800–1850 (New York: Schocken, 1977); Epstein, The Politics of Domesticity; Jensen, Loosening the Bonds.

12. See, for example, "Systematic Charity," Missionary Herald 19 (1823), 367: "The first article in the constitution for the Auxiliaries, is so formed, that the subscription is but for one year, and, of course, must be repeated annually. Supposing, what ought to be supposed, that there is an active, faithful body of Collectors, this will be the best arrangement—1. It will tend to create a feeling of responsibility in the Collectors. Unless they act, the Association dies." The extent of lay responsibility for moralist reform led to elaborate committee structures in many churches. In one of the most active, Boston's Park Street Church, the minister and deacons were supplemented in 1824 by a nine-member Standing Committee; a five-man auditing committee; six others charged with collecting Sunday evening lecture contributions; a committee to rent out pews and cellar space; and a committee "to aid the pastor in attending to inquiries" (H. Crosby Englizian, Brimstone Corner: Park Street Church, Boston [Chicago: Moody Press, 1968], 75).

13. Lawrence, Joel Hawes, 220. Of course, the moralists' success in winning adherents to their banner of reformed behavior did revive the optimism of the churches, especially in comparison with the gloomy state of the 1790s. See Increase N. Tarbox, The Religious and Ecclesiastical Contrast within the Bounds of Suffolk West Conference, between the Years 1776 and 1876 (Boston: Suffolk West Conference, 1876).

14. Lawrence, Joel Hawes, 220; Joseph R. Gusfield, Symbolic Crusade: Status Politics and the American Temperance Movement (Urbana: University of Illinois Press, 1963), 44–46; Clifford S. Griffin, Their Brothers' Keepers: Moral Stewardship in the United States, 1800–1865 (New Brunswick, N.J.: Rutgers University Press, 1960), 49–60; cf. Muriel Jaegar, Before Victoria: Changing Standards and Behaviour, 1787–1837 (London: Chatto and Windus, 1956); and Walter E. Houghton, The Victorian Frame of Mind, 1830–1870 (New Haven: Yale University Press, 1957).

15. Gusfield, Symbolic Crusade, 46; the 1826 statement is in Hallock, Justin Edwards, 194; on the difference between consecration and conversion, see Foster, An Errand of Mercy, 167–168.

16. Paul E. Johnson, A Shopkeeper's Millennium: Society and Revivals in Rochester, New York, 1815–1837 (New York: Hill and Wang, 1978); Anthony F. C. Wallace, Rockdale: The Growth of an American Village in the Early Industrial Revolution (New York: Knopf, 1978), esp. 296–471; Leonard L. Richards, "Gentlemen of Property and Standing": Anti-Abolition Mobs in Jacksonian America (New York: Oxford University Press, 1970), 166–169.

17. Beecher, The Practicability of Suppressing Vice, 20, 17–18.

18. Beecher, "A Reformation of Morals," Works, 2:95.

19. Beecher, "The Remedy of Intemperance," Works, 1:391–392.

20. Beecher, "The Remedy for Duelling," Works, 2:45.

21. Wyatt-Brown, "Prelude to Abolitionism," 339–340.

22. See Aileen S. Kraditor, Means and Ends in American Abolitionism: Garrison and His Critics on Strategy and Tactics, 1834–1850 (New York: Pantheon, 1969).

23. Friedman, Gregarious Saints, 37, 36; Robert H. Abzug, Passionate Liberator: Theodore Dwight Weld and the Dilemma of Reform (New York: Oxford University Press, 1980).

24. Of the 354 cities and towns in Massachusetts in 1910, fully 233 had

one or more memorials of the Civil War; the total expended for these came to more than $35,000,000. This information, and descriptions of all the memorials in the Commonwealth, can be found in Alfred S. Roe, comp., *Monuments, Tablets and Other Memorials Erected in Massachusetts to Commemorate the Services of Her Sons in the War of the Rebellion, 1861–1865* (Boston: Wright & Potter, 1910).

Notes to Chapter Twelve

1. The best source for Payson's life is the memoir compiled by Asa Cummings, published in Boston in 1830, reprinted by the American Tract Society about 1835, and included in vol. 1 of *Memoir of Payson;* the passages cited in this paragraph are at 1:18, 21. Also see *Our Pastor; or Reminiscences of Rev. Edward Payson, D.D.* (Boston: Tappan & Whittemore, 1855).

2. William Willis, *The History of Portland*, 2d ed. (Portland: Bailey and Noyes, 1865), 660.

3. Population statistics are from J. D. B. DeBow, *Statistical View of the United States* (Washington: Tucker, 1854), 192; Dwight, *Travels*, 2:141; also see Oliver Wendell Holmes's comparison of Portland with its southern rivals in *Elsie Venner: A Romance of Destiny* (1861; rpt. Boston, Houghton Mifflin, 1891), chap. 2; and Edward C. Kirkland, *Men, Cities and Transportation: A Study in New England History, 1820–1900* (Cambridge: Harvard University Press, 1948), 1:192–222.

4. Cummings, *Memoir of Payson*, 1:142, 143.

5. Ibid., 143, 144, 167; customs duties are from Dwight, *Travels*, 2:114.

6. Cummings, *Memoir of Payson*, 1:256.

7. Ibid., 143.

8. Ayer, *Diary*, 201, 206–207.

9. Cummings, *Memoir of Payson*, 1:42.

10. Ibid., 44.

11. Ibid., 56, 57–58; cf. the rules of "unyielding rectitude" discussed in chap. 9, above; the devotionalist attitude toward rules, stressing the superiority of communion with God over social proprieties, is seen in W. E. Boardman, *The Higher Christian Life* (Boston: Henry Hoyt, 1859), 156: "There is nowhere in the bible one single line or precept of rigid requirement binding the Christian to any rigid rules about living and dress, or anything of the sort."

12. Cummings, *Memoir of Payson*, 1:71.

13. Ibid., 92.

14. Ibid., 60; Wisner, *Memoirs of Susan Huntington*, 114–115; Cummings, *Memoir of Payson*, 1:198.

15. Cummings, *Memoir of Payson*, 1:221; Frederick Morgan Davenport, *Primitive Traits in Religious Revivals: A Study in Mental and Social Evolution* (New York: Macmillan, 1905), 203.

16. Cummings, *Memoir of Payson*, 1:222.

17. Ibid., 223–224.

18. Ibid., 224. The metaphor of the mind (or of the imagination, the memory, or other mental faculties) as a fountain, rather than as a storehouse or a machine, is a key romantic usage in the nineteenth century.

19. Ibid.

20. Ibid., 228.

21. Ibid., 226, 227.

22. The notion of performance has been explored most powerfully in Erving Goffman, *The Presentation of Self in Everyday Life* (Garden City, N.Y.: Doubleday Anchor, 1959); and in Elizabeth Burns, *Theatricality: A Study of Convention in the Theatre and in Social Life* (New York: Harper & Row, 1972).

23. Tyler, *Lectures on Theology*, 52.

24. Beecher, *Autobiography*, 1:263, on the religion of these Beecher children, see Charles H. Foster, *The Rungless Ladder: Harriet Beecher Stowe and New England Puritanism* (Durham, N.C.: Duke University Press, 1954), which is also one of the best studies of "devotionalist" religion; William G. McLoughlin, *The Meaning of Henry Ward Beecher: An Essay on the Shifting Values of Mid-Victorian America* (New York: Knopf, 1970); Rugoff, *The Beechers*; and Caskey, *Chariot of Fire*.

25. Stockbridge, *Baron Stow*, 69; also see *Our Pastor*, 347–360.

Notes to Chapter Thirteen

1. Henry Clay Fish, *Primitive Piety Revived, or The Aggressive Power of the Christian Church* (Boston: Congregational Board of Publication, 1855), 91.

2. Stockbridge, *Baron Stow*, 244–245.

3. Thomas C. Upham, *Principles of the Interior or Hidden Life*, 4th ed. (Boston: Waite, Peirce, 1845), 140, 141.

4. Theo[dore] Spencer, *Conversion; Its Theory and Process, Practically Delineated* (New York: Dodd, 1854), 38; cf. William James, *The Principles of Psychology* (1890; rpt. New York: Dover, 1950), chap. 26 ("Will").

5. Spencer, *Conversion*, 44–45.

6. The passage appears in the Conclusion of *Walden*. *The Congregationalist* asked in 1849 whether one should obey the dictates of an unenlightened conscience. The answer was yes, even if one's acts were sinful, so long as one accepted the responsibility to undertake enlightenment first (1, no. 31 [Dec. 21, 1849], 122).

7. Upham, *Interior Life*, 240.

8. Stockbridge, *Baron Stow*, 247; William James's theory of the will is a milestone in the development of this epistemology (see n. 4, above). In modern psychology, the idea of "cognitive dissonance" is based upon many of the same premises. See Leon Festinger, *A Theory of Cognitive Dissonance* (Stanford: Stanford University Press, 1957), for an account of how the mind acts to justify difficult decisions by retrospectively foreclosing the options available earlier. Moralists, of course, argued for man's "power to [choose] the contrary," thereby taking the opposite tack and emphasizing the options available even though they had already been disavowed.

9. See Arthur O. Lovejoy, "Coleridge and Kant's Two Worlds," in *Essays on the History of Ideas* (Baltimore: Johns Hopkins University Press, 1948), 254–276; and Lovejoy, *The Reason, The Understanding and Time* (Baltimore: Johns Hopkins University Press, 1961).

10. George L. Prentiss, ed., *Life and Letters of Elizabeth Prentiss* (New York: Randolph, 1882), 54.

11. See Perry Miller, *The New England Mind: The Seventeenth Century* (Cambridge: Harvard University Press, 1954), chap. 9, esp. 257–259; Terence Martin, *The Instructed Vision: Scottish Common Sense Philosophy and the Origins of American Fiction* (Bloomington: Indiana University Press, 1961); also chap. 2, above.

12. An interesting example among evangelicals is Henry M. Dexter, *Street Thoughts* (Boston: Crosby, Nichols, 1859), a book of observations, eavesdroppings, and portraits of eccentricities; the most famous historical cases are Poe's "The Man of the Crowd" and Baudelaire's *Fleurs du Mal;* a brilliant commentary is Walter Benjamin, "On Some Motifs in Baudelaire," in *Illuminations,* ed. Hannah Arendt, trans. Harry Zohn (New York: Schocken, 1969), 155–200.

13. Jerome L. Singer, *The Inner World of Daydreaming* (New York: Harper & Row, 1975), 3; also see Eric Klinger, *Structure and Functions of Fantasy* (New York: Wiley-Interscience, 1971); and Gaston Bachelard, *The Poetics of Reverie,* trans. Daniel Russell (New York: Orion, 1969).

14. [Mrs. Joel Hawes], *Memoir of Mrs. Mary E. Van Lennep* (Hartford: Belknap and Hamersley, 1848), 105–106.

15. Henry A. Boardman, *Suggestions to Young Men Engaged in Mercantile Business* (Philadelphia: Lippincott, Grambo, 1851), 17.

Notes to Chapter Fourteen

1. Bouton, *Autobiography,* 15–16.

2. Israel P. Warren, *The Sisters: A Memoir of Elizabeth H., Abbie A., and Sarah F. Dickerman* (Boston: American Tract Society, 1859), 176.

3. Ibid., 31; also see Upham, *Interior Life,* passim.

4. Warren, *The Sisters,* 34.

5. Ibid., 254.

6. "Now let us look around your parlors, and see how many of these splendid engravings convey any moral or religious impressions" ("Home Furniture," *The Congregationalist* 11, no. 2 [Jan. 14, 1859], 6); see Neil Harris, *The Artist in American Society: The Formative Years, 1790–1860* (New York: Braziller, 1966); the house referred to is described in Ruth Davidson, "Roseland, a Gothic Revival Mansion," *Antiques* 81 (1962), 510–514.

7. James Hastings Nichols, *Romanticism in American Theology: Nevin and Schaff at Mercersburg* (Chicago: University of Chicago Press, 1961), 94; also see Welch, *Protestant Thought,* part 2.

8. On the controversy between Hodge and Nevin, see Nichols, *Romanticism in American Theology,* 84–106; and Nichols, ed., *The Mercersburg Theology* (New York: Oxford University Press, 1966), 197–259; also Sydney E. Ahlstrom, "Theology in America," in *The Shaping of American Religion,* ed. Smith and Jamison, 270–271.

9. Edwards, "Influence of Eminent Piety on the Intellectual Powers," in *Writings,* 2:490.

10. Ibid.

11. Warren, *The Sisters,* 219.

12. Anne T. Drinkwater, *Memoir of Mrs. Deborah H. Porter* (Portland: Sanborn & Carter, 1848), 71.

13. Payson, "Christ Rejects None Who Come Unto Him," in Cummings, *Memoir of Payson,* 2:485.

14. Upham, *Interior Life,* 216.

15. Fish, *Primitive Piety Revived,* 47, 61–62, 40.

16. Phoebe Palmer, *The Way of Holiness* (New York: Lane and Tippett, 1847), 58.

Notes to Chapter Fifteen

1. Edwards, "Influence of Eminent Piety on the Intellectual Powers," in *Writings*, 2:481–482.

2. Beecher, intro. to *Narratives of Remarkable Conversions*, by Conant, xvi-xvii.

3. *Biography*, according to the *Oxford English Dictionary*, referred to "the history of lives of individual men, as a branch of literature" as early as 1683; a hundred years later, it took on the meaning of a record of an individual life, considered by itself. By the middle of the nineteenth century, it had finally become a synonym for "life history." *Auto-biography*, despite its later application to the *Life of Dr. Franklin*, was first recorded in 1809. A *memoir*, which began life as a simple memorandum, was a "written account of the incidents in his own life" in 1673. By 1826, these incidents appeared less significant in the telling than the larger story of the life history, and *memoir* became identical with *biography* (in time, it might be added, for the appearance of the dozens of evangelical "memoirs" we have referred to in this study). *Career*, the dictionary tells us, escaped its racetrack pedigree and became "the course of one's life" only around 1803.

4. Beecher, intro. to *Narratives of Remarkable Conversions*, by Conant, xiv-xv.

5. Chandler Robbins, *A Memoir of Mary Elizabeth Clapp*, 4th ed. (Boston: Crosby, Nichols, 1859), 91–92.

6. Conant, *Narratives of Remarkable Conversions*, 113–115, 134.

7. See Edward N. Kirk, *Effectual Prayer* (Boston: Tappan & Whittemore, 1853).

8. Stockbridge, *Baron Stow*, 247–248.

9. Spencer, *Conversion*, 17–18; Kirk, *Effectual Prayer*, 17: "The efficacy of prayer is proportioned to its fervid energy."

10. Robert Meredith, *The Politics of the Universe: Edward Beecher, Abolition, and Orthodoxy* (Nashville: Vanderbilt University Press, 1968), 48; Edward Beecher, *The Conflict of Ages; or the Great Debate on the Moral Relations of God and Man*, 5th ed. (Boston: Phillips, Sampson, 1854), 552.

11. Beecher, *The Conflict of Ages*, 552; Boardman, *The Higher Christian Life*, 134; Philip Rieff, *Freud: The Mind of the Moralist* (New York: Viking, 1959), 355; also see Rieff, *The Triumph of the Therapeutic: Uses of Faith after Freud* (New York: Harper & Row, 1966).

12. See Philip Rieff, *Fellow Teachers* (New York: Harper & Row, 1973).

13. Daphne S. Giles, *The Religious and Political Influence of Educated and Uneducated Females* (Boston: Howe, 1849), 128; in the Baptist Society of Sturbridge, Mass., where John Phillips (see Introduction, above) was a deacon, 27 were converted (9 men, 18 women) in 1810. Of the 21 whose ages are known, the mean age was 30.83, the median 29. In 1831–1832, 29 were converted (11 men, 18 women) in another revival. Of the 21 traced, the mean age was 20.71, the median 16. Though the correlations of church membership and birth records are harder for later years, all the evidence suggests that the pattern of early affiliation continues through the pre-Civil War years. Source: Sturbridge Baptist Society Records, in the possession of the clerk of the Society.

14. Horace Bushnell, *Christian Nurture* (1916; rpt. New Haven: Yale University Press, 1947), 4, 30; Barbara Cross, *Horace Bushnell: Minister to a Changing America* (Chicago: University of Chicago Press, 1958), 67.

15. On the clash with Tyler, see Cross, *Bushnell*, 70–71.

16. Mary Bushnell Cheney, comp., *Life and Letters of Horace Bushnell* (New York: Harper, 1880), 191–192, 192–193.

17. Timothy L. Smith, *Revivalism and Social Reform in Mid-Nineteenth-Century America* (New York: Abingdon, 1957), 104; Boardman, *The Higher Christian Life*, passim; Robbins, *Memoir of Clapp*, 90.

18. Prentiss, ed., *Elizabeth Prentiss*, 63.

19. Palmer, *The Way of Holiness*, 69–70.

20. Hervé Carrier, *The Sociology of Religious Belonging*, trans. Arthur J. Arrieri (New York: Herder and Herder, 1965), 289.

21. Ada R. Parker, *Letters* (Boston: Crosby and Nichols, 1863), 163; Powell and Wolcott, both cited in *The Advance* (Chicago) 1, no. 8 (Oct. 24, 1867), 1.

22. Park, *The Theology of the Intellect and of the Feelings: A Discourse Delivered before the Convention of the Congregational Ministers of Massachusetts, . . . May 30, 1850* (Boston: Perkins & Whipple, 1850), 17, 37; see Douglas, *The Feminization of American Culture*, 149–151, passim; Kuklick, *Churchmen and Philosophers*, 203–215.

23. Park, *Theology*, 26; Austin Phelps, *The Still Hour; or Communion with God* (Boston: Gould and Lincoln, 1860), 59; Boardman, *The Higher Christian Life*, 172.

24. Robbins, *Memoir of Clapp*, 34–37. The year cannot be verified absolutely.

25. See Phoebe B. Stanton, *The Gothic Revival and American Church Architecture: An Episode in Taste, 1840–1856* (Baltimore: Johns Hopkins University Press, 1968).

Notes to Chapter Sixteen

1. Robbins, *Memoir of Clapp*, 34–37.

2. Hampton, Conn., Congregational Church Records, Connecticut State Library, 2:73.

3. Warren, *The Sisters*, 180–181.

4. Fish, *Primitive Piety Revived*, 207–208.

5. Warren, *The Sisters*, 197.

6. Robbins, *Memoir of Clapp*, 81.

7. Ibid.

8. Cheney, comp., *Horace Bushnell*, 248.

9. Lasch, "Two 'Kindred Spirits': Sorority and Family in New England, 1839–1846," in *The World of Nations*, 18; also see Carroll Smith-Rosenberg, "The Female World of Love and Ritual: Relations between Women in Nineteenth-Century America," *Signs: Journal of Women in Culture and Society* 1 (1975), 1–29. Smith-Rosenberg argues that women occupied a sphere of their own in American culture, which had "an essential integrity and dignity that grew out of women's shared experiences and mutual affection" (10). She understands this sphere as unaltered from the 1760s through the following century.

10. Robbins, *Memoir of Clapp*, 75–76.

11. Ibid., 88.

12. Carol F. Karlsen and Laurie Crumpacker, eds., *The Journal of Esther Edwards Burr* (New Haven: Yale University Press, 1984), 33–40, passim; Cott, *Bonds of Womanhood*, 186.

13. See Sklar, *Catharine Beecher;* Lasch attributes the "restlessness" of women in the 1830s and 1840s (and the consequent importance of female friendship) to the unsettling effects of geographical mobility and the ensuing breakdown of "all agencies of social cohesion—not merely the family, but church, state, and social classes" ("Two 'Kindred Spirits,'"in *The World of Nations*, 19, 27); Douglas, *The Feminization of American Culture*, 44–79, also emphasizes the defensive impulse of feminine spirituality; the most supple analysis is Cott's chapter, "Sisterhood," in *The Bonds of Womanhood*, 160–196.

14. A typical attack is "Sentimental Religion," *The Congregationalist* 1, no. 8 (July 13, 1849), 30; a good start in developing a history of social awkwardness is Christopher Ricks, *Keats and Embarrassment* (Oxford: Clarendon Press, 1974).

15. Richard B. Sewall, *The Life of Emily Dickinson* (New York: Farrar, Straus and Giroux, 1974), 2:393, 392, 394.

16. Prentiss, ed., *Elizabeth Prentiss*, 46, 70.

17. Ibid., 54.

18. Ibid., 80.

19. William Rounseville Alger, *The Friendships of Women* (Boston: Roberts, 1868), 10.

20. Parker, *Letters*, 76–77.

21. "Imaginative projection" is similar to the "habit of incorporation" attributed to American nineteenth-century writers and savagely attacked in them by Quentin Anderson, *The Imperial Self* (New York: Knopf, 1971).

22. Smith, *Revivalism and Social Reform*, 175–176.

23. Richard R. Niebuhr, *Experiential Religion* (New York: Harper & Row, 1972), 3–4; also see Berger, Berger, and Kellner, *The Homeless Mind*, chap. 3, on the notion of a "life plan."

24. See Michael Young and Peter Willmott, *The Symmetrical Family* (New York: Pantheon, 1973).

25. Cf. Cotton Mather, *Bonifacius: An Essay upon the Good*, ed. David Levin (Cambridge: Harvard University Press, 1966).

26. Thorstein Veblen, *The Theory of the Leisure Class* (New York: Macmillan, 1889); Daniel Calhoun, *The Intelligence of a People* (Princeton: Princeton University Press, 1973), 186; Colleen McDannell, *The Christian Home in Victorian America, 1840–1900* (Bloomington: Indiana University Press, 1986).

27. Eli Zaretsky, *Capitalism, The Family, and Personal Life* (New York: Harper & Row, 1976).

28. Prentiss, ed., *Elizabeth Prentiss*, 80.

Notes to Conclusion

1. Tyler, *New England Revivals*, x; see Miller, "Declension in a Bible Commonwealth," in *Nature's Nation*, 14–49; another contemporary view is Parsons Cooke, *A Century of Puritanism and a Century of Its Opposites* (Boston: Whipple, 1855).

2. Tracy, *The Great Awakening*, 145.

3. Henry David Aiken, "Levels of Moral Discourse," in *Reason and Conduct: New Bearings in Moral Philosophy* (New York: Knopf, 1962), 65–87.

4. Peter Brown, "The Rise and Function of the Holy Man in Late Antiquity," *Journal of Roman Studies* 61 (1971), 80–101. Mary Douglas argues, "The contrast of secular with religious has nothing whatever to do with the contrast of modern with traditional or primitive. The idea that primitive man is by nature deeply religious is nonsense. The truth is that all the varieties of scepticism, materialism and spiritual fervour are to be found in the range of tribal societies" (*Natural Symbols: Explorations in Cosmology* [New York: Vintage, 1973], 36; this passage is not in the hardbound edition [New York: Pantheon, 1970] cited earlier).

5. Horwitz, *Transformation of American Law*, 8.

6. Meyer, *Democratic Enlightenment*, 181; though the "New Divinity" men "felt no need to make Calvinism palatable, they did in the late eighteenth century have to make it ultimately rational" (May, *Enlightenment in America*, 59); on the impact of the French Revolution, see Rollins, *The Long Journey of Noah Webster*, 75ff.

7. Webster, "On the Education of Youth in America," in *Essays on Education in the Early Republic*, ed. Frederick Rudolph (Cambridge: Harvard University Press, 1965), 45.

8. These paragraphs are based upon careful readings of period (manuscript) diaries and account books in the Old Sturbridge Village Research Library, and on conversations with staff members there. See Rodney C. Loehr, "Self-Sufficiency on the Farm," *Agricultural History* 26 (April 1952), 37–41, and Andrew Hill Clark, "Suggestions for the Geographical Study of Agricultural Change in the United States, 1790–1840," in *Farming in the New Nation: Interpreting American Agriculture, 1790–1840*, ed. Darwin P. Kelsey (Washington: Agricultural History Society, 1972), 165–172; also see other essays in this volume. A contrasting, but still useful, work is Percy Wells Bidwell, "Rural Economy in New England at the Beginning of the Nineteenth Century," *Transactions of the Connecticut Academy of Arts and Sciences* 20 (1916), 241–399; and Bidwell, "The Agricultural Revolution in New England," *American Historical Review* 26 (1921), 683–702.

9. Horwitz, *Transformation of American Law*, 167.

10. Dwight, *Greenfield Hill*, 36, 143, 127.

11. Crowley, *This Sheba, Self: The Conceptualization of Economic Life in Eighteenth-Century America* (Baltimore: Johns Hopkins University Press, 1974), 155–156.

12. Dwight, *Greenfield Hill*, 169.

13. Secretary of the Treasury [Louis McLane], *Documents Relative to the Manufactures in the United States* (1833; rpt. New York: Kelley, 1969), 1:623, 805; see Christopher Clark, "The Household Economy, Market Exchange and the Rise of Capitalism in the Connecticut Valley," *Journal of Social History* 13 (1979), 169–189; Taylor, *The Transportation Revolution*, 211–220.

14. Marx, *Capital: A Critical Analysis of Capitalist Production*, ed. Frederick Engels and trans. Samuel Moore and Edward Aveling (Moscow: Foreign Languages Publishing House, 1961), 1:72; also see Horwitz, *Transformation of American Law*, 180; Stuart Bruchey, *The Roots of American Economic Growth* (New York.: Harper & Row, 1965), 74–91, passim; and Karl Polanyi, *The Great Transformation: The Political and Economic Origins of Our Time* (New York: Rinehart, 1944); on chicanery,

see Neil Harris, *Humbug: The Art of P. T. Barnum* (Boston: Little, Brown, 1973), 9–30, 61–89.

15. Horwitz, *Transformation of American Law*, 185.

16. Sounding like an impatient evangelical moralist bored with the abstruse reasonings of orthodox Calvinism, one late eighteenth-century jurist complained that "many common-law doctrines were formulated 'in an age when the minds of men were fettered in forms [and] when forms were held to be substances, and abstractions real entities.' As a result, at common law, 'technical reasoning and unmeaning maxims . . . frequently supplied the place of principles'" (ibid., 24); for the "reason and principle'" passage, see ibid., 25–26.

17. Ibid., 31, 38; the historical background is traced in Gary Kulik, "Dams, Fish, and Farmers: Defense of Public Rights in Eighteenth-Century Rhode Island," in Steven Hahn and Jonathan Prude, ed., *The Countryside in the Age of Capitalist Transformation* (Chapel Hill: University of North Carolina Press, 1985), 3–50.

18. Hannah Arendt, *The Human Condition* (Chicago: University of Chicago Press, 1958), 22–78.

19. See Arthur M. Schlesinger, *Learning How to Behave: A Historical Study of American Etiquette Books* (New York: Macmillan, 1946), 20.

20. Paul H. Mattingly, *The Classless Profession: American Schoolmen in the Nineteenth Century* (New York: New York University Press, 1975), 44.

21. Ibid., 62–63.

22. See Michael Zuckerman, "The Nursery Tales of Horatio Alger," *American Quarterly* 24 (1972), 201.

23. For a brief account, see Carl Bode, *The Anatomy of American Popular Culture, 1840–1861* (Berkeley: University of California Press, 1960), 119–131.

24. Lydia Marie Child, *The Frugal Housewife: Dedicated to Those Who Are Not Ashamed of Economy* (Boston: Marsh & Capen, 1829), often reprinted under the title *The American Frugal Housewife*.

25. Meyer, *The Democratic Enlightenment*; Bryson, *Man and Society*.

26. Mattingly, *The Classless Profession*, 73; Monte A. Calvert, *The Mechanical Engineer in America, 1830–1910: Professional Cultures in Conflict* (Baltimore: Johns Hopkins University Press, 1967), 53.

27. Foster, *An Errand of Mercy*.

28. Calhoun, *The Intelligence of a People*, 319–320; among the more specialized manuals, of which there are hundreds, see, for example, S. Annie Frost, *The Godey's Lady's Book Receipts and Household Hints* (Philadelphia: Evans, Stoddart, 1870); Charles L. Flint, *Milch Cows and Dairy Farming . . .* (Boston: Williams, 1858); *The Grocer's Companion and Merchant's Hand-Book* (Boston: Johnson, 1883); and Edward Shaw, *The Modern Architect; or Every Carpenter His Own Master . . .* (Boston: Dayton and Wentworth, 1854).

29. Welter, *The Mind of America, 1820–1860* (New York: Columbia University Press, 1975), 159.

30. Mattingly, *The Classless Profession*, 83.

31. On mothers, see Barbara Welter, "The Cult of True Womanhood," *American Quarterly* 18 (1966), rpt. in *The American Family in Social-Historical Perspective*, ed. Michael Gordon (New York: St. Martin's Press, 1973), 224–250; Mattingly,

The Classless Profession, 81; on bridge building, etc., see Calhoun, *The Intelligence of a People*, 319.

32. Horwitz, *Transformation of American Law*, 43.

33. Welter, *The Mind of America*, 159; Thorstein Veblen's *The Theory of Business Enterprise* (1904; rpt. New York: Scribner's, 1932) is still the richest analysis of the conflict between the two key elements of the modern economy, "the machine process and investment for a profit" (1).

34. See, for example, Thomas Snell, *A Discourse, Containing a Historical Sketch of the Town of North Brookfield* (West Brookfield, Mass.: Cooke, 1854), 17.

35. Melville, *The Confidence-Man: His Masquerade*, ed. Harrison Hayford, Hershel Parker, and G. Thomas Tanselle (Evanston: Northwestern University Press, 1984), 133 (chap. 24).

36. See Max Horkheimer, *The Eclipse of Reason* (1947; rpt. New York: Seabury, 1974).

37. On mind cure, see Gail Thain Parker, *Mind Cure in New England: From the Civil War to World War I* (Hanover, N.H.: University Press of New England, 1973); Donald Meyer, *The Positive Thinkers: A Study of the American Quest for Health, Wealth and Personal Power from Mary Baker Eddy to Norman Vincent Peale* (Garden City, N.Y.: Doubleday, 1965); the best study of contemporary variations is Donald Stone, "The Human Potential Movement," in *The New Religious Consciousness*, ed. Charles Y. Glock and Robert N. Bellah (Berkeley: University of California Press, 1976), 93–115. Though the modern devotees of the Thoreauvian alternative are numerous and articulate (e.g., Robert Pirsig, *Zen and the Art of Motorcycle Maintenance* [New York: Morrow, 1974]), the movement has not been studied historically.

38. On the traditional builder, Elting E. Morison, *From Know-How to Nowhere: The Development of American Technology* (New York: Basic Books, 1974), 17–18; on visual intuition, Calhoun, *The Intelligence of a People*, 244; also see n. 31 above. Devotionalists loved the analogy between technical religiosity and industrial power. In 1860, the *Atlantic Monthly* asked, "Is the Religious Want of the Age Met?" and found "our age an age of daring and of doing."

> We are ready to discard the word *impossible* from our vocabulary; we deny that anything is the less probable because of being unprecedented. For doing new things we look about for new means,—being full charged with the belief that for all worthy and desirable ends there must be adequate and available means. In this regard, it is an age of unprecedented faith, of *expectation of success;* and we all know the natural and necessary influence of such an expectation. . . . The world has advanced, in our age, from a speed of 5 miles per hour, to 20 to 30, or more. . . . Our age is an age of great devotion to secular affairs,—of men who are great in the conduct of such affairs,—in every department of life. To counterbalance this, our ministry must be filled with an equally earnest devotion to God and salvation" (5 [March, 1860], 358–360).

See the response, "Preaching by Steam," *Congregational Quarterly* 2 (April 1860), 215–219.

Henry Ward Beecher's preaching often inspired such analogies: for example,

There is no earthly necessity for working a church, by hand power, no more than there is a printing press. All it needs is that the great engineer should lubricate the machine once every Sunday, not with the fire-water of a Whitefield or Wesley, which dries up as fast as poured on, and then corrodes all it touches, or the patent friction oil of the established church, which gums, and has to be removed and renewed every little while, but with the genuine concentrated extract of the kerosene of the Rev. H.W. Beecher, which is warranted to run smooth for a week at least, and a high pressure machine which can do a power of work without human assistance. . . . To be sure, the paper turned out in this manner can hardly be called vellum, nor the printed matter pass the scrutiny of the great critic, but as society goes, it will answer the purpose as long as it presents a smooth type, and does not outrage the laws of the land. . . ." (*The Crayon* [New York], 6, pt. 5 [May, 1869], 155)

39. Calhoun, *The Intelligence of a People,* 306; see Richard Poirier, *A World Elsewhere: The Place of Style in American Literature* (New York: Oxford University Press, 1966); the link between the romantic imagination and the concurrent technical enthusiasm of the nineteenth century is developed in different ways in Walter J. Ong, *Rhetoric, Romance, and Technology: Studies in the Interaction of Expression and Culture* (Ithaca, N.Y.: Cornell University Press, 1971); and by Horkheimer, *The Eclipse of Reason.*

40. The distinctions drawn by Karl R. Popper between natural science, which works by "expectations," and prophetic or historicist social science, which operates by (what I call) "projections," have been suggestive here; see *Conjectures and Refutations: The Growth of Scientific Knowledge,* 2d ed. (New York: Basic Books, 1965), 47. Walter J. Ong acutely sees the analogy of romance and technology in their common rejection of the restraining bonds of prior knowledge; see *Rhetoric, Romance, and Technology,* 255–283.

41. A mid-nineteenth-century compendium of sentimentalist consolation is Mrs. H. Dwight Williams, *Voices from The Silent Land; or, Leaves of Consolation for the Afflicted* (Boston: Jewett, 1854); the most famous contemporary account of a glimpse of heaven is Elizabeth Stuart Phelps, *The Gates Ajar* (Boston: Fields, Osgood, 1869); see Melville, *Mardi and a Voyage Thither,* ed. Harrison Hayford, Herschel Parker, and G. Thomas Tanselle (Evanston: Northwestern University Press, 1970), 587; also see the critical comments of a contemporary reviewer in the *Democratic Review,* ibid., 669; and Douglas, *The Feminization of American Culture,* 200–226. George Santayana once wrote, "This is the secret of that extra-ordinary vogue which the transcendental philosophy has had for nearly a century in Great Britain and America; it is a method which enables a man to renovate all his beliefs, scientific and religious, from the inside, giving them a new status and interpretation as phases of his own experience or imagination; so that he does not seem to himself to reject anything, and yet is bound to nothing, except to his creative self" (*Character and Opinion in the United States* [New York: Scribners, 1920], 12–13).

42. Melville's comment appeared in his review of "Hawthorne and his Mosses," rpt. in *The Portable Melville,* ed. Jay Leyda (New York: Viking, 1952), 406.

43. Key documents of postwar orthodoxy are Will Herberg, *Protestant-Catholic-Jew: An Essay in American Religious Sociology* (Garden City, N.Y.: Doubleday,

1955); and Arthur M. Schlesinger, Jr., *The Vital Center: The Politics of Freedom* (Boston: Houghton Mifflin, 1949).

44. Boorstin, *The Americans: The Democratic Experience*, 165–244.

45. See Langdon Winner, *Autonomous Technology: Technics-Out-of-Control as a Theme in Political Thought* (Cambridge: MIT Press, 1977).

46. Unger, *Knowledge and Politics*, 26–27.

47. Homans, *Theology after Freud: An Interpretive Inquiry* (Indianapolis: Bobbs-Merrill, 1970), 211.

Select Bibliography

Primary Sources: Personal Narratives

Ambrose, Samuel. *A Brief Account of the Life and Conversion of Peggy Walker, Who Died at Parristown, State of New-Hampshire; on Sunday, May 13, 1784.* Norwich, Conn.: J. Trumbull, 1785.

An Authentic Account of the Conversion and Experience of a Negro. To which is added, A Faithful Narrative of the Wonderful Dealings of God, towards Polly Davis, of New-Granthan, in the State of New-Hampshire. Windsor, Vt.: Alden Spooner, 1793. [American Antiquarian Society]*

Ayer, Sarah Connell. *Diary of Sarah Connell Ayer.* Portland, Me.: Lefavor-Tower, 1910.

Bangs, Heman. *The Autobiography and Journal of Rev. Heman Bangs.* New York: Tibbals, 1872.

Beecher, Lyman. *The Autobiography of Lyman Beecher.* Edited by Barbara M. Cross. 2 vols. Cambridge: Harvard University Press, 1961.

Biography of Mrs. Lydia B. Bacon. Boston: Massachusetts Sabbath School Society, 1856.

Birney, George Hugh, Jr. "The Life and Letters of Asahel Nettleton." Ph.D. diss., Hartford Theological Seminary, 1943.

Bond, Alvan. Diaries and Papers. Alvan Bond Collection, Old Sturbridge Village Research Library, Sturbridge, Mass.

————. *Memoir of the Rev. Pliny Fisk.* Edinburgh: Waugh & Innes, 1829.

Bouton, Nathaniel. *Autobiography of Nathaniel Bouton, D.D.* Edited by John Bell Bouton. New York: Randolph, 1879.

[Brown, Letitia J. S.] *Memoir of Elder Elijah Shaw.* 3d ed. Boston: L. J. Shaw, 1852.

Brownson, Orestes Augustus. *The Convert: or, Leaves from my Experience.* New York: Dunigan, 1857.

Bryant, Blanche Brown, and Gertrude Elaine Baker, eds. *The Diaries of Sally and Pamela Brown, 1832–1838, and Hyde Leslie, 1887.* Springfield, Vt.: Bryant Foundation, 1970.

Channing, William H. *Memoir of William Ellery Channing with Extracts from his Correspondence and Manuscripts.* 2d ed. 3 vols. Boston: Crosby and Nichols, 1848.

Cheney, Mary Bushnell, comp. *Life and Letters of Horace Bushnell.* New York: Harper, 1880.

Cogswell, E. C. *Memoir of the Rev. Samuel Hidden.* Boston: Crocker & Brewster, 1842.

*Bracketed material after an entry gives the location of a very rare or hard-to-find publication.

Colby, John. *The Life, Experience and Travels of John Colby, Preacher of the Gospel. With an Appendix, Containing Remarks on the Character and Labors of the Author, &c.* 3d ed., revised and corrected. 2 vols. bound together. Cornish, Me.: S. W. and C. C. Cole, 1829.

Conant, William C. *Narratives of Remarkable Conversions and Revival Incidents: Including . . . an account . . . of the Great Awakening of 1857–'8.* New York: Derby & Jackson, 1858.

The Conversion of an Infidel, being the Confession and Exhortation of an Old Man, who wishes well to his fellow Mortals, near the Close of his life. Enfield, Mass.: John Howe, 1830. [American Antiquarian Society]

Cooley, Timothy Mather. *Sketches of the Life and Character of the Rev. Lemuel Haynes, A.M.* New York: Taylor, 1839.

Cowles, Anna Roosevelt, and Laura Hadley Mosely, eds. *The Diaries of Julia Cowles: A Connecticut Record.* New Haven: Yale University Press, 1931.

Cummings, Asa. *A Memoir of the Rev. Edward Payson, D.D., Late of Portland, Maine.* Evangelical Family Library, Vol. 12. New York: American Tract Society, [c. 1835].

Cummings, Asa, comp. *Memoir, Select Thoughts and Sermons of the Late Rev. Edward Payson, D.D., Pastor of the Second Church in Portland.* 3 vols. Portland, Me.: Hyde, Lord and Duren, 1846.

Dewey, Orville. *Autobiography and Letters.* Edited by Mary E. Dewey. Boston: Roberts, 1883.

"Diary of Archelaus Putnam of New Mills." *Danvers Historical Society Collections*, 4 (1916), 51–72; 5 (1917), 49–69; 6 (1918), 11–29.

Dickinson, Thomas A. "Biographical Sketch and Extracts from the Journal of Rev. Timothy Dickinson." *Proceedings of the Worcester Society of Antiquity* 6 (1883), 63–89.

Dow, Lorenzo. *The Dealings of God, Man, and the Devil, as Exemplified in the Life, Experience, and Travels of Lorenzo Dow in a Period of More than a Half Century; With Reflections on Various Subjects, Religious, Moral, Political and Prophetic.* 4th ed., revised. Norwich, Conn.: Wm. Faulkner, 1833.

Dow, Peggy. *Vicissitudes in the Wilderness; Exemplified, in the Journal of Peggy Dow, to which is added, An Appendix of Her Death, and also, Reflections on Matrimony, by Lorenzo Dow.* 5th ed. Norwich, Conn.: Wm. Faulkner, 1833.

Drinkwater, Anne T. *Memoir of Mrs. Deborah H. Porter, Wife of Rev. C. G. Porter, of Bangor.* Portland, Me.: Sanborn & Carter, 1848.

Emerson, Joseph, ed. *Writings of Miss Fanny Woodbury, Who Died at Beverly, Nov. 15, 1814, Aged Twenty-Three Years.* 4th ed. Boston: Armstrong, 1819.

Emmons, F. W., et al. *The Biography and Phrenological Character of Deacon John Phillips: With the Addresses, Poem, and Original Hymns, of the Celebration of His C [One-Hundredth] Birthday.* Southbridge, Mass.: O. D. Haven, 1860.

Finney, Charles G. *Memoirs.* New York: A. S. Barnes, 1876.

Goodrich, S[amuel] G[oodrich]. *Recollections of a Lifetime, or Men and Things I Have Seen: In a Series of Familiar Letters to a Friend, Historical, Biographical, Anecdotal, and Descriptive.* 2 vols. 1857. Reprint. Detroit: Gale Research, 1967.

Hallock, William A. *Memoir of Harlan Page; or the Power of Prayer and Personal Effort for the Souls of Individuals.* New York: American Tract Society, 1835.

————. *A Sketch of the Life and Labors of the Rev. Justin Edwards, D. D., The Evangelical Pastor; The Advocate of Temperance, the Sabbath, and the Bible.* New York: American Tract Society, 1855.

Hatfield, Edwin F. *A Memoir of Elihu W. Baldwin, D. D.* New York: Jonathan Leavitt, 1843.

[Hawes, Mrs. Joel]. *Memoir of Mrs. Mary E. Van Lennep, Only Daughter of the Rev. Joel Hawes, D. D., and Wife of the Rev. Henry J. Van Lennep, Missionary in Turkey.* Hartford: Belknap and Hammersley, 1848.

Hopkins, Samuel, comp. *The Life and Character of Miss Susanna Anthony, who died, in Newport (R. I.) June 23, MDCCXCI, in the sixty fifth year of her age. Consisting Chiefly in Extracts from her Writings, with some brief observations on them.* Worcester: Worcester, 1796.

————. *Memoirs of the Life of Mrs. Sarah Osborn, Who Died at Newport, Rhodeisland, on the Second Day of August, 1796, in the Eighty-Third Year of Her Age.* Worcester: Worcester, 1799.

Hyde, Alvan. *Memoir of Rev. Alvan Hyde, D. D., of Lee, Massachusetts.* Boston: Perkins & Marvin, 1835.

Jessee, Dean C. "The Early Accounts of Joseph Smith's First Vision." *Brigham Young University Studies* 9 (1969), 275–294.

Johnson, Clifton H., ed. *God Struck Me Dead: Religious Conversion Experiences and Autobiographies of Ex-Slaves.* Philadelphia: Pilgrim Press, 1969.

Karlsen, Carol F., and Laurie Crumpacker, eds. *The Journal of Esther Edwards Burr, 1754–1757.* New Haven: Yale University Press, 1984.

Knight, H. C. *Memorial of Rev. Wm. A. Hallock, D. D., First Secretary of the American Tract Society.* New York: American Tract Society, [1882].

Lawrence, Edward A. *The Life of Rev. Joel Hawes, D. D., Tenth Pastor of the First Church, Hartford, Conn.* Hartford: Hammersley, 1871.

Long, Pierce, ed. *From the Journal of Zadoc Long.* Caldwell, Idaho: Caxton Printers, 1943.

Lyon, Benjamin. Religious diary, 1763–1767. Connecticut Historical Society, Hartford.

Marks, David. *The Life of David Marks, To the 26th Year of His Age.* Limerick, Me.: Morning Star, 1831.

Mathews, Lyman. *Memoir of the Life and Character of Ebenezer Porter, D. D., Late President of the Theological Seminary, Andover.* Boston: Perkins & Marvin, 1837.

Morris, Robert Clark, ed. *Memoirs of James Morris of South Farms in Litchfield.* New Haven: Yale University Press for the Aline Brothier Morris Fund, 1933.

Morton, Daniel O. *Memoir of Rev. Levi Parsons.* 1824. Reprint. New York: Arno Press, 1977.

Munger, Hiram. *The Life and Religious Experience of Hiram Munger, Including Many Singular Circumstances Connected with Camp-Meetings and Revivals.* Boston: Advent Christian Publication Society, 1881.

Our Pastor; or Reminiscences of Rev. Edward Payson, D. D., Pastor of the Second Congregational Church in Portland, Me. By One of His Flock. Boston: Tappan & Whittemore, 1855.

Park, Edwards A. *Memoir of the Life and Character of Samuel Hopkins, D. D.* 2d ed. Boston: Doctrinal Tract and Book Society, 1854.

————. *Memoir of Nathanael Emmons; with Sketches of His Friends and Pupils.* Boston: Congregational Board of Publication, 1861.

Parker, Ada R. *Letters.* Boston: Crosby and Nichols, 1863.

Prentiss, George L., ed. *Life and Letters of Elizabeth Prentiss.* New York: Randolph, 1882.

Robbins, Chandler. *Portrait of a Christian, Drawn from Life: A Memoir of Maria Elizabeth Clapp.* 4th ed. Boston: Crosby, Nichols and Company, for the Sunday-School Society, 1859.

Seely, Catharine. *Memoir of Catharine Seely, Late of Darien, Connecticut.* New York: Collins, Brother & Co., 1843.

Sewall, Jotham. *A Memoir of Rev. Jotham Sewall, of Chesterville, Maine.* Boston: Tappan & Whittemore, 1853.

Smith, E. Goodrich. *Memoir of Charles Henry Porter.* New York: n.p., 1849.

Sprague, William B., comp. *Annals of the American Pulpit.* 9 vols. New York: Carter, 1856–1869.

————. *Memoir of the Rev. Edward D. Griffin, D.D., Compiled Chiefly from his own Writings.* New York: Taylor & Dodd, 1839.

Stearns, W. A. *Life of Samuel H. Stearns.* New ed. Boston: James Munroe, 1846.

Stockbridge, John C. *The Model Pastor: A Memoir of the Life and Correspondence of Rev. Baron Stow, D.D.* Boston: Lee and Shepard, 1871.

Storrs, Richard S. *Memoir of the Rev. Samuel Green.* Boston: Perkins & Marvin, 1836.

Tarbox, Increase N., ed. *Diary of Thomas Robbins, D.D., 1796–1854.* 2 vols. Boston: Beacon Press, 1886.

Thrift, Minton. *Memoir of the Rev. Jesse Lee, With Extracts from His Journals.* New York: N. Bangs and T. Mason, for the Methodist Episcopal Church, 1823.

Todd, John E., ed. *John Todd: The Story of His Life Told Mainly by Himself.* New York: Harper, 1876.

Tyler, Bennet. *Lectures on Theology. With a Memoir by Rev. Nahum Gale, D.D.* Boston: J. E. Tilton, 1859.

————. *Memoir of the Life and Character of Rev. Asahel Nettleton, D.D.* 3d ed. Boston: Doctrinal Tract and Book Society, 1850.

Tyler, Bennet, comp. *Remains of the Late Rev. Asahel Nettleton, D.D.* Hartford: Robins and Smith, 1845.

Waite, Eliza. *Life and Writings of Eliza Waite, who died at Freeport, (Me.) January 13, 1819, in the 20th year of her age.* Hallowell, Me.: E. Goodale, 1819.

Warren, Israel P. *The Sisters: A Memoir of Elizabeth H., Abbie A., and Sarah F. Dickerman.* Boston: American Tract Society, 1859.

Winslow, Calvin. *The Experience of Calvin Winslow.* N.p. [1807?]. [American Antiquarian Society]

Winslow, Miron. *Memoir of Mrs. Harriet L. Winslow, Thirteen Years a Member of the American Mission in Ceylon.* New York: American Tract Society, 1840.

Wisner, Benjamin B. *Memoirs of the Late Mrs. Susan Huntington, of Boston, Mass., Consisting Principally of Extracts from Her Journal and Letters; With the Sermon Occasioned by Her Death.* 2d ed. Boston: Crocker & Brewster, 1826.

Worcester, Samuel M. *The Life and Labors of Rev. Samuel Worcester, D.D.* 2 vols. Boston: Crocker and Brewster, 1852.

Wright, Henry Clarke. *Human Life: Illustrated in My Individual Experience as a Child, a Youth, and a Man.* Boston: Bela Marsh, 1849.

Yale, Cyrus. *Life of Rev. Jeremiah Hallock, Late Pastor of the Congregational Church in Canton, Conn.* New York: John P. Haven, 1828.

Other Primary Sources

[Abbott, Jacob.] *New England, and Her Institutions.* London: R. B. Seeley and W. Burnside, 1835.

Alger, William Rounseville. *The Friendships of Women.* Boston: Roberts, 1868.

Backus, Azel, and Chauncey Prindle. *Bethlem in 1812 & Watertown in 1801.* Hartford: Acorn Club, 1961.

Backus, Charles. *The Faithful Ministers of Jesus Christ Rewarded. A Sermon, Delivered at the Ordination of the Rev. Azel Backus, to the Pastoral Care of the Church in Bethlem, April 6, 1791.* Litchfield: Collier & Buel, [1792].

———. *The Scripture Doctrine of Regeneration Considered, in Six Discourses.* Hartford: Hudson and Goodwin, 1800.

———. *A Sermon Delivered Jan. 1, 1801; Containing a Brief Review of Some of the Distinguishing Events of the Eighteenth Century.* Hartford: Hudson and Goodwin, 1801.

Backus, Isaac. *A History of New England, With Particular Reference to the Denomination of Christians called Baptists.* 2d ed. Edited by David Weston. Vol. 2. Newton, Mass.: Backus Historical Society, 1871.

Baldwin, Thomas. *A Brief Sketch of the Revival of Religion in Boston, 1803–5.* Boston: Lincoln & Edmands, 1826.

———. *A Sermon Delivered at Boston, on Tuesday, April 2, 1799, at a Quarterly Meeting of Several Churches for Special Prayer.* Boston: Manning & Loring, 1799.

Bancroft, Aaron. *A Discourse on Conversion.* Worcester: William Manning, 1816.

———. *The Duties Enjoined by the Fourth Commandment, Illustrated in a Discourse Delivered January, 1877.* 2d ed. Worcester: William Manning, 1817.

Barber, John Warner. *Connecticut Historical Collections, Being a General Collection of Interesting Facts, Traditions, Biographical Sketches, Anecdotes, &c., Relating to the History and Antiquities of Every Town in Connecticut, With Geographical Descriptions.* 2d ed. New Haven: Durrie & Peck and J. W. Barber, 1837.

———. *Massachusetts Historical Collections, Being a General Collection of Interesting Facts, Traditions, Biographical Sketches, Anecdotes, &c., Relating to the History and Antiquities of Every Town in Massachusetts, with Geographical Descriptions.* Worcester: Dorr, Howland, 1839.

Barnard, Henry. *School Architecture, or Contributions to the Improvement of Schoolhouses in the United States.* 6th ed., Cincinnati: Derby, 1854.

Beecher, Catharine E. *A Treatise on Domestic Economy For the Use of Young Ladies at Home, and at School.* Revised ed. New York: Harper, 1851.

Beecher, Edward. *The Conflict of Ages; or the Great Debate on the Moral Relations of God and Man.* 5th ed. Boston: Phillips, Sampson and Co., 1854.

Beecher, Lyman. *The Practicability of Suppressing Vice, By Means of Societies Instituted for That Purpose: A Sermon, Delivered before the Moral Society, in East-*

Hampton (*Long-Island*), *September 21, 1803.* New London: Samuel Green, 1804.

———. *The Remedy for Duelling. A Sermon Delivered before the Presbytery of Long-Island, at the Opening of their Session at Aquebogue, April 16, 1806.* New York: Williams and Whiting, 1809.

———. *Works.* 3 vols. Boston: Jewett, 1852.

Beecher, Thomas K. *Our Seven Churches.* New York: J. B. Ford, 1870.

Bellamy, Joseph. *True Religion Delineated, or, Experimental Religion.* Boston: S. Kneeland, 1750.

———. *The Works of Joseph Bellamy, D.D.* Edited by Tryon Edwards. 2 vols. Boston: Doctrinal Tract and Book Society, 1853.

Boardman, Henry A. *Suggestions to Young Men Engaged in Mercantile Business.* Philadelphia: Lippincott, Grambo and Co., 1851.

Boardman, W. E. *The Higher Christian Life.* Boston: Henry Hoyt, 1859.

Bowen, Francis. *The Metaphysics of Sir William Hamilton, Collected, Arranged, and Abridged, for the use of Colleges and Private Students.* Cambridge, Mass.: Sever and Francis, 1868.

[Bradford, Ebenezer.] A *Dialogue between Philagathus, a young divine, and Pamela, his sister, a young convert, upon the work of God's Holy Spirit.* Newburyport: John Mycall, [1795].

Bradford, James. *An Address Delivered September 5, 1839, at the Celebration of the Second Centennial Anniversary of its Settlement.* In *The History of Rowley, Anciently Including Bradford, Boxford, and Georgetown, from the year 1639 to the Present Time,* by Thomas Gage. Boston: Ferdinand Andrews, 1840.

Bristol, Conn. First Congregational Church Records, 1742–1897. Connecticut State Library, Hartford.

Buell, Samuel. *A Faithful Narrative of the Remarkable Revival of Religion, in the Congregation of Easthampton, on Long-Island, In the year of our Lord, 1764; With some reflections.* . . . *And, also, An Account of the Revival of Religion in Bridgehampton & Easthampton, In the year 1800.* Sag Harbor, N.Y.: Alden Spooner, 1808.

Burton, Asa. *Essays on Some of the First Principles of Metaphysicks, Ethicks, and Theology.* Portland, Me.: Mirror, 1824.

Bushman, Richard L., ed. *The Great Awakening: Documents on the Revival of Religion, 1740–1745.* New York: Atheneum, 1970.

Bushnell, Horace. *Work and Play; or Literary Varieties.* New York: Scribner, 1864.

———. *Views of Christian Nurture.* 1916. Reprint (as *Christian Nurture*). New Haven: Yale University Press, 1947.

Calvin, John. *Institutes of the Christian Religion.* Edited by John T. McNeill. Translated by Ford Lewis Battles. Library of Christian Classics, 20–21. 2 vols. Philadelphia: Westminster Press, 1960.

Channing, William E. *Works.* 6 vols. Boston: George C. Channing, 1849.

Chase, Philander. *The Ingrafted Word; or the Ingrafted Branch Grafted Upon: a Sermon, Delivered in Christ-Church, Hartford, Connecticut, February 6, A.D 1814.* Hartford: Hale & Hosmer, 1814.

Child, Lydia Maria. *The Frugal Housewife: Dedicated to Those Who Are Not Ashamed of Economy.* Boston: Marsh & Capen, 1829.

Codman, John. *A Sermon, on Prayer, Preached at Dorchester, December 12, 1813.* Boston: Armstrong, 1814.

Colton, Calvin. *Thoughts on the Religious State of the Country; with Reasons for Preferring Episcopacy.* 2d ed. New York: Harper, 1836.

Contributions to the Ecclesiastical History of Connecticut; Prepared Under the Direction of the General Association, to Commemorate the Completion of One Hundred and Fifty Years Since Its First Annual Assembly. New Haven: Kingsley, 1861.

Cooke, Jacob E., ed. *The Federalist.* Middletown: Wesleyan University Press, 1961.

Cooke, Parsons. *A Century of Puritanism, and A Century of Its Opposites; With Results Contrasted to Enforce Puritan Principles, and to Trace What is Peculiar in the People of Lynn to What is Peculiar in Its History.* Boston: S. K. Whipple, 1855.

The Cooper. London: Houlston and Stoneman, n.d. [Old Sturbridge Village Research Library]

Crofut, Florence S. Marcy. *Guide to the History and the Historic Sites of Connecticut.* 2 vols. New Haven: Yale University Press, 1937.

DeBow, J. D. B. *Statistical View of the United States, . . . Being a Compendium of the Seventh Census.* Washington: Beverley Tucker, 1854.

[Dewey, Orville.] *Letters of an English Traveller to His Friend in England, on the "Revivals of Religion," in America.* Boston: Bowles and Dearborn, 1828.

Dexter, Henry M. *Street Thoughts.* Boston: Crosby, Nichols, 1859.

Downing, Andrew Jackson. *The Architecture of Country Houses; Including Designs for Cottages, Farm-houses, and Villas.* New York: Appleton, 1850.

Dwight, Timothy. *Greenfield Hill: A Poem, in Seven Parts.* New York: Childs and Swaine, 1794.

————. *A Sermon on Duelling, Preached in the Chapel of Yale College, New-Haven, September 9th, 1804, and in the Old Presbyterian Church, New-York, January 21st 1805.* New York: Collins, Perkins, 1805.

————. *Theology Explained and Defended, in a Series of Sermons.* 12th ed. 4 vols. New York: Harper, 1850.

————. *Travels in New England and New York.* Edited by Barbara M. Solomon. 4 vols. Cambridge: Harvard University Press, 1969.

Edwards, Bela Bates. *Writings. With a Memoir by Edwards A. Park.* 2 vols. Boston: Jewett, 1853.

Edwards, Jonathan. *Freedom of the Will.* Edited by Paul Ramsey. Vol. 1 of *The Works of Jonathan Edwards.* New Haven: Yale University Press, 1957.

————. *The Great Awakening: A Faithful Narrative, The Distinguishing Marks, Some Thoughts Concerning the Revival.* Edited by C. C. Goen. Vol. 4 of *The Works of Jonathan Edwards.* New Haven: Yale University Press, 1972.

————. *Original Sin.* Edited by Clyde Holbrook. Vol. 3 of *The Works of Jonathan Edwards.* New Haven: Yale University Press, 1970.

————. *Religious Affections.* Edited by John E. Smith. Vol. 2 of *The Works of Jonathan Edwards.* New Haven: Yale University Press, 1959.

————. *Works.* 8 vols. Worcester: Isaiah Thomas, Jr., 1808–1809.

Emerson, Ralph Waldo. "Historic Notes of Life and Letters in New England." In Vol. 10, *Lectures and Biographical Sketches, Works.* Boston: Houghton Mifflin, 1883.

————. *Nature, Addresses, and Lectures.* Rev. ed. Vol. 1 of *Works.* Edited by J. E. Cabot. 12 vols. Boston: Houghton Mifflin, 1883.

Emmons, Nathanael. *A Discourse, Delivered, September 3, MCDDXCII, to the Society for the Reformation of Morals in Franklin.* Worcester: Worcester, 1793.

————. *Sermons, on Various Important Subjects of Christian Doctrine and Practice.* Boston: Armstrong, 1812.

————. *Works.* Edited by Jacob Ide. 6 vols. Boston: Crocker & Brewster, 1842.

Finney, Charles G. *Lectures on Revivals of Religion.* Edited by William G. McLoughlin. Cambridge: Harvard University Press, 1960.

Fish, Henry Clay. *Primitive Piety Revived, or The Aggressive Power of the Christian Church.* Boston: Congregational Board of Publication, 1855.

Flint, Charles L. *Milch Cows and Dairy Farming.* Boston: A. Williams, 1858. [Old Sturbridge Village Research Library]

Frost, S. Annie. *The Godey's Lady's Book Receipts and Household Hints.* Philadelphia: Evans, Stoddart, 1870.

General Association of Connecticut. *Acts and Proceedings . . . in the Year 1801.* (In succeeding years called *Minutes, Extracts,* etc.) Hartford: various publishers, 1801–1850.

————. *An Address . . . to the Congregational Ministers and Churches of the State, on the Importance of United Endeavors to Revive Gospel Discipline.* Litchfield, Conn.: Hosmer and Goodwin, 1808.

————. *An Address of the General Association of the Pastors of the Consociated Churches, of the Colony of Connecticut, to the Consociated Pastors and Churches in said Colony.* New York, 1776.

General Association of Massachusetts Proper. *Extracts from the Minutes,* etc. Boston: various publishers, 1811–1850. ("Proper" dropped after Maine set apart in 1820.)

General Association of New-Hampshire. *Extracts from the Minutes,* etc. Boston, Concord, N.H., Dover, N.H.: various publishers, 1811–1820.

General Convention of Congregational and Presbyterian Ministers in Vermont. *Extracts from the Minutes,* etc. N.p., 1811, 1816.

Giles, Daphne S. *The Religious and Political Influence of Educated and Uneducated Females.* Boston: J. Howe, 1849.

Goshen, Conn. Transactions of the Society for the Promotion of Good Morals, in the Town of Goshen, 1812–1816. Connecticut State Library, Hartford.

Griffin, Edward D. *The Doctrine of Divine Efficiency, Defended against Certain Modern Speculations.* New York: Jonathan Leavitt, 1833.

————. *A Letter to a Friend on the Connexion between the New Doctrines and the New Measures.* Albany: Hosford & Wait, 1833.

————. *A Letter to the Rev. Ansel D. Eddy, of Canandaigua, N.Y., on the Narrative of the Late Revivals of Religion, in the Presbytery of Geneva.* Williamstown, Mass.: Ridley Bannister, 1832.

The Grocer's Companion and Merchant's Hand-Book. Boston: Benjamin Johnson, 1883. [Old Sturbridge Village Research Library.]

Hampton, Conn. Congregational Church Records. Connecticut State Library, Hartford.

Hart, Levi. *The Earnest Desire and Endeavour of the True, and Evangelical Minister, That*

His Hearers May Have a Proper Remembrance of the Gospel After His Death.
New London: Green, 1786.

———. *Liberty Described and Recommended; in a Sermon, Preached to the corporation of Freemen in Farmington, at Their Meeting on Tuesday, September 20, 1774.* Hartford: Watson, 1775.

Hawes, Joel. *Lectures Addressed to the Young Men of Hartford and New Haven, and Published at their United Request.* 2d ed. Hartford: Oliver D. Cooke, 1828.

Heimert, Alan, and Perry Miller, eds. *The Great Awakening: Documents Illustrating the Crisis and its Consequences.* Indianapolis: Bobbs, Merrill, 1967.

Hitchcock, Edward. *The Religion of Geology and its Connected Sciences.* Boston: Phillips, Sampson, 1851.

Holmes, Oliver Wendell. *Elsie Venner: A Romance of Destiny.* 1861. Reprint. Boston: Houghton Mifflin, 1891.

Hopkins, Samuel. *The System of Doctrines, Contained in Divine Revelation, Explained and Defended.* 2 vols. Boston: Thomas and Andrews, 1793.

———. *Treatise on the Millennium.* In Vol. 2 of *The System of Doctrines.* Boston: Thomas and Andrews, 1793.

Humphrey, Heman. *Revival Sketches and Manual.* New York: American Tract Society, 1859.

Hyde, Alvan. "The Purpose of God Displayed in Abasing the Pride of Nation." In *Sermons on Important Subjects.* Hartford: Hudson & Goodwin, 1797.

Ide, Jacob. *The Nature and Tendency of Balls, Seriously and Candidly Considered, in Two Sermons, Preached in Medway, the First, December 21: The Second, December 28, 1818.* Dedham, Mass.: H. & W. H. Mann, n.d.

Jericho, Vermont. First Congregational Church Papers. Congregational Library, Boston.

Keep, John. *A Narrative of the Origin and Progress of the Congregational Church in Homer, Cortland County, N.Y., With Remarks.* Homer, N.Y.: Kinney & Aikin, 1833.

Kirk, Edward N. *Effectual Prayer.* Boston: Tappan & Whittemore, 1853.

Lanier, Sidney. *The English Novel and Essays on Literature.* Vol. 4 of the Centennial Edition of *The Works of Sidney Lanier.* Baltimore: Johns Hopkins University Press, 1945.

Leonard Family Papers. Old Sturbridge Village Research Library, Sturbridge, Mass.

Letters of the Rev. Dr. Beecher and Rev. Mr. Nettleton, on the "New Measures" in Conducting Revivals of Religion. New York: G. & C. Carvill, 1828.

Locke, John. *An Essay Concerning Human Understanding.* Edited by Alexander Campbell Fraser. 2 vols. New York: Dover, 1959.

M'Cosh, James. *The Method of the Divine Government, Physical and Moral.* New York: Carter, 1852.

Marsh, James. "Preliminary Essay" to *Aids to Reflection, in the Formation of a Manly Character, On the Several Grounds of Prudence, Morality, and Religion . . . ,* by Samuel Taylor Coleridge. Burlington, Vt.: Chauncey Goodrich, 1829.

Mather, Cotton. *Bonifacius: An Essay upon the Good.* Edited by David Levin. Cambridge: Harvard University Press, 1966.

Melville, Herman. *The Confidence-Man: His Masquerade.* Edited by Harrison Hayford, Herschel Parker, and G. Thomas Tanselle. Vol. 10 of *The Writings of Her-*

man Melville. Evanston, Ill.: Northwestern University Press and the Newberry Library, 1984.

———. *Mardi and a Voyage Thither.* Edited by Harrison Hayford, Herschel Parker, and G. Thomas Tanselle. Vol. 3 of *The Writings of Herman Melville.* Evanston, Ill.: Northwestern University Press and the Newberry Library, 1970.

———. *Moby-Dick, or The Whale.* Edited by Luther S. Mansfield and Howard P. Vincent. New York: Hendricks House, 1952.

———. *The Portable Melville.* Edited by Jay Leyda. New York: Viking Press, 1952.

Moore, George. Diaries, 1828–1836. 4 vols. Harvard University Archives, Cambridge, Mass.

A Narrative of the Religious Controversy in Fitchburg. With Comments on a Pamphlet, Entitled "Facts and Documents," & c. Published by the Church under the Late Care of the Rev. Samuel Worcester, and General Remarks. Worcester: Isaiah Thomas, Jr., 1804.

Nettleton, Asahel. Papers. Case Memorial Library, Hartford Seminary Foundation, Hartford, Connecticut.

Nevin, John W. *The Anxious Bench.* 2d ed. Chambersburg, Pa.: Publication Office of the German Reformed Church, 1844.

New Hartford, Conn. First Congregational Church Records. Connecticut State Library, Hartford.

Noah Webster's First Edition of an American Dictionary of the English Language. 1828. Reprint. Anaheim, Calif.: Foundation for American Christian Education, 1967.

Nott, Samuel. *Franklin in 1800.* Ed. Thompson R. Harlow. Hartford: Acorn Club, 1949.

[Ogden, John C.] *An Appeal to the Candid, upon the Present State of Religion and Politics in Connecticut.* N.p. [1798?]. [American Antiquarian Society]

Old South Chapel Prayer Meeting: Its Origin and History; with Interesting Narratives, and Instances of Remarkable Conversions in Answer to Prayer. Boston: J. E. Tilton, 1859.

Palmer, Phoebe. *The Way of Holiness, with Notes by the Way; Being a Narrative of Religious Experience Resulting from a Determination to be a Bible Christian.* New York: Lane and Tippett, 1847.

Park, Edwards A., ed. *The Atonement: Discourses and Treatises.* Boston: Congregational Board of Publications, 1859.

———. *The Theology of the Intellect and of the Feelings: A Discourse Delivered before the Convention of the Congregational Ministers of Massachusetts, . . . May 30, 1850.* Boston: Perkins & Whipple, 1850.

Payson, Edward. *Sermons, by the late Rev. Edward Payson, D.D., Pastor of the Second Church in Portland.* Portland: Shirley and Hyde, 1828.

———. *Sermons, by the late Rev. Edward Payson, D.D., Pastor of the Second Church in Portland.* Vol. 2. Portland: Gershom Hyde, 1831.

Perkins, Nathan. *The Character of a Faithful Minister of the Gospel Delineated—in a Discourse, Delivered January 16, 1805, at the Ordination of the Rev. Joab Brace, to the Work of the Christian Ministry, over the Church and Congregation in Newington, a parish in Wethersfield.* Hartford: Hudson and Goodwin, 1807.

———. *A Half Century Sermon, Delivered at West-Hartford, on the 15th Day of October,*

1822: *In which a Church and Congregation are Commended to God, and the Word of his Grace.* Hartford: Goodwin, 1822.

————. *A Narrative of a Tour Through the State of Vermont, From April 27 to June 12, 1789.* Rutland, Vt.: Tuttle, 1964.

————. *Two Discourses on the Grounds of the Christian's Hope; Containing a Brief Account of the Work of God's Holy Spirit in a Remarkable Revival of Religion in West-Hartford, in the Year 1799. Delivered on the First Sabbath of the Year 1800.* Hartford: Hudson and Goodwin, 1800.

Phelps, Austin. *My Portfolio: A Collection of Essays.* New York: Scribner's 1882.

————. *The Still Hour; or Communion with God.* Boston: Gould and Lincoln, 1860.

Phelps, Elizabeth Stuart. *The Gates Ajar.* Boston: Fields, Osgood, 1869.

Pleasing Tracts Selected for the Benefit of Youth. Boston: Timothy Fletcher, 1808.

Pond, Enoch. *Apology for Religious Conferences; Letter to Rev. Aaron Bancroft, D.D., on his Discourse on the Fourth Commandment.* Worcester, n.p., 1817.

Porter, Ebenezer. *Letters on the Religious Revivals which Prevailed about the Beginning of the Present Century.* Boston: Congregational Board of Publication, 1858.

Porter, Noah. *The Human Intellect: With an Introduction upon Psychology and the Soul.* 4th ed. New York: Scribner, 1872.

Potter, Alonzo, and George B. Emerson. *The School and the Schoolmaster: A Manual for the Use of Teachers, Employers, Trustees, Inspectors, &c., &c., of Common Schools.* Boston: Fowle and Capen, 1843.

Prentice, Charles. *A Sermon, delivered September 20, 1829, at the Twenty-Fifth Anniversary of his Ordination, to which is added, A Brief Narrative of a Revival of Religion.* Litchfield, Conn.: Henry Adams, 1830.

Rice, Charles B. "History of the First Parish in Danvers." *Proceedings at the Celebration of the Two Hundredth Anniversary of the First Parish at Salem Village, now Danvers, October 8, 1872.* Boston: Congregational Publication Society, 1874.

Rudolph, Frederick, ed. *Essays on Education in the Early Republic.* Cambridge: Harvard University Press, 1965.

Schaff, Philip. *America: A Sketch of its Political, Social, & Religious Character.* Edited by Perry Miller. Cambridge: Harvard University Press, 1961.

Secretary of the Treasury [Louis McLane]. *Documents Relative to the Manufactures in the United States.* 2 vols. 1833. Reprint. New York: A. M. Kelley, 1969.

A Sermon, entitled "The Remedy for Dueling," by Rev. Lyman Beecher, D.D., Applied to the Crime of Slaveholding. Boston: Isaac Knapp, 1838.

Sermons on Important Subjects, Collected From a Number of Ministers in Some of the Northern States of America. Hartford: Hudson and Goodwin, 1797.

Shaw, Edward. *The Modern Architect; or Every Carpenter His Own Master.* Boston: Dayton and Wentworth, 1854. [Old Sturbridge Village Research Library, Sturbridge, Mass.]

Shrewsbury, Mass. First Congregational Church. Sabbath School Records, 1833–1876. Old Sturbridge Village Research Library, Sturbridge, Mass.

————. Record Books for Local Organizations, 1814–1898. Old Sturbridge Village Research Library, Sturbridge, Mass.

————. Shrewsbury and Boylston Baptist Society Records, 1812–1837. Old Sturbridge Village Research Library, Sturbridge, Mass.

Smiles, Samuel. *Character.* Chicago: Belford, Clarke, 1883.

Snell, Thomas. *A Discourse, Containing a Historical Sketch of the Town of North Brook-field.* West Brookfield, Mass.: Cooke, 1854.

Somers, Conn. Congregational Church Records and Miscellaneous Papers, 1727–1890. Vol. 4. Connecticut State Library, Hartford.

Spencer, Theo[dore]. *Conversion; Its Theory and Process, Practically Delineated.* New York: M. W. Dodd, 1854.

Sprague, William B. *Lectures on Revivals of Religion.* Albany: Webster & Skinners, 1832.

A *Statistical Account of the Towns and Parishes in the State of Connecticut.* Vol. 1, no. 1. New Haven: Connecticut Academy of Arts and Sciences, 1811.

Stevens, Abel. *Memorials of the Introduction of Methodism into the Eastern States.* 2 vols. Boston: Charles H. Peirce, 1848, 1852.

Stowe, Harriet Beecher. *The Minister's Wooing.* 1859. Reprint. Boston: Houghton Mifflin, 1896.

———. *Oldtown Folks.* Edited by Henry F. May. Cambridge: Harvard University Press, 1966.

———. *Poganuc People: Their Loves and Lives.* Boston: Houghton Mifflin, 1878.

Strong, Nathan. *The Character of a Virtuous and Good Woman, a Discourse, Delivered by the Desire and in the Presence of the Female Beneficent Society, in Hartford, October 4th, A.D. 1809.* Hartford: Hudson and Goodwin, 1809.

———. *A Sermon, On the Use of Time; Addressed to Men at Several Ages of Life. Delivered at Hartford, January 10th, 1813.* Hartford: Peter B. Gleason, 1813.

———. *Sermons, on Various Subjects, Doctrinal, Experimental and Practical.* Vol. 1. Hartford: Hudson and Goodwin, 1798.

———. *Sermons, on Various Subjects, Doctrinal, Experimental and Practical.* Vol. 2. Hartford: John Babcock, for Oliver D. & I. Cooke, 1800.

Sturbridge, Mass. Baptist Church Records. In the possession of the clerk of the Sturbridge Baptist Society.

———. Congregational Church Records. In the possession of the clerk of the Sturbridge Congregational Society.

Tarbox, Increase N. *The Religious and Ecclesiastical Contrast within the Bounds of Suffolk West Conference, between the Years 1776 and 1876.* Boston: Suffolk West Conference, 1876.

Taylor, Nathaniel W. *Regeneration the Beginning of Holiness in the Human Heart.* New Haven: Nathan Whiting, 1816.

Tracy, Joseph. *The Great Awakening. A History of the Revival of Religion in the Time of Edwards and Whitefield.* Boston: Charles Tappan, 1841.

[Tudor, William.] *Letters on the Eastern States.* New York: Kirk & Mercein, 1820.

Tyler, Bennet. *New England Revivals As They Existed at the Close of the Eighteenth and the Beginning of the Nineteenth Centuries. Compiled Principally from Narratives First Published in the Conn. Evangelical Magazine.* Boston: Massachusetts Sabbath School Society, 1846.

Upham, Thomas C. *Principles of the Interior or Hidden Life; Designed Particularly for the Consideration of Those Who are Seeking Assurance of Faith and Perfect Love.* 4th ed. Boston: Waite, Peirce, 1845.

Vital Records of Sturbridge, Mass., to the Year 1850. Boston: New England Historic Genealogical Society, 1906.

Washburn, Joseph. *Sermons on Practical Subjects. To which is Added, a Sermon of the*

Rev. Asahel Hooker, Delivered at Farmington, on the Occasion of Mr. Washburn's Death. Hartford: Lincoln & Gleason, 1807.

Webster, Daniel. *Works.* 6 vols. Boston: Little and Brown, 1851.

Webster, Noah. *Noah Webster's First Edition of an American Dictionary of the English Language.* 1828. Reprint. Anaheim, Calif.: Foundation for American Christian Education, 1967.

Williams, Mrs. H. Dwight. *Voices from the Silent Land; Or, Leaves of Consolation for the Afflicted.* Boston: John P. Jewett, 1854.

Willis, William. *The History of Portland, from 1632 to 1864.* 2d ed. Portland, Me.: Bailey and Noyes, 1865.

Woodward, William W., comp. *Surprising Accounts of the Revival of Religion in the United States of America, in Different Parts of the World, and among Different Denominations of Christians. With a Number of Interesting Occurrences of Divine Providence.* Philadelphia: Woodward, 1802.

Yale, Cyrus. *A Discourse before the North Consociation of Litchfield County, at Their Annual Meeting in Goshen, Conn., September 25, 1849.* New Haven: B. L. Hamlen, 1849.

Periodicals

Articles in these religious periodicals are not listed separately in the Bibliography.

The Advance. Vol. 1. Chicago, 1867.

Christian Spectator. Vols. 1–2. Hartford, 1819–1821.

Congregational Quarterly. Vols. 1–11. Boston, 1858–1869.

The Congregationalist. Vols. 1–11. Boston, 1849–1859.

Connecticut Evangelical Magazine. Vols. 1–7. And New Series, called *Connecticut Evangelical Magazine and Religious Intelligencer,* Vols. 1–8. Hartford, 1800–1815.

Massachusetts Missionary Magazine. Vols. 1–5. Boston, 1803–1809.

Missionary Herald. Vols. 1–19. Boston, 1805–1823.

The Panoplist. Vols. 1–9. Andover and Boston, 1805–1813. Later called *The Panoplist and Missionary Magazine,* Vol. 13. Boston, 1817.

The Spirit of the Pilgrims. Vols. 1–6. Boston, 1828–1833.

Secondary Works

Abzug, Robert H. *Passionate Liberator: Theodore Dwight Weld and the Dilemma of Reform.* New York: Oxford University Press, 1980.

Adams, Robert Martin. *Nil: Episodes in the Literary Conquest of Void During the Nineteenth Century.* New York: Oxford University Press, 1966.

Ahlstrom, Sydney E. *A Religious History of the American People.* New Haven: Yale University Press, 1972.

———. "The Scottish Philosophy and American Theology." *Church History* 24 (1955), 257–272.

———. "Theology in America: A Historical Survey." In *The Shaping of American Religion,* ed. James Ward Smith and A. Leland Jamison. Princeton: Princeton University Press, 1961.

Aiken, Henry David. *Reason and Conduct: New Bearings in Moral Philosophy.* New York: Knopf, 1962.

Allen, William. *The American Biographical Dictionary: Containing an Account of the Lives, Characters, and Writings of the Most Eminent Persons Deceased in North America, from its first Settlement.* 3d ed. Boston: Jewett, 1857.

Allport, Gordon W. *The Individual and His Religion: A Psychological Interpretation.* New York: Macmillan, 1950.

———. *The Use of Personal Documents in Psychological Science.* Bulletin 49. New York: Social Science Research Council, 1942.

Ammidown, Holmes. *Historical Collections.* 2 vols. New York: privately pub., 1874.

Anderson, Quentin. *The Imperial Self: An Essay in American Literary and Cultural History.* New York: Knopf, 1971.

Arendt, Hannah. *The Human Condition.* Chicago: University of Chicago Press, 1958.

Ariès, Philippe. *Centuries of Childhood: A Social History of Family Life.* Translated by Robert Baldick. New York: Knopf, 1962.

Armstrong, John B. *Factory under the Elms: A History of Harrisville, New Hampshire, 1774–1969.* Cambridge: MIT Press, 1969.

Bachelard, Gaston. *The Poetics of Reverie.* Translated by Daniel Russell. New York: Orion Press, 1969.

Bainton, Roland H. *Christian Unity and Religion in New England.* Collected Papers in Church History, Series 2. Boston: Beacon Press, 1964.

Banner, Lois W. "Religious Benevolence as Social Control: A Critique of an Interpretation." *Journal of American History* 60 (1973), 23–41.

Barbu, Zevedei. *Problems of Historical Psychology.* New York: Grove Press, 1960.

Barker-Benfield, G. J. *The Horrors of the Half-Known Life: Male Attitudes Toward Women and Sexuality in Nineteenth-Century America.* New York: Harper & Row, 1976.

Bellah, Robert N. *Beyond Belief: Essays on Religion in a Post-Traditional World.* New York: Harper & Row, 1970.

Benes, Peter, ed. *New England Meeting House and Church: 1630–1850.* Annual Proceedings for 1979 of the Dublin Seminar for New England Folklife. Boston: Boston Univ., n.d.

Benes, Peter, and Philip D. Zimmerman. *New England Meeting House and Church: 1630–1850: A Loan Exhibition held at the Currier Gallery of Art, Manchester, New Hampshire.* Boston: Boston University and the Currier Gallery for the Dublin Seminar for New England Folklife, 1979.

Benjamin, Walter. *Illuminations.* Edited by Hannah Arendt. Translated by Harry Zohn. New York: Schocken, 1969.

Bercovitch, Sacvan. *The Puritan Origins of the American Self.* New Haven: Yale University Press, 1975.

Berger, Peter L. *The Sacred Canopy: Elements of a Sociological Theory of Religion.* Garden City, N.Y.: Doubleday, 1967.

Berger, Peter L., Brigitte Berger, and Hansfried Kellner. *The Homeless Mind: Modernization and Consciousness.* New York: Random House, 1973.

Berk, Stephen E. *Calvinism versus Democracy: Timothy Dwight and the Origins of American Evangelical Orthodoxy.* Hamden, Conn.: Archon Books, 1974.

Bernstein, Richard J. *Praxis and Action: Contemporary Philosophies of Human Activity.* Philadelphia: University of Pennsylvania Press, 1971.

Berthoff, Rowland T. *An Unsettled People: Social Order and Disorder in American History*. New York: Harper & Row, 1971.

Bidwell, Percy Wells. "The Agricultural Revolution in New England." *American Historical Review* 26 (1921), 683–702.

———. "Rural Economy in New England at the Beginning of the Nineteenth Century." *Transactions of the Connecticut Academy of Arts and Sciences* 29 (1916), 241–399.

Birdsall, Richard D. "The Second Great Awakening and the New England Social Order." *Church History* 39 (1970), 354–364.

Bledstein, Burton J. *The Culture of Professionalism: The Middle Class and the Development of Higher Education in America*. New York: Norton, 1976.

Bloch, Marc. *Feudal Society*. Translated by L. A. Manyon. London: Routledge & Kegan Paul, 1961.

Bode, Carl. *The Anatomy of American Popular Culture, 1840–1861*. Berkeley: University of California Press, 1960.

Boisen, Anton T. *Religion in Crisis and Custom: A Sociological and Psychological Study*. New York: Harper, 1955.

Boles, John B. *The Great Revival, 1787–1805: The Origins of the Southern Evangelical Mind*. Lexington: University Press of Kentucky, 1972.

Boorstin, Daniel J. *The Americans: The Democratic Experience*. New York: Random House, 1973.

———. *The Americans: The National Experience*. New York: Random House, 1965.

Bowen, Clarence Winthrop. *The History of Woodstock, Connecticut*. 1926. Reprint. Woodstock: Woodstock Libraries, 1973.

Brauer, Jerald C. "Conversion: From Puritanism to Revivalism." *Journal of Religion* 58 (1978), 227–243.

Breitenbach, William. "The Consistent Calvinism of the New Divinity Movement." *William and Mary Quarterly*, 3d ser., 41 (1984), 241–264.

———. "New Divinity Theology and the Idea of Moral Accountability." Ph.D. diss., Yale University, 1978.

———. "Unregenerate Doings: Selflessness and Selfishness in New Divinity Theology." *American Quarterly* 34 (1982), 479–502.

Bronowski, Jacob. *The Common Sense of Science*. New York: Random House, 1959.

Brown, Peter. "The Rise and Function of the Holy Man in Late Antiquity." *Journal of Roman Studies* 61 (1971), 80–101.

Brown, Richard D. "The Emergence of Urban Society in Rural Massachusetts, 1760–1820." *Journal of American History* 61 (1974), 29–51.

———. *Modernization: The Transformation of American Life, 1600–1865*. New York: Hill & Wang, 1976.

Bruchey, Stuart W. *The Roots of American Economic Growth, 1607–1861: An Essay in Social Causation*. New York: Harper & Row, 1965.

Bryson, Gladys. *Man and Society: The Scottish Inquiry of the Eighteenth Century*. Princeton: Princeton University Press, 1945.

Buell, Lawrence. *Literary Transcendentalism: Style and Vision in the American Renaissance*. Ithaca: Cornell University Press, 1973.

———. *New England Literary Culture: From Revolution to Renaissance*. Cambridge, Eng.: Cambridge University Press, 1986.

Bullock, F. W. B. *Evangelical Conversion in Great Britain, 1696–1845.* St. Leonards on Sea, Eng.: Budd & Gillatt, 1959.

Bumsted, J. M. "Religion, Finance, and Democracy in Massachusetts: The Town of Norton as a Case Study." *Journal of American History* 57 (1971), 817–831.

Burke, Kenneth. *A Grammar of Motives.* 1945. Reprint. Berkeley: University of California Press, 1969.

———. *The Rhetoric of Religion: Studies in Logology.* 1961. Reprint. Berkeley: University of California Press, 1970.

Burns, Elizabeth. *Theatricality: A Study of Convention in the Theatre and in Social Life.* New York: Harper & Row, 1972.

Bushman, Richard L. *Joseph Smith and the Beginnings of Mormonism.* Urbana: University of Illinois Press, 1984.

Caldwell, Patricia. *The Puritan Conversion Narrative: The Beginnings of American Expression.* New York: Cambridge University Press, 1983.

Calhoun, Daniel. *The Intelligence of a People.* Princeton: Princeton University Press, 1973.

———. *Professional Lives in America: Structure and Aspiration, 1750–1850.* Cambridge: Harvard University Press, 1965.

Calvert, Monte A. *The Mechanical Engineer in America, 1830–1910: Professional Cultures in Conflict.* Baltimore: Johns Hopkins University Press, 1967.

Candee, Richard M. "The Early New England Textile Village in Art." *Antiques* 98 (1970), 910–915.

Carrier, Hervé. *The Sociology of Religious Belonging.* Translated by Arthur J. Arrieri. New York: Herder and Herder, 1965.

Carwardine, Richard. "The Second Great Awakening in the Urban Centers: An Examination of Methodism and the 'New Measures.'" *Journal of American History* 54 (1972), 327–340.

Caskey, Marie. *Chariot of Fire: Religion and the Beecher Family.* New Haven: Yale University Press, 1978.

Chadwick, Owen. *The Victorian Church, Part II.* Vol. 7 of An Ecclesiastical History of England. Edited by J. C. Dickinson. London: Adam and Charles Black, 1970.

Charvat, William. *The Origins of American Critical Thought, 1810–1835.* Philadelphia: University of Pennsylvania Press, 1936.

Clark, Christopher. "The Household Economy, Market Exchange and the Rise of Capitalism in the Connecticut Valley." *Journal of Social History* 13 (1979), 169–189.

Clark, Elmer T. *The Psychology of Religious Awakening.* New York: Macmillan, 1929.

Cohen, Charles Lloyd. *God's Caress: The Psychology of Puritan Religious Experience.* New York: Oxford University Press, 1986.

Cole, Charles C., Jr. *The Social Ideas of the Northern Evangelists.* New York: Columbia University Press, 1954.

Conforti, Joseph A. *Samuel Hopkins and the New Divinity Movement: Calvinism, the Congregational Ministry, and Reform in New England between the Great Awakenings.* Grand Rapids, Mich.: Christian University Press, 1981.

Cott, Nancy F. *The Bonds of Womanhood: "Women's Sphere" in New England, 1780–1835.* New Haven: Yale University Press, 1977.

Cross, Barbara M. *Horace Bushnell: Minister to a Changing America*. Chicago: University of Chicago Press, 1958.

Cross, Whitney R. *The Burned-Over District: The Social and Intellectual History of Enthusiastic Religion in Western New York*. Ithaca: Cornell University Press, 1950.

Crowley, J. E. *This Sheba, Self: The Conceptualization of Economic Life in Eighteenth-Century America*. Johns Hopkins University Studies in Historical and Political Science, 92d ser., no. 2. Baltimore: Johns Hopkins University Press, 1974.

Cummings, Abbott Lowell. *Architecture in Early New England*. Old Sturbridge Village Booklet Series, 7. Sturbridge, Mass.: Old Sturbridge Village, 1958.

Cuningham, Charles E. *Timothy Dwight, 1752–1817*. New York: Macmillan, 1942.

Cushing, John D. "Notes on Disestablishment in Massachusetts, 1780–1833." *William and Mary Quarterly*, 3d ser., 26 (1969), 169–190.

————. "Town Commons of New England." *Old-Time New England* 51 (1961), 86–94.

Davenport, Frederick Morgan. *Primitive Traits in Religious Revivals: A Study in Mental and Social Evolution*. New York: Macmillan, 1905.

Davidson, Ruth. "Roseland, a Gothic Revival Mansion." *Antiques* 81 (1962), 510–514.

Davis, Fred C., and Richard W. Davis. *Somers: The History of a Connecticut Town*. Somers, Conn.: Somers Historical Society, 1973.

Davis, George. *A Historical Sketch of Sturbridge and Southbridge*. West Brookfield, Mass.: O. S. Cooke, 1856.

Davis, Joe Lee. "Mystical versus Enthusiastic Sensibility." *Journal of the History of Ideas* 4 (1943), 301–319.

Davis, Merrell R. "Emerson's 'Reason' and the Scottish Philosophers." *New England Quarterly* 27 (1944), 209–228.

Delattre, Roland André. *Beauty and Sensibility in the Thought of Jonathan Edwards: An Essay in Aesthetics and Theological Ethics*. New Haven: Yale University Press, 1968.

Demos, John. *A Little Commonwealth: Family Life in Plymouth Colony*. New York: Oxford University Press, 1970.

Deshen, Shlomo A. "On Religious Change: The Situational Analysis of Symbolic Action." *Comparative Studies in Society and History* 12 (1970), 260–274.

Desroche, Henri. *Jacob and the Angel: An Essay in Sociologies of Religion*. Translated by John K. Savacool. Amherst: University of Massachusetts Press, 1973.

Dolan, Rex Robert. "An Analysis of Religious Commitment." Ph.D. diss., Columbia University, 1955.

Donnelly, Marian Card. *The New England Meeting Houses of the Seventeenth Century*. Middletown: Wesleyan University Press, 1968.

Douglas, Ann. *The Feminization of American Culture*. New York: Knopf, 1977.

Douglas, Mary. *Natural Symbols: Explorations in Cosmology*. New York: Pantheon Books, 1970.

————. *Natural Symbols: Explorations in Cosmology*. New York: Random House, Vintage Books, 1973.

————. *Purity and Danger: An Analysis of Concepts of Pollution and Taboo*. London: Routledge & Kegan Paul, 1966.

Douglas, Mary, ed. *Rules and Meanings: The Anthropology of Everyday Knowledge*. Harmondsworth, Eng.: Penguin, 1973.

Douglas, Mary, and Baron Isherwood. *The World of Goods: Towards an Anthropology of Consumption*. New York: Basic Books, 1979.

Douglas, Mary, and Steven Tipton, eds. *Religion and America: Spiritual Life in a Secular Age*. Boston: Beacon Press, 1983.

Englizian, H. Crosby. *Brimstone Corner: Park Street Church, Boston*. Chicago: Moody Press, 1968.

Epstein, Barbara Leslie. *The Politics of Domesticity: Women, Evangelism, and Temperance in Nineteenth Century America*. Middletown: Wesleyan University Press, 1981.

Erikson, Erik H. *Life History and the Historical Moment*. New York: Norton, 1975.

———. *Young Man Luther: A Study in Psychoanalysis and History*. New York: Norton, 1958.

Erikson, Kai T. *Wayward Puritans: A Study in the Sociology of Deviance*. New York: Wiley, 1966.

Faust, Clarence H. "The Decline of Puritanism." In *Transitions in American Literary History*. Edited by Harry Hayden Clark. Durham: Duke University Press, 1953.

Febvre, Lucien. *A New Kind of History: From the Writings of Febvre*. Edited by Peter Burke. Translated by K. Folca. London: Routledge & Kegan Paul, 1973.

Fennelly, Catherine. *Town Schooling in New England, 1790–1840*. Old Sturbridge Village Booklet Series, 15. Sturbridge, Mass.: Old Sturbridge Village, 1962.

Festinger, Leon. *A Theory of Cognitive Dissonance*. Stanford, Calif.: Stanford University Press, 1957.

Fiering, Norman. *Jonathan Edwards's Moral Thought and Its British Context*. Chapel Hill: University of North Carolina Press, 1981.

———. "Will and Intellect in the New England Mind." *William and Mary Quarterly*, 3d ser., 29 (1972), 306–327.

Fischer, David Hackett. *The Revolution of American Conservatism: The Federalist Party in the Era of Jeffersonian Democracy*. New York: Harper & Row, 1965.

Flaherty, David H. *Privacy in Colonial New England*. Charlottesville: University Press of Virginia, 1972.

Foner, Eric. *Free Soil, Free Labor, Free Men: The Ideology of the Republican Party before the Civil War*. New York: Oxford University Press, 1970.

Forbes, Harriette Merrifield. *New England Diaries, 1602–1800*. Topsfield, Mass.: privately pub., 1923.

Foster, Charles H. *The Rungless Ladder: Harriet Beecher Stowe and New England Puritanism*. Durham: Duke University Press, 1954.

Foster, Charles I. *An Errand of Mercy: The Evangelical United Front, 1790–1837*. Chapel Hill: University of North Carolina Press, 1960.

Foster, Frank Hugh. *A Genetic History of the New England Theology*. 1907. Reprint. New York: Russell and Russell, 1963.

Foucault, Michel. *History of Sexuality, Volume I: An Introduction*. New York: Pantheon, 1978.

French, Stanley. "The Cemetery as Cultural Institution: The Establishment of Mount

Auburn and the 'Rural Cemetery' Movement." *American Quarterly* 26 (1974), 37–59.

Friedman, Lawrence J. *Gregarious Saints: Self and Community in American Abolitionism, 1830–1870.* New York: Cambridge University Press, 1982.

Gates, Paul W. *The Farmer's Age: Agriculture, 1815–1860.* Vol. 3 of The Economic History of the United States. New York: Holt, Rinehart and Winston, 1960.

Gaustad, Edwin S. *The Great Awakening in New England.* New York: Harper, 1957.

Geertz, Clifford. *The Interpretation of Cultures: Selected Essays.* New York: Basic Books, 1973.

Geib, Susan. "Changing Works: Agriculture and Society in Brookfield, Massachusetts, 1785–1820." Ph.D. diss., Boston University, 1981.

Goen, C. C. *Revivalism and Separatism in New England, 1740–1800.* New Haven: Yale University Press, 1962.

Goffman, Erving. *The Presentation of Self in Everyday Life.* Garden City, N.Y.: Doubleday Anchor, 1959.

Goodenough, Erwin Ramsdell. *The Psychology of Religious Experiences.* New York: Basic Books, 1965.

Gordon, Michael, ed. *The American Family in Social-Historical Perspective.* New York: St. Martin's Press, 1973.

Greven, Philip J. *Four Generations: Population, Land, and Family in Colonial Andover, Massachusetts.* Ithaca: Cornell University Press, 1970.

———. *The Protestant Temperament: Patterns of Child-Rearing, Religious Experience, and the Self in Early America.* New York: Knopf, 1977.

———. "Youth, Maturity, and Religious Conversion: A Note on the Ages of Converts in Andover, Massachusetts, 1711–1749." *Essex Institute Historical Collections* 108 (1972), 119–134.

Griffin, Clifford S. *Their Brothers' Keepers: Moral Stewardship in the United States, 1800–1865.* New Brunswick: Rutgers University Press, 1960.

Gross, Robert A. *The Minutemen and Their World.* New York: Hill and Wang, 1976.

Gura, Philip F. *The Wisdom of Words: Language, Theology, and Literature in the New England Renaissance.* Middletown: Wesleyan University Press, 1981.

Gusfield, Joseph R. *Symbolic Crusade: Status Politics and the American Temperance Movement.* Urbana: University of Illinois Press, 1963.

Hahn, Steven, and Jonathan Prude, eds. *The Countryside in the Age of Capitalist Transformation: Essays in the Social History of Rural America.* Chapel Hill: University of North Carolina Press, 1985.

Halttunen, Karen. *Confidence Men and Painted Women: A Study of Middle-class Culture in America, 1830–1870.* New Haven: Yale University Press, 1982.

Hambrick-Stowe, Charles E. *The Practice of Piety: Puritan Devotional Disciplines in Seventeenth-Century New England.* Chapel Hill: University of North Carolina Press, 1982.

Handlin, Oscar, and Mary F. Handlin. *Facing Life: Youth and the Family in American History.* Boston: Little, Brown, 1971.

Hareven, Tamara K., ed. *Anonymous Americans: Explorations in Nineteenth-Century Social History.* Englewood Cliffs, N.J.: Prentice-Hall, 1971.

Haroutunian, Joseph. *Piety versus Moralism: The Passing of the New England Theology.* 1932. Reprint. New York: Harper & Row, 1970.

Harris, Neil. *The Artist in American Society: The Formative Years, 1790–1860.* New York: Braziller, 1966.

————. *Humbug: The Art of P. T. Barnum.* Boston: Little, Brown, 1973.

Harvey, Van Austin. *The Historian and the Believer: The Morality of Historical Knowledge and Christian Belief.* New York: Macmillan, 1966.

Hatch, Nathan O. *The Sacred Cause of Liberty: Republican Thought and the Millennium in Revolutionary New England.* New Haven: Yale University Press, 1977.

Hatch, Nathan O., and Mark A. Noll, eds. *The Bible in America: Essays in Cultural History.* New York: Oxford University Press, 1982.

Haynes, George H. *Historical Sketch of the First Congregational Church, Sturbridge, Massachusetts.* Worcester, Mass.: Davis, 1910.

Heimert, Alan. *Religion and the American Mind from the Great Awakening to the Revolution.* Cambridge: Harvard University Press, 1966.

Henry, Stuart C. *Unvanquished Puritan: A Portrait of Lyman Beecher.* Grand Rapids, Mich.: Eerdmans, 1973.

Herberg, Will. *Protestant-Catholic-Jew: An Essay in American Religious Sociology.* Garden City, N.Y.: Doubleday, 1955.

Hofstadter, Richard. *Anti-Intellectualism in American Life.* New York: Knopf, 1963.

Homans, Peter. *Theology After Freud: An Interpretive Inquiry.* Indianapolis: Bobbs-Merrill, 1970.

Horkheimer, Max. *The Eclipse of Reason.* 1947. Reprint. New York: Seabury, 1974.

Horwitz, Morton J. *The Transformation of American Law, 1780–1860.* Cambridge: Harvard University Press, 1977.

Houghton, Walter E. *The Victorian Frame of Mind, 1830–1870.* New Haven: Yale University Press, 1957.

Howard, Leon. *The Connecticut Wits.* Chicago: University of Chicago Press, 1943.

Howe, Daniel Walker. "The Decline of Calvinism: An Approach to its Study." *Comparative Studies in Society and History* 14 (1972), 306–327.

————. *The Political Culture of the American Whigs.* Chicago: University of Chicago Press, 1979.

————. *The Unitarian Conscience: Harvard Moral Philosophy, 1805–1861.* Cambridge: Harvard University Press, 1970.

Howland, Franklyn. *A History of the Town of Acushnet.* New Bedford, Mass.: privately pub., 1907.

Huber, Richard M. *The American Idea of Success.* New York: McGraw-Hill, 1971.

Hummel, Charles F. *With Hammer in Hand: The Dominy Craftsmen of East Hampton, New York.* Charlottesville: University Press of Virginia for the Henry Francis du Pont Winterthur Museum, 1968.

Jaegar, Muriel. *Before Victoria: Changing Standards and Behaviour, 1787–1837.* London: Chatto and Windus, 1956.

James, Sydney V. *A People Among Peoples: Quaker Benevolence in Eighteenth-Century America.* Cambridge: Harvard University Press, 1963.

James, William. *The Principles of Psychology.* 2 vols. 1890. Reprint. New York: Dover, 1950.

————. *The Varieties of Religious Experience: A Study in Human Nature*. New York: Longmans, Green, 1902.

————. *The Will to Believe and Other Essays in Popular Philosophy*. New York: Dover, 1956.

Jedrey, Christopher M. *The World of John Cleaveland: Family and Community in Eighteenth-Century New England*. New York: Norton, 1979.

Jensen, Joan M. *Loosening the Bonds: Mid-Atlantic Farm Women, 1750–1850*. New Haven: Yale University Press, 1986.

Johnson, Paul E. *A Shopkeeper's Millennium: Society and Revivals in Rochester, New York, 1815–1837*. New York: Hill & Wang, 1978.

Jonas, Hans. *Philosophical Essays: From Ancient Creed to Technological Man*. Englewood Cliffs, N.J.: Prentice-Hall, 1974.

Jones, Howard Mumford. *Belief and Disbelief in American Literature*. Chicago: University of Chicago Press, 1967.

Kaplan, Louis, comp. *A Bibliography of American Autobiographies*. Madison: University of Wisconsin Press, 1961.

Keller, Charles Roy. *The Second Great Awakening in Connecticut*. New Haven: Yale University Press, 1942.

Kelley, Mary. *Private Women, Public Stage: Literary Domesticity in Nineteenth-Century America*. New York: Oxford University Press, 1984.

Kelly, J. Frederick. *Early Connecticut Meetinghouses: Being an Account of the Church Edifices Built before 1830 Based Chiefly upon Town and Parish Records*. 2 vols. New York: Columbia University Press, 1948.

Kelsey, Darwin P. "Farming and Farm Crops: Agriculture in New England, 1790–1840." Research report. Sturbridge, Mass.: Old Sturbridge Village, 1967.

Kelsey, Darwin P., ed. *Farming in the New Nation: Interpreting American Agriculture, 1790–1840*. Washington: Agricultural History Society, 1972.

Kett, Joseph F. *Rites of Passage: Adolescence in America, 1790 to the Present*. New York: Basic Books, 1977.

Kilby, Kenneth. *The Cooper and His Trade*. London: John Baker, 1971. [Old Sturbridge Village Research Library]

King, John Owen, III. *The Iron of Melancholy: Structures of Spiritual Conversion in America from the Puritan Conscience to Victorian Neurosis*. Middletown: Wesleyan University Press, 1983.

Kirkland, Edward Chase. *Men, Cities and Transportation: A Study in New England History, 1820–1900*. 2 vols. Cambridge: Harvard University Press, 1948.

Kirkpatrick, Doris. *The City and the River*. Vol. 1. Fitchburg, Mass.: Fitchburg Historical Society, 1971.

Klinger, Eric. *Structure and Functions of Fantasy*. New York: Wiley-Interscience, 1971.

Knox, R. A. *Enthusiasm: A Chapter in the History of Religion, With Special Reference to the XVII and XVIII Centuries*. Oxford: Clarendon Press of Oxford University Press, 1950.

Kraditor, Aileen S. *Means and Ends in American Abolitionism: Garrison and His Critics on Strategy and Tactics, 1834–1850*. New York: Pantheon, 1969.

Kuklick, Bruce. *Churchmen and Philosophers: From Jonathan Edwards to John Dewey*. New Haven: Yale University Press, 1985.

Kulik, Gary, Roger Parks, and Theodore Z. Penn, eds. *The New England Mill Village, 1790–1860.* Cambridge: MIT Press, 1982.

Larkin, Jack. "The View from New England: Notes on Everyday Life in Rural America to 1850." *American Quarterly* 34 (1982), 244–261.

Larned, Ellen D. *History of Windham County, Connecticut.* 2 vols. Worcester, Mass.: privately pub., 1874–1880.

Lasch, Christopher. *The World of Nations: Reflections on History, Politics, and Culture.* New York: Knopf, 1973.

Leeuw, G. van der. *Religion in Essence and Manifestation.* Translated by J. E. Turner. 2 vols. New York: Harper & Row, 1963.

Lefebvre, Henri. *Everyday Life in the Modern World.* Translated by Sacha Rabinovitch. New York: Harper & Row, 1971.

Lenski, Gerhard. *The Religious Factor: A Sociological Study of Religion's Impact on Politics, Economics, and Family Life.* Revised ed. Garden City, N.Y.: Doubleday Anchor, 1963.

Levine, Herbert J. "In Pursuit of the Nucleated Village." Research report. Sturbridge, Mass.: Old Sturbridge Village, 1971.

Levy, Leonard W. *The Law of the Commonwealth and Chief Justice Shaw.* Cambridge: Harvard University Press, 1957.

Lockridge, Kenneth A. "Social Change and the Meaning of the American Revolution." *Journal of Social History* 6 (1973), 403–439.

Loehr, Rodney C. "Self-Sufficiency on the Farm." *Agricultural History* 26 (1952), 37–41.

Lovejoy, Arthur O. *Essays in the History of Ideas.* Baltimore: Johns Hopkins University Press, 1948.

———. *The Reason, the Understanding, and Time.* Baltimore: Johns Hopkins University Press, 1961.

Luckmann, Thomas. *The Invisible Religion: The Problem of Religion in Modern Society.* New York: Macmillan, 1967.

McDannell, Colleen. *The Christian Home in Victorian America, 1840–1900.* Bloomington: Indiana University Press, 1986.

McLoughlin, William G. *The Meaning of Henry Ward Beecher: An Essay on the Shifting Values of Mid-Victorian America.* New York: Knopf, 1970.

———. *New England Dissent, 1630–1833: The Baptists and the Separation of Church and State.* 2 vols. Cambridge: Harvard University Press, 1971.

McLoughlin, William G., ed. *The American Evangelicals, 1800–1900: An Anthology.* New York: Harper & Row, 1968.

McNeill, John T. *The History and Character of Calvinism.* New York: Oxford University Press, 1954.

Macpherson, C. B. *The Political Theory of Possessive Individualism: Hobbes to Locke.* London: Oxford University Press, 1962.

McPherson, James M. *Battle Cry of Freedom: The Civil War Era.* New York: Oxford University Press, 1988.

Madden, Edward H. *Civil Disobedience and Moral Law in Nineteenth-Century American Philosophy.* Seattle: University of Washington Press, 1968.

Marini, Stephen A. *Radical Sects of Revolutionary New England.* Cambridge: Harvard University Press, 1982.

Marsden, George M. *The Evangelical Mind and the New School Presbyterian Experience: A Case Study of Thought and Theology in Nineteenth-Century America.* New Haven: Yale University Press, 1970.

Martin, David. *The Religious and the Secular: Studies in Secularization.* London: Routledge & Kegan Paul, 1969.

Martin, Terence. *The Instructed Vision: Scottish Common Sense Philosophy and the Origins of American Fiction.* Indiana University Humanities Series, no. 48. Bloomington: Indiana University Press, 1961.

Marty, Martin E. "Religious Behavior: Its Social Dimension in American History." *Social Research* 41 (1974), 241–264.

———. *Righteous Empire: The Protestant Experience in America.* New York: Dial, 1970.

Marx, Karl. *Capital: A Critical Analysis of Capitalist Production.* Edited by Frederick Engels. Translated by Samuel Moore and Edward Aveling. 3 vols. Moscow: Foreign Languages Publishing House, 1961.

Mathews, Donald G. "The Second Great Awakening as an Organizing Process, 1780–1830: An Hypothesis." *American Quarterly* 21 (1969), 23–43.

Matthews, William, comp. *American Diaries: An Annotated Bibliography of American Diaries Written Prior to the Year 1861.* 1945. Reprint. Boston: J. S. Canner, 1959.

———. *American Diaries in Manuscript, 1880–1954: A Descriptive Bibliography.* Athens: University of Georgia Press, 1974.

Mattingly, Paul H. *The Classless Profession: American Schoolmen in the Nineteenth Century.* New York: New York University Press, 1975.

Mattson, John Stanley. "Charles Grandison Finney and the Emerging Tradition of 'New Measures' Revivalism." Ph.D. diss., University of North Carolina at Chapel Hill, 1970.

May, Henry F. *The Enlightenment in America.* New York: Oxford University Press, 1976.

Mazmanian, Arthur B. *The Structure of Praise: A Design Study, Architecture for Religion from the 17th Century to the Present.* Barre, Mass.: Barre Publishers, 1973.

Mead, George Herbert. *Mind, Self, and Society from the Viewpoint of a Social Behaviorist.* Edited by Charles W. Morris. Vol. 1 of *Works.* Chicago: University of Chicago Press, 1962.

———. *Movements of Thought in the Nineteenth Century.* Edited by Merritt H. Moore. Vol. 2 of *Works.* Chicago: University of Chicago Press, 1936.

Mead, Sidney E. *The Lively Experiment: The Shaping of Christianity in America.* New York: Harper & Row, 1963.

———. *Nathaniel William Taylor, 1786–1858: A Connecticut Liberal.* 1942. Reprint. Hamden, Conn.: Archon Books, 1967.

Melder, Keith E. *Beginnings of Sisterhood: The American Woman's Rights Movement, 1800–1850.* New York: Schocken, 1977.

Meredith, Robert. *The Politics of the Universe: Edward Beecher, Abolition and Orthodoxy.* Nashville: Vanderbilt University Press, 1968.

Merz, John Theodore. *A History of European Scientific Thought in the Nineteenth Century.* 2 vols. 1904. Reprint. New York: Dover, 1965.

Mesthene, Emmanuel G. "Technological Change and Religious Unification." *Harvard Theological Review* 65 (1972), 29–51.

Meyer, Donald. *The Positive Thinkers: A Study of the American Quest for Health, Wealth and Personal Power from Mary Baker Eddy to Norman Vincent Peale.* Garden City, N.Y.: Doubleday, 1965.

Meyer, Donald H. *The Democratic Enlightenment.* New York: Putnam's 1976.

————. *The Instructed Conscience: The Shaping of the American National Ethic.* Philadelphia: University of Pennsylvania Press, 1972.

Michaelsen, Robert S. *The American Search for Soul.* Baton Rouge: Louisiana State University Press, 1975.

Miller, George A., Eugene Galanter, and Karl H. Pribram. *Plans and the Structure of Behavior.* New York: Holt, 1960.

Miller, J. Hillis. *The Disappearance of God: Five Nineteenth-Century Writers.* Cambridge: Harvard University Press, 1963.

Miller, Perry. *Errand into the Wilderness.* Cambridge: Harvard University Press, 1956.

————. *Jonathan Edwards.* New York: Sloane, 1949.

————. "Jonathan Edwards on the Sense of the Heart." *Harvard Theological Review* 41 (1948), 123–145.

————. *The Life of the Mind in America from the Revolution to the Civil War. Books One through Three.* New York: Harcourt, Brace and World, 1965.

————. *Nature's Nation.* Cambridge: Harvard University Press, 1967.

————. *The New England Mind: From Colony to Province.* Cambridge: Harvard University Press, 1953.

————. *The New England Mind: The Seventeenth Century.* Cambridge: Harvard University Press, 1954.

Miyakawa, T. Scott. *Protestants and Pioneers: Individualism and Conformity on the American Frontier.* Chicago: University of Chicago Press, 1964.

Morgan, Edmund S. *The Gentle Puritan: A Life of Ezra Stiles, 1727–1795.* New Haven: Yale University Press, 1962.

————. *Visible Saints: The History of a Puritan Idea.* New York: New York University Press, 1963.

Morison, Elting E. *From Know-How to Nowhere: The Development of American Technology.* New York: Basic Books, 1974.

Morse, James King. *Jedidiah Morse: A Champion of New England Orthodoxy.* New York: Columbia University Press, 1939.

Nash, Gary B. "The American Clergy and the French Revolution." *William and Mary Quarterly,* 3d ser., 22 (1965), 392–412.

Nelson, William E. *Americanization of the Common Law: The Impact of Legal Change on Massachusetts Society, 1760–1830.* Cambridge: Harvard University Press, 1975.

Nichols, James Hastings. *The Mercersburg Theology.* New York: Oxford University Press, 1966.

————. *Romanticism in American Theology: Nevin and Schaff at Mercersburg.* Chicago: University of Chicago Press, 1961.

Niebuhr, Reinhold. *The Self and the Dramas of History.* New York: Scribner's, 1955.

Niebuhr, Richard R. *Experiential Religion.* New York: Harper & Row, 1972.

Nock, A. D. *Conversion: The Old and the New in Religion from Alexander the Great to Augustine of Hippo.* 1933. Reprint. Oxford: Oxford University Press, 1969.

North, Douglass C. *The Economic Growth of the United States, 1790–1860.* Englewood Cliffs, N.J.: Prentice-Hall, 1961.

Nye, Russel Blaine. *The Cultural Life of the New Nation, 1776–1830.* New York: Harper, 1963.

Oberholzer, Emil, Jr. *Delinquent Saints: Disciplinary Action in the Early Congregational Churches of Massachusetts.* New York: Columbia University Press, 1956.

Ong, Walter J., S. J. *Rhetoric, Romance, and Technology: Studies in the Interaction of Expression and Culture.* Ithaca: Cornell University Press, 1971.

Osterud, Nancy, and John Fulton. "Family Limitation and Age at Marriage: Fertility Decline in Sturbridge, Massachusetts, 1730–1850." *Population Studies* 30 (1976), 481–494.

Parker, Gail Thain. *Mind Cure in New England: From the Civil War to World War I.* Hanover, N.H.: University Press of New England, 1973.

Parks, Roger N. *Roads and Travel in New England, 1790–1840.* Old Sturbridge Village Booklet Series, 24. Sturbridge, Mass.: Old Sturbridge Village, 1967.

Pettit, Norman. *The Heart Prepared: Grace and Conversion in Puritan Spiritual Life.* New Haven: Yale University Press, 1966.

Poirier, Richard. *A World Elsewhere: The Place of Style in American Literature.* New York: Oxford University Press, 1966.

Polanyi, Karl. *The Great Transformation: The Political and Economic Origins of Our Time.* New York: Rinehart, 1944.

Pope, Robert G. *The Half-Way Covenant: Church Membership in Puritan New England.* Princeton: Princeton University Press, 1969.

Popper, Karl R. *Conjectures and Refutations: The Growth of Scientific Knowledge.* 2d ed. New York: Basic Books, 1965.

Porte, Joel. *Emerson and Thoreau: Transcendentalists in Conflict.* Middletown: Wesleyan University Press, 1966.

Proudfoot, Wayne. *Religious Experience.* Berkeley: University of California Press, 1985.

Pruyser, Paul W. *A Dynamic Psychology of Religion.* New York: Harper & Row, 1968.

Rabinowitz, Richard. "The Crisis of the Classroom: Architecture and Education." *History of Education Quarterly* 14 (1974), 115–123.

———. "Soul, Character, and Personality: The Transformation of Personal Religious Experience in New England, 1790–1860." Ph.D. diss., Harvard University, 1977.

Ranulf, Svend. *Moral Indignation and Middle Class Psychology: A Sociological Study.* 1938. Reprint. New York: Schocken, 1964.

Reed, Walter J. "The Pattern of Conversion in Sartor Resartus." *ELH* 38 (1971), 411–431.

Richards, Leonard L. *"Gentlemen of Property and Standing": Anti-Abolition Mobs in Jacksonian America.* New York: Oxford University Press, 1970.

Ricks, Christopher. *Keats and Embarrassment.* Oxford: Clarendon Press, 1974.

Rieff, Philip. *Fellow Teachers.* New York: Harper & Row, 1973.

———. *Freud: The Mind of the Moralist.* New York: Viking, 1959.

———. *The Triumph of the Therapeutic: Uses of Faith after Freud.* New York: Harper & Row, 1966.

Roe, Alfred S., comp. *Monuments, Tablets and Other Memorials Erected in Massachusetts* to Commemorate the Services of Her Sons in the War of the Rebellion, 1861–1865. Boston: Wright & Potter, 1910.

Rollins, Richard M. *The Long Journey of Noah Webster.* Philadelphia: University of Pennsylvania Press, 1980.

Rorabaugh, W. J. *The Alcoholic Republic: An American Tradition.* New York: Oxford University Press, 1979.

Rothman, David J. *The Discovery of the Asylum: Social Order and Disorder in the New Republic.* Boston: Little, Brown, 1971.

Rourke, Constance Mayfield. *Trumpets of Jubilee: Henry Ward Beecher, Harriet Beecher Stowe, Lyman Beecher, Horace Greeley, P. T. Barnum.* New York: Harcourt, Brace, 1927.

Royster, Charles. *A Revolutionary People at War: The Continental Army and American Character, 1775–1783.* Chapel Hill: University of North Carolina Press, 1979.

Rugoff, Milton. *The Beechers: An American Family in the Nineteenth Century.* New York: Harper & Row, 1981.

Russell, Howard S. *A Long, Deep Furrow: Three Centuries of Farming in New England.* Hanover, N.H.: University Press of New England, 1976.

Santayana, George. *Character and Opinion in the United States.* New York: Scribner's, 1920.

Schlesinger, Arthur M. *Learning How to Behave: A Historical Study of American Etiquette Books.* New York: Macmillan, 1946.

Schlesinger, Arthur M., Jr. *The Vital Center: The Politics of Freedom.* Boston: Houghton Mifflin, 1949.

Schutz, Alfred. *Collected Papers, I: The Problem of Social Reality.* Edited by Maurice Natanson. The Hague: Martinus Nijhoff, 1962.

Scott, Donald M. *From Office to Profession: The New England Ministry, 1750–1850.* Philadelphia: University of Pennsylvania Press, 1978.

Sellers, Charles Coleman. *Lorenzo Dow: The Bearer of the Word.* New York: Minton, Balch, 1928.

Sewall, Richard B. *The Life of Emily Dickinson.* 2 vols. New York: Farrar, Straus and Giroux, 1974.

Shea, Daniel B., Jr. *Spiritual Autobiography in Early America.* Princeton: Princeton University Press, 1968.

Shiels, Richard D. "The Second Great Awakening in Connecticut: Critique of the Traditional Interpretation." *Church History* 49 (1980), 401–415.

Simmel, Georg. *The Sociology of Georg Simmel.* Translated and edited by Kurt H. Wolff. Glencoe, Ill.: Free Press, 1950.

Singer, Jerome L. *The Inner World of Daydreaming.* New York: Harper & Row, 1975.

Sklar, Kathryn Kish. *Catharine Beecher: A Study in American Domesticity.* New Haven: Yale University Press, 1973.

Smith, Elwyn A., ed. *The Religion of the Republic.* Philadelphia: Fortress Press, 1971.

Smith, James Ward, and A. Leland Jamison, eds. *The Shaping of American Religion.* Vol. 1 of *Religion in American Life.* Princeton: Princeton University Press, 1961.

Smith, Timothy L. "Congregation, State, and Denomination: The Forming of the

American Religious Structure." *William and Mary Quarterly*, 3d ser., 25 (1968), 155–176.

———. *Revivalism and Social Reform in Mid-Nineteenth-Century America*. New York: Abingdon Press, 1957.

Smith-Rosenberg, Carroll. "The Female World of Love and Ritual: Relations between Women in Nineteenth-Century America." *Signs: Journal of Women in Culture and Society* 1 (1975), 1–29.

———. *Religion and the Rise of the American City: The New York City Mission Movement, 1812–1870*. Ithaca: Cornell University Press, 1971.

Solberg, Winton U. *Redeem the Time: The Puritan Sabbath in Early America*. Cambridge: Harvard University Press, 1977.

Stanton, Phoebe B. *The Gothic Revival and American Church Architecture: An Episode in Taste, 1840–1856*. Baltimore: Johns Hopkins University Press, 1968.

Starbuck, Edwin Diller. *The Psychology of Religion: An Empirical Study of the Growth of Religious Consciousness*. New York: Scribner's, 1900.

Stark, Rodney, and Charles Y. Glock. *American Piety: The Nature of Religious Commitment*. Vol. 1 of *Patterns of Religious Commitment*. Berkeley: University of California Press, 1968.

Stauffer, Vernon. *New England and the Bavarian Illuminati*. Studies in History, Economics and Public Law 82, no. 1. New York: Columbia University Press, 1918.

Stilgoe, John R. *Common Landscape of America, 1580 to 1845*. New Haven: Yale University Press, 1982.

Stone, Donald. "The Human Potential Movement." In *The New Religious Consciousness*, edited by Charles Y. Glock and Robert N. Bellah, 93–115. Berkeley: University of California Press, 1976.

Stout, Harry S. "The Great Awakening in New England Reconsidered: The New England Clergy." *Journal of Social History* 8 (Fall 1974), 21–41.

———. *The New England Soul: Preaching and Religious Culture in Colonial New England*. New York: Oxford University Press, 1986.

Strout, Cushing. *The New Heavens and the New Earth: Political Religion in America*. New York: Harper & Row, 1974.

Syrett, Harold C., and Jean G. Cooke, eds. *Interview in Weehawken: The Burr-Hamilton Duel as told in the Original Documents*. Middletown: Wesleyan University Press, 1960.

Szatmary, David P. *Shays' Rebellion: The Making of an Agrarian Insurrection*. Amherst: University of Massachusetts Press, 1980.

Tate, Allen. *Essays of Four Decades*. Chicago: Swallow Press, 1959.

Taylor, George Rogers. *The Transportation Revolution, 1815–1860*. Vol. 4 of The Economic History of the United States. New York: Holt, Rinehart and Winston, 1951.

Thompson, E. P. "Time, Work-Discipline, and Industrial Capitalism." *Past and Present* 38 (1967), 56–97.

Tolles, Frederick B. *Quakers and the Atlantic Culture*. New York: Macmillan, 1960.

Torrey, Rufus C. *History of the Town of Fitchburg, Massachusetts*. Fitchburg: Fitchburg Centennial Committee, 1865.

Tracy, Patricia J. *Jonathan Edwards, Pastor: Religion and Society in Eighteenth-Century Northampton*. New York: Hill & Wang, 1979.

Trayser, Donald G., ed. *Barnstable: Three Centuries of a Cape Cod Town*. Hyannis, Mass.: Goss, 1939.

Trilling, Lionel. *Sincerity and Authenticity*. Cambridge: Harvard University Press, 1972.

Tuveson, Ernest Lee. *The Imagination as a Means of Grace: Locke and the Aesthetics of Romanticism*. Berkeley: University of California Press, 1960.

Underwood, Francis H. *Quabbin: The Story of a Small Town*. 1893. Reprint. Boston: Northeastern University Press, 1986.

Unger, Roberto Mangabeira. *Knowledge and Politics*. New York: Free Press, 1975.

Updegraff, Harlan. *The Origin of the Moving School in Massachusetts*. 1907. Reprint. New York: Arno Press, 1969.

Veblen, Thorstein. *The Theory of Business Enterprise*. 1904. Reprint. New York: Scribner's, 1932.

———. *The Theory of the Leisure Class*. New York: Macmillan, 1889.

Wagenknecht, Edward. *Ambassadors for Christ: Seven American Preachers*. New York: Oxford University Press, 1972.

Walker, George Leon. *Some Aspects of the Religious Life of New England with Special Reference to Congregationalists*. New York: Silver, Burdett, 1897.

Wallace, Anthony F. C. *Rockdale: The Growth of an American Village in the Early Industrial Revolution*. New York: Knopf, 1978.

Warren, Austin. *New England Saints*. Ann Arbor: University of Michigan Press, 1956.

Weber, Max. *From Max Weber: Essays in Sociology*. Translated and edited by H. H. Gerth and C. Wright Mills. New York: Oxford University Press, 1946.

Welch, Claude. *Protestant Thought in the Nineteenth Century: Vol. I, 1799–1870*. New Haven: Yale University Press, 1972.

Welter, Rush. *The Mind of America, 1820–1860*. New York: Columbia University Press, 1975.

Whicher, Stephen E. *Freedom and Fate: An Inner Life of Ralph Waldo Emerson*. Philadelphia: University of Pennsylvania Press, 1953.

Willey, Basil. *The Eighteenth Century Background: Studies on the Idea of Nature in the Thought of the Period*. 1939. Reprint. Boston: Beacon Press, 1961.

Williams, Daniel Day. *The Andover Liberals: A Study in American Theology*. New York: King's Crown Press, 1941.

Winner, Langdon. *Autonomous Technology: Technics-Out-of-Control as a Theme in Political Thought*. Cambridge: MIT Press, 1977.

Wolin, Sheldon S. *Politics and Vision: Continuity and Innovation in Western Political Thought*. Boston: Little, Brown, 1960.

Worthley, Harold Field. *An Inventory of the Records of the Particular (Congregational) Churches of Massachusetts Gathered 1620–1805*. Harvard Theological Studies 25. Cambridge: Harvard University Press, 1970.

Wright, Conrad. *The Beginnings of Unitarianism in America*. Boston: Beacon Press, 1966.

———. *The Liberal Christians: Essays on American Unitarian History*. Boston: Beacon Press, 1970.

Wyatt-Brown, Bertram. *Lewis Tappan and the Evangelical War against Slavery.* New York: Atheneum, 1971.

———. "Prelude to Abolitionism: Sabbatarianism and the Rise of the Second Party System." *Journal of American History* 58 (1971), 316–341.

Yinger, J. Milton. *Religion, Society and the Individual: An Introduction to the Sociology of Religion.* New York: Macmillan, 1957.

Young, Michael, and Peter Willmott. *The Symmetrical Family.* New York: Pantheon, 1973.

Zaretsky, Eli. *Capitalism, the Family, and Personal Life.* New York: Harper & Row, 1976.

Zetterberg, Hans L. "The Religious Conversion as a Change of Social Roles." *Sociology and Social Research* 36 (1952), 159–166.

Zijdervald, Anton. *The Abstract Society: A Cultural Analysis of Our Time.* Garden City, N.Y.: Doubleday, 1970.

Zuckerman, Michael. "The Nursery Tales of Horatio Alger." *American Quarterly* 24 (1972), 191–209.

———. *Peaceable Kingdoms: New England Towns in the Eighteenth Century.* New York: Knopf, 1970.

Index of Names